TRANSMISSION AND DISTRIBUTION
(ELECTRICAL POWER-I)

FOR POLYTECHNIC STUDENTS

Er. Tarlok Singh

TRANSMISSION AND DISTRIBUTION
(Electrical Power-I)

by
Er. Tarlok Singh
Principal
Yamuna Polytechnic for Engineering
Gadholi, (Haryana)

S.K. KATARIA & SONS®
Publisher of Engineering Books
4885/109, Prakash Mahal, Dr. Subhash Bhargav Lane,
Opposite Delhi Medical Association, Daryaganj, New Delhi-110002 (INDIA)
Phone: +91-11-43551243, *Mobile:* +91-9871775858
e-mail: katariabook@gmail.com, katariabooks@yahoo.com
Website: www.skkatariaandsons.com
(e-books, subscriptions and bulk buying also available on our website)

Published by:

S.K. Kataria & Sons®

4885/109, Prakash Mahal, Dr. Subhash Bhargav Lane,
Opposite Delhi Medical Association, Daryaganj, New Delhi-110002 (INDIA)
Phone: +91-11-43551243 Mobile: +91-9871775858
e-mail: katariabook@gmail.com, katariabooks@yahoo.com
Website: www.skkatariaandsons.com

First Edition: 2001; Third Edition: 2019, Reprint: 2023

***Price :* ₹ 395/-**

Laser Typesetting by:
SARA ASSIGNMENTS

Printed at:
A.S. OFFSET PRINTERS

Preface to the Third Edition

The author feels great pleasure in presenting the Third Edition of the book with marked improvements over the previous one. The book has been thoroughly revised enlarged with additions of chapters and topic so as to meet the needs of degree and Electrical Engineering Diploma students.

This book is written entirely according to the syllabus of all the polytechnics of Delhi, Haryana, Punjab, Himachal, J&K, and Rajasthan who follow this syllabus.

Although sincere efforts have been made to make the subject simple, brief and clear, still readers may find few things here not to as per their taste and hope for their valuable suggestions in this regard shall be very much appreciated.

A large number of worked out examples have been given as illustrations and this will help the readers in understanding the basic theory.

Any suggestion for the improvement of the book will be thankful acknowledge.

Author is thankful to M/S S.K. Kataria & Sons, Publishing House for bringing out the book in such a short time.

July, 2019

Er. Tarlok Singh
(Author)

Preface to the First Edition

This book is written according to new syllabus introduced in Punjab Polytechnic by the T.T.T.I. Chandigarh, and therefore, shall be useful also to the students of all the Polytechnics of Haryana, Himachal Pradesh who has already follows this syllabus.

A large number of worked out example have been taken from previous year papers of State Board of Haryana. It is earnestly hoped that the book will serve the purpose it is meant for selected numerical problems with answers given at the end of each chapter will help the students in evaluating their understanding of the subject.

I would like to thank my family for their patience and encouragement.

Author is also grateful to *M/s. S.K. Kataria & Sons*, Publish of Engineering books, Delhi bringing out the book in the present nice form.

Suggestions regarding improvement, correction and misprint are welcome.

January, 2001 **Er. Tarlok Singh**

Contents

1

Power Generation

INSIDE THIS CHAPTER

- Introduction
- Different Energy Sources
- Generation of Electrical Energy
- Main Generating Stations
- Importance of Non-Conventional Energy Sources in Present Scenario
- Solar Energy
- Solar Thermal Power Generation
- Solar Cookers
- Solar Water Heaters
- Wind Energy
- Selection of Site for a Wind Power Plant
- Natural Sources of Energy
- Non-renewable and Renewable Sources of Energy
- Sources of Energy
- Gas Turbine Power Plant
- Solar Cells
- Solar Pond
- Solar Water Heating
- BIO-Energy
- Applications of Wind Energy

1.1 INTRODUCTION

Electrical energy is generated by conversion of energy available in different forms from different natural sources such as kinetic energy of blowing winds, pressure head of water, chemical energy of fuels and nuclear energy of radioactive substances. Conventional methods of power generation generally prime movers such as petrol engines, steam engines, diesel engines, steam turbines, gas turbine and hydraulic turbines are used to convert mechanical energy into electrical energy. The machines which generate D.C are called *generators* and electrical machines employed for generating AC are called *alternators*.

The alternate methods of generating electrical energy without the use of prime movers are called non-conventional methods of power generation. Various non-conventional methods of power generation may be such as solar cells, wind power generation, tidals power generation, Magneto-hydrodynamic (MHD) power generation and geothermal energy generation etc.

1.1.1 Advantages of Electrical Energy

Electrical energy finds its application in the fields where energy is required. Electrical energy is increasingly being used in industrial, commercial and domestic fields due to its advantages over other forms of energies. The few advantages of electrical energy over other types of energy are:

1. It is cleaner.
2. It can easily be controlled.
3. It is more flexible.
4. It has high efficiency.
5. It can be easily transmitted over long distances.
6. It is environmental friendly as no smoke or fumes are produced.
7. Its operation is noiseless.
8. It can be easily converted from one form to the other.
9. Electrical energy can be utilized instantaneously just by the press of a button. There is no time gap.
10. Equipments operated on electrical energy are more reliable and safe to use.

1.2 NATURAL SOURCES OF ENERGY

The following are the main natural sources of energy which may be converted into electrical.

1. **Coal:** Coal is used for generating steam in the boiler and steam turbine drives the generator. Such type of power plants are called thermal or steam power plants.
2. **Water:** Water at a high pressure or flowing with a high velocity can be used to run the water turbines which are coupled to the generation. Such type of power station, in which electrical energy is generated by the pressure of water is called hydroelectric power plant. The main requirement for this type of power plant is that water is available at some height and throughout the year.

   This method of power generation is very popular because it is reliable and requires minimum maintenance and care.
3. **Fuels:** The fuels may be solid, liquid or gas such as coal, oil and fuel gases. Oil and gas are used as fuel for I.C. engines by which the generators are driven. The generators run by diesel engines are called diesel power stations and are used as standby power stations, or as peak load power stations or in interconnected grid system. For generating small power, petrol engines are used as prime mover and for generating large blocks of power diesel engines are commonly used. Modern trend is to use gas turbine prime movers. The gas can also be used by burning it and producing steam from the water in the boiler. The super heated steam under pressure is then injected into steam turbine thereby running the steam turbine and hence the generator.
4. **Nuclear Substances:** Nuclear energy is also used for power generation in nuclear power plants. A very large amount of heat energy is produced by the fission process of the nuclear substances (high atomic weight substances) in the nuclear reactor. The nuclear substance are Uranium (U_{235}), Thorium (TH_{232}) and Plutonium (PU_{239}). The heat energy obtained by fission of 1 kg of U_{235} is roughly equivalent to that produeed by burning 2500 tons of high grade coal.

   The tremendous amount of heat produced in the nuclear reactor by the fission process of uranium or other nuclear substance is utilized to heat up the liquid sodium metal which is called the working substance. The liquid sodium metal carries the heat to the heat exchanger and the heat is used to heat up the water and convert it into steam, which is utilized to run the alternator.

5. **Sun:** Sun is the primary source of energy. Sun radiates energy in the form of electro-magnetic waves such as heat, light etc. Generally, for small energy convertion solar cells are used. The solar cells panel converts solar energy directly into electrical energy. The solar energy is used for various electronics circuits such as street lights, watches, calculators etc. This energy is utilized for charging of batteries.
6. **Wind:** Wind pressure got sufficient energy which can be used in wind mills to drive small generators. Such generators are used for charging of batteries for continuous use. The great advantages of this source of energy is that it is in plenty, inexhaustable, non-polluting and it does not require any operator. Also it does not required any maintenance for a longer periods.
7. **Tides:** Tides are generated by the action of gravitational forces of sun and moon on the oceans. Electrical energy is generated by the tides by oceans. A small dam with larger gates can be male across the bay and low head turbines are installed in it to generate electrical energy.
8. **Biomass:** Biomass is the organic matter from plants, animals. Energy obtained from biomass is called bio-energy. It is considered as renewable energy source. Biomass resources are wood, dung, vegetable waste etc. A wide variety of convertion techniques is available for manufacturing fuel from biomass. A better method is to convert biomass into a gas called biogas.

1.3 DIFFERENT ENERGY SOURCES

Energy source can be classified into two types.

1. **Primary sources:** The primary sources are: sun, wind, tides and sea waves. These sources are used originally without processing, Moreover these sources are commercially not converted into electrical energy.
2. **Secondary sources:** The secondary sources are like water, fuel and nuclear energy. These sources are commercially electrical energy is generated from these sources.

1.4 NON-RENEWABLE AND RENEWABLE SOURCES OF ENERGY

1. **Non-Renewable energy sources:** The energy source which cannot be reused is called renewable source of energy is coal, oil etc.
2. **Renewable energy sources:** The source of energy which can be used again and again is called renewable source of energy i.e., hydro energy, wind energy etc.

Merits of Renewable Sources

1. Renewable sources are inexhaustible.
2. The power plant based on renewable almost have no fuel cost.
3. Renewable sources are used for local processing and applications. Hence transmission and distribution of power is not required.
4. There is no-pollution problem with the use of renewable sources.
5. The use of renewable energy can help to generate local employment.

Demerits in use of Renewable Sources of Energy

1. It needs large sizes of the plant resulting in increased cost of delivered energy.
2. Efficiency is low due to low energy density.

3. More chances of environment pollution.
4. Large instrument is required before deriving any perfect benefit from it.

1.4.1 Conventional Energy Sources

The source of energy which is in common use is called *conventional energy source.* Coal oil gas etc., are conventional energy sources.

1.4.2 Non-conventional Energy Sources

The source of energy which is not in common use is called *non-conventional* use due to lack of **awareness** and may be major source of energy in future i.e., solar, wind, biomass etc.

Various conventional sources of energy are:

(i) Wood
(ii) Coal
(iii) Natural gas
(iv) Oil
(v) Hydro energy

Various non-conventional sources are:

(i) Solar energy
(ii) Wind energy
(iii) Tidal energy
(iv) Biomass
(v) Geothermal energy
(vi) Magneto hydrodynamic generation
(vii) Fuel cells

Difference between Conventional Energy Sources and Non-conventional Energy Sources

S.No	Conventional energy sources	Non-conventional energy sources
1.	These sources will exhaust in next century.	These sources can't be exhausted in many thousand years.
2.	Cost is paid to have these sources.	These sources are available free of cost.
3.	They pollute the environment other hydro-electric plant.	These sources does not pollute the environment.
4.	They have high energy density.	They have low energy density.
5.	Easy to design plant.	Difficult to design plant.
6.	It is produced fossil fuel, uranium etc.	It is produced from animal dung, solar, tide and agriculture wastage etc.

1.5 GENERATION OF ELECTRICAL ENERGY

Electrical energy is generated by conversion of energy available in different forms from different natural sources such as kinetic energy of blowing winds, pressure head of water, chemical energy of fuels and nuclear energy etc.

1.5.1 Power Plant Layout and Equipment

Introduction: These days the dependence on electricity is so much that it has become part and parcel of our life. The use of electric power for domestic and industrial purposes is increasing day by day and therefore, it is very essential to generate bulk electric power economically.

The conversion of one type of energy available from natural sources such as water, fuels oils, nuclear substances, sun winds, tides, etc., to electrical energy is called generation of electric power.

Electrical energy is generated by a generator in a power station. The power stations are located at favourable places generally away from the load centres. The mechanically equipment driving the generator in called a prime-mover.

The prime-mover gets its energy from the various sources. The electric power generated by the power stations is transmitted and distributed by overhead lines to the various consumers.

1.6 SOURCES OF ENERGY

The sources of energy may be classified as follows:

1.6.1 Primary Source

Sun, wind and tides are the primary source. The sun is the primary source of energy and the heat energy radiated by the sun can be utilized for the generation of electric power.

The winds have got sufficient energy which can be utilized in wind mills to drive small generators between 2 to 5 kW capacity. Such generators are used for the charging of batteries for continuous use. The generators run by wind are called wind generators.

Tidal wave are produced when there is disturbance in sea. The energy of these tidal waves can be utilized for running small rating generators to generate electric power.

Primary sources of energy are not economical because the natural conditions like sun, wind and tides can be used for limited time and being uncertain make the generation uneconomical. On economical basis, secondary sources of energy are generally used for power generation.

1.6.2 Secondary Sources

(i) **Coal:** Coal is used for generating steam in the boiler and steam turbine drives the generator. Such type of power plants are called thermal or steam power plants.

(ii) **Water:** Water at a high pressure or flowing with a high velocity can be used to run the water turbines which are coupled to the generators. Such type of power station, in which electrical energy is generated by the pressure of water, is called hydro-electric power plant. The main requirement for this type of power plant is that water is available at some height and throughout the year.

This method of power generation is very popular because it is reliable and requires minimum maintenance and care.

(iii) **Fuels:** The fuels may be solid, liquid, or gas such as coal, oil, and fuel gases. Oil and gas are used as fuel for I.C. engines by which the generators are driven. The generators run by diesel engines are called diesel power stations and are used as stand by power stations or as peak load power stations or in interconnected grid system.

For generating small power petrol engines are used as prime mover and for generating large blocks of power diesel engines are commonly used. Modern trend is to use gas turbine prime movers. The gas can also be used by burning it and producing steam from the water in the boiler. The super heated steam under pressure is then injected into steam turbine thereby running the steam turbine and hence the generator.

(iv) **Nuclear Substances:** Nuclear energy is also used for power generation in nuclear power plants.

A very large amount of heat energy is produced by the fission process of the nuclear substances (high atomic weight substances) in the nuclear reactor. The nuclear substances are Uranium (U_{235}), Thorium (Th_{232}) and Plutonium (Pu_{239}). The heat energy obtained by fission of 1 kg of U_{235} is roughly equivalent to that produced by burning 2500 tonnes of high grade coal.

The tremendous amount of heat produced in the nuclear reactor by the fission process of uranium of other nuclear substance is utilized to heat up the liquid sodium metal which is called the *working substance*. The liquid sodium metal carries the heat to the heat exchanger and the heat is used to heat up the water and convert it into steam. After giving up the heat the liquid sodium metal i.e., working substance again fed to the reactor.

1.7 MAIN GENERATING STATIONS

The plants where bulk power energy is produced are known as generating power stations. The following are the main generating stations.

1. Thermal power stations.
2. Hydroelectric power stations.
3. Nuclear power stations.
4. Diesel power stations.

1.7.1 Thermal Power Station

Out of the total power developed in India roughly 50% is thermal. In a thermal power plant, coal is used as fuel. To increase the efficiency of the boiler the coal is burnt in the powdered form. The heat of combustion of coal is utilized to convert water into steam, which runs the steam turbine. To steam turbine is coupled the alternator from which electrical energy is obtained.

This power station is also known as *coal-fired power station* and is adopted only where large amount of power is required to be generated, coal is available in plenty and at responsible cost. The operating cost is about ₹200/- per kW of installed capacity and ₹0.10 per unit generated.

The heat given out by burning 1 kg. of coal completely is called its calorific value. The modern power stations consume about 0.4 to 0.8 kg. of coal per unit depending upon the calorific value and design of the power station. It has been found that hardly 15 to 20% of the heat given out by coal can be usefully utilized. In other words thermal efficiency of these power plants is about 15 to 20%. The average heat value of Indian coal may be taken as 6700 kcal/kg. Over all efficiency of the power station, which is the product of thermal efficiency and electrical efficiency, is quite low and varies from 20% to 30% due to the following reasons:

(i) Heat lost in the condenser.
(ii) Heat lost in various stages.

The schematic line diagram of a modern steam power station is shown in Fig. 1.1. The arrangement can be divided into the following stages:

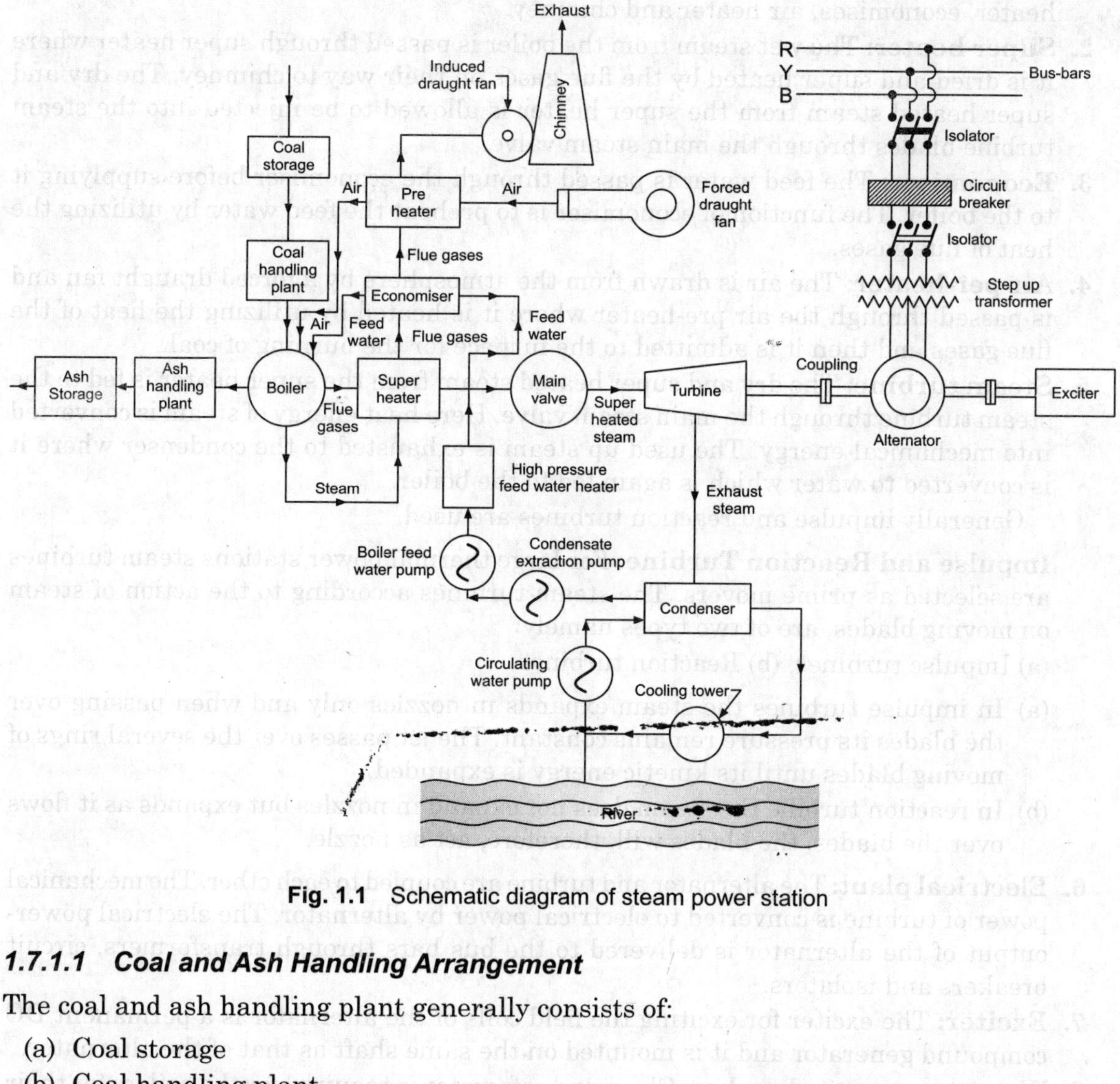

Fig. 1.1 Schematic diagram of steam power station

1.7.1.1 Coal and Ash Handling Arrangement

The coal and ash handling plant generally consists of:

(a) Coal storage
(b) Coal handling plant
(c) Ash handling plant
(d) Ash storage

The coal is stored in the coal storage plant and from there it is delivered to the coal handling plant where it is crushed into small pieces for proper burning. The coal in the powdered form is burnt in the boiler. The ash produced due to burning of coal is delivered to ash handling plant and then removed to ash storage plant. The ash is removed from the boiler for the proper burning of coal.

1. **Boiler:** The heat of combustion produced by burning coal in the boiler is used to heat up water and to convert it into steam. The steam so formed is wet and wet steam is harmful for turbine blades. The wet steam is passed through super heater where it dries and gets super heated. The flue gases pass out to atmosphere through super heater, economises, air heater and chimney.
2. **Super heater:** The wet steam from the boiler is passed through super heater where it is dried and super heated by the flue gases on their way to chimney. The dry and super heated steam from the super heater is allowed to be injected into the steam turbine blades through the main steam valve.
3. **Economiser:** The feed water is passed through the economiser before supplying it to the boiler. The function of economiser is to preheat the feed water by utilizing the heat of flue gases.
4. **Air per-heater:** The air is drawn from the atmosphere by a forced draught fan and is passed through the air pre-heater where it is heated by utilizing the heat of the flue gases and then it is admitted to the furnace for the burning of coal.
5. **Steam turbine:** The dry and super heated steam from the super heater is fed to the steam turbine through the main steam valve. Here heat energy of steam is converted into mechanical energy. The used up steam is exhausted to the condenser where it is converted to water which is again fed to the boiler.

   Generally impulse and reaction turbines are used.

   Impulse and Reaction Turbine: For large thermal power stations steam turbines are selected as prime movers. The steam turbines according to the action of steam on moving blades, are of two types namely:

   (a) Impulse turbines, (b) Reaction turbines

   (a) In impulse turbines the steam expands in nozzles only and when passing over the blades its pressure remains constant. The jet passes over the several rings of moving blades until its kinetic energy is expanded.

   (b) In reaction turbine the steam does not expand in nozzles but expands as it flows over the blades, the blades will, therefore, act as nozzle.
6. **Electrical plant:** The alternator and turbine are coupled to each other. The mechanical power of turbine is converted to electrical power by alternator. The electrical power-output of the alternator is delivered to the bus bars through transformers, circuit breakers and isolators.
7. **Exciter:** The exciter for exciting the field coils of the alternator is a permanent DC compound generator and it is mounted on the same shaft as that of the alternator.
8. **Water treatment chamber:** Clean and soft water is required for the boilers for their long life. The water taken from the river is stored in the storage tanks and chemical treatment is done to make it soft and clean. Clean and soft water is delivered to the boiler by means of feed water pump.

9. **Control room:** The control room houses all the measuring instruments for each panel of alternator and feeder, synchronizing gear, protective gear, automatic voltage regulator etc.
10. **Switch yard:** The switch yard houses transformers, circuit breakers and switches for connecting and disconnecting. The supply to the bus bars from the alternator is taken through transformers and circuit breakers of suitable ratings.

    The power station also requires workshop, store, library and residential accommodation for operating staff.

1.7.1.2 Selection of Site of Thermal Power Station

While selecting site for a thermal power plant, following considerations play the dominant part.

1. Nearness of load so that transmission losses can be cut down.
2. Nearness of coal mines so that transporting charges can be cut down. It may be noted that it is cheaper and convenient to transmit power than transport coal. Hence, as far as possible, thermal power stations should be located near coal mines.
3. Ample supply of water for cooling. The water requirement of a thermal power plant varies from 5 to 8 litres per minute per kW.
4. Availability of adequate land. The land requirement varies from 250 sq. meter to 500 sq meter per megawatt.
5. Means for ash disposal.
6. Transportation facilities.

Advantages

1. The fuel used is quite cheap. To generate 1 kWh of electrical energy about 0.5 kg of coal is necessary.
2. Less space is required as compared to hydroelectric power station.
3. It can be located near the load centres.
4. It can be installed at any place.
5. Cheaper in production cost in comparison with that of diesel power station.
6. Less initial cost as compared to other power stations (hydroelectric and nuclear).

Disadvantages

1. Costlier in running cost as compared to hydroelectric power plant.
2. Atmosphere is polluted (made dirty) due to smoke and fumes.

Thermal Efficiency

$$\text{Thermal efficiency} = \frac{\text{Heat quivatent of mechanical energy transmitted to turbine shaft}}{\text{Heat of combustion}}$$

$$\text{Overall efficiency} = \frac{\text{Heat equivalent of electrical output}}{\text{Heat of combustion}}$$

$$= \text{Generator efficiency} \times \text{Turbine efficiency} \times \text{Boiler efficiency}$$

$$= 18\% \text{ to } 30\%$$

While calculating the overall efficiency of the station, alternator efficiency is also taken into account. More than half of total heat of combustion is lost as heat rejected to condenser. The useful output is about 25 to 35% in a well designed station.

EXAMPLE 1.1 A thermal power station consumes 0.7 kg of coal to generate 1 kWh of electrical energy. If the thermal efficiency of the station is 16.5%. Calculate the calorific value of coal.

Solution: Calorific value of coal is defined as the amount of heat produced in calories by complete combustion of 1 kg of coal.

Let us assume that coal has calorific value of x calories per kg.

Heat contained in 0.7 kg of coal = 0.7 x calories

But 1 calorie = 4.2 joules or watt seconds

Energy contained in 0.7 kg coal = 0.7 x × 4.2 watt seconds

= 2.94 x watt seconds

Energy output = 1 kWh = 1000 × 3600 watt seconds

Thermal efficiency η = 16.5%

So,
$$\frac{1000 \times 3600}{2.94x} = \frac{16.5}{100} \left[\eta = \frac{\text{Output}}{\text{Input}}\right]$$

$$x = \left[\frac{100 \times 1000 \times 3600}{16.5 \times 2.94}\right]$$

x = 7440 kilo calories per kg. **Ans.**

1.7.1.3 Major Thermal Power Plants in Northen Region

1. Guru Nanak thermal power station at Bhatinda.
2. Guru Govind Singh super power plant, Ropar.
3. National thermal power house at Delhi.
4. Inderprastha power house at Delhi.
5. Thermal power plant, Badarpur.
6. Faridabad thermal power plant.
7. Thermal power plant at Panipat.
8. Thermal power plant at Yamuna Nagar

1.7.2 Hydroelectric Power Plant

In hydro power plant the energy contained in water is utilized to rotate hydraulic turbines to which are coupled electrical generators. Water lying at height contains potential energy where as fast moving rivers contain kinetic energy. For satisfactory operation, sufficient quantity of water at a reasonable head or reasonable quantity of water at a very high height must be available. Power P which can be produced at 100% efficiency is given by

$$P = 8.5 \times Q \times H \text{ kW}$$

where Q is the discharge in cubic metre per second and H is the head in metres.

In these power stations, water is stored at a suitable place by constructing a dam and water head is obtained. The kinetic and potential energies of water are utilized to turn the water turbine. Alternator is coupled to the hydraulic turbine and hence electrical energy is obtained from the alternator.

The water stored at a high altitude is allowed to fall on the turbine blades through the penstock. The potential and kinetic energy of water is first converted into mechanical energy and then into electrical energy. Continuous flow of water throughout the year is necessary for proper operation of this plant. Therefore, when planning the site of this power station, the study of rainfall, stream flow, available head and facilities of storing water etc., are to be studied.

These power stations are generally located in hilly areas where large reservoir can be built easily. The operating cost of the plant is ₹250 per kW of installed capacity and 15 paisa per unit generated.

1.7.2.1 Elements of Hydroelectric Power Plant

The schematic diagram of a hydroelectric power plant and whole arrangement is shown in Fig. 1.2 and can be divided into the following major components:

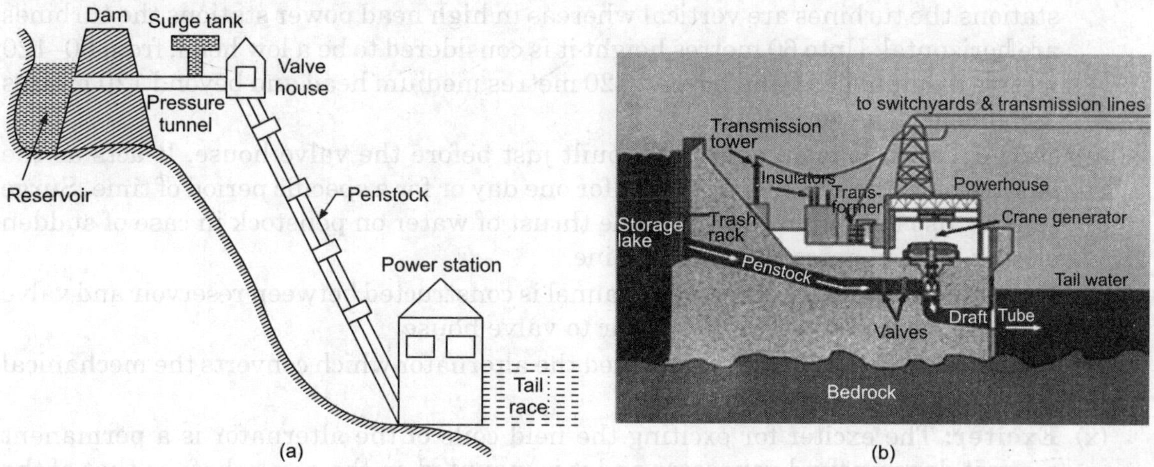

Fig. 1.2 Schematic arrangement of a hydroelectric power plant

(i) Catchment area	(ii) Water reservoir
(iii) Dam	(iv) Valve house
(v) Penstock	(vi) Hydraulic turbine
(vii) Surge tank	(viii) Pressure channel
(ix) Alternator	(x) Exciter
(xi) Tail race	(xii) Draft tube
(xiii) Spillway	(xiv) Control room
(xv) Switch yard	

(i) **Catchment Area**: It is the area over which rainfall is collected and led to the reservoir.

(ii) **Water Reservoir**: A dam is constructed across a river at a suitable place and water is stored in the catchment area in large quantity from where it is led to the water reservoir. The main sources of water are rainfall and melting of ice in the mountains.

(iii) **Dam**: It is generally a masonry structure and its functions are to create water head and to store water in the catchment area. The dam should be able to resist failure against sliding, overturning and rupturing. The water from the reservoir is brought to the surge tank through the pressure channel.

(iv) **Valve House**: At the start of the penstock there is a valve house which contains main sluice valves for controlling the water flow. In addition to this there are also provided automatic isolating valves which come into operation when the penstock bursts, which cuts off further supply of water.

(v) **Penstock**: The huge steel or concrete pipe that conveys the water from valve house to water turbine.

(vi) **Hydraulic Turbine**: From the penstock water is taken to the turbine. The turbine converts the water energy into mechanical energy. Water turbine may be broadly classified into:

(a) Impulse turbines (Pelton wheel)

(b) Reaction turbines (Kaplans, Francis turbines).

Impulse turbines are used for high head power stations and reaction turbines are used for low and medium head power stations. In low and medium head power stations the turbines are vertical whereas in high head power stations the turbines are horizontal. Upto 60 metres height it is considered to be a low head, from 60–120 metres medium head and beyond 120 metres medium head and beyond 120 metres a high speed power station.

(vii) **Surge Tank:** It is an open tank built just before the valve house. It acts as the storage of water which is sufficient for one day or for a specific period of time. Surge tank is also helpful in reducing the thrust of water on penstock in case of sudden closing of fixed gates of water turbine.

(viii) **Pressure Channel:** A pressure channel is constructed between reservoir and valve house to carry water from reservoir to valve house.

(ix) **Alternator:** To the turbine is coupled the alternator which converts the mechanical energy into electrical energy.

(x) **Exciter:** The exciter for exciting the field coils of the alternator is a permanent magnet dc compound generator and it is mounted on the same shaft as that of the alternator.

(xi) **Tail Race:** After the water has done its useful work in the turbine, it is discharged to the tail race which may lead it to the same stream.

(xii) **Draft Tube:** An air tight pipe of suitable diameter attached to the runner outlet and conducting water down from the wheel and discharging it under the surface of water to the tail race is known as draft tube.

(xiii) **Spillway:** It is normally constructed at the top of the dam acting as a safety valve by discharging the overflow of water to the downstream when the reservoir is full during rainy season. This is generally constructed of concrete and provided with water discharge openings shut off by metal control gates. By changing the degree to which the gates are opened the discharge of water head can be accomplished in order to maintain the water level in the reservoir.

(xiv) **Control Room:** All controlling equipment, protective devices, indicating instruments are placed on the panel.

(xv) **Switch Yard:** The open space where various electrical equipment like transformers, CTs, PTs etc., are installed.

Advantages

1. It is quite neat and clean.
2. It is economical in large sizes.
3. Running costs are less since no fuel is required.
4. It can be started in no time.
5. It is simple in construction, robust and requires low maintenance.
6. It has higher efficiency and long life.
7. It can meet wide fluctuating loads without any difficulty.
8. It helps in irritation and controlling of the floods.

Disadvantages

1. High capital cost.
2. High cost of transmission lines.
3. Power supply may be effected during dry season.
4. Skilled and experienced hands are required to build the plant.

Selection of Site

1. It should be selected where sufficient water at a reasonable head is available.
2. Reservoir should have large catchment area.
3. Transportation facilities should be adequate.
4. Possibility of constructing the dam should be there.
5. The land should be cheap.
6. The bearing capacity of the soil should be sufficient so that heavy equipment can be installed.
7. The site selected should be near the load centres as far as possible to reduce the cost of transmission.
8. Possibility of steam diversion during period of construction should be examined.

1.7.2.2 *Classification of Hydro-electric Power Plants*

Hydro-electric plant can be classified as:

(i) Low head hydro-electric plant
(ii) Medium head hydro-electric plant
(iii) High head hydro-electric plant

1. Low Head Power Plant

The water head upto 50 m is considered as low head plant. In the low head plants Kaplan turbines are used. The penstock used are of large diameters and short length. Such a plant is shown in Fig. 1.3.

Generators employed in such plants are of low speed and large diameters.

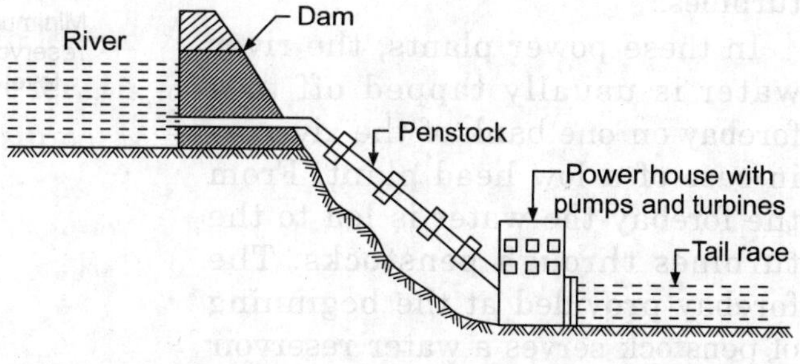

Fig. 1.3 Arrangement of low head hydro-electric plant

2. Medium Head Power Plant

The layout of medium head (300 m) plant is shown in Fig. 1.4. In such plants horizontal shaft Francis turbines are employed.

In medium head plant river consists essentially of a dam across the stream to back up the river and create a fall, the water flowing through the turbines and rejoining the river below the dam. A dam or barrage constructed across the river creates the necessary head. The power plant is located near the dam and therefore, no surge tank is required. The schematic arrangement of medium head hydroelectric power plant is shown in Fig. 1.4.

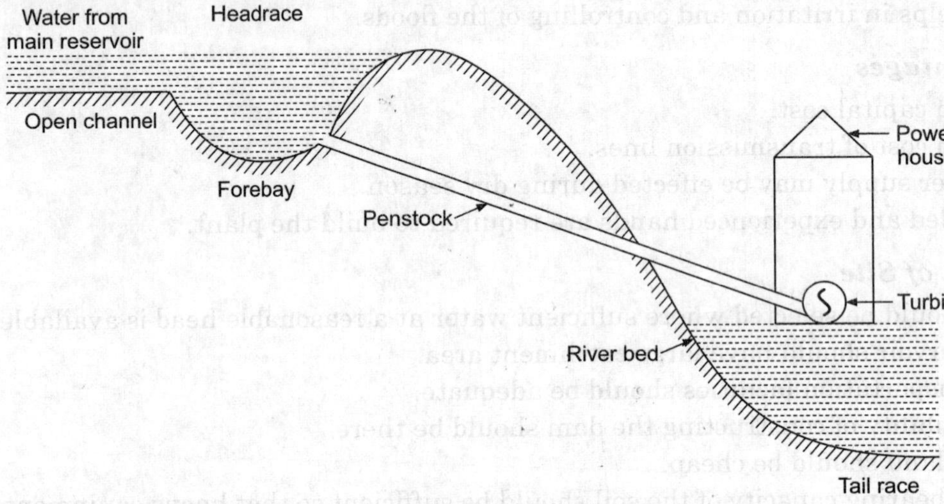

Fig. 1.4 Arrangement of medium head hydroelectric power plant

3. High Head Power Plant

Figure 1.5 shows the layout of high head plant (above 300 m). A pressure tunnel is constructed between reservoir to valve house at the start of penstock. It is used to carry water from reservoir to valve house. A surge tank is built in between the penstock and valve house. Surge tank also serves as a ready reservoir from which the turbine can draw water in case of sudden increased in demand. Penstocks are steel pipes and carry the water from the valve house to the turbines.

In these power plants, the river water is usually tapped off to a forebay on one bank of the river as in case of a low head plant. From the forebay the water is led to the turbines through penstocks. The forebay provided at the beginning of penstock serves a water reservoir

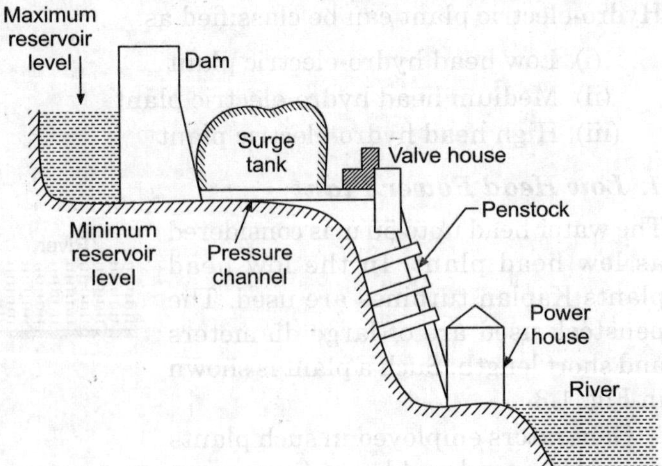

Fig. 1.5 Arrangement of high hydroelectric power plant

for such power plants. In these plants water is usually carried in open channel from main reservoir to the forebay and then to the turbines through the penstock. The forebay itself serves as the surge tank in this case.

1.7.2.3 Classification According to the Type of Load Supplied

According to the load supplied hydroelectric power stations may be classified into:

(i) Base load
(ii) Peak load and
(iii) Pumped storage plants.

Base Load and Peak Load Power Stations

The consumer load on a power station varies from time to time. Therefore, a power station has a cope with the varying demand of the consumers. The generators are pressed into service if load demand increases and shut down when load demand decreases. But there is always some minimum load on the power station which remains constant throughout the day. This unvarying load is known as base load and the maximum load occurring in load curve, excluding the base load, is known as peak load. In short the minimum load which remains almost the whole day on a station is known as base load.

It is not economical and advisable to design the power station on the basis of peak load because if the power station is designed on the basis of peak load then for most of the time many generators will remain idle thus reducing the load factor and increasing the cost of generation.

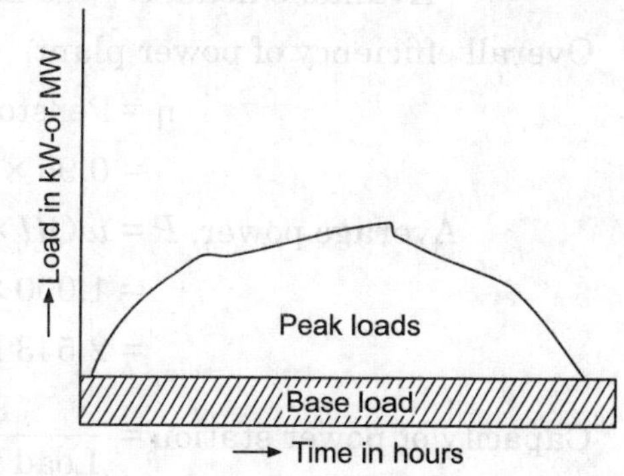

Fig. 1.6 Time-load curve

(i) **Base Load:** The power stations which are designed for base loads and are required throughout the day are known as *base load stations.* In short the maximum load on a power station at a particular time is known as its *base load.*

(ii) **Peak Load:** The power stations which are installed to share the load of base load stations during peak hours are called peak load stations.

Thermal and hydroelectric power stations are used as base load stations because of their low running cost and diesel power stations, are best suited for peak load stations due to quick starting and high running cost.

(iii) **Pumped Storage Plant:** This is a unique design of peak load plant. A pumped storage plant works much like a conventional hydroelectric station, except the same water can be used over and over again.

1.7.2.4 Hydro-plant Auxiliaries

The following are the main auxiliaries required for hydro-electric plants.

1. Governer
2. Cranes
3. Air compressor
4. Cooling water pumps
5. Lubricating oil pumps
6. Valves

7. Drainage pumps
8. CO_2 cylinders
9. Battery charging units

EXAMPLE 1.2 A hydroelectric station is to be designed for a catchment area of 400 km², rainfall for which is 125 cm/annum. The head available is 30 m. If 75% of the total rainfall is available, rest is lost to evaporation. Penstock efficiency 95% Turbine efficiency 85% and generator efficiency is 90% and load factor 40%. Determine the capacity of the station.

Solution: Quantity of water available for utilization per second,

$$= \frac{\text{Catchment area in km}^2 \times 10^6 \times \text{average annual rainfall in } m \times \text{yield factor}}{365 \times 24 \times 60 \times 60}$$

$$= \frac{400 \times 10^6 \times 1.25 \times 0.75}{8{,}760 \times 3{,}600} = 11.89 \text{ m}^3$$

Available head, $H = 30$ m

Overall efficiency of power plant,

$$\eta = \text{Penstock efficiency} \times \text{turbine efficiency} \times \text{generator efficiency}$$

$$= 0.95 \times 0.85 \times 0.9 = 0.72675$$

$$\text{Average power, } P = wQH \times 9.81 \times \eta \times 10^{-6} \text{ MW}$$

$$= 1{,}000 \times 11.89 \times 30 \times 9.81 \times 0.72675 \times 10^{-6}$$

$$= 2.543 \text{ MW}$$

$$\text{Capacity of power station} = \frac{P}{\text{Load factor}}$$

$$= \frac{2.543}{0.4} = 6.36 \text{ MW} \quad \textbf{Ans.}$$

1.7.3 Nuclear or Atomic Power Station

In this power station there is no steam boiler but a nuclear reactor is used as the source of heat. Uranium (U_{235}), Thorium (Th_{232}) and Plutonium (PU_{239}) are main nuclear fuels. The nuclear fuel are a highly concentrated form of energy and are high atomic weight metals. By fission process in a nuclear reactor, the above metals become unstable and become metals of lower atomic weight like silicon, nickel etc. The heat energy obtained by the fission of 1 kg of U_{235} is roughly equal to that produced by burning 2500 tonnes of high quality coal. The heat energy produced is utilized in raising steam which runs the steam turbine. Alternator is coupled to the steam turbine.

The schematic diagram of a nuclear power plant is shown in Fig. 1.7 and whole arrangement can be divided into the following stages:

1. Nuclear reactor
2. Heat exchanger
3. Steam turbine
4. Alternator

High atomic weight substance (U_{235}) undergoes the process of nuclear fission in the nuclear reactor. The substance becomes disintegrated and enormous amount of heat is produced. The heat produced in the nuclear reactor by the fission process is given to liquid sodium metal which carries the heat to heat exchanger. The liquid sodium metal is called working substance. In the heat exchanger the heat of working substance is utilized to heat up the water and convert it into steam. After giving up heat, the working substance is again fed to the reactor.

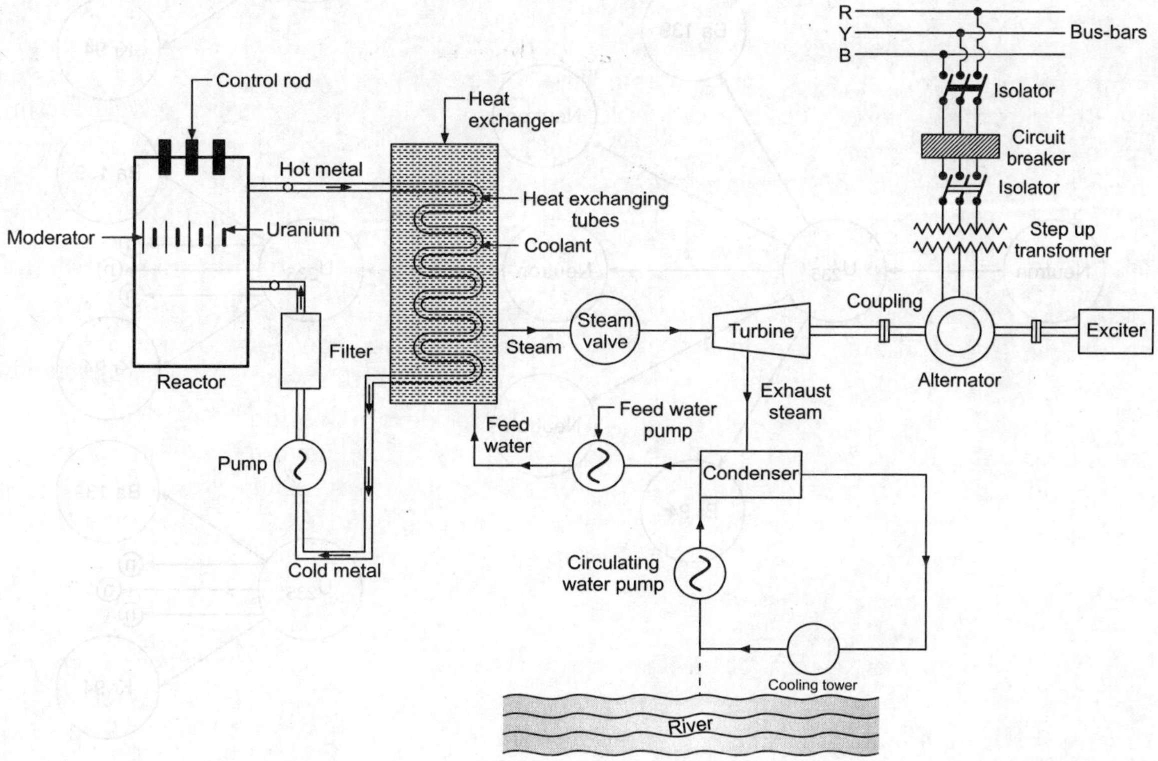

Fig. 1.7 Schematic diagram of Nuclear Power Station

The steam produced in the heat exchanger is fed to the steam turbine through the steam valve. Here the heat energy is converted to mechanical energy. To the steam turbine is coupled the alternator and from the alternator, electrical energy output is carried on to the bus bars through a step up transformers isolator and circuit breaker.

1.7.3.1 Chain Reaction

In the nuclear power plant nuclear energy is converted into electrical energy. In these power plant heavy nuclear material such as U_{235} is placed in the nuclear reactor and bombarded by neutron, resulting in U_{235} split into two lighter atoms (barium and krypton) along with a very huge amount of energy.

U235 + neutron $\xrightarrow{\text{Fusion}}$ Ba139 + Kr94 + 3 neutron + energy. Above reaction shows that during reaction, three new neutrons are released. These neutrons further react with uranium and produce same product. Thus chain reaction takes place and can be controlled by moderator.

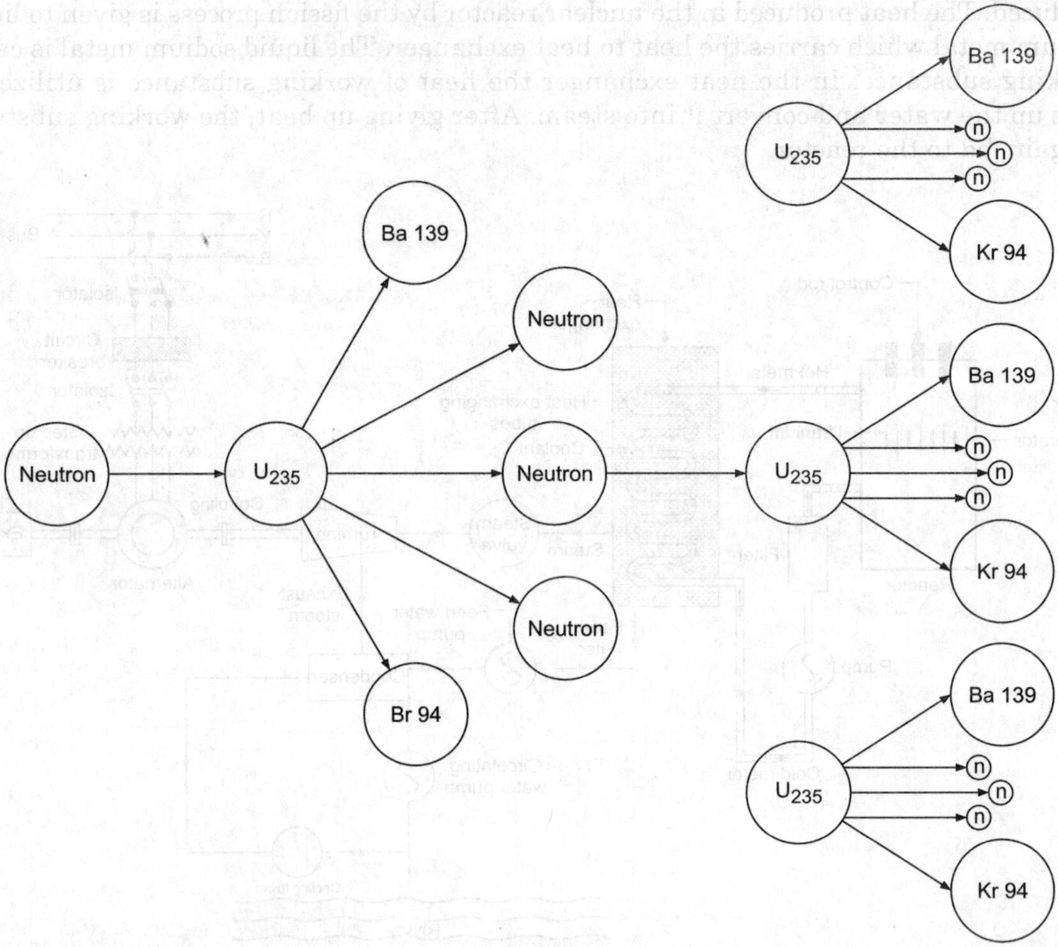

Fig. 1.8 Chain reaction

1.7.3.2 Main Parts of Nuclear Plant

The two main parts of a nuclear plant are Heat exchanger and a Nuclear reactor. The heat exchanger together with the steam turbine, condenser and alternator is similar to an ordinary thermal power plant with the difference that in this power plant the heat exchanger has replaced the boiler of thermal power plant.

Main parts of nuclear reactor are:

1. **Reactor Core:** It is the apparatus where controlled nuclear fission chain reaction is carried out so that released energy can be utilized. It is in the form of sphere or a cylinder and contains a number of fuel rods of radioactive elements.
2. **Moderator:** Moderators are the substances which are capable of slowing down neutrons. The process of slowing down the speed of the neutrons is known as moderation. The slow neutrons are more effective. Moderator rods are made of graphite in triggering fission in natural uranium than the fast neutrons. Heavy water; light water and graphite are more commonly used moderating materials.

3. **Shielding:** Reactor is properly shielded so that deadly α and β particle radiations and γ rays which are released during the process of nuclear fission, remain inside the reactor only and there is proper protection outside.
4. **Coolant:** It is the medium through which the heat produced in reactor is transferred to the heat exchanger for production of steam. Coolant also keeps the internal surface of the reactor at the prescribed temperature. Sometimes the same materials is used as the coolant as well as the moderator but commonly air, helium, CO_2 or molten sodium are the materials which are used as coolant.
5. **Reflectors:** These are the substances which have good scattering and low absorbing power for neutrons striking against them. These are used to reflect the neutrons back into reactor core and are a mean of controlling the chain reaction. Moderators are usually good reflectors also.
6. **Control System:** All power plant reactors are provided with the means to regulate the fission process so that energy is generated according to the load requirements and in an emergency the reactor can be shut down quickly. Generally central rods, i.e., the metal rods containing strong neutrons absorbers such as cadmium and boron are used. Various electronic and electromagnetic devices are used to regulate the position of the central rods.

Nuclear Power Plant in India

1. 1400 MW Tarapur Nuclear Power Plant at Tarapur near Mumbai.
2. 1400 MW Rana Partap Atomic Power Station at Kota (Rajasthan).
3. 440 MW Madras Power Station at Kalpakkam.
4. 220 MW Kakrapar Atomic Power Station Gujarat.

Advantages

1. Amount of fuel required is very small.
2. Low running cost.
3. Very economical in large capacity.
4. Generation cost is small.
5. The plants can be located near the load centre, therefore, primary distribution cost is reduced.
6. The output control is extremely flexible.

Disadvantages

1. High capital cost (about 2 to 2.5 times that of thermal power plants).
2. Fuel is very costly.
3. Greater technical knowledge is required.
4. Not suitable for variable load operation as the reactors cannot be easily controlled to respond quickly to load changes.
5. It pollutes the environment.
6. It has high maintenance cost.

Location of Site

Some of the factors which should be considered in deciding the location of a nuclear power station are as under :

1. Adequate supply of water for cooling.
2. Away from habitation due to radioactive radiations.
3. Near to the load centre as far as possible to reduce the primary distribution cost.
4. Safety of area from danger of floods.
5. Approach to the site by rail and road.

Due to high capital cost these stations can be competitive only if they operate at high load factor (about 80%).

1.7.4 Diesel Power Station

A diesel power plant is installed where:

(i) Supply of coal and water is not available in sufficient quantity.
(ii) Power is to be generated in small quantity.
(iii) Standby sets are required for continuity of supply such as in radio stations, telephone exchanges, hospitals and cinema houses.
(iv) Peak loads are to be supplied for small duration or for seasonal loads in a medium size power installation.
(v) Power supply is required for auxiliaries in the event of failure of the main working units in steam power plant.
(vi) A few machines are to be run in case of road construction and building construction.
(vii) Consumers like to have their own power supply for emergency reasons.

In this power station, heat of combustion of diesel oil is used to run the diesel engine. The diesel engine is coupled the alternator from where electrical energy is obtained.

With average calorific value of diesel oil as 10800 kcal/kg and efficiency between 32 to 38%, the fuel consumption comes out to be 0.3 liters/kWh.

The prime mover of diesel power plant is compression ignition engine usually working on 4 stroke cycle. During first stroke air is sucks in, during second stroke it is compressed and its temperature and pressure rises. At the end of compression stroke fuel is injected in the cylinder which burns and expansion of gases takes place. Then third stroke starts which is called power stroke. After work is done, the gases of combustion are exhausted during fourth stroke. Hence the stage of a 4 stroke internal combustion engine are:

(i) Suction stroke
(ii) Compression stroke
(iii) Working stroke or power stroke
(iv) Exhaust stroke.

Diesel power plant as shown in Fig. 1.9 consists of the following auxiliary system in addition to diesel engine:

1. **Air intake system and exhaust system:** The air is led to the engine cylinder through air filters. Exhaust gases are discharged into atmosphere outside the building through silencer to reduce noise.
2. **Fuel system:** The diesel oil delivered to the plant is stored in the storage tank which has usually a capacity to store oil for 2 or 3 months. From the storage tank, oil is

transferred to smaller all day tank by means of transfer pump. Fuel injection oil pump then draws its oil supply from all day fuel tank through filter and feeds it to the diesel engine.

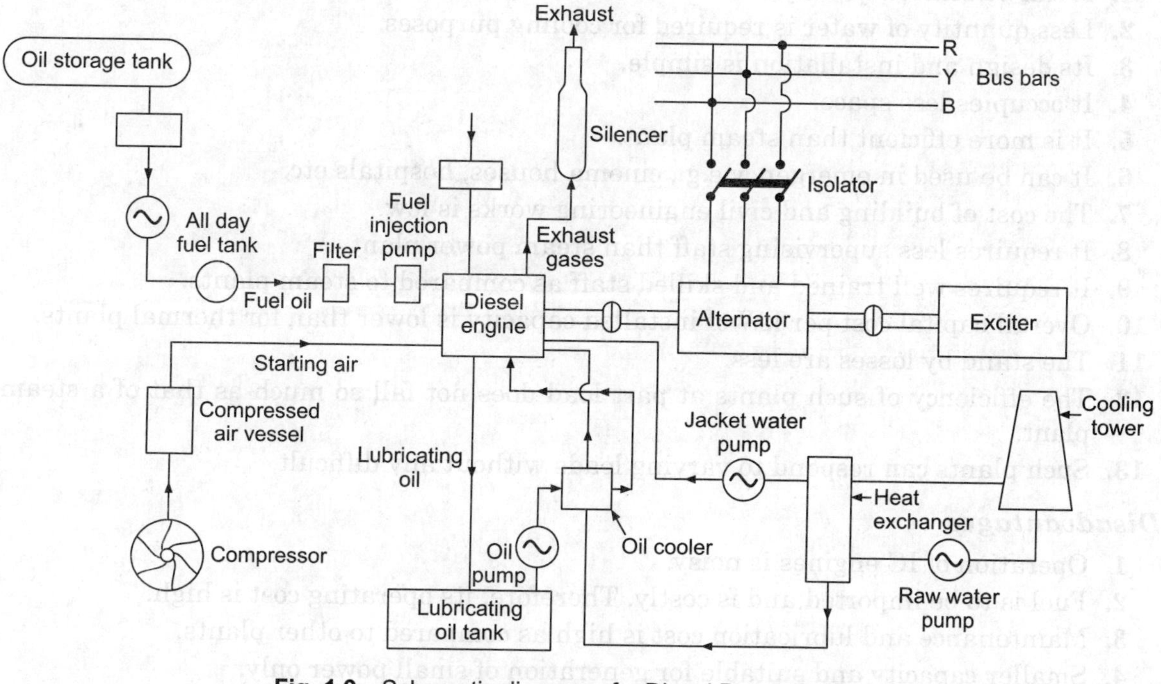

Fig. 1.9 Schematic diagram of a Diesel Power Station

3. **Engine starting system:** Diesel engines are started by sending compressed air at 18-20 kg/sq cm pressure in the engine cylinder. Compressed air is obtained with the help of a compressor. Fuel oil is admitted in the engine cylinder which starts burning and converts chemical energy of fuel into mechanical energy. Small engines are, however, started by battery.
4. **Alternator:** To the diesel engine is coupled the alternator. The mechanical energy available at the diesel engine shaft is converted into electrical energy.
5. **Engine cooling system:** Due to constant running, the engine become sufficiently hot which may damage the cylinder liners, heads and walls and piston and its rings. Therefore, it is essential that the engine is cooled property. This is done by circulating cold water in the cylinder jacket by means of jacket water pump. Cooling water should by soft. If soft water is not available, water softening plant is installed. Cylinder jacket output water is cooled in heat exchanger. The cold water output of heat exchanger on its way to cylinder jacket cools the lubricating oil in cooler.
6. **Lubricating oil system:** Lubricating oil being circulated by oil pump through oil cooler performs the following functions :

   (i) Lubricates bearings and cylinder.
   (ii) Removes heat from cylinder and bearings.
   (iii) Carries away solid matter from rubbing moving parts.
   (iv) Provides gas tight seal between piston rings and cylinder.

The advantages and disadvantages of diesel-electric power station are given below:

Advantages

1. It can be started quickly.
2. Less quantity of water is required for cooling purposes.
3. Its design and installation is simple.
4. It occupies less space.
5. It is more efficient than steam plant.
6. It can be used in emergency e.g., cinema houses, hospitals etc.
7. The cost of building and civil engineering works is low.
8. It requires less supervising staff than steam power plant.
9. It requires well trained and skilled staff as compared to steam plants.
10. Overall capital cost per kW of installed capacity is lower than for thermal plants.
11. The stand by losses are less.
12. The efficiency of such plants at part load does not fall so much as that of a steam plant.
13. Such plants can respond to varying loads without any difficult.

Disadvantages

1. Operation of IC engines is noisy.
2. Fuel is to be imported and is costly. Therefore, its operating cost is high.
3. Maintenance and lubrication cost is high as compared to other plants.
4. Smaller capacity and suitable for generation of small power only.
5. Diesel plants cannot supply overloads continuously whereas steam plant can work under 25% overload continuously.

Choice of Site

The diesel power station can be installed at any place.

1.7.4.1 Applications of Diesel Power Plant

Thermal, hydro and atomic power plants are commonly used for generating bulk power but diesel electric power plant is sometimes exclusively used at the places where demand is too less or to supplement hydroelectric plants. They have also been used as house service sets in large thermal power plants. The main applications of diesel electric plants are as follows:

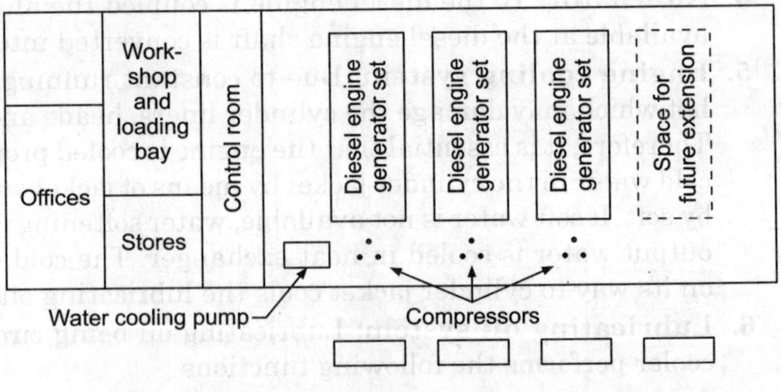

Fig. 1.10 Typical layout of a Diesel Power Plant

(i) As standby plant for continuity of electric supply such as in hospitals, telephone exchanges, TV and ratio stations and cinemas houses diesel plant supplies power when power supply from main station plants (hydro, thermal or atomic) fails due to certain faults.

(ii) As peak load plant to supply peak load on the power system while the basic load is supplied either by thermal or hydro station.

(iii) **As private power plant for small industries:** These plants have applications as private industrial plants to supply power to factories. It can be conveniently run for shorter period when required for seasonal loads.

(iv) **Power to sparsely populated areas:** For sparsely populated areas which are remote from the existing transmission facilities, it may be many time cheaper to take power from Local Diesel Stations.

1.7.4.2 Starting Diesel Engine

Small engines may be started by cranking them by hand, with an arrangement to relieve compression during cranking. But large and medium size engines are started either by using a petrol driven auxiliary engine or by using compressed air at 16-20 kg/cm^3. A compressor driven by an induction motor or diesel engine with a reservoir tank and inter connecting piping is installed for the purpose.

1. Diesel Oil Storage

Diesel is stored steel over head tanks or under ground steel tanks. A masonry tank capable to contain the entire oil is constructed all round the over ground tank. The storage capacity should be sufficient for about eight to twelve weeks of operations. Diesel is transferred from the main storage tank or by motor operated pump through filters to the overhead day tank placed near each engine.

2. Cooling Water

The circulating water should not be hard water, so before use it should be analysed for the presence of sulphates, bicarbonates and silicate of calcium and magnesium which result in scale formation with in the cooling jackets. Hard water is passed through cooling towers and heat exchanger only. Water is cooled either in open tanks with or without spray nozzles or in cooling tower which employ natural, forced or induced draft.

1.7.4.3 Operation of Diesel Engine

For smooth operation of diesel engine at maximum efficiency, observe the following points:

(i) Note exhaust temperature from all the cylinders.

(ii) Watch the temperature of inlet and outlet water. The difference between the two should not exceed 8–12°C.

(iii) Watch the temperature and pressure of lubricating oil.

(iv) Fuel, air and lubricating oil filters should be periodically checked and they may be cleaned or replaced as and when necessary; so that diesel, air and lubricating oil remains always clean.

(v) Check and calibrate injection periodically. The colour of exhaust smoke is a good guide to the state of engine. Black smoke means incomplete combustion.

EXAMPLE 1.3 A diesel power station has fuel consumption of 0.26 kg per kWh, the calorific value of the oil being 10,000 kcals for kg. Determine the overall efficiency of the power station.

Solution: We know

$$\text{Overall efficiency} = \frac{\text{Output}}{\text{Input}}$$

$$\text{Input} = \text{Fuel consumption/kWh output} \times \text{Calorific value of the fuel}$$

$$= 0.26 \times 10000 \text{ kcals} = 2600 \text{ kcals}$$

$$\text{Overall efficiency} = \frac{\text{Output}}{\text{Input}} \times 100$$

$$= \frac{860}{2600} \times 100 \text{ (1 kWh = 860 kcals)} = 33.06\%$$

1.8 GAS TURBINE POWER PLANT

Introduction: Gas turbine electric power plant is a power plant in which a gas turbine is used as the prime-mover for the generation of electrical energy.

In steam power plants, the products of combustion do not form the working medium. These are utilized to produce an intermediate fluid, called the steam which is expanded in the turbine. The principle employed in gas turbine electric power plant in which gas is directly expanded in the turbine. The gas turbine is different from the diesel engine in this respect that the combustion region is eternal to the prime-mover.

In a gas turbine, the working medium is either a mixture of combustion products and air or heated air at a certain pressure and a higher initial temperature. With respect to design, a gas turbine is quite similar to a steam turbine. In the turbine blading, working gas expands and the heat energy is converted first into the kinetic energy and then to the work of the turbine shaft rotation.

The principle of a gas turbine power plant is that a turbo-compressor compresses working medium to a high pressure and then it is brunt in the combustion chamber where the combustion takes place at a constant pressure and temperature of working medium is raised. The high pressure and high temperature working medium is then expanded in a gas turbine coupled to the alternator. The overall efficiency of a gas turbine as a prime-mover is limited due to the fact that a large portion of the power developed by the turbine is used in driving the compressor and also by the temperature safely attainable.

1.8.1 Elements of Simple Gas Turbine Power Plants

A simple gas turbine power plant essentially consists of the reaction type non-condensing turbine, a compressor mounted on the same shaft and coupled to the turbine, the combustion chamber, an alternator coupled to the turbine itself and auxiliaries such as starting motor, auxiliary lubrication pumps, oil system, fuel system and duct system etc. A schematic arrangement for simple gas turbine power plant is illustrated in Fig. 1.11.

1. Compressor

The compressor used in the gas turbine power plant is usually of rotary type. The air is sucked in by the compressor from the atmosphere through the filter, which removes the

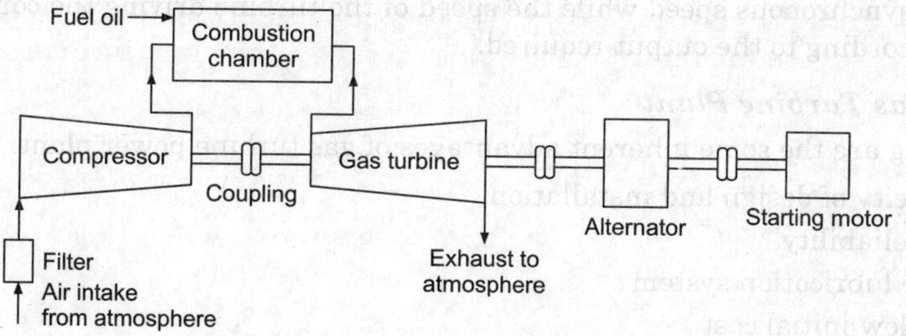

Fig. 1.11 Schematic arrangement of a simple Gas Turbine Power Plant

dust from the air. The rotary blades of the compressor push the air between the stationary blades to raise its pressure to 4–5 atmospheres. Thus air is available at high pressure at the output of the compressor.

2. Combustion Chamber

The combustion chamber consists to a vessel into which the air at high pressure from the compressor is fed. Fuel is injected into the combustion chamber and burnt in the stream of air supplied from the compressor. A part of the air is delivered ahead of the burning fuel of order to cool the very hot combustion products (at temperature of around 1.650°C) and bring them to a temperature around 800°C when these can be allowed to enter the turbine without causing damage to the first few rows of blades.

The products of combustion comprising of mixture of gases at high temperature and pressure are passes through the gas turbine. These gases in passing over the turbine blades expand and thus result in motion of rotor and finally discharged to the atmosphere at a temperature of about 540°C.

Part of the power development by the gases in passing through the turbines is used to run the compressor and auxiliaries and the rest is used to generate electrical energy driving the generator.

3. Alternator

The alternator is coupled to the gas turbine, converts mechanical energy of the turbine into electrical energy and feeds is to the bus-bars through transformers, circuit breakers and isolators etc.

4. Electric Motor

An electric motor used for starting the compressor (compressor is required to be started before starting of turbine) is mounted on the same shaft as that of the turbine. Once the unit starts, a part of mechanical power output of the turbine drives the compressor and there is no need of motor now. The motor is energized by the batteries.

5. Gas Turbine

The gas turbine has to drive the compressor as well as the alternator. In some cases, these two functions of gas turbines are separated and two different turbines are employed. High pressure turbine drives the compressor and a low pressure turbine drives the alternator. This arrangement has the advantage that the speed of the power turbine can be kept constant at synchronous speed while the speed of the turbine driving the compressor can be varied according to the output required.

Merits of Gas Turbine Plant

The following are the some inherent advantages of gas turbine power plant:

1. Simplicity of design and installation
2. High reliability
3. Simple lubrication system
4. It has low initial cost
5. Compact and has no standby losses
6. It requires small building space
7. It needs little cooling waters
8. Gas turbine can be quickly started
9. It can be operated by remote control and need little attention while operating and shut low
10. Higher efficiency

Demerits

The gas turbine has got some limitations also which are listed below:

1. Low net output
2. Low overall efficiency
3. Noisy operation
4. High specific fuel consumption and limited unit capacity
5. The unit has got starting problems as the compressor has to be started before the starting turbine.

1.8.2 Selection of Site for Gas Turbine Power Plants

Following factors should be considered while selecting site for gas turbine power plant:

1. **Distance from load centre:** The site should be as near to the load centre as possible so that the transmission costs and losses are minimized.
2. **Availability of land:** The land should be easily available and at reasonable rate.
3. **Availability of fuel:** The fuel should be easily available and at reasonable rate.
4. **Availability of transportation facilities:** The transportation facilities should be available.
5. **Distance from populated facilities:** The site should be away from thickly populated area because of noisy operation.
6. **Type of land:** The land should be of high bearing capacity to withstand the load of the plant and also the vibrations transmitted to the foundation from compressors and turbines.

1.8.3 Fuels for Gas Turbines

The most important requirement of the fuel used in gas turbine is that its products of combustion should contain a minimum of matter which might get deposited on the turbine blades or the heat exchanger.

A variety of fuels-solid, liquid and gaseous are available for use in gas turbines. Though coal and peat can be employed as gas turbine fuels but these are not used mainly because of coal handling and ash handling problems. The petroleum fuels such as kerosene, gas oil, diesel oil, residual oil, are quite suitable for use in gas turbines but their use is limited because of their higher costs. Natural gas which is mainly methane, has a very high calorific value and is generally used for auxiliary power generation in oil fields.

Nowadays the gas turbine power plants use mainly natural gas and liquid petroleum fuels. Natural gas contains 80% methane and small fraction of other gases.

1.8.4 Applications

1. Majority of such power plants are usually used for driving generators and supplying peak loads in other types of power plants (steam and hydroelectric power plants), because they can be started and loaded quickly. Other reasons for it are low initial costs and higher fuel costs.
2. Such a plant is used as a starting plant of driving auxiliaries in other power plants.
3. A large number of such plants are also used as base-load power plants where fuel oil or natural gas are cheap and easily available, water supply is scare and load factor is very low, say 15-18%. Base-load gas turbine power plants are likely to play significant role in future.
4. Such plants can be used in parallel with tidal power plants.
5. These plants are used to operate as combination plants with conventional steam boilers.

The overall efficiency of such power plants called the open cycle plants is very low as greater part (around 65%) of the power developed by the turbine is used in driving the compressor. The fact that the hot gases from the combustion chamber are cooled to a safe temperature before admitting it to the turbine, also reduces the efficiency. The overall efficiency of the plant, owing to above reasons seldom exceeds 20%.

1.8.5 Merits and Demerits of Open Cycle Gas Turbine Power Plants

Open cycle gas turbine power plants are simple in design, small in size, light in weight, do not need any warm up time, possibility of great variety in the system arrangement and self contained. The combustion chamber can be designed to burn any of the hydrocarbon fuels including solid fuels.

However, the open-cycle gas turbine power plants have drawbacks of higher air rate in comparison to other prime movers, sensitivity to changes in component efficiencies and erosion and corrosion of turbine blades.

Comparison of Generating Stations on the Basis of Running Cost, Site, Starting and Maintenance

S.No.	*Particulars*	*Steam power station*	*Hydro-electric power station*	*Nuclear power station*	*Diesel power station*
1.	Site	These plants are located near coal mines of rivers	These plants should be constructed to such a place where huge quantity of water at a sufficient head is available	These plants are located near the load centre and away from populated area due to radioactivity	It can be installed anywhere
2.	Initial cost	Initial cost is low as compared to hydroelectric and Nuclear power plant (₹500 to 800/kW capacity)	Initial cost is very high as compared to steam power plant (₹700 to 800/kW)	The capital cost is very high than all other types due to nuclear reactor (₹400 + 0.04/kWh)	Initial cost is less than all other plants
3.	Running cost	More than hydroelectric and nuclear plants	Running cost is low as water is used as fuel	Running cost is low as very small quantity of fuel is required	High, due to high cost of diesel
4.	Cost of Transmission	Low, as it can be located near the load centre	Long transmission lines are required hence cost is transmission is very high	Its cost of transmission is low	Cost of transmission is low as compared to hydroelectric power plant
5.	Cleanliness	Atmosphere is polluted by the fumes and dust	It is clean and does not pollute the atmosphere	It is also neat and clean	Atmosphere is polluted
6.	Space	Large space is required	It also required large space	Large space is required	Small space is required
7.	Cost of transmission of fuel	Heavy cost of transmission of fuel as the plant is located away from the coal mines etc.	Cost of transmission of fuel is nil as no fuel is needed	Very low cost of transmission of fuel because small quantity of fuel is required	Cost of transmission is very higher than hydro-electric plants but lower than steam power plant
8.	Reliability	Steam power plants are less reliable	Hydroelectric plants are more reliable because they are simple and robust	These plants are more relible	These are less reliable

(Contd...)

S.No.	Particulars	Steam power station	Hydro-electric power station	Nuclear power station	Diesel power station
9.	Starting condition	It is not quick starting	It is quick starting	It is also not quick starting	It is quick starting
10.	Maintenance cost	Higher as compared to hydroelectric power plants because more skilled engineers are required	Maintenance cost is low comparatively	Maintenance cost is comparatively higher as well trained staff is required for its operation and maintenance	Low maintenance cost because few operating staff is required
11.	Field of application	More economical near coal mines and by the side of river	More economical where huge quantity of water is available at a sufficient head	These power plants are more feasible and adopted, where neither water nor coal as a source of power is available	These power plants are installed to supply power in case of emergency

1.9 IMPORTANCE OF NON-CONVENTIONAL ENERGY SOURCES IN PRESENT SCENARIO

Energy is the important input in all sectors of any country's economy. The power demand is increasing day-by-day moreover it is the most important factor that deflects the growth of given country. So we are depending on conventional energy sources so far. The conventional sources of energy i.e., coal, gas and oil are based on fossil fuels. Coal and oil reserves in the world will get exhausted by the end of this century. Therefore, in order to pressure coal and oil for longer duration. The use of non-conventional sources of energy has gained importance in present scenario. Hydro power is variable and depends upon rain and successful in hilly areas only.

Since fossil fuels are main fuel for thermal power and get exhausted in next century, therefore, it is demand of time that we should try non-conventional energy sources in order to meet demand. The power plants based on non-conventional sources such as solar energy wind energy and tide energy do not require any fuel and their running and maintenance cost is very little. Therefore the main focus of government is to popularise the use of these sources. Governments offering also subsidy for the installation of solar and wind based plants. In short non-conventional sources are available in nature and can't be exhausted in many thousand years.

1.10 SOLAR ENERGY

Introduction

The sun is a source of enormous energy. The energy from the sun in the form of radiations is called solar energy. Solar energy is the most promising of the unconventional energy sources. Moreover solar energy is a very large, inexhaustible source of energy.

In India the energy problem is very serious. Inspite of discoveries of oil and gas, the import of crude oil continues to increase. Therefore, it is necessary to develop energy alternation. One of the most promising option is to make use of renewable sources of energy derived from the sun. The energy radiated from the sun in all directions and a very small fraction of it reaches the earth.

Solar energy can the used both directly or indirectly. Directly the solar energy can be used for heating water or air, cooking drying etc. The heated fluids can be used in turn for certain applications like generation.

A second way in which the solar energy can be used directly is through the photovoltaic effect in which it can be converted into electrical energy. Indirect method include the use of water power, the winds and biomass etc.

The solar energy source is a environmentally clean source of energy. Secondly, it is free and available in abundant quantities in almost all parts of the world where people live.

The main problem associated with the use of solar energy is that its availability varies widely with time. It is entirely depends upon the weather conditions. Consequently, the energy can be stored when the sun is shining and used during periods when it is not available.

1.10.1 Solar collectors

A solar collector is a receiving device which absorbs the incident solar radiation and heat a fluid like water or air. The solar radiation further can be converted into electrical power. The followings are the main types of collectors:

(a) Flat plate collector
(b) Concentrating collectors

1.10.1.1 Flat Plate Collector

Flat plate collectors are used for temperature below 100°C they are always installed in a fixed tilted position oriented towards the equator. The concentrating collectors are used for medium and high temperature collectors.

These are mainly used in solar plants for power generation.

The main components of a flat plate collector are shown in Fig. 1.12.

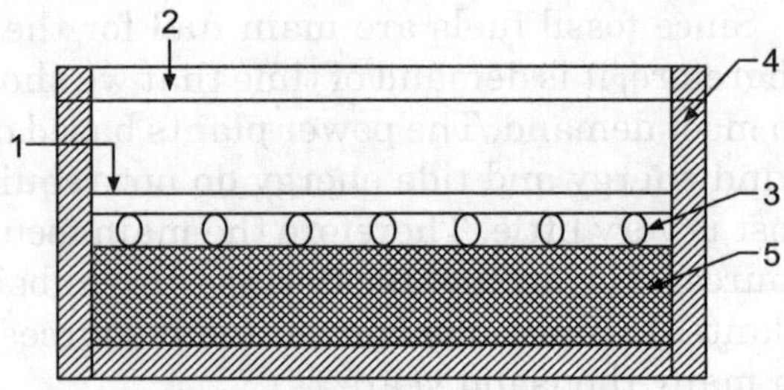

1. Absorber plate, 2. Transparent cover, 3. Heat transfer fluid tube, 4. Casing 5. Thermal insulation.

Fig. 1.12 Flat plate collector

The absorber plate with second parallel tubes is fabricated from copper tubes. The plate is blackened in order to absorb maximum amount of sun light. The plate in enclosed in a box to insulate it on the sides and bottom so as to present losses to attain high temperatures. The complete structure is placed at a proper inclination to the sum so as to absorb solar radiations. The heat absorbed by plate is removed by circulating water of fluid through the tubes. The flat plate collector gives a temperature of about 60°C so flat plate collector is mainly used for water heating.

The most common material used for the absorber is copper because of high conductivity and resistance to corrosion. The material used for the insulation is glass wool, calcium silicate, cellular foam etc.

For cover plate tempered glass is most common material which is generally transparent.

1.10.1.2 *Concentrating Collectors*

These are used for medium and high temperature applications. ***Various types of concentrating type solar collector are shown in Fig. 1.13 below:***

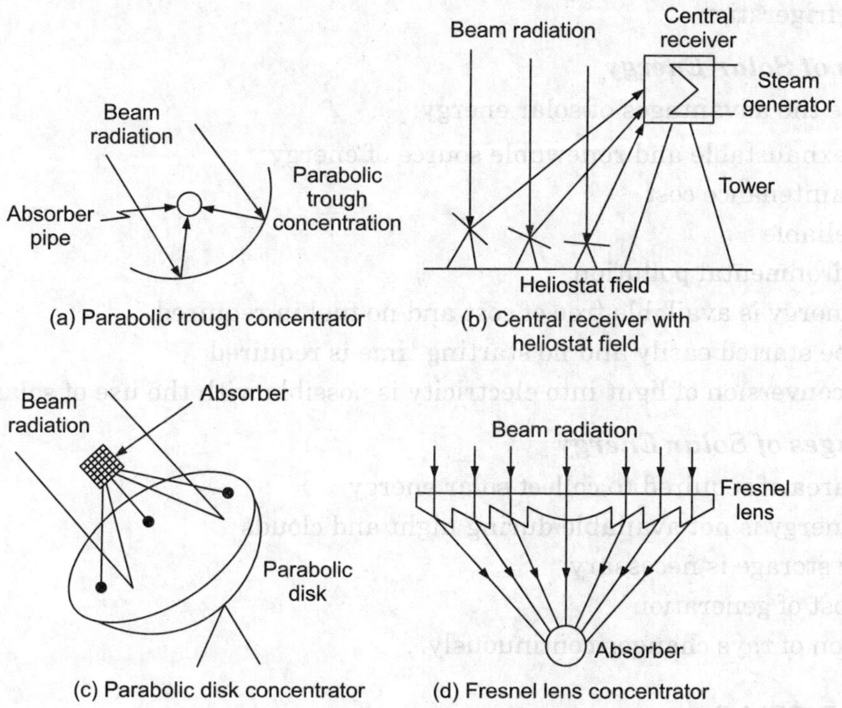

Fig. 1.13 Various types of concentrating collectors

It consists of a concentrating device which may be a reflecting mirror of Fresnel lens. The beam radiations are concentrated and focused on to the absorber. ***Different types of collectors have different values of concentration ratio which is given as:***

$$C = \frac{A_a}{A_r}$$

where A_a = Aperture area of the concentrator

A_r = Area of absorber.

A parabolic trough concentrator is a linear concentrators for which the value of C may be 20 to 100. Parabolic disk concentrator is a point focus concentrator for which the value of C may be 100 to 4000. The mirror and Fresnel lenses can focus only beam radiations. These concentrators are rotated through tracking mechanism to follow the motion of the sun in the sky. Temperature as high as 1000°C can be achieved. These are used in solar power generation and process heating.

Various Applications of Solar Energy

The following are the main applications of solar energy:

1. Solar energy generation
2. Solar heating and cooling
3. Solar drying of animal and agriculture products
4. Solar pumping
5. Solar furnaces
6. Food refrigeration.

Advantages of Solar Energy

Following are the advantages of solar energy:

1. It is inexhaustable and renewable source of energy
2. Low maintenance cost
3. High reliable
4. No environmental pollution
5. Solar energy is available free of cost and no fuel in required
6. It can be started easily and no starting time is required
7. Direct conversion of light into electricity is possible with the use of solar cells.

Disadvantages of Solar Energy

1. Large area of required to collect solar energy
2. Solar energy is not available during night and clouds
3. Energy storage is necessary
4. High cost of generation
5. Direction of rays changes continuously.

1.11 SOLAR CELLS

Solar cells are device which directly convert incident solar radiation to electric current. Moreover in solar photovoltaic system, the electricity is generated directly from solar energy. It works on the principle of photoelectric effect. This is also called *photovoltaic cells*.

If electrical contacts are made with two semiconductor material (p and n type) and the contacts are connected through an external electrical conductor the free electrons will move from the n-type material through the conductor to the p-type material. The free electrons will enter the holes and become bound electrons; thus both free electrons and holes will be removed.

The flow of electrons through the external conductor constitutes an electric current and will continue as long as there is solar radiation. This is the basic of photovoltaic conversion, that is, the conversion of solar energy into electrical energy single converter cell is called a *solar cell* or *photovoltaic cell* and combination of such cell designed to increase the electric power output is called a solar array.

Photovoltaic cells are made of semiconductors that generate electricity when they absorb light.

Figure 1.14 shows a silicon photovoltaic cell which consists of single crystal of p-type silicon with a surface layer of n-type silicon. When light falls on such a junction electrons and holes moves in opposite direction across the junction and if an external circuit is connected across the junction an electric current will flow. The efficiency of such cell is generally in the range 12-16%.

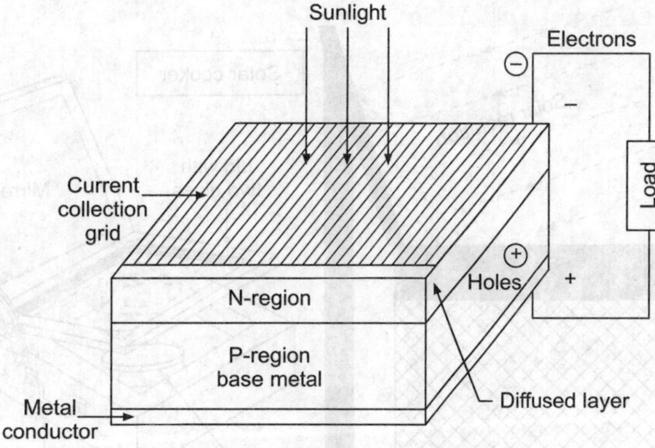

Fig. 1.14 Solar photovoltaic cell

In practice the maximum voltage of solar cell is about 0.6 V when no power is produced. The maximum power of a silicon cell occurs at an output voltage of approximately 0.45 volt.

By assembling a large number of cells in an array an electricity generating system can be constructed and 5000 industrial solar water heating system : 2.30 lakh solar cookers have already been installed. At Medical College, Rohtak, the solar water heating system is capable of heating 26000 litres of water per day at 65°.

A solar thermal power plant of 22 MW capacity, using focus collectors and steam turbine is in operation at Solajipally village in Andhra Pradesh.

At present the SPV (Solar Photovoltaic) system in India are being used for powering a variety of low power applications in rural, remote areas for lighting and water pumping, rural telecommunication system, TV transmission, power for railway signaling and water for irrigation purpose.

1.11.1 Applications of Solar Photovoltaic System

The following are the main applications of solar photovoltaic:

1. Irrigation water pumping.
2. Railway signaling equipment.
3. Battery charging.
4. Street lighting.
5. Weather monitoring.
6. Community radio and television sets.

Advantages of Photovoltaic Solar Energy Conversion

1. Conversion of light to electricity through simple solid state device.
2. Cost of maintenance is low.
3. Easy of operate.
4. No supervision is required for a longer period due to absence of moving parts.
5. They are free from pollution.
6. They have longer life.

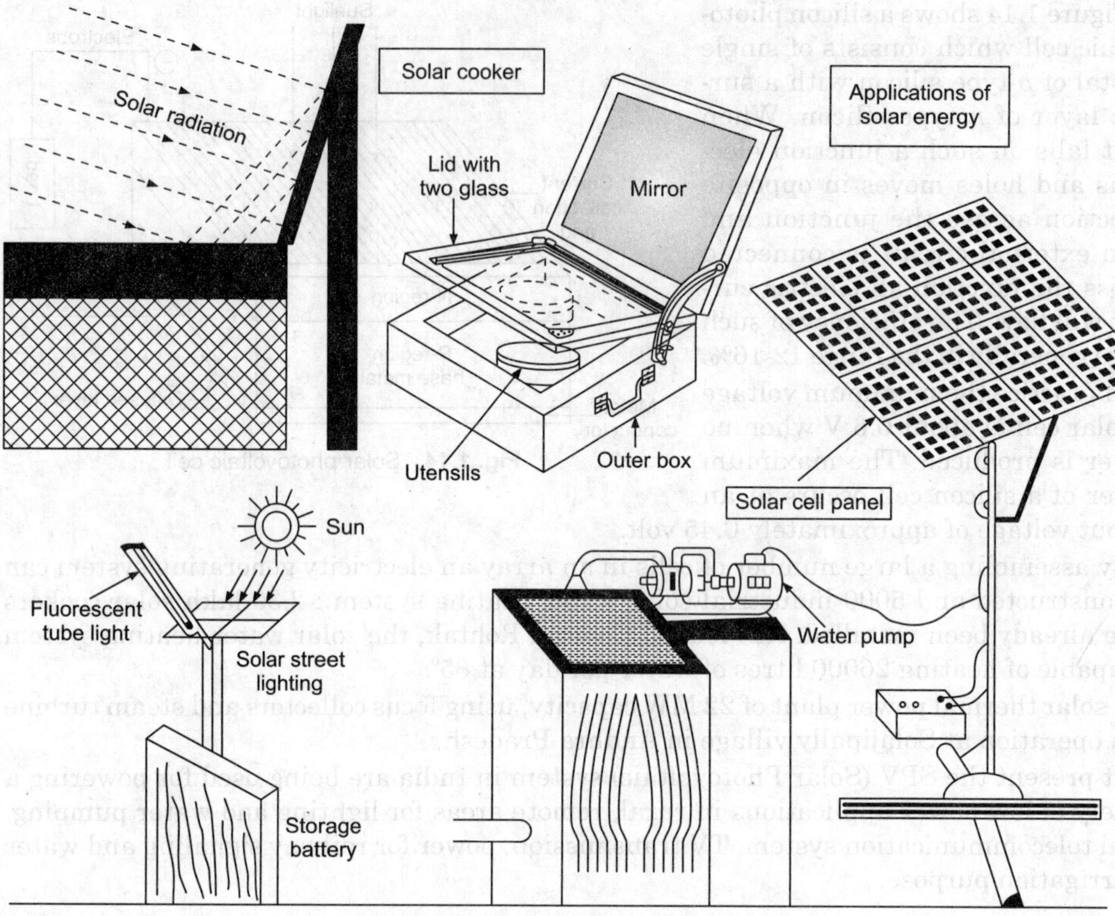

Fig. 1.15 Applications of solar energy

7. They are more reliable.
8. As the sun's energy is free hence they consume no fuel in their operation.
9. They are easy to fabricate being simplest semiconductor device. The main disadvantage is high initial cost.
10. Highly reliable
11. There can be used with or without sun tracking.

Disadvantages

1. High cost
2. Solar power plants require very large land areas
3. Electrical generation cost is very high
4. The initial cost of the plant is very high and still requires a long gas station period
5. The energy spent in manufacture of solar cells is very high.

1.12 SOLAR THERMAL POWER GENERATION

The generation of electrical or mechanical power is one of the most important applications of solar energy. In this system generally the solar energy is converted into thermal or heat energy. Here the heat can be converted directly into electrical energy by solar cells. The most practical thermal electrical procedure is adopted for solar energy is to utilize to heat the water or gas. This heat energy produced by solar energy is then converted into mechanical energy by using turbine which is further coupled to the generator produces electrical energy. Such type of mechanical power generation system is called the solar thermal power production system.

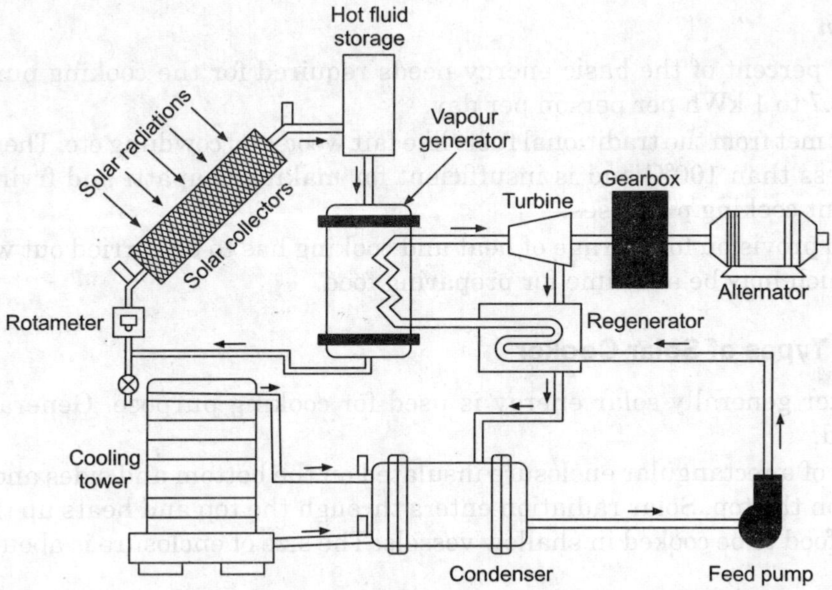

Fig. 1.16 Solar power plant

Solar thermal power generation employs power cycles which may be low, medium and high temperature cycles.

In low temperature working system, the energy of the sun is collected by water flowing through an array of flat-plate collector. In order to get maximum possible temperature booster mirrors which reflect-radiation on the flat-plates collectors sometimes used.

The hot water at temperature about 100°C is stored in a well insulated storage tank. From here, it flows through vapour generated, through which the working fluid of the Rankine cycle is also passed. This vapour then executes a regular rankine cycle by flowing through a prime mover, a condenser and liquid pump to generate the electric energy. However, the efficiency of this system is rather low.

1.13 SOLAR POND

Solar pond is one of the most promising technologies in solar energy utilization for various purposes. It is a large scale solar energy collector with integral heat energy storage for supplying thermal energy. This thermal energy can be used in various ways, such as drying, thermal electricity generation.

A simplest type of solar pond is very shallow, about 5 to 10 cm deep, with a radiation absorbing material such as black plastic bottom. The bottom warm water is used as the heart source and top cool water as the heat sink. The hot bottom water is pumped through an evaporator and back to the bottom. The fluid is evaporated and drives a turbogenerator which in turn produces electrical energy.

The main applications of solar ponds are power generation and crop drying and the main limitations are availabilities of water, sunny climate etc.

1.14 SOLAR COOKERS

Introduction

About eighty percent of the basic energy needs required for the cooking purpose, which amounts to 0.7 to 1 kWh per person per day.

It is mostly met from the traditional fuels like fair wood and cowdung etc. The temperature obtained is less than 100ºC and is insufficient for making chapatti and frying which are very important cooking processes.

There is no provision for storage of heat and cooking has to be carried out while the sun is shining which may be add time for preparing food.

1.14.1 Box Types of Solar Cooker

In solar cooker generally solar energy is used for cooking purpose. Generally box type cooker is used.

In consists of a rectangular enclosure insulated on the bottom and sides and having two glass covers on the top. Solar radiation enters through the top and heats up the enclosure in which the food to be cooked in shallow vessels. The size of enclosure is about 50 cm^2 and 12 cm deep.

The reflector mirror has a provision adjustment of reflector different angles with solar cooker. With the help of reflector mirror, a temperature rise of 15 to 20ºC can be obtained inside the solar cooker.

The pulses, rice, vegetables etc., can be readily cooked in box type cooker. The time taken for cooking depends upon the solar radiation and varies from 1/2 to 2 hours. A sketch of such a cooker is shown in Fig. 1.17.

Box type cookers with one reflector is most commonly used because it is simple and require less attention.

With some experience, the operator does not have to spend much time in the sun for cooking. In such type of cooker the item to be cooked has only to be placed inside and taken out easily. Typical cost of such type of cooker is about ₹ 400.

In India in most places solar cooker can be used at least for 240 days in a year and saving in fuel cost is about ₹ 120 per year and the cost of cooker is received back within period of two to three years.

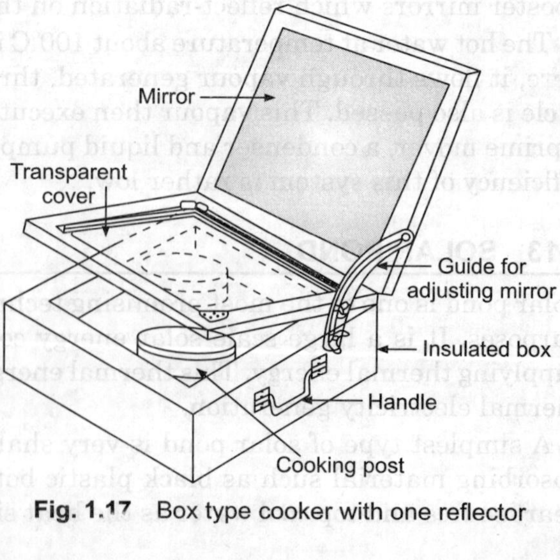

Fig. 1.17 Box type cooker with one reflector

Advantages of Solar Cooker

Following are the some advantages of a solar cooker:

1. No fuel is required.
2. Maintenance cost is negligible.
3. No attention is needed during cooking as compared to other devices.
4. Free from pollution.
5. The biggest advantage of solar cooker is that nutritional value of the cooked food is way high, vitamins of food are not destroyed and food is cooked with natural taste and no overflowing of food takes place.

Disadvantages

1. Meal cannot be cooked at short notice.
2. It takes comparatively time.
3. Food cannot be prepared in the night or during cloudy days.
4. Chapatis are required high temperature for baking. Therefore, they cannot be cooked solar-cooker and also needs manipulation at the time of baking.
5. Cooking has to be carried out in the open without privacy and in the sun which is very inconvenient to the housewife.

1.15 SOLAR WATER HEATING

The principle usually followed is to expose a dark surface to solar radiation so that the radiation is absorbed. A part of the absorbed radiation is than transferred to a fluid like air or water.

Figure 1.18 shows simple, small capacity natural circulation system for domestic purpose. The main two components of the system are the liquid flat-plate collector and the storage tank. The tank is located above the level of collector.

As water in the collector is heated by solar energy, it flows automatically to the top of the water tank. The place vacated by this water is taken by colder water from the bottom of the tank. How water for use is withdrawn from top of the tank. Whenever this is done, cold water automatically enters at the bottom. Such a system have capacities ranging from 100 to 200 liters which is sufficient for the needs of family of four to six persons. The temperature of the hot water delivered ranges from 50 to 70ºC.

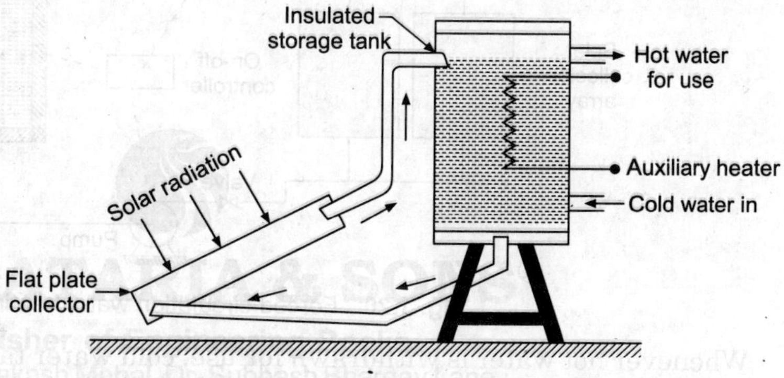

Fig. 1.18 Natural circulation solar water heating system

1.16 SOLAR WATER HEATERS

Small capacity domestic solar water heaters are also available. A schematic diagram of one such unit is shown in Fig. 1.19. It consists box 5 to 12 cm deep, made of sheet steel. The box is insulated around the bottom and sides the box is filled with water in the morning which heats up through the day and is withdrawn for use in the evening.

A storage type solar water heater has the advantage of being less cost than the natural circulation system. However, it is less efficient.

The basic elements of the system are:

(i) Flat plate collector
(ii) Storage tank
(iii) Circulation system
(iv) Control of the system

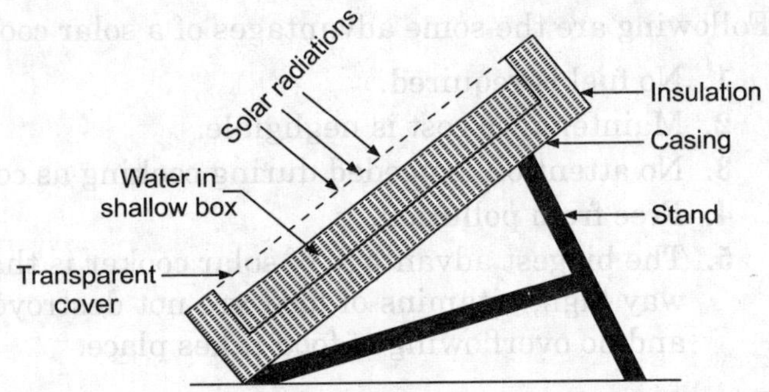

Fig. 1.19 Storage type solar water heater

Solar radiations pass through the transparent cover of flat plate collector and is absorbed by collector plate. Water flowing in contact with the collector is heated and the heat from water is extracted for use. The circulating pump keeps a continuous circulation of water through collector and storage tank.

1.16.1 Forced Circulating Solar Water Heater

A schematic diagram of a typical system is shown in Fig. 1.20. In this water heating system large arrays of flat plate collectors are used. The forced circulation is maintained with a water pump. In this system of water heating, it is not bound to keep the storage tank at a higher level. Generally ball-float control system is used.

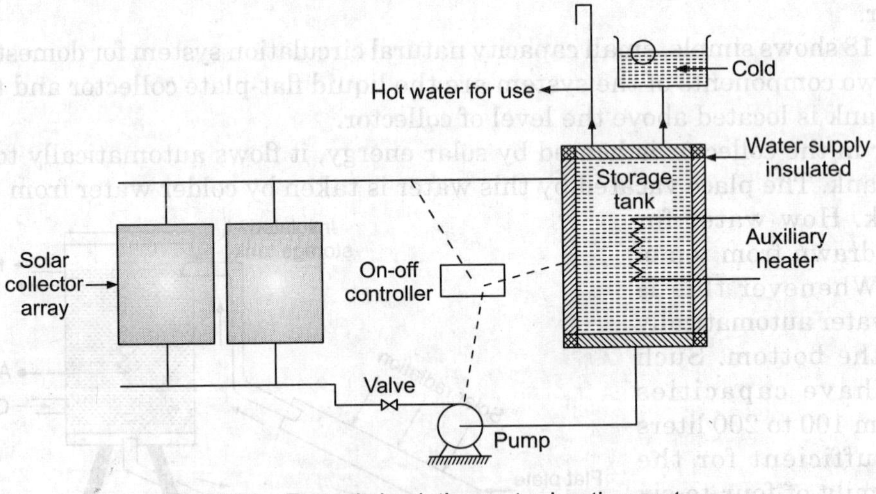

Fig. 1.20 Forced circulation water heating system

Whenever hot water is withdrawn for use, cold water takes its place because of the ball-float control system as shown in Fig. 1.20. The pump is operated by on-off controller which senses the difference between the temperature of the water at collector $\frac{8.5}{7}$ exit and inside the storage tank.

Uses: It is used in hospitals, hotels, factories, colleges and offices.

1.17 BIO-ENERGY

Energy obtained from bio-mass is called *bio-energy*. Biomass is a renewable energy resources derived from plants, animals and micro-organism grown on land and water. Bio-mass is produced by the power of photosynthesis. Biomass is available in three forms.

(i) **Terrestrial crops:** Non-woody plants which are easily converted into liquid or gas. Tervestrial crops have energy potential of 3×10^{12} foules.

(ii) **Aquatic crops:** Grown in fresh sea and backsish water. These include seaweeds etc.

(iii) **Animal and human waste:** Animal and human waste are indirect terrestorial crops from which biogass can be produced while retaining the fertilizers value of man use. The daily produce of cow dung is 13.5 kg/cattle which can be used to produce 0.48 m^3 of biogas in gobar gas plant. This can produce 1 kWh of electricity in a biogas engine. Human waste can also be used to produce biogas.

1.17.1 Materials used for Biogas Generation

The following material is used for the production of biogas.

1. **Animal wastes:** It includes cattle dung, urine, goat and poultry droppings, wood wastes, piggery wastes etc.
2. **Human wastes:** Faces, urine and other wastes emanating from human occupations.
3. **Agricultural wastes:** Aquatic and terrestrial weeds crop-residues sugar cane trash, press mud, cotton and textile wastes etc.
4. **Industrial wastes:** Sugar factory, tannery, paper etc.

1.17.2 How Biogas is Produced?

Bio-gas produced by anaerobic digestion of biomass. Common materials used as a feed stock include animal wastes, crop residues and urban waste. Fig. 1.21 shows the schematic diagram of biogas plant.

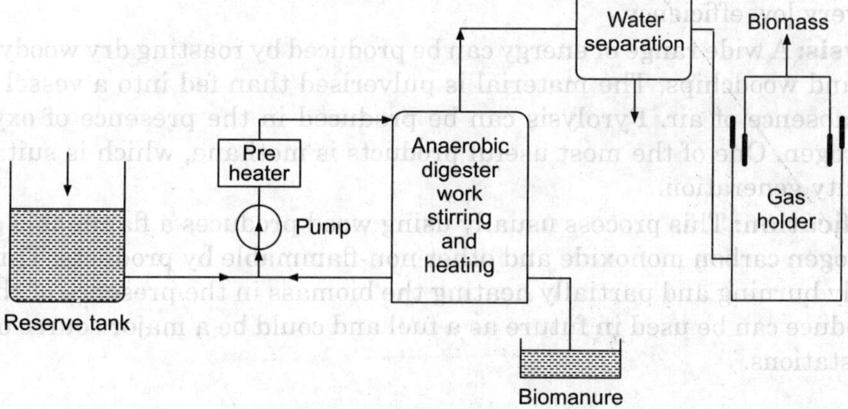

Fig. 1.21 Biogas plant

1.17.3 Biogas Digester

Biogas is produced by digestion in the presence of anaerobic organisms in the absence of oxygen at ambient pressure and temperature of 40–70°C. The container in which digestion takes place is called digester.

Advantages of Biogas Plant

1. The intial cost is low due to simple construction of plant.
2. The raw materials for digester can be grown and cultivated like agriculture.
3. Biogas is generated locally and can be distributed for domestic use.
4. Biogas is very suitable for rural areas.
5. The raw material used also helps to keep the village clean.

Disadvantages

1. Large area is required for cultivation of biomass.
2. It is difficult to distribute the biogas as the same cannot be liquefied.

1.17.4 Methods of Obtaining Energy from Biomass

Bio-chemical conversion of biomass into full is a slow process. It involves two process to convert biomass into energy.

(i) Anaerobic digestion, (ii) Fermentation

1. **Anaerobic digestion:** Anaerobic is a micro-organise on that can live and grow without oxygen. It gets oxygen by decomposition at low temperature upto 65°C. It generates a gas consisting CO_2, methane and H_2S. The gas can be directly burnt.
2. **Fermentation:** It is the process of breaking down of complex molecules in organic compounds under the influence of ferment such as yeast, bacteria etc. Fermentation is widely used technology for conversion of grains and sugar crops into ethanol.
3. **Combustion:** Combustion system is the suitable way of extracting energy from biomass. Combustion system virtually obtained by burning any kind of fuel from chicken manure, scrape tyres and municipal refuse. The disadvantages of this method is the very low efficiency.
4. **Pyrolysis:** A wide range of energy can be produced by roasting dry woody matter like straw and woodchips. The material is pulverised than fed into a vessel and heated in the absence of air. Pyrolysis can be produced in the presence of oxygen, water or hydrogen. One of the most useful products is methane, which is suitable fuel for electricity generation.
5. **Classification:** This process usually using wood produces a flammable gas mixture of hydrogen carbon monoxide and other non-flammable by products. This is done by partially burning and partially heating the biomass in the presence of charcoal. The gas produce can be used in future as a fuel and could be a major source of energy for power stations.

1.17.5 Difference Between Biomass and Biogas

Biomass can be considered a renewable energy source and Biomass is also organic matter produced by various types of plants. It includes forest crops and residues, crops grown especially for their energy content on energy farms and animal manure. It can also be considered a form of solar energy.

Biogas is the process which is to ferment the biomass anaerobically to obtain a gaseous fuel called *biogas*. Biogas is obtained from biomass.

Gasifier

It is an equipment which can gasify a variety of biomass such as wood waste, agricultural waste like stalks and roots of various cropes, maize etc. The gasifier essentially a chemical reactor where various complex physical and chemical process takes place. Biomass get dried, heated, pyrolysed, partially oxidized and reduced, as it flows through it. The gas produced in the gasifier is a clean fuel burning fuel having heating value of about 900–1200 kcal/m^3.

Advantages of Gasifier

1. Its maintenance to easy
2. It is sturdy in construction
3. It is reliable in operation
4. It is very easy to operate the gasifier.

Applications of Biogas

The main products of the biogas plant are fuel gas and organic manure. Biogas is a flammable gas. The biogas can be utilized effectively by household cooking, lighting, pumping water and grinding flour.

1.18 WIND ENERGY

Introduction

It is also one of the most effective non-conventional energy used in rural areas. Wind power development has proved to be an effective environmental friendly way of producing electricity area in India where wind energy is in abundance like Kaniyakumari in Tamil Nadu etc.

Wind power is used as an effective way to give water to lands, where earlier engines were employed to the well, which fetch water from land and pass the water to fields, but now the fresh ideas come into the minds of people and they are using non-conventional technique like using windmills to fetch water from wells to pass on their fields.

Wind energy is a renewable source of non-polluting energy and is emerging as one of the most exciting potential sources of alternate energy which will be helpful to great extent in reducting the gap between the energy demand and supply.

Basically wind is essentially air in motion, possess the finite energy by virtue of the movement of large masses of air caused by differential heating of atmosphere by the sun.

Wind turbine can be used to generate electricity for lifting water from wells, for direct water from wells, for direct water pumping etc.

1.18.1 Windmill

The windmill works on the principle of connecting kinetic energy of the wind to mechanical energy or the basic function of windmill is to extract energy from the wind and to produce mechanical energy which may be converted into other forms of energy like electrical energy by using ac generators. Many types of windmills have been designed and out of them few have been found to be practically useful. The windmill may be horizontal axis and vertical axis.

A windmill is a machine for converting the wind energy in electrical energy. Basically a wind turbine converts the kinetic energy of the winds motion to mechanical energy to which the a generator is coupled to convert into electrical energy.

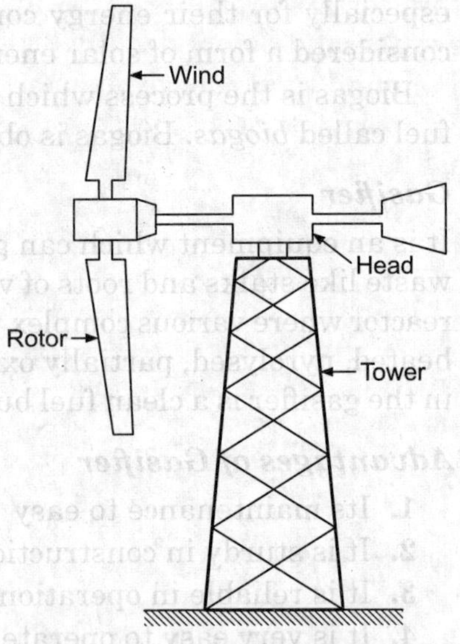

Fig. 1.22 Two blades horizontal axis type windmill

1.18.2 Horizontal Axis Type Mill

Figure 1.22 shows a horizontal axis with two aerodynamic blades type windmill. This mill is made by suitable shaping/sheets. It may have two or four blades depending upon the requirements. The speed of windmill may be 300 to 400 rpm.

Wind machines intended for generating substantial amount of power should have large rotors and be located in areas of high wind speeds.

In such type of windmills rotor drives the generator through a step up gear-box. The blade of rotor is designed to be projected downward of the tower. The components are mounted on a bed plate which is further attached on a pintle at the top of the tower. Moreover the blades of the rotor are continuously flexed by gravitational and inertia loads, when the windmill is in operation. During operation there should not be any vibration in the rotor.

Wind turbine basically consists of few blades radiating from central axis. As the wind blows against blades, the blade rotates about the axis. The rotational option is then utilized to some useful works, i.e., mechanical energy is converted into electrical energy.

1.18.3 Horizontal Axis, Dutch Type Windmill

Figure 1.23 shows the sketch of one of the oldest design four blades Dutch type windmill. The blades are hinged at a point on the top of the windmill in such a manner that they have equal space. The blade surface are made from an array of wooden slats which feather at high wind speeds.

The performance of a windmill is strongly dependent on its location because the value of wind speed can be vary significantly

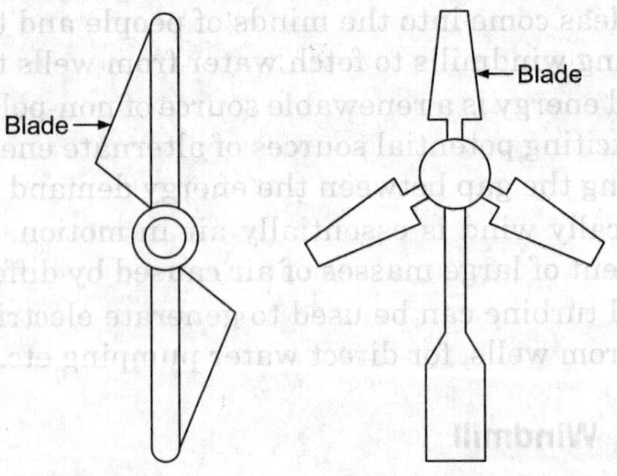

(a) Two blade profile. (b) Three blade high speed horizontal axis windmill

Fig. 1.23 Horizontal axis dutch type windmill

within certain area due to the topography of land. Therefore it is necessary to do carefully survey of land before deciding the location for windmill.

For wind turbines with power outputs upto 20 kW, dc generators can be used to charge the batteries directly. For higher power it is necessary to use ac generator and current must be rectified before charging the battery.

1.19 APPLICATIONS OF WIND ENERGY

As we know that the wind energy basically in the form of rotary or translational mechanical motion. This mechanical motion can be further converted into electricity or heat etc. The main applications of wind energy are storage of electricity in batteries, hot water, pumped hydro system. It is also used to pump irrigation water.

1.19.1 Merits of Wind Energy

1. It is a renewable and non-polluting source of energy.
2. It is an important renewable source of energy and available free from cost.
3. No fuel is required hence transport changes are nil.
4. No time is required for the start of generation.
5. Power generation is cheaper as compared to other sources.
6. Low capital cost.
7. It is helpful in supplying power to remote and rural areas.

1.19.2 Demerits of Wind Energy

1. It has noisy operation.
2. Wind energy is available in fluctuating in nature.
3. It is variable, unsteady and irregular.
4. Windmills can be installed only in vast open areas which are generally away from load centre.
5. Overall weight of wind power systems is high because they involve the construction of a high tower, a generator coupling shaft etc.

1.20 SELECTION OF SITE FOR A WIND POWER PLANT

1. Building, forests generally offers the resistance to the air movement, therefore, wind mills are located away from cities and forests.
2. Adequate and uniform wind velocity throughout the year should be available.
3. Flat open area should be selected, as the wind velocities are high in flat open area.
4. For the site selection it is desirable to have average wind speed. Since wind velocity is not constant, the average velocity should be calculated from the reading taken over a period of one year by average hourly, daily, weekly monthly readings are suitable.
5. Altitude of the proposed site should be considered. Higher ground experience strong winds than lower ground. Thus, altitude affects the electricity output from wind energy.
6. Site selected should be near the consumer, which minimize the cost and losses.
7. Land selected for the wind mills should be cheap.

1.20.1 Types of Wind Power Plant

The wind power plants can be classified as per different parameter:

(i) **Axis of Rotation:** There are vertical axis and horizontal axis turbines. They use either lift or drag forces to harness the wind energy majority of modern wind turbibes are the horizontal axis lift machines.

Figure 1.24 shows simple diagrams of different types of wind turbine.

(ii) **Size of machine:** According to power output wind power plants are divided into the following classes:

(a) **Small wind power plants:** The output of 10 to 50 kW and rotor diameter of 1 to 16 m.

(b) **Medium wind power plants:** The power output of 50 to 500 kW and a rotor diameter of 16 to 50 m.

(c) **Large wind power plants:** The power output or 500 to 5000 kW and a rotor diameter of 50 to 130 m.

The tower (hub) height is usually 1 to 2 times the rotor diameter.

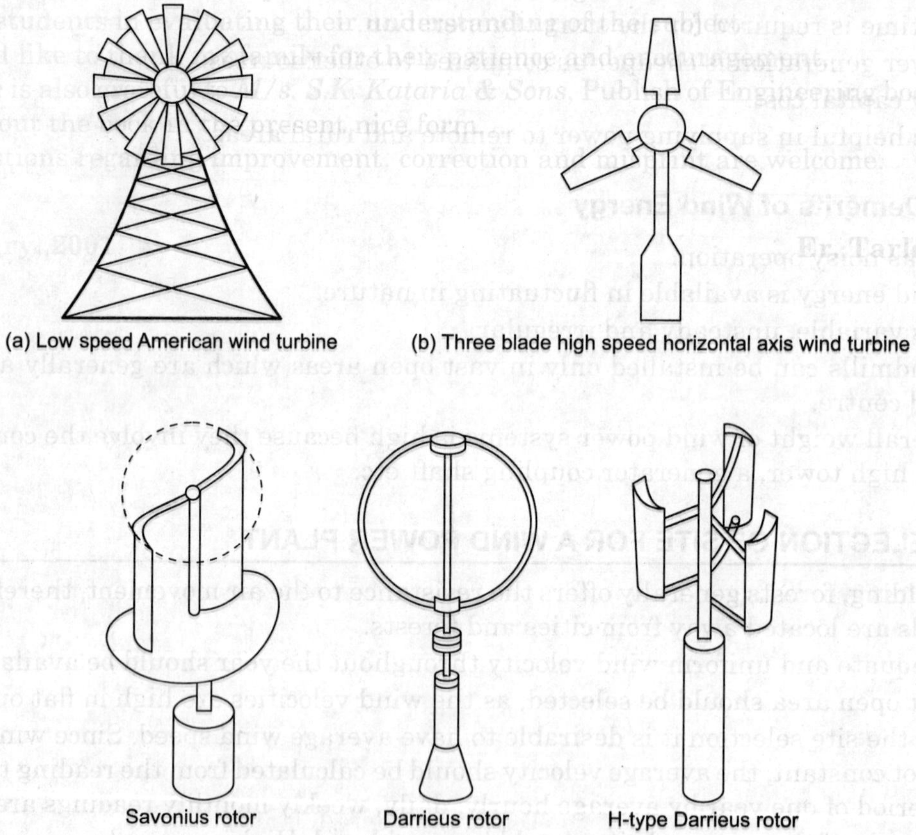

(a) Low speed American wind turbine

(b) Three blade high speed horizontal axis wind turbine

Savonius rotor

Darrieus rotor

H-type Darrieus rotor

Fig. 1.24 Types of rotor in wind mill

1.20.2 Horizontal Axis Wind Turbine

Horizontal axis wind turbines (HAWT) are of monoblade type, twin bladed and three bladed type. Fig. 1.25 shows such types of HAWT.

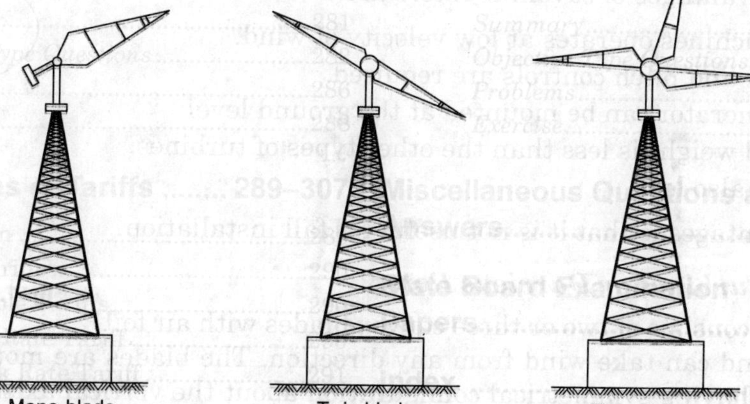

Fig. 1.25 Horizontal axis wind turbines blades

The propeller are of two types (i) Upwind type (ii) Downwind type. In upwind the blades are slanted and wind approaching the blades from front side and nacelle is placed on rare side of the blade. Necelle having propeller gears and generators.

The monoblades wind turbine have lighter rotor. The blades are lighter in weight. Length of blades varies from 15 m to 25 m.

Twin blades horizontal axis wind turbine (HAWT) having two blades in order to face the difficulty of vibration.

At higher wind speeds the force on the blade in upper position are more than lower position. Due to this difference in forces rotor experiences severe vibrations. To avoid this teething control is provided.

In three blades HAWT, the rotor has three blades. The blades are long and mounted on hub. The shaft is mounted on the bearing. The step up gear box changes the speed of the turbine shaft to the required speed of the generator. The generator, turbine, bearing etc. are mounted in nacelle. The portion of nacelle changes automatically according to the direction of wind.

1.20.3 Vertical Wind Turbine Generator

These are also known as cross wind axis machines. Here axis of rotation is perpendicular to the direction of wind. In a vertical axis machine the rotor looks like an upright egg beater.

Vertical axis machines are of two types:

1. Savonius Rotor Turbine

The savonius rotor is S-shaped it viewed from above. This is drage type VAWT turns relatively slow, but yields a high torque Fig. 1.26 shows the savonius rotor.

It consists of two S-shaped metal air foils supported between top and bottom by circular plates. Savonius rotor rotates for air flow in any direction. They are self starting, low speed and have low efficiency around 15%.

The main advantages of savonius rotors are:

(i) The machines operates at low velocity of wind.
(ii) No yaw and pitch controls are required.
(iii) The generator can be mounted at the ground level.
(iv) Overall weight is less than the other types of turbines.
(v) Cost is also low.

The disadvantages is that it is not useful for fall installation.

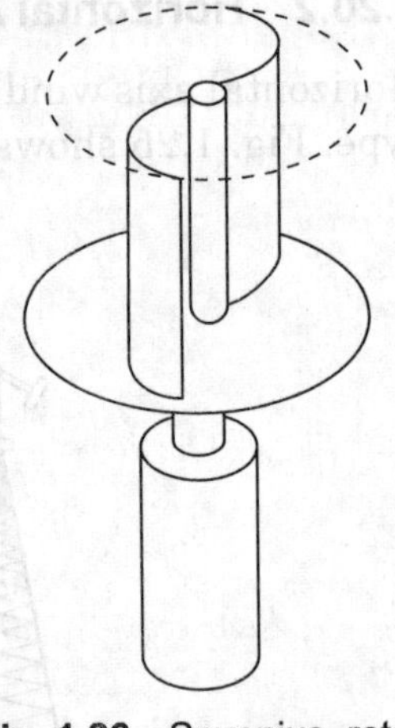

Fig. 1.26 Savonius rotor

2. Darrieus Turbines or Darrieus Rotor

Darrieus rotor consists of two or three convex blades with air foil cross-section and can take wind from any direction. The blades are mounted on vertical shaft. Rotor is having symmetrical configuration about the vertical axis. This rotor looks like an eggbeater. The vertical shaft is hollow and mounted on lower bearing and upper bearing. The upper part of the rotor is supported by the guy cables. The force in the blade due to rotation is pure tension, thus blade can be made lighter than in the propeller type.

Figure 1.27 shows a Darrieus rotor turbine. These rotors are not self starting and require auxiliary starter. The efficiency is about 35%. The capital cost of such type of rotor is low. This type of rotor (machine) is mounted on the ground which eliminates the tower structures and other assemblies. No pitch control is required. At very high speeds, stalling may occurs and rotation may stop. As these machines are not self starting, an auxiliary starter required. The generator can serve as the motor to start the turbine. The efficiency of Darrieus rotor machines are lower than the conventional horizontal rotor.

Fig. 1.27 Darrieus rotor

Advantages of Vertical Axis Wind Turbine Over Horizontal Axis Turbines

Following are the main advantages of vertical axis wind turbine over horizontal axis ones:

1. The will react to wind from any direction and therefore do not need yawing equipment to turn the rotor into the wind.
2. They required less structure sport because heavy components like gearbox and generator can be located at ground level. Therefore installation and maintenance.
3. Since the blade do not turn end over end, the rotor is not subjected to continuous cyclic gravity load.

1.20.4 Main Parts of Wind Turbine

There are four main parts to a wind turbine, the base, tower, needle and blades. The blade capture, the wind energy spinning a generator in the needle and provides access to the needle for maintenance. The base made of concreted and steel, supports the whole structure.

1. **The blades:** Wind turbine blades are lift to capture the wind energy. Because of the blades special shape, the wind creates a pocket of pressure as it passes behind the blade. This pressure pulles the blades causing the turbine to rotate. The Fig 1.28 shows a wind turbine coupled to a generator.
2. **The needle:** The needle houses a generator and gearbox. The spinning blades are attached to the generator through a series of grass. The gears increases the rotational speed of the blades to the generator speed of over 1500 rpm. As the generator spins, electricity is produced.
3. **The tower:** The tower is a white steel cylinders about 200 feet tall and 10 feet in diameter. Towers have a ladder running up the inside and a hoist of tools and equipment.
4. **The base:** Bases are made of concrete reinforced with steel bars. There are two types of base. One is a shallow flat disk about 40 feet diameter and 3 feet thick the other is a deeper cylinder about 15 inch diameter and 16 feet deep.

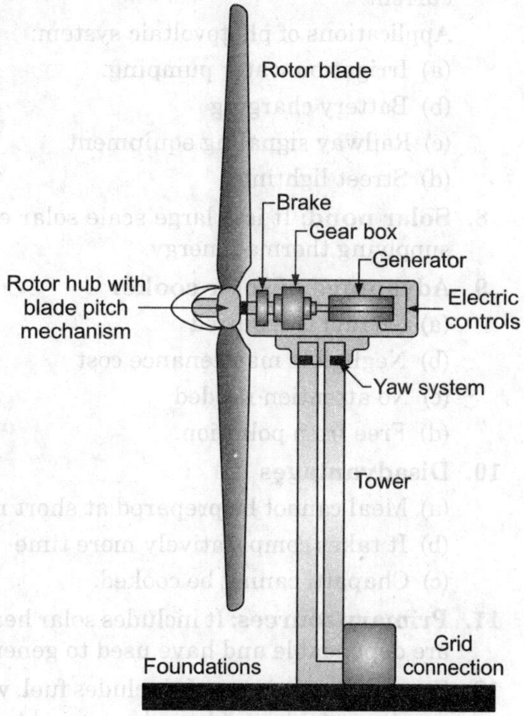

Fig. 1.28 Main parts of wind turbine

Applications of Wind Plant

The main applications of wind plants are:

1. Water pumping
2. Generation of electricity
3. Saw milling
4. Drainage
5. Battery charging
6. Grinding grains

SUMMARY

Main Resources of Energy

1. **Renewable resources:** For example, sunlight, water, water plants and animals.
2. **Non-renewable sources:** These sources are related to earth e.g., minerals fossils fuels.
3. **Conventional energy resources:** These include fossile fuel such as coal, petroleum, natural gas, water and nuclear energy.
4. **Non-conventional energy resources:** These include solar, wind, tide, biomass and geothermal etc.

5. **Advantages of renewable sources**

   (a) Renewable are exhaustible

   (b) No pollution problem with the use of resources.

   Disadvantages

   (a) Large size of the plant

   (b) Low efficiency

   (c) Large investment is required

6. **Solar Energy:** The sun is a source of energy. The energy from the sun in the form of radiations is called solar energy.

7. **Solar photovoltaic:** It is called solar cell, which convert incident solar radiations to electric current.

   Applications of photovoltaic system:

   (a) Irrigation water pumping.

   (b) Battery charging

   (c) Railway signaling equipment

   (d) Street lighting

8. **Solar pond:** It is a large scale solar energy collectors with integral heat energy storage for supplying thermal energy.

9. **Advantage of solar cooker**

   (a) No fuel is required

   (b) Negligible maintenance cost

   (c) No attention needed

   (d) Free from pollution.

10. **Disadvantages**

    (a) Meal cannot be prepared at short notice

    (b) It takes comparatively more time

    (c) Chapatti cannot be cooked.

11. **Primary sources:** It includes solar heat, wind power and tidal power. These sources of energy are dependable and have used to generate energy.

12. **Secondary sources:** It includes fuel, water power and nuclear power. These sources of energy are dependable and have been used to generate energy.

13. **Wind energy:** Wind energy is a renewable source of non-polluting energy of and is emerging as one of the most exciting potential sources of alternating energy.

14. **Windmill:** The windmill works on the principle of converting kinetic energy of the wind to mechanical energy which may be converted into electrical energy.

15. **Applications of wind energy:** Battery charging, hot water, pumped hydro system. It is also used to pump irrigation water, saw milling etc.

16. **Merits of wind energy**

    (a) No fuel is required.

    (b) No time is required for the start of generation.

    (c) Power generation is cheaper.

Demerits

(a) It has noisy operation.

(b) Wind energy is available in fluctuating in nature.

17. Types of wind power plants

(a) Small wind power plants.

(b) Medium wind power plants.

(c) Large wind power plants.

18. Thermal power station: The generating stations using solid fuel are known as thermal power stations.

Main components of thermal power stations.

(i) Boiler
(ii) Turbine
(iii) Economiser
(iv) Super heater
(v) Air preheater
(vi) Condensers
(vii) Cooling tower
(viii) Generaters

Selection of site

1. Nearness to load centres
2. Nearness coal mines
3. Ample supply of water for cooling
4. Availability of adequate land
5. Transportation facilities.

Advantages

(i) The fuel used is quite cheap
(ii) Less space is required
(iii) It can be located near load centres
(iv) It can be installed at any placed.

Disadvantages

(i) Costlier in running cost as compared to hydroelectric power plant
(ii) Atmosphere is polluted due to smoke and fumes.

19. Hydro-electric power plant: The generating stations using energy contained in water are hydro-power stations.

20. Classification of hydro-power plants

(i) Low head power plant below 50 m
(ii) Medium head power plant above 50 m and upto 300 m
(iii) High head power plant above 300 m.

21. Important elements of hydroelectric power plant

(i) Dam
(ii) Spillway
(iii) Penstock
(iv) Surge tank
(v) Tail race
(vi) Alternator

22. Type of turbines used

(i) Impulse turbine
(ii) Reaction turbine
(iii) Propeller.

Advantages

(a) Quite neat and clean
(b) Economical
(c) Less running cost as no fuel is used
(d) Simple in construction
(e) High efficiency
(f) It helps in irrigation

Disadvantages

(a) High capital cost
(b) High cost of transmission.

Selection of site

(a) Installed where sufficient water head is available.
(b) The land should be cheap.
(c) Adequate transportion facilities.
(d) Site selected should be cheap.

23. Nuclear power station: The generating stations using energy obtained from nuclear fission are called nuclear power station.

Advantages

(a) Less fuel is required
(b) Low running cost
(c) Generation cost is small
(d) Plant can be located near the load centre

Disadvantages

(a) High capital cost
(b) Costly fuel
(c) High technical skill is required

Selection of site

(i) Adequate supply of water
(ii) Approach to the site by rail and road

24. Main parts of nuclear plant

(i) Reactor core
(ii) Moderator
(iii) Shielding
(iv) Coolant
(v) Reflector
(vi) Control system

25. Diesel power station. The generating stations using liquid fuels are known as diesel power stations.

A diesel power station is installed where

(i) Sufficient supply of coal and water is not available
(ii) As a standby unit
(iii) A few consumers like to have their own power supply for emergency reasons.

Components of diesel engine power station

(i) Air intake and exhaust system
(ii) Fuel system
(iii) Engine starting system

(iv) Alternator
(v) Engine cooling system
(vi) Lubricating oil system

Advantages

(i) It can be quickly started
(ii) It occupies less space
(iii) For cooling less quantity of water is needed
(iv) It can be used in emergency
(v) Installation is simple

Choice of site: The diesel power station can be installation at any place.

26. Gas turbine power plant: Gas turbine power plant is device for conversion of heat energy into mechanical work which is further used to convert into electrical energy.

Advantages of gas turbine plant

(i) No warm up time
(ii) Quickly start up and shut up
(iii) High efficiency
(iv) Less floor space
(v) Much little cooling water is required

Application:

(i) For supplying peak loads in other types of power plants.

27. Interconnected grid system: When number of generating stations are connected to each other, it forms an interconnected grid system. There are several advantages of interconnecting the large generating stations. Fews are given below:

(i) The reliability of supply is increased.
(ii) By interconnecting large generating stations, the amount of reseve plant capacity in the system is reduced and hence the load factor and efficiency of operation are improved.
(iii) The diversity factor of the whole system is improved thereby increasing the effective capacity of the whole system.
(iv) When the hydroelectric station and thermal power station are interconnected, their operation become more economical. When water is insufficient quantity in rainy season, the hydroelectric power station is used as a base load and thermal power station as a peak load station because the running cost of hydroelectric plant is low. On the other hand when the level of water is low in summer season, the thermal power station is used as a base load and hydro-electric power station as a peak load.

Objective Type Questions

1. Multiple Choice Type Questions

1. Which of the non-conventional energy sources?

(a) Wind energy
(b) Solar energy
(c) Biomass
(d) Geothermal
(e) All the above

2. Conventional energy sources are:
(a) Available free of cost (b) Cost paid to use these sources
(c) Not producing any pollution (d) None of the above

3. The secondary sources of energy are:
(a) Sun (b) Wind
(c) Tides (d) All the above

4. Which is a conventional source of energy?
(a) Solar (b) Wind
(c) Geothermal (d) Radioactive substances

5. Which of the following power plants is the heat reliable?
(a) Wind (b) Tides
(c) Solar (d) Geothermal

6. In a thermal power station, water is used for cooling purpose in
(a) Super heater (b) Condenser
(c) Boiler (d) Turbine

7. The efficiency of a modern thermal power station is nearly.
(a) 10% (b) 28%
(c) 60% (d) 90%

8. In steam power plant, cooling towers are used for:
(a) Cooling condenser outlet water (b) Cooling exhaust steam
(c) Cooling feed water (d) None of the above

9. Hydroelectric power stations are generally installed in:
(a) Swamps (b) Desert area
(c) Hilly areas (d) Grassland

10. The function of the surge tank is to:
(a) Relieve water hammer pressures in the penstock pipe
(b) Supply water at a constant pressure
(c) Produce surge in the pipe line
(d) All of the above

11. Nuclear power stations have:
(a) High running cost (b) Low running cost
(c) Both (a) and (b) (d) None of the above

12. Nuclear reactors usually employ
(a) Fussion (b) Fission
(c) Both (a) and (b) (d) None of the above

13. Heavy water is used in nuclear power plant as
(a) Coolant (b) Moderator
(c) Shield (d) Fuel

14. Diesel power plant is generally used as a
(a) Base load (b) Standby plant
(c) Peak load plant

15. A diesel power station is mostly used as a standby generating station because of
(a) Higher cost of fuel (b) Poor efficiency
(c) Poor power factor (d) High capital cost

16. A gas turbine plant usually suits for as a
(a) Peak load (b) Base load
(c) Permanent (d) None ot these

17. Which of the following generating stations has the maximum efficiency
(a) Thermal power plant (b) Hydro-electric power plant
(c) Nuclear power plant (d) Diesel power palnt

18. Which of the following generating stations has the minimum running cost.
(a) Hydro-electric station (b) Thermal power station
(c) Diesel power station (d) Nuclear power station

19. The capital cost of thermal power plant will depend upon:
(a) The size of the plant (b) The fuel cost
(c) (a) and (b) both (d) None of the above

ANSWERS

1. (e)	**2.** (b)	**3.** (d)	**4.** (a)	**5.** (a)	**6.** (b)	**7.** (b)	**8.** (a)	**9.** (c)
10. (a)	**11.** (b)	**12.** (b)	**13.** (a)	**14.** (b)	**15.** (a)	**16.** (a)	**17.** (b)	**18.** (a)
19. (a)								

2. Fill in the Blanks

1. The primary source of energy are __________ and __________
2. Sun is a __________ conventional source of energy.
3. The biomass is converted into __________ which run engine.
4. Wind is the __________ source of energy.
5. The thermal efficiency of the steam power station is __________
6. The hydroelectric plants are located in __________ area.
7. Steam turbine converts __________ energy into __________ energy.
8. The __________ power plants do not require any fuel.
9. Economizers are used to heat __________
10. Running cost of __________ power station is lowest.
11. The function of the nuclear reactor is to control __________.
12. Graphite is used in nuclear power plant as a __________
13. Diesel is a __________ renewable source of energy.
14. The fuel mostly used in nuclear plants is __________

ANSWERS

1. sun, wind	**2.** non	**3.** biogas	**4.** primary	**5.** 25%
6. hilly	**7.** mechanical, electrical		**8.** hydro	
9. feed water	**10.** hydro	**11.** atomic chain reaction		
12. coolant	**13.** non	**14.** uranium		

3. True-False Type Questions

1. Modern thermal power station has efficiency more than 60%.
2. Thermal power stations are preferably located near the load centre.
3. Thermal stations use water as a fuel.
4. Condenser converts steam into water.
5. The capital cost of hydroelectric power stations is low.
6. Penstock is employed in hydroelectric plant.
7. Hydroelectric plant have longest life.
8. Atomic chain reaction is controlled by reactor.
9. In a nuclear reactor power plant, the power is produced by nuclear fission of heavy atom.
10. Diesel power plants are used as standby unit.
11. Diesel power plants is the most reliable.
12. Gas turbine power plant is more efficient than steam power plant.
13. In a gas electric power plant prime mover is a steam turbine.

ANSWERS

1. False	2. True	3. False	4. True	5. False	6. True	7. True	8. True
9. True	10. True	11. False	12. True	13. False			

SHORT ANSWER TYPE QUESTIONS

Q.1. Write the name of four sources of non-conventional energy.

Ans. (i) Solar (ii) Wind, (iii) Biomass (iv) Geothermal

Q.2. Write the name of four primary sources of energy.

Ans: (i) Coal (ii) Natural gas (iii) Uranium (iv) Oil

Q.3. Define biomass.

Ans. Biomass means organic matter and produced by plants and their derivatives.

Q.4. What is conventional source of energy?

Ans: It includes fossil fuels, hydro and nuclear power.

Q.5. Name the factor on which total wind generation depend.

Ans: (i) wind speed (ii) turbine shaft (iii) conversion energy efficiency of the rotor.

Q.6 Write the demerits of diesel power plant.

Ans. (i) High running cost
(ii) Pollute the atmosphere
(iii) Cost of lubricant is high

Q.7. Why thermal power plants are located near river or canal?

Ans: Since an huge amount of water is required for condenser hence these plants are located near the river or canal.

Q.8. What is the function of economizer?

Ans: Economiser is used to heat the feed water supplied to boiler by utilizing fuel gases on the way to chimney.

Q.9. What is the function of condenser?

Ans: It condenses the steam into water.

Q.10. Define spillway.

Ans: Spillway is used to discharge the surplus water of reservoir into downstream side of dam.

Q.11 Which type of energy is possessed by water stored in a dam?

Ans. Potential energy.

Q.12 What is penstock?

Ans. Closed pipe connecting water turbine with the valve house in hydro plant is called penstock.

Q.13 Which fuel is used in nuclear power plant?

Ans. U_{235}

Q.14 What is nuclear fission?

Ans. When nucleas of U_{235} is bombarded with slow moving neutrons, it breaks up into two parts. The process is called nuclear fission. In this process, three additional neutrons are produced and energy is released.

Q.15 Name the material used as a coolant in nuclear power plant.

Ans. Heavy water, gas or liquid.

Q.16 Define dam.

Ans. The structure which obstructs the flow of water in a river is called dam.

Q.17 Name the various types of hydroelectric plants:

Ans.
(i) Low head upto 70 m
(ii) Medium head from 70 m to 300 m
(iii) High head above 300 m.

Q.18 What are the advantages and disadvantages of diesel power station?

Ans. Advantages :

(i) Less space is required for installation
(ii) Installation is simple
(iii) More efficient than steam plants
(iv) Cost of transmission lines is less.

Disadvantages:

(i) Diesel is costly, therefore, running cost is very high
(ii) Maintenance cost is high.

EXERCISE

1. What are the main sources from which electrical power can be generated?
2. Classify different energy sources. List various conventional and non-conventional energy sources.
3. What is wind energy? Describe the main components of a wind power plants.
4. What is the importance of non-conventional source of energy in present scenario?
5. Write a note on conventional and non-conventional energy source.

6. What is biomass and how it is useful for bio-energy production?
7. What is solar energy? Explain in brief the solar power plant.
8. Draw a neat layout diagram of a thermal power plant. Name the various major parts. Give function of each.
9. Explain the functions of the following in a thermal power station: (i) Economiser, (ii) Air pre-heater, (iii) Condenser, (iv) Super heater
10. Draw and explain the layout of a hydroelectric station.
11. Draw the layout of an atomic power station and explain the function of moderator, control rods, coolant and reflector.
12. What are the major consideration to be taken into account before making a choice of power station?
13. Sketch the schematic layout of diesel power station and explain the main parts.
14. Explain the advantages of interconnection of different power.
15. What are the advantages and disadvantages of a diesel power station?
16. Compare the performance of hydro, thermal and nuclear power station on the basis of starting time, maintenance, space, capital cost and pollution.

Economics of Generation

2

INSIDE THIS CHAPTER

- Introduction
- Cost of Generation
- Concept of Regional and National Grid
- Concept of Power Factor
- Interconnection of Power Stations and Its Advantages

2.1 INTRODUCTION

The generation of electrical energy economically is not an ordinary matter, rather it requires a long experience to decide about type, location and rating of generating stations. The other considerations for the design of the power station are reliability, minimum capital and operating costs. For this, it is necessary that the layout should be such that the maintenance and repairs can be carried out easily.

For deciding the type and rating of generating plant it is necessary that Engineer may be familiar with the following important terms.

2.1.1 Fixed Cost

The cost, which is independent of maximum demand and energy output is called fixed cost.

This cost is due to interest on the capital cost of land used for the generating station and kept for future expansion and salaries of high officials.

2.1.2 Semi-fixed Cost

The cost which depends upon the maximum demand and independent of energy output is called semi-fixed cost.

This cost is only due to annual interest and depreciation on the capital cost of building and other equipment installed at the station, insurance, taxes and salaries of management and electrical staff.

2.1.3 Running Cost

It is the cost which depends only upon the number of units generated. This running cost is due to the annual cost of fuel, lubricating oil, maintenance, repairs, wages and salaries of operating staff. This cost is proportional to the number of unit generated.

While deciding any scheme to execute, the operating cost i.e., sum of fixed, semi fixed and running cost is considered which should be minimum.

$$\text{Total annual cost of energy} = R_S\,(a + b\text{ kW} + C\text{ kWh})$$

where a = fixed cost

b kW = semi fixed cost

c kWh = running cost

2.1.4 Per Unit Cost

The cost of generation per unit is called per unit cost of generation. To determine per unit cost of generation the total operating cost is divided by the number of units generated.

$$\text{Per unit cost} = \frac{\text{Total operating cost}}{\text{Number of unit generated/annum}}$$

$$= R_S\,\frac{a + b\text{kW} + c\text{kWh}}{\text{kWh}}$$

Definition of Important Terms

1. **Connected load:** The sum of the continuous ratings of all the equipment connected to the supply system is called connected load.
2. **Maximum demand:** The greatest of all the demands (loads) which occur during a given period in called maximum demand. It is not necessary that all the consumers switch on whole of connected load at a time, it varies according to the requirement of the consumers.
3. **Load factor:** It is defined as the ratio of average load to maximum demand.

$$\text{Load factor} = \frac{\text{Average load}}{\text{Maximum demand}}$$

$$\text{Daily load factor} = \frac{\text{kWh supplied in a day}}{\text{Maximum demand} \times 24}$$

$$\text{Yearly load factor} = \frac{\text{kWh supplied in whole of year}}{\text{Maximum demand} \times 365 \times 24}$$

The load factor will be always less than one.

If the load factor is high, the maximum demand will be low. Thus at high load factor the generation cost will be less and vice versa.

4. **Diversity factor:** The maximum demands of all consumers don't occur at the same moment, thus maximum demand on power plant will be always less than the sum of individual maximum demands of all consumers connected to the power plant.

Diversity factor is defined as the ratio of sum of the individual maximum demands of all the consumers connected to the power plant to the maximum demand of the power station.

$$\text{Diversity factor} = \frac{\text{Sum of individual maximum demands}}{\text{Maximum demand of power station}}$$

It is always greater than unity.

If the diversity factor is high, the demand will be low and the capacity of plant will be smaller resulting in reduction in capital cost. Hence the generation per kWh of energy will also be less.

5. **Demand factor:** It is defined as the ratio between maximum demand to connected load of a power station.

It may be noted that load factor and demand factor are always less than unity, whereas the diversity factor is always greater than unity.

$$\text{Demand factor} = \frac{\text{Maximum demand}}{\text{Connected load}}$$

If the demand factor is low, the maximum demand will be less. Thus cost of generation will be less at low value of the demand factor and vice versa.

6. **Plant factor or capacity factor:** As the demand of electrical power is increasing day by day, so every plant should keep a reserve capacity so as to take care of future expansions to meet the demand of increasing load. Keeping this thing in view, the capacity of plants is usually greater than the required capacity.

Plant or capacity factor is defined as the ratio of average load to the rated capacity of the power plant.

$$\text{Plant factor} = \frac{\text{Average load}}{\text{Rated capacity of power plant}}$$

7. **Load curve:** The load on the power station is seldom constant. It varies from time to time.

The curve plotted between load on the power station on y-axis and time on x-axis is called **load curve.**

When the load curve is plotted for a period of 24 hours as shown in Fig. 2.1, it is known as *daily load curve*. If the daily average values are plotted for one month, the curve so obtained is known as monthly load curve and if the monthly average values are plotted for a year, the curve is known as yearly load curve.

Load curve has great importance in generation and it supplies the following information.

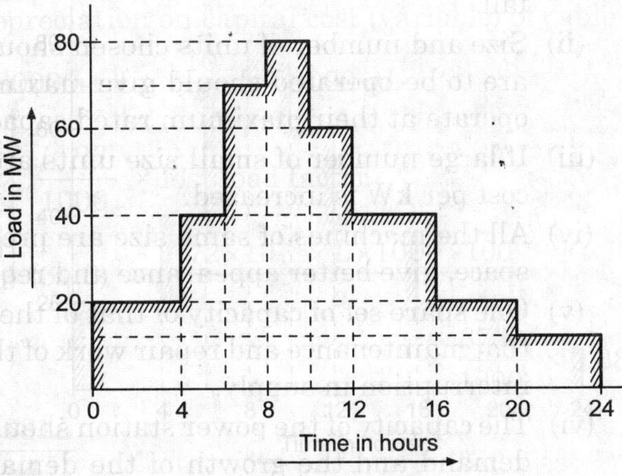

Fig. 2.1 Load curve

(i) It indicates the variation of load time to time in a day.

(ii) Area under the curve i.e., shaded portion shown in Fig. 2.1 represents the total energy generated in a day.

(iii) The peak of the curve represents the maximum demand on the generating station in a day.

(iv) The area under the curve divided by the number of hours in that period represents the average load on the generating station.

(v) The ratio of area under the load curve to the total area of the rectangle in which it is contained gives the load factor.

Thus, the above informations help in deciding the size and number of units to be installed and their schedule of operation.

8. **Utilization factor:** It is defined as the ratio of maximum demand to the rated capacity of the power station. It is always less than unity.

$$\text{Utilization factor} = \frac{\text{Maximum demand}}{\text{Rated capacity of power plant}}$$

$$1\text{m}^3 \text{ of water weighs} = 1000 \text{ kgm}$$

$$1 \text{ kWh} = 860 \text{ kcals}$$

9. **Average load** $= \dfrac{\text{No. of units generated/annum}}{\text{No. of hours in a year}}$

2.1.5 Size and Number of Generating Units

The size and number of generating units depend upon the load curve of the generating station. The initial cost of the power plant depends upon the choice of size and number of units to be installed and the running cost depends upon their working schedule. While deciding the size of units, their number and operating schedule, the following important points must be kept in view.

(i) A single unit of maximum capacity should not be chosen because it will given very poor efficiency at light loads and in case of break down, whole of the supply will fail.

(ii) Size and number of units chosen should be such that at all loads, the units which are to be operated should give maximum efficiency. This is only possible if they operate at their maximum rated capacity or so.

(iii) If large number of small size units are chosen, the floor area required and initial cost per kW is increased.

(iv) All the machines of same size are preferred due to the fact that they require less space, give better appearance and require less spare parts.

(v) One spare set of capacity of that of the largest unit is installed as stand by unit; so that maintenance and repair work of the working units may be carried out without interruption in supply.

(vi) The capacity of the power station should be 20% more than the expected maximum demand and the growth of the demand expected in near future should also be considered.

2.1.6 Significance of Load and Diversity Factor Generation

The load factor and diversity factor have an important role to play in the cost of energy generated at the power station. Higher the value of load factor and diversity factor, lower will be the cost per unit of energy generated.

Higher the diversity factor of the station, lower will be the maximum demand of the station, therefore, smaller will be the capacity of the plant required to meet with the individual demands of the consumers. As the capital cost of the generating station depends upon the capacity of the plant, therefore, the fixed charges due to capital investment will be much reduced with higher diversity factor. Thus, the cost of energy generated will be quite less.

Similarly, higher the load factor, more will be the average load and more number of units will be generated for a given maximum demand and therefore, overall cost per unit of electrical energy generated is reduced due to distribution of fixed charges over more number of units generated, which are proportional to the maximum demand and independent of the energy generated.

EXAMPLE 2.1 If a generating station had maximum load for the year of 18000 kW and a load factor of 30.5% and the maximum load on the substations were 7500, 5000, 3400, 4600 and 2800 kW. Calculate the units generated for the year and the diversity factor.

Solution:

$$\text{Maximum load} = 18000 \text{ kW}$$

$$\text{Load factor} = 30.5\% = 0.305$$

$$\text{Average load} = \text{Max. load} \times \text{load factor}$$

$$= 18000 \times 0.305 = 5490 \text{ kW}$$

$$\text{Energy generated/year} = 5490 \times 8760 = \mathbf{48092400 \text{ kWh (Ans.)}}$$

$$\text{Sum of individual max. demands} = 7500 + 5000 + 3400 + 4600 + 2800 = 23300 \text{ kW]}$$

$$\text{Diversity factor} = \frac{\text{Sum of individual max. demands}}{\text{Maximum demand}}$$

$$= \frac{23300}{18000} = \mathbf{1.2944 \text{ (Ans.)}}$$

EXAMPLE 2.2 A generating station has a maximum demand of 40 MW and a connected load of 75 MW. If the number of units generated in a year are 250 × 10^6. Calculate load factor and demand factor.

Solution:

$$\text{Maximum demand} = 40 \text{ MW} = 40 \times 10^3 \text{ kW}$$

$$\text{Connected load} = 75 \text{ MW} = 75 \times 10^3 \text{ kW}$$

$$\text{No. of units generated/year} = 250 \times 10^6$$

$$\text{Average load} = \frac{\text{Energy generated/year}}{8760}$$

$$= \frac{250 \times 10^6}{8760} = 28.54 \times 10^3 \text{ kW}$$

$$\text{Load factor} = \frac{\text{Average load}}{\text{Maximum load}}$$

$$= \frac{28.54 \times 10^3}{40 \times 10^3} = 0.7135 = \mathbf{71.35\% \text{ (Ans.)}}$$

$$\text{Demand factor} = \frac{\text{Maximum demand}}{\text{Connected load}}$$

$$= \frac{40 \times 10^3}{75 \times 10^3} = 0.5334 = \mathbf{53.34\% \text{ (Ans.)}}$$

EXAMPLE 2.3 A generating station has a maximum demand of 3550 kW and has a connected load of 65000 kW. The number of units generated are annually 25.6 × 10^7. Calculate: (a) load factor, (b) demand factor.

Solution:

$$\text{Maximum demand} = 3550 \text{ kW} = 35.5 \times 10^3 \text{ kW}$$

$$\text{Connected load} = 65000 \text{ kW} = 65 \times 10^3 \text{ kW}$$

$$\text{No of units generated per year} = 25.6 \times 10^7$$

$$\text{Average load} = \frac{\text{Energy generated year}}{8760}$$

$$= \frac{25.6 \times 10^7}{8760} = 29.224 \times 10^3 \text{ kW}$$

$$\text{Load factor} = \frac{\text{Average load}}{\text{Maximum load}}$$

$$= \frac{29.224 \times 10^3}{35.5 \times 10^3} = 0.8232$$

$$= 82.32\% \textbf{ (Ans.)}$$

$$\text{Demand factor} = \frac{\text{Maximum demand}}{\text{Connected load}}$$

$$= \frac{35.5 \times 10^3}{65 \times 10^3} = 0.5461 = 54.61\% \textbf{ (Ans.)}$$

EXAMPLE 2.4 A diesel generating station supplies 500 kW, 480 kW, 300 kW and 180 kW loads and has maximum demands of 750 kW calculate:

(i) Annual load factor; (ii) the diversity factor; (iii) the demand factor. The number of units supplied annually are 16 × 10^5.

Solution:

$$\text{Maximum demand} = 750 \text{ kW}$$

$$\text{Units supplied/year} = 16 \times 10^5$$

$$\text{Average load} = \frac{16 \times 10^5}{8760} = 182.65 \text{ kW}$$

$$\text{Load factor} = \frac{\text{Average load}}{\text{Maximum load}}$$

$$= \frac{182.65}{750} = 0.24353$$

$$= 24.353\% \textbf{ (Ans.)}$$

$$\text{Diversity factor} = \frac{\text{Sum of individual maximum loads}}{\text{Maximum load}}$$

$$= \frac{500 + 480 + 300 + 180}{750} = \frac{1460}{750}$$

$$= 1.9467 \textbf{ (Ans.)}$$

$$\text{Demand factor} = \frac{\text{Maximum demand}}{\text{Connected load}}$$

$$= \frac{750}{500+480+300+180} = \frac{750}{1460}$$

$$= 05137 = \mathbf{51.37\%\ (Ans.)}$$

EXAMPLE 2.5 Estimate the generating cost per unit of a power station with the following data:

Plant capacity = 100 MW
Annual load factor = 60%
Capital cost = ₹1250/kW installed
Maximum demand = 80 MW
Annual cost of fuel taxation, salaries etc. = ₹60 lacs
Interest and depreciation/annum = 6% each of capital cost

Solution: Capital cost = ₹1250 × 100 × 10^3 = ₹1250 × 10^5

Fixed charges i.e., interest and depreciation/annum

$$= ₹\left(\frac{6+6}{100}\right) 1250 \times 10^5 = ₹150 \times 10^5$$

Running charges/annum = ₹60 lacs

= ₹60 × 10^5

Total charges/annum = ₹(150 + 60) × 10^5

= ₹210 × 10^5

Average load = Max. demand × Load factor

$$= \frac{80 \times 10^3 \times 60}{100} = 48 \times 10^3 \text{ kW}$$

Energy generated/year = Average load × 8760

= 48 × 10^3 × 8760 = 42.48 × 10^6 kWh

$$\text{Cost of generation/unit} = ₹\frac{210 \times 10^5}{42.48 \times 10^6} = \mathbf{4.994\ P\ (Ans.)}$$

EXAMPLE 2.6 A bulk supply of 100 MW is taken at ₹60 per kW and 5 paise per unit for 400 hrs. Calculate the cost per kWh if the load factor is: (*i*) 100% (*ii*) 40%. Comment on the results.

Solution: Maximum demand = 100 MW = 100 × 10^3 kW

No. of hours = 400

(i) When the load factor = 100% = 1

Average load = Max. load × load factor

= 100 × 10^3 × 1 = 100 × 10^3 kW

Energy generated = Average load × No. of hours

100 × 10^3 × 400 = 40 × 10^6 kWh

Fixed charges = ₹60 × 100 × 10^2 = ₹60 × 10^5

$$\text{Running charges} = ₹\,\frac{5}{100} \times 40 \times 10^6 = ₹\,20 \times 10^5$$

$$\text{Total charges} = ₹\,(60 + 20) \times 10^5 = ₹\,80 \times 10^5$$

$$\text{Cost of energy/kWh} = ₹\,\frac{80 \times 10^5}{40 \times 10^6} = \textbf{20 P (Ans.)}$$

(ii) When the load factor = 40% = 0.4

$$\text{Average load} = 100 \times 10^3 \times 0.4 = 40 \times 10^3 \text{ kW}$$

$$\text{Energy generated} = 40 \times 10^3 \times 400 = 16 \times 10^6 \text{ kWh}$$

$$\text{Fixed charges} = ₹\,60 \times 100 \times 10^3 = ₹\,60 \times 10^5$$

$$\text{Running charges} = \frac{5}{100} \times 16 \times 10^6 = ₹\,80 \times 10^5$$

$$\text{Total charges} = ₹\,(60 + 8) \times 10^5 = ₹\,68 \times 10^5$$

$$\text{Cost of energy/kWh} = ₹\,\frac{67 \times 10^5}{16 \times 16} = \textbf{42.5 P (Ans.)}$$

Comments: *At higher load factor, per unit cost of energy is less since the fixed charges are distributed over more number of units.*

EXAMPLE 2.7 A power station has to supply loads as follows:

Time	*kW*	*Time*	*kW*
11 pm to 5 am	500	12 noon to 1 pm	1500
5 pm to 6 am	750	1 pm to 5 pm	2500
6 pm to 7 am	1000	5 pm to 7 pm	2000
7 pm to 9 am	2000	7 pm to 9 pm	2500
9 pm to 12 noon	2500	9 pm to 11 pm	1000

Determine load factor. Choose the number and size of alternator units for meeting this load demand.

Soluton: Maximum load on the power station = 2500 kW

Energy generated/day

$$= 500 \times 6 + 750 \times 1 + 1000 \times 1 + 2000 \times 2 + 2500 \times 3 + 1500 \times 1 + 2500 \times 4 + 2000 \times 2 + 2500 \times 2 + 1000 \times 2$$

$$= 3000 + 750 + 1000 + 4000 + 7500 + 1500 + 10000 + 4000 + 5000 + 2000$$

$$= 38750 \text{ kW}$$

$$\text{Average load} = \frac{\text{Energy generate/day}}{\text{No.of hours in a day}} = \frac{38750}{24} = 1614.583 \text{ kW}$$

$$\text{Load factor} = \frac{\text{Average load}}{\text{Maximum load}}$$

$$= \frac{1614.583}{2500} = \textbf{0.6458} = \textbf{63.58\% (Ans.)}$$

Since the minimum and maximum load on the power station is 500 kW and 2500 kW respecting. Six alternator operating at 0.8 p.f. with an output of 500 kW (625 kVA) may be selected. One of them will act as a stand by unit.

2.2 CONCEPT OF POWER FACTOR

Alternating current drawn by any electrical machine consists of two components. One component of current I_w is always in phase with the applied voltage and is called wattful component. This is the component of the current which does the useful work. The second component of current $I\mu$, is in quadrature with the applied voltage and is called watt less component. This component of the current does not do useful work but it is merely the magnetizing current. The two components of the current are shown in Fig. 2.2(a).

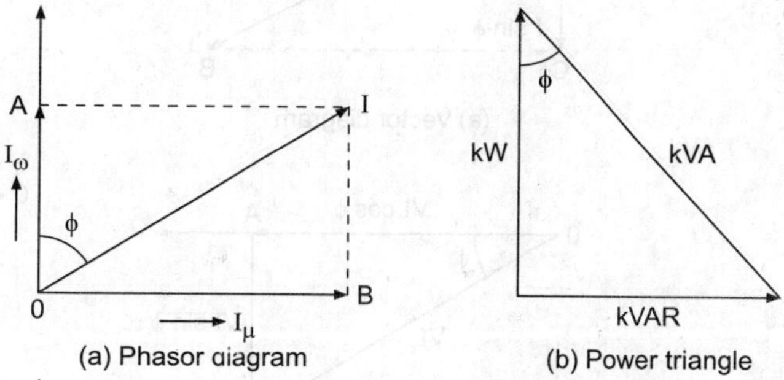

Fig. 2.2 Phasor diagram and power triangle

$$I^2 = I^2_{\mu} + I^2_{w}$$

Multiplying both sides by $\left(\frac{V}{1000}\right)^2$; we get

$$\frac{V^2 I^2}{(1000)^2} = \frac{V^2 I_{\mu^2} - V^2 I_{\omega^2}}{(1000)^2} = \frac{V^2 I^2 \sin^2\phi}{(1000)^2} + \frac{V^2 I^2 \cos^2\phi}{(1000)^2}$$

$$(\text{kVA})^2 = (\text{kVAR})^2 + (\text{kW})^2 : (\text{Reactive power kVAR})$$

$$= \text{kVA} \sin\phi = \text{kW} \tan\phi$$

Figure 2.2(b) shows the power triangle. From this triangle we can write down as following:

$$\text{Power factor } \cos\phi = \frac{\text{kW}}{\text{kVA}} \text{ and also } \cos\phi = \frac{I_w}{I}$$

Thus power factor is defined as the cosine of the phase angle difference between voltage and current vectors. It is expressed as the ratio of useful or wattful current to total current.

Consider an inductive circuit which draws a current from the supply mains lagging behind the supply voltage V by an angle ϕ, the vector diagram is shown in Fig. 2.3(a).

The current 'I' can be resolved into two components, one along the voltage vector and other perpendicular to it. The component along the voltage vector, $I\cos\phi$ is called the in phase or active component of current and perpendicular to the voltage $I\sin\phi$ is called the out of phase or reactive component of current.

If all the three sides of the triangle OAB multiply voltage 'V' Then

$OA = VI \cos\phi$ represent the true power in kW

$AB = VI \sin\phi$ represent the reactive power in kVAR

$OB = VI$ represent the apparent power kVA

The power triangle is shown in Fig. 2.3(d).

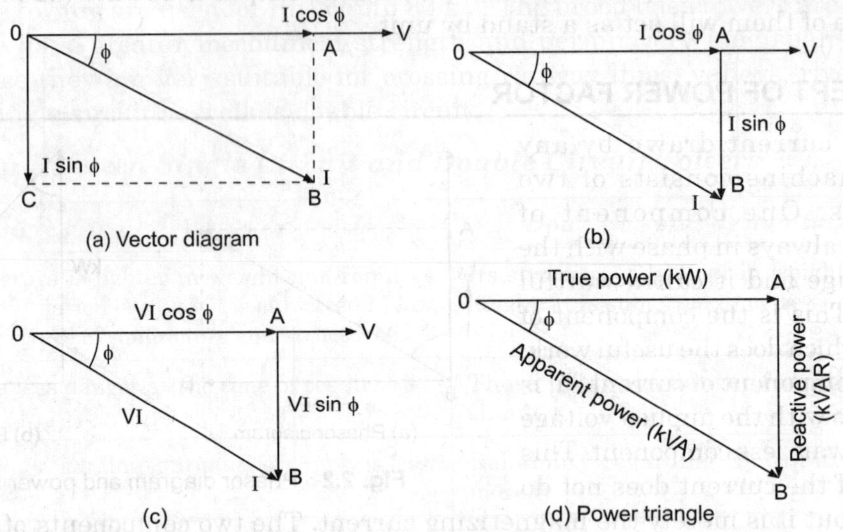

Fig. 2.3

2.2.1 Effect of Power Factor on Cost Generation

When the power factor is improved by installation on either by using synchronous condensers or by static capacitors then it involves an investment and expenditure which have to be incurred every year in the shape of interest and depreciation on account of investment made for purchasing the equipment. However, improved power factor means reduction in maximum demand and hence reduced electricity bill. The limit of the power factor at which the net annual saving (Saving in electricity bill less annual interest and depreciation charges) is maximum, is known as most economical power factor.

It is given by the equation

$$\text{Economical power factor} = \sqrt{1-\left(\frac{B}{A}\right)^2}$$

where B = Annual expenditure per kVAR of the power factor improvement equipment,

A = Annual maximum demand tariff charges per kVA.

In actual practice it is quite economical to work with an average power factor of 0.92 to 0.95.

Proof: Consider a consumer taking a peak load of P kW at a power factor of $\cos \phi_1$ and charged at the rate of ₹ A per kVA of maximum demand per annum. Let the expenditure per kVAR per annum of the power factor correction equipment be ₹ B.

Corresponding to maximum demand of P kW at power factor of $\cos \phi_1$

Maximum demand in kVA,

$$\text{kVA}_1 = \frac{P}{\cos \phi_1} = P \sec \phi_1$$

$$\text{Reactive power, kVAR}_1 = P \tan \phi_1$$

Let the power factor become $\cos\phi_2$ by installing the power factor correction equipment such as phase advancer.

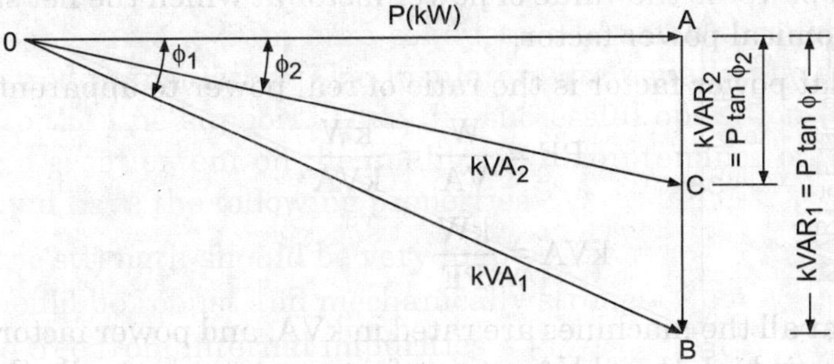

Fig. 2.4 Economics of power factor

New maximum demand in kVa,

$$kVA_2 = \frac{P}{\cos\phi_2} = P\sec\phi_2$$

New reactive power, $kVAR_2 = P\tan\phi_2$

Annual saving in maximum demand charge

$$= ₹\, A\,(kVA_1 - kVA_2)$$
$$= ₹\, A\,(P\sec\phi_1 - P\sec\phi_2)$$
$$= ₹\, AP\,(\sec\phi_1 - \sec\phi_2)$$

Leading kVAR supplied by the power factor correction equipment

$$= P\,(\tan\phi_1 - \tan\phi_2)$$

Annual expenditure on pf correction equipment

$$= BP\,(\tan\phi_1 - \tan\phi_2)$$

Net annual saving;

$$S = AP\,(\sec\phi_1 - \sec\phi_2) - BP\,(\tan\phi_1 - \tan\phi_2)$$

This saving will be maximum if the differentiation of it with respect to ϕ_2 is zero,

i.e., $$\frac{ds}{d\phi_2} = 0$$

or $$\frac{d}{d\phi_2}[AP(\sec\phi_1 - \sec\phi_2) - BP\,(\tan\phi_1 - \tan\phi_2)] = 0$$

or $$-AP\sec\phi_1\tan\phi_2 + BP\sec^2\phi_2 = 0 \quad \text{(Assuming } \phi_1 \text{ as constant)}$$

or $$\tan\phi_2 = \frac{B}{A}\sec\phi_2$$

or $$\sin\phi_2 = \frac{B}{A} = \frac{\text{Annual cost of phase advancing plant per kVAR}}{\text{Annual cost per kVA of max. demand}}$$

$\therefore$ $$\cos\phi_2 = \sqrt{1-\sin^2\phi_2} = \sqrt{1-\left(\frac{B}{A}\right)^2}$$

From the above expression the value of most economical power factor $\cos \phi_2$ can be determined.

Most economical power is the value of power factor at which the net saving is maximum is called most economical power factor.

Also we know that power factor is the ratio of real power to apparent power

i.e.,
$$PF = \frac{W}{VA} = \frac{kW}{kVA}$$

$\therefore$
$$kVA = \frac{kW}{PF}$$

Also we know that all the machines are rated in kVA, and power factor is also involved in it. If the power factor is high then kVA rating of ac generator is smaller hence capital lost is reduced. Moreover the cost of generation of electrical energy per kWh will also be reduced.

If the pf is low, cost of generation will be more. Due to this reason the pf of the load should be high at the substation.

EXAMPLE 2.8 A factory is equipped with three-phase induction motor, taking a total load of 1000 kW at pf of 0.85. A synchronous motor is installed taking 160 kW. Estimate the power factor at which the synchronous motor should operate in order that the whole factory may be run at full load with a power factor of 0.9, and find the kVA supplied to the synchronous motor.

Solution: Load of induction motor

$$P_1 = 1000 \text{ kW}$$

$$\text{Power factor, } \cos \phi_1 = 0.85$$

or
$$\phi_1 = 31° \, 48'$$

$$\text{Reactive power of the load} = P_1 \tan \phi_1 = 1000 \times \tan 31° \, 48'$$
$$= 1000 \times 0.62 = 620 \text{ kVAR}$$

Factory load after improved power factor

$$= 1000 + 160 = 1160 \text{ kW}$$

New improved power factor $\cos \phi_2 = 0.9$

or
$$\phi_2 = 25° \, 50'$$

Reactive power of the factory after improving power factor

$$= 1160 \tan 25° \, 50' = 1160 \times 0.4841 = 561.5 \text{ kVAR}$$

Reactive power supplied by the synchronous motor

$$= 620 - 561.5 = 58.5 \text{ kVAR}$$

kVA rating of the motor

$$= \sqrt{kW^2 + kVAR^2}$$

$$= \sqrt{160 + 58.5^2}$$

$$= 170.4 \text{ kVA}$$

$$\text{Power factor of synchronous motor} = \frac{160}{170.4} = 0.939 \text{ leading } \textbf{Ans.}$$

EXAMPLE 2.9 An industrial concern consists of the following loads:

(i) A lighting load of 300 kW.

(ii) An induction motor of 200 metric H.P.; efficiency 80% and working at a power factor 0.7 lagging.

(iii) A synchronous motor of 100 metric H.P.; efficiency 90%. Calculate the power factor of the motor so that the station power factor may be unity.

Solution: The total load on the station can be determined as follows:

Load	*Active component* $kW = kVA \cos \phi$	*Reactive component* $kVAR = kW \tan \phi$
1. Lighting	300	0
(P.F. is unity)		
$\cos \phi = 1$ and $\phi = 0$		
2. Input of the induction		
Motor $= \frac{200 \times 735.5}{0.8} = 184$	184	184 tan ($\cos^{-1}$ 0.7)
Power factor = 0.7 lag		184 × 1.02 = – 187.68
Total	484 kW	– 187.68 kVAR

$$\text{Input to synchronous motor} = \frac{200 \times 735.5}{0.9} = 81.7 \text{ kW}$$

Since the station is to work at unity power factor, the total reactive component of the station must be neutralized i.e., the synchronous motor must have a leading component = 187.68 kVAR

$$\tan \phi = \frac{187.68}{81.7} = 2.296$$

$$\phi = 66^\circ\, 30'$$

$$\cos \phi = 0.3987 \text{ leading, } \textbf{Ans.}$$

EXAMPLE 2.10 A supply system has the following tariff in force ₹ 200 per kVA of maximum demand plus 10 paisa per unit. A consumer intends to improve the power factor of his installation with the help of a phase advancing plant which costs ₹ 80 per kVAR. Calculate the most economical power factor to which it should be improved. Assume interest and depreciations as 10%.

Solution: The annual expenditure per kVAR of phase advancing plant

$$₹\, 80 \times \frac{10}{100} = ₹\, \frac{80}{10} = ₹\, 8.0$$

Most economical power factor

$$\cos\phi = \sqrt{1-\left(\frac{B}{A}\right)^2}$$

$$B = ₹8.00$$

$$A = ₹200$$

$$\cos\phi = \sqrt{1-\left(\frac{8}{200}\right)^2}$$

$$\cos\phi = \sqrt{0.9984}$$

Hence most economical power factor = 0.999 **Ans.**

EXAMPLE 2.11 Factory takes a peak load of 1000 kW at a p.f. of 0.7 lagging and is charged ₹ 500 per year per kVA of maximum demand. If the phase advancing plant costs ₹ 1200 per kVAR, find the limit to which the power factor can be economically improved. Interest and depreciation is 10% of the capital cost.

Solution: Factory load, $P = 1000$ kW

Power factor, $\cos\phi = 0.7$

$$\text{Maximum demand in kVA} = \frac{1000}{0.7} = 1428.5$$

Annual charges of maximum demand, A ₹ 500/kVA

Annual charges of phase advancing

Plant, $B = 1200$/kVAR

$$\text{Interest and depreciation, } B = ₹\frac{10}{100}\times 1200 = ₹120$$

Most economical power factor

$$\cos\phi_2 = \sqrt{1-\left(\frac{B}{A}\right)^2} = \sqrt{1-\left(\frac{120}{500}\right)^2} = 0.9707 \text{ lagging} \quad \textbf{Ans.}$$

2.2.2 Significance of Demand Factor and Power Factor

The demand factor is defined as the ratio of maximum demand to connected load on the power station. For the same connected load, if the demand factor is low, lower is the maximum demand and smaller will be plant capacity. Since the capital cost of the generating station depends upon the capacity of the plant, therefore, the fixed charges due to capital investment will be much reduced with lower demand factor.

Thus, the cost of energy generated will be quite less.

Hence, per unit cost of generation will be less at lower demand factor.

The power factor is defined as the ratio of true power to apparent power i.e.,

$$\text{Power factor} = \frac{\text{True power}}{\text{Apparent power}}$$

or $$\text{pf} = \frac{\text{kW}}{\text{kVA}}$$

or $$\text{kVA} = \frac{\text{kW}}{\text{pf}}$$

The alternators installed at the generating stations are rated in kVA. Therefore, for the same power to be delivered if the power factor at the generating station is high, the alternators of lower rating (or capacity) are required. This reduces the capital cost which in turn reduces the fixed charges and the cost of energy generated.

Thus, at higher power factor the cost of generation per unit will be less.

2.2.3 Significance of Load Factor and Diversity Factor

The values of load factor and diversity factor play a very important part on the cost of electrical energy produced by a power house. If the diversity factor and load factor are more, the cost per kWh will be less. The capital cost of the power station depends upon the capacity of the power station. Lower the maximum demand of the power station, the lower is the capacity required and therefore, lower is the capital cost of the plant. It can be explained as below.

If the value of diversity factor is high, then for the same maximum demands of different consumers, maximum demand on the power house will be less necessitating small size of generating set which means initial cost will be less; and thereby cost per kWh will be reduced. Hence, higher the diversity factor smaller will be the capacity of the plants required; hence capital cost is reduced.

It the load factor is increased then the same power house will generate more electrical energy; but the cost of generation remains the same. Thus more number of energy units will share the total cost of generation, resulting in reduced cost per kWh. Higher load factor means better utilization of the plants.

2.3 COST OF GENERATION

The total capital required in a project can be subdivided into: (a) Fixed capital; (b) Running capital.

2.3.1 Fixed Capital

The fixed capital comprises that part of the capital which is to be spent for the purchase of assets such as land, plant and equipment etc. It may be grouped under the following heads:

(i) Capital cost of generating equipment.
(ii) Capital cost of transmission system.
(iii) Capital cost of distribution system, both HT and LT. The fixed capital also include freight, cartage, octroi and labour charges.

2.3.2 Running Capital

The capital required for the purchase or fuel (if any), payment of salaries, wages etc., for continuous and smooth operation of the project makes up the running capital.

Cost of generation will include charges towards both, the fixed capital and running capital. So annual cost of generation can be subdivided into the following two heads:

(i) **Fixed charges:** It includes annual charge on assets covered under fixed capital, taxes, salaries of management and clerical staff and interest on the total capital.

(ii) **Running charges:** It includes fuel cost, maintenance and repair cost, cost of lubricating oil and wages of operation cost.

Interest and Depreciation

Usually for big projects money is borrowed from banks or other financial institutions and at the end of the year, the undertaking of the project is required to pay the interest on capital cost.

If a capital outlay required for a project is ₹ P and the rate of interest per year is r% then an amount of $\frac{rP}{100}$ per year must be provided as interest payment.

Depreciation of Plant

The power plant and equipment in the station will have a certain period of usual life. After years of use, the equipment loses its efficiency or it becomes obsolete and needs replacement. Sometimes even fairly new equipment may have to be changed, if more efficient equipment has come into the market. To enable this to be done, when necessary, some money is put aside annually which is known as *Depreciation fund.*

EXAMPLE 2.12 Calculate the rating of a capacitor required to improve the pf of a 5 kW. Load from 0.6 to 0.8.

Solution:

$$\cos\phi_1 = 0.6$$

$$\therefore \quad \phi_1 = 53° - 8' = \cos^{-1} 0.6$$

$$\therefore \quad \tan\phi_1 = \tan 53° - 8' = 1.333$$

$$\cos\phi_2 = 0.8$$

$$\phi_2 = \cos^{-1} 0.8 = 36° - 52'$$

$$\therefore \quad \tan\phi_2 = \tan 36° - 52' = 0.73$$

$$\text{Load } P = 5 \text{ kW}$$

$$\therefore \text{ kVAR supplied by the capacitor} = P(\tan\phi_1 - \tan\phi_2) = 5.00\,(1.333 - 0.75)$$

$$= 5 \times 0.583 = 2.915 \text{ kVAR}$$

$\therefore$ kVA rating of the capacitor = 2.915

(for capacitors kVA and kVAR are same)

$$\text{kVAR} = \text{kVA} \sin\phi = \text{kVA}$$ **Ans.**

EXAMPLE 2.13 An induction motor of a tubewell is taking a load of 5 kW at 0.6 pf Calculate the lamp load to be connected by the user so that pf rises to 0.8.

Solution:

$$\cos\phi = 0$$

$$\therefore \quad \phi_1 = \cos^{-1} 0.6 - 53° - 8' = 1.133$$

$$\therefore \quad \tan\phi_1 = \tan 53° - 8'$$

$$\cos\phi_2 = 0.8$$

$$\therefore \quad \phi_2 = \cos^{-1} 0.8 = 36^\circ - 52$$

$$\tan \phi_1 = \tan 36^\circ - 52' = 0.75$$

$$\text{Load } P = 5 \text{ kW}$$

$\therefore$ kVAR supplied by the lamp load

$$= P(\tan \phi_1 - \tan \phi_2) = 5\,(1.333 - 0.75)$$

$$= 5 \times 0.583 = 2.915 \text{ kVA}$$

$$\therefore \quad \text{kVA rating of the lamp load} = \sqrt{(\text{kW})^2 + (\text{kVAR})^2}$$

$$= \sqrt{(5)^2 + (2.915)^2} = 5.8 \text{ kVA } \textbf{Ans.}$$

2.4 INTERCONNECTION OF POWER STATIONS AND ITS ADVANTAGES

In North India, Himachal Pradesh has great potential for the development of hydroelectric power; but its own power requirement is too small and may not be much in near future; whereas in Haryana, total power requirement is much more than the available sources of power generation. In these circumstances it will be the best course to transfer surplus power of Himachal Pradesh to Haryana. This is possible by connecting the power systems of Haryana and Himachal Pradesh by means of transmission lines called *The Line*. The two systems thus connected are known as *interconnected system*. If more than two systems are thus connected then it is known as GRID FORMATION.

Whenever steam power station and hydroelectric power stations are interconnected then hydroelectric power plant acts as a capacity plant, i.e., it is used to supply power during peak load hours and steam station may be used as base load station.

Advantages of Interconnection of Power Stations

The following are the major advantages of inter-connected power stations.

1. **Less reserve plant capacity:** If the generating station work independently, the overall reserve plant capacity would be very high by interconnecting the generating stations reserve plant capacity can be reduced.
2. **Reduction in capital cost:** In an interconnected grid system it is possible to go in for large generating units, which means reduction in capital cost per kW.
3. **Better reliability:** The reliability of supply is increased in interconnected system. If plant fails to supply due to any fault, the supply is maintained from other plant.
4. **Better diversity factor:** Since the load curves of different stations are likely to differ, therefore, diversity factor of the whole system is improved.
5. **Reduction in running cost:** By interconnection of power station, the running cost of generating plant is reduced.

EXAMPLE 2.14 **The cost of an alternator installed in a generating plant is ₹7.5 lac and its normal life span is 30 years. At the end of this time it is expected that the alternator will have a scrap value of ₹50,000. (a) Calculate by sinking fund depreciation method, the annual charge to be set aside in order to replace the present plan with a new one at the end of life span. (b) Compare this with that calculated by straight line depreciation method. Assume the rate of compound interest as 10%.**

Solution: (*a*) Cost of replacement afters 30 years

$\therefore \quad C = 7,50,000 - 50,000 = ₹\,7,00,000$

$\therefore \quad n = 30$ years

$$r = \frac{10}{100} = 0.1$$

Annual deposit
$$X = \frac{Cr}{(1+r)^n - 1}$$

$$X = \frac{7,00,000}{(1.1)^{30} - 1} = \frac{7,00,000}{17.46-1} = \frac{70,000}{16.46} = ₹\,4,252.7$$

(*b*) Straight line depreciation method

The total amount to be collected after 30 years

$$= ₹\,(7.5 \times 10^5 - 50,000)\ ₹\,7 \times 10^5$$

$$\text{Amount to be set aside each year} = \frac{7,00,000}{30} = ₹\,23,333 \text{ Ans.}$$

EXAMPLE 2.15 An electric supply undertaking with a firm capacity of 5 MW has a maximum demand of 4 MW. It supplies the following categories of load.

(i) Domestic load : 3000 kW is the maximum demand at a load factor of 15%.

(ii) Street light : 200 kW is the maximum demand at a load factor of 30%.

(iii) Power load : 1800 kW is the maximum demand at a load factor of 40%.

The cost data is:

Capital cost of equipment = ₹ 1,31,40,000

Annual cost of fuel, wages, salary, repairs and maintenance

= ₹ 5,38,740

Rate of interest and depreciation is 12%

Calculate the cost per kWh for each category of load.

Solution: Capital cost = ₹ 1,31,40,000

Interest and depreciation = 12%

$$\therefore \quad \text{Annual fixed charges payable} = \frac{1,31,40,000 \times 12}{100} = ₹\,15,76,800$$

Annual cost of fuel, wages etc. = ₹ 5,38,740

Total amount payable per year = 15,76,800 + 5,38,740 = ₹ 21,15,540

Total M.D. of all categories = 3000 + 200 + 1800 = 5000 kW

$$\text{Cost per kW} = \frac{21,15,540}{5000} = ₹\,423.108$$

Domestic Load:

Maximum demand = 3000 kW

Load factor = 15%

$$\text{Units consumed per year} = \frac{3000 \times 15}{100} \times 8760 = 39{,}42{,}000$$

Total cost payable for domestic load in a year

$$= 3000 \times 423.108 = ₹\,12{,}69{,}324$$

$$\text{Cost per kWh} = \frac{12{,}69{,}324}{39{,}42{,}000} \times 100 = 32.2 \text{ paise}$$

Street Load:

$$\text{Maximum demand} = 200 \text{ kW}$$

$$\text{Load factor} = 30\%$$

$$\text{Units consumed per year} = \frac{200 \times 30}{100} \times 8760 = 5{,}25{,}600 \text{ kWh}$$

$$\text{Total cost payable for street load} = 200 \times 423.108 = 84621.6$$

$$\text{Cost per kWh} = \frac{84{,}621.6}{5{,}25{,}600} \times 100 = 16.1 \text{ paise}$$

Street Load:

$$\text{Maximum demand} = 1800 \text{ kW}$$

$$\text{Load factor} = 40\%$$

$$\text{Units consumed per year} = \frac{1800 \times 40}{100} \times 8760 = 8{,}76{,}000 \times 72 \text{ kWh}$$

$$\text{Total cost payable for power} = 1800 \times 423.108 = 7{,}61{,}594.4$$

$$\text{Cost per kWh} = \frac{7{,}61{,}594.4}{8{,}76{,}000 \times 72} \times 100 = 12.1 \text{ paise } \textbf{Ans.}$$

EXAMPLE 2.16 A generating station has a maximum demand of 35,500 kW and has a connected load of 65,000 kW. The number of units generated annually is 25.6 × 10⁷. Calculate:

(i) Load factor, and

(ii) Demand factor.

Solution:

$$\text{Maximum demand} = 35{,}500 \text{ kW}$$

$$\text{Connected load} = ₹\,65{,}000 \text{ kW}$$

$$\text{No. of units generated} = ₹\,25.6 \times 10^7 \text{ per annum}$$

$$\therefore \quad \text{Average load} = \frac{\text{No. of units generated per annum}}{\text{No. of hours in a year}} = \frac{25.6 \times 10^7}{8{,}760} \text{ kW}$$

(i) $$\text{Load factor} = \frac{\text{Average load}}{\text{Maximum demand}} = \frac{25.6 \times 10^7}{8760} \times \frac{1}{35{,}500} = 0.822$$

(ii) $$\text{Demand factor} = \frac{\text{Maximum demand}}{\text{Connected load}} = \frac{35{,}500}{65{,}000} = 0.546 \quad \textbf{Ans.}$$

EXAMPLE 2.17 The output of the generating station is 390 × 10^5 units per annum and installed capacity is 80,000 kW. If the annual fixed charges are ₹18 per kW of installed plant and running charges are 5 paise per kWh. What is the cost per unit at generating station?

Solution:

$$\text{Total annual fixed charges} = ₹18 \times 80{,}000 = ₹144 \times 10^4$$

$$\text{Annual running charges} = 390 \times 10^5 \times \frac{5}{100} = ₹195 \times 10^4$$

$$\text{Total annual charges} = \text{Fixed charges} + \text{Running charges}$$
$$= ₹(144 \times 10^4) + ₹(195 \times 10^4) = ₹339 \times 10^4$$

Total number of units generated per annum

$$= 390 \times 10^5$$

∴ Cost per unit at the generating station

$$= ₹\frac{339 \times 10^4}{390 \times 10^5} = \frac{339 \times 10^4}{390 \times 10^5} \times 100 \text{ paise}$$

$$= \frac{339}{39} = 8.7 \text{ paise } \textbf{Ans.}$$

EXAMPLE 2.18 (a) What are the factors considered while selecting the units of generating station? (b) Find the cost of generation per kWH for a generating station running at an annual load factor of 40% and having a maximum demand of 60 MW.

The total capital cost of the plant is ₹1 crore and coal and lubricants expenditure is ₹9 lakh per year. The annual charges towards wages and salaries are 1/20th of capital cost. Assume rate of interest and depreciation as 10%.

Solution: (*a*) Factors to be considered for selection of unit:

The following factors influence the selection of units in a power station:

1. The units selected should be the such that the load factor is high.
2. The number of units should at least be two, but should not be too many. If only two units are selected, size of each should be such that they can supply the maximum demand individually.
3. Provisions for reserve capacity should be made.
4. Provisions for future expansion in load demand should be made.
5. Units of equal size should preferably be selected, so that the number of supports is minimum, maintenance becomes easy.

(*b*) Given, annual load factor = 40% or 0.4

$$\text{Maximum demand} = 60 \text{ MW}$$

$$\text{Total capital cost} = ₹1 \text{ crore}$$

$$\text{Coal and lubricants cost} = ₹9 \text{ lakh/year}$$

$$\text{Annual charges of wages} = \frac{1}{20} \times \text{Capital cost}$$

$$\text{Interest and depreciation} = 10\%$$

We have,

$$\text{Annual expenditure} = \frac{1}{20} \times 10^7 + 0.1 \times 10^7 + 9 \times 10^5$$

$$= (0.5 + 1 + 0.9) \times 10^6$$

$$= ₹\,2 \times 10^6$$

$$\text{Units generated/annum} = \text{L.F} \times \text{M.D.} \times 8760$$

$$= 0.4 \times 60 \times 10^3 \times 8760 \text{ kWh}$$

$$= 210 \times 10^6 \text{ kWh}$$

$$\therefore \quad \text{Cost/unit generated} = ₹\,\frac{2 \times 10^6}{210 \times 10^6}$$

$$= 0.95 \text{ paisa} \quad \textbf{Ans.}$$

EXAMPLE 2.19 ***(a)*** **How does the increase in diversity factor reduce the cost of installation? *(b)* There are four loads each of 100, 200, 300 and 400 kVA. The diversity factor is 2.5 among the loads. Calculate the percentage saving in the single transformer supplying the total load.**

Solution: (*a*) Greater diversity factor means that the overall maximum demand is much less than arithmetic sum of the individual maximum demands. That means a plant of lesser installed capacity can supply these loads. Thus the installation cost is reduced due to reduced plant capacity.

(*b*) Given, diversity factor = 2.5

$$\text{Sum of individual M.DS} = 100 + 200 + 300 + 400$$

$$= 1000 \text{ kVA}$$

$$\therefore \quad \text{Overall M.D.} = \frac{\text{Sum of individual maximum demands}}{\text{Diversity factor}}$$

$$= \frac{1000}{2.5} = 400 \text{ kVA}$$

That is, one single transformer of 400 kVA capacity can supply all the loads as against a transformer of 1000 kVA capacity if all the loads were to occur at the same time.

$$\text{Saving in capacity} = 1000 - 400$$

$$= 600 \text{ kVA}$$

$$\%\text{ Saving in capacity} = \frac{60}{1000} \times 100$$

$$= 60\% \quad \textbf{Ans.}$$

2.5 CONCEPT OF REGIONAL AND NATIONAL GRID

2.5.1 Concept of Regional Grid

Electrical grid is defined as the network which interconnects the generation, transmission and distribution unit. A large amount of power is transmitted for the generating station to load centre at 220 kV or higher.

Regional Grid

The regional grid is formed by interconnecting the different transmission system of a particular area through the transmission line. It supplies the electrical power from generating unit to the distribution unit. A large amount of power is transmitted from the generating station to load centre at 220 kV or higher.

The power station of the grid is located near the fuel source which reduces the transportation cost of the system. But it is located far away from the populated area.

2.5.2 Concept of National Grid

The system of power that joins the places where electricity is produced, and takes electricity to all parts of country. The national grid is the high-voltage electric power transmission network in main land India connecting power stations and major substations and ensuring that electricity generated anywhere in India can be used to satisfy demand. The national grid is owned, operated, and maintained by state-owned Power Grid Corporation of India.

Individual state grids were inter connected to 5 regional grid covering main land India. The grids were the Northern, Eastern, Western, North-eastern and Southern grids. These regional links were established to enable transmission of surplus electricity between states in each region.

SUMMARY

1. **Fixed cost:** This is due to the interest on capital cost of land used for the station and for future expansion.
2. **Semi-fixed cost:** This cost is due to the annual interest on the capital cost of the building and equipment.
3. **Running cost:** It is also called operating cost and dependent upon the energy output of the station.
4. **Load curve:** It is a graph which shows the variation of load on the power from time to time. Hourly time is plotted along x-axis and load on system along y-axis.
5. **Connected load:** Sum of the continuous ratings of all the appliances connected to system.
6. **Maximum demand:** Greatest of all demands occurs during a given period on powers station.
7. **Load factor** $= \dfrac{\text{Average load}}{\text{Maximum demand}}$
8. **Diversity factor** $= \dfrac{\text{Sum of individual consumers maximum demand}}{\text{Maximum demand of a station}}$
9. **Capacity factor** $= \dfrac{\text{Average demand on the station}}{\text{Total connected load to the station}}$

10. Base load: The unvarying load is known as base load or maximum load which remains constant for the whole of the station.

11. Peak load: The maximum load occurring in the load curve excluding the base load is called peak load or maximum demand on a station at a particular time is called peak load.

12. Interconnection of power stations: When two stations of different states are connected together so that extra power generated in one state can be transmitted to other state when these states need it.

13. Grid: When number of power stations interconnected is more than two, the GRID is said to have been formed.

14. Power factor: It is defined as cosine of angle between voltage and current.

15. Disadvantages of low power factor

(a) Large kVA rating of equipment
(b) Greater conductor size
(c) Large copper loss
(d) Excessive heating of conductor materials
(e) Voltage regulation is poor
(f) Uneconomical power generation and transmission

16. Causes of lower power factor

(a) A transformer working on light loads draws magnetizing current at a low power factor.
(b) Induction motors working at loads less than full load draw currents at low power factor, through the power factor of induction motor at full load is about 0.85.
(c) Arc lamps work at low power factor due to their very nature.

17. Methods of improving power factor

(i) By the use of static capacitor
(ii) By the method of synchronous condenser
(iii) By the use of phase advancer

(i) **Static capacitor**. Either star or delta connected. These are mostly used in shunt connection. Series connected capacitors pose more operational problem and are bulky in size.

(ii) **Synchronous condenser**. Synchronous motors working with over excitation draw leading current thus compensating for the lagging current component. Such motors work at no load and very high speeds (to obtain an economical design).

(iii) **Phase advancers**. A special machine which may be connected in the rotor circuit of induction motor to improve its power factor.

18. Location of power factor improvement apparatus: Best location for power factor improvement apparatus causing low power factor. If synchronous condensers are used they are best located at receiving end; this would relieve generators and also transmission lines of carrying excessively large lagging current causing great losses.

Objective Type Questions

1. Multiple Choice Type Questions

1. The ratio of maximum demand on the system to rated connected load is called.

(a) Demand factor (b) Load factor
(c) Diversity factor (d) Utilization factor

2. The cost which is independent of maximum demand and depends upon the energy output is called?

(a) Fixed cost (b) Running cost
(c) Semi-fixed cost (d) All these above

3. The total electrical energy delivered in a given period divided by the time in that period is known as :

(a) Connected load (b) Load factor
(c) Diversity factor (d) Utilization factor

4. Demand factor is defined as the ratio of :

(a) Average load to maximum load (b) Maximum load to connected load
(c) Maximum load to average load (d) Connected load to maximum load

5. Demand factor on a power system is :

(a) Always lesser than unity (b) Always greater than unity
(c) Normally greater than two (d) None of the above

6. Load factor is defined as the ratio of :

(a) Maximum load to connected load. (b) Average load to maximum load
(c) Maximum load to average load (d) Average load to installed capacity.

7. All high demand factor the cost of generation is per unit will be

(a) high (b) low
(c) moderate (d) all these above

8. During which system the load on the power system is maximum?

(a) Autum (b) summer
(c) winter (d) rainy

9. Diversity factor is difined as the ratio of

(a) Sum of individual maximum demands of all the consumers supplied by a power system
(b) Maximum demand to average load
(c) Installed capacity to maximum load of power station.
(d) All of above.

10. Utilization factor is defined as the ratio of :

(a) Average demand on power plant
(b) Maximum demand to rated capacity
(c) Rated capacity to maximum demand of the power plant
(d) None of the above

11. Knowledge of diversity factor helps in computing.

(a) Plant capacity (b) Average load
(c) Peak demand (d) kWh generation

ANSWERS

1. (a) **2.** (b) **3.** (c) **4.** (b) **5.** (a) **6.** (b) **7.** (b) **8.** (d) **9.** (a)
10. (b) **11.** (a)

2. Fill in the Blanks

1. Demand factor is the ratio of __________ to connected load.
2. The value of load factor is always less than __________
3. Load factor is the ratio of average load to __________
4. The connected load is generally __________ than the maximum demand.
5. The value of demand factor __________ than unity.
6. The higher the load factor power station the __________ the cost of generating station.
7. In an interconnected grid system, the diversity factor of the whole system __________
8. Base load occurs on the power station for __________ hours in a day.
9. In an annual load curve __________ is taken along y-axis and __________ is taken along x-axis.
10. The demand above the __________ load of station is known as beak load.
11. The ratio of average load to the maximum load is called __________
12. The ratio of maximum demand to the rated connected load is called __________
13. Diversity factor is always __________ than one.
14. The load curve is plotted between load and __________
15. The capacity of power station should be __________ more than the maximum demand.

ANSWERS

1. maximum demand	2. one	3. maximum load
4. more	5. less	6. lesser
7. increases	8. 24	9. load, hours
10. base	11. load factor	12. demand factor
13. more	14. time	15. 20%

3. True-False Type Questions

1. Fixed cost is independent of maximum demand and energy output.
2. Demand factor is the ratio of maximum demand to the rated connected load.
3. Load factor is the ratio of maximum demand to average value.
4. The ratio of average load to the maximum load is called utilization factor.
5. Load curve is a graph between load and time.
6. Semi-fixed charges of generating plant are independent of the energy output.
7. Cost of generation per unit will be high at high demand factor.
8. The ratio of maximum demand and rated capacity of station is called utilization factor.
9. Connecting load factor is the ratio of average demand to maximum demand.
10. Running charges of generating plant is directly proportional to the number of kWh generated.
11. Diversity factor has direct effect on the load factor.
12. Plant capacity factor is the product of load factor and utilization factor.

ANSWERS

1. False	2. True	3. False	4. False	5. True	6. True	7. False	8. True
9. False	10. True	11. True	12. True				

SHORT ANSWER TYPE QUESTIONS

Q.1. Explain fixed and running cost of generation.

Ans. **Fixed cost:** The cost which is independent of maximum demand and energy output is called fixed cost.

Running cost: The cost which is independent of maximum demand but depends upon the energy output is called running cost.

Q.2. Define connected load.

Ans. The sum of continuous rating of all the equipments connected to the supply system is called connected load.

Q.3. Define demand factor.

Ans. The ratio of maximum demand on the system to the rated connected load to the system is called demand factor what is load factor? Its value is always less than unity.

The ratio of average to the maximum load is called demand factor.

Q.4. Define the following terms maximum demand and diversity factor.

Ans. **Maximum demand:** The greatest of all demands (load) which occur during a given period is called maximum demand.

Diversity factor: The ratio of the sum of individual maximum demands of all the consumers connected to the generations station to the maximum demand on the power station is called diversity factor. Its value is always more than one.

Q.5. What items constitute the fixed and running charges of generation of electrical energy?

Ans. The fixed charges include the annual interest and depreciation on the capital cost of generating plant, transmission and distribution network, buildings and other civil works, all types of taxes and insurance charges and salaries of high officials, management and clerical staff and compensation given to the workers.

The running or operating cost includes annual costs of fuel, lubricating oil, water maintenance and repairs of equipment and salaries of operational and maintenance staff and salaries of supervisory staff engaged in the running of the plant.

Q.6. What is depreciation reserve?

Ans. The depreciation charge represents the amount which is set aside from income every year and the amount so accumulated is called the depreciation reserve.

Q.7. How does the load duration curve differ from chronological load curve?

Ans. The daily variations in load on the power station from time to time hourly or half hourly, can be plotted on a graph taking load on a graph taking load on y-axis and time on x-axis. The curve so obtained is known as chronological load curve. The load duration curve indicates the variation of load, but with the load arranged in descending order of magnitude i.e., the greatest load on the left, lesser loads towards the right hand and the least load at the extreme light.

Q.8. What informations can be supplied by load curves?

Ans. The informations that can be had from load curves are: (*i*) variations of load during different hours of the day, (*ii*) total number of units generated in a day, (*iii*) maximum demand on the power station, (*iv*) average load, and (*v*) load factor.

Q.9. How does energy load curve differ from mass curve?

Ans. The curve drawn between demand in kW or MW on y-axis and units generated (kWh) on

x-axis is known as integrated load duration curve energy load curve while mass curve is plotted with units (kWh) generated as ordinate and time as abscissa.

Q.10. What is diversity factor and how does it influence the cost of generation?

Ans. The ratio of the sum of individual maximum demands of all the consumers supplied by it to the maximum demand of the power station is called the diversity factor. It is always greater than unity. Higher the diversity factor better it is with a given number of consumers; the higher the diversity factor of their loads, the smaller will be capacity of the power plant required and consequently the fixed charges due to capital investment will be much reduced.

Q.11. What are the advantages of using industrial/agricultural loads during night hours?

Ans. During night hours a large portion of the generating and distribution equipment remains idle due to extremely low demand. In case industrial and agricultural consumers are encouraged to use electricity during night and other off peak hours by giving a special discount, the energy can be supplied without incurring any additional capital cost.

Q.12. What are the different types of loads?

Ans. The main types of loads on a power system are domestic, commercial, agricultural, industrial, municipal, traction etc.

Q.13. What is the necessity of power factor improvement?

Ans. Low power factor causes the rating of generators and transformers, cross-sectional area of the bus-bars and the contact surface of the switchgear, the size of the feeders and distributors, energy losses, voltage drops in generators, transformers, transmission lines and distributors to increase.

Q.14. What factors determine the economical limit of power factor correction?

Ans. Economical limit of power factor correction is governed by the relative costs of the supply and power factor correcting equipment.

LONG ANSWER TYPE QUESTIONS

Q.1. Define the load factor, demand factor and diversity factor. What are their effects on the cost of generation?

Ans.

1. **Load factor:** In electrical engineering the load factor is defined as the average load divided by maximum load in a given period. Its value is always less than one because maximum demand is always more than average demand since we will not connected all the loads at a time.
2. **Demand factor:** The ratio of maximum demand on the system to the rated connected load to the system is called demand factor. The actual maximum demand is always less than the rated load connected to the system, therefore, demand factor is always less than unity. The knowledge of demand factor is generally used for determining the capacity and hence cost of the power equipment required to serve the given load.
3. **Diversity factor:** It is defined as the ratio of sum of individual maximum demands of all the consumers connected to the generating station to the maximum demand on it.

   Higher the diversity factor of the station lower will be the maximum demand on the station, hence smaller will be the capacity of the plant required to meet the individual demand of the consumers. As the capital cost of the generating station depends upon the capacity of the plant, therefore, the fixed charges due to capital investment will be reduced to large extent with higher diversity factor. Thus, the cost of energy generated will be lower at higher diversity factor.

Q.2. Define power factor. State significance of power factor.

Ans. Power factor is defined as a cosine angle between voltage and current or the power factor in defined as the ratio of real power to apparent power in the circuit and it has no unit. Real power is the capacity of circuit for performing work in particular time. Apparent power is the product of voltage and current of the circuit. A negative power factor occurs when the device generates power which then flows back towards the source.

Significance of power factor: The significance of power factor lies in the fact that utility companies supply customers with watt-amperes, but bill them for watts. Power factor below one requires a utility to generate more than the minimum volt-amperes necessary to supply real power (watts). This increases generation and transmission cost.

For example, if the load power factor were as low as 0.7, the apparent power would be 1.4 times the real power used by the load. Line current in the circuit would also be 1.4 times the current required at 1.0 power factor, so the losses in the circuit would be doubled. Hence all the components of the system such as generators, transformers, conductors and switch gears would be increased in size to carry extra current.

Engineers are often interested in the power factor of a load as one of the factors that affects the efficiency of power transmission.

PROBLEMS

Q.1. A generating station has a maximum demand of 40 MW and has a connected load of 75 MW. The number of units generated annually are 200×10^6. Calculate

(a) Load factor

(b) Demand factor **[Ans.** (a) 0.57 (b) 0.533]

Q.2. The annual output of a generating station is 526.6×10^6 kWh and the average load factor is 60%. If the annual fixed charges are ₹ 20 per kW of the installed plant, and the annual running charge 2 paise per unit, what would be the cost at the bus bar.

[Ans. 2.38 paise per kWh]

Q.3. A generating station has a maximum demand of 35500 kW and has a connected load of 65,000 kW. The number of units generated in a year are 25.6×10^7. Calculate:

(a) Load factor

(b) Demand factor **[Ans.** (a) 0.822, (b) 0.546]

Q.4. Calculate the total units consumed per year by a consumer if its maximum demand is 50 kW and annual load factor is 70%. **[Ans.** 306, 600 kWh]

Q.5. The maximum demand of a power plant is 40 MW. The capacity factor is 0.5 and utilization factor is 0.8. Find the: (i) load factor, (ii) Plant capacity, (iii) annual energy consumption.

[Ans. (i) 0.625, (ii) 50 MW, (iii) 2.19×10^9 kWh]

Solution of Problems

Solution 1:

No. of unit generated annually = 200×10^6

$$\text{Average demand} = \frac{200\times10^6}{8760} = 2.28 \times 10^4 \text{ kW}$$

Maximum demand = 40 MW = 40×10^3 kW

(*a*) $$\text{Load factor} = \frac{\text{Average demand}}{\text{Maximum demand}} = \frac{2.28 \times 10^4}{40 \times 10^3} = 0.57 \textbf{ Ans.}$$

(*b*) $$\text{Demand factor} = \frac{\text{Maximum demand}}{\text{Total connected load}} = \frac{40}{75} = 0.533 \textbf{ Ans.}$$

Solution 2:

$$\text{Output of the generating station} = 525.6 \times 10^6 \text{ kWh}$$

$$\text{Load factor} = \frac{\text{Average load}}{\text{Maximum demand}}$$

$$\text{Annual maximum demand in kWh} = \frac{\text{Average load}}{\text{Load factor}} = \frac{525.6 \times 10^6}{0.6} = 876 \times 10^6 \text{ kWh}$$

$$\text{Maximum demand in kW} = \frac{876 \times 10^6}{8760} = 10^6 \text{ kW}$$

Fixed charges per kW = ₹20.

$\therefore$ Total fixed charges = 20×10^5

$$\text{Annual running changes} = \frac{2}{100} \times 525.6 \times 10^6 = 1051.2 \times 10^4 = 105.12 \times 10^5$$

Total annual charges = Fixed charges + Running charges

$$= 20 \times 10^5 + 105.12 \times 10^5 = 125.12 \times 10^5$$

Total annual generation = 525.6×10^6 kWh

$\therefore$ Cost of generation per kWh at bus bar

$$= ₹\frac{125.12 \times 10^5}{525.6 \times 10^6} = \frac{125.12 \times 10^5 \times 10^2}{525.6 \times 10^6}$$

= 2.38 paise per kWh **Ans.**

Solution 3:

Maximum demand = 35,000 kW

Connected load = 65,000 kW

No. of units generated = 25.6×10^7 per annum

$$\text{Average load} = \frac{\text{No. of units generated per annum}}{\text{No. of hour sin a year}}$$

$$= \frac{25.6 \times 10^7}{8760} \text{ kW}$$

$$\text{Load factor} = \frac{\text{Average load}}{\text{Maximum demand}}$$

$$= \frac{25.6 \times 10^7}{8760} \times \frac{1}{35500} = 0.822 \textbf{ Ans.}$$

$$\text{Demand factor} = \frac{\text{Maximum demand}}{\text{Connected load}} = \frac{35,500}{65,000} = 0.546 \textbf{ Ans.}$$

Solution 4:

$$\text{Maximum demand} = 50 \text{ kW}$$

$$\text{Load factor} = 70\% = 0.7$$

$$\text{Average load} = \text{Maximum demand} \times \text{Load factor}$$

$$= 50 \times \frac{70}{100} = 35 \text{ kW}$$

$$\text{Energy generated in a year} = \text{Average load} \times 8760$$

$$= 35 \times 876^{\circ} = 306,\ 600 \text{ kWh } \textbf{Ans.}$$

Solution 5:

$$\text{Maximum demand} = 40 \text{ MW}$$

$$\text{Utilization factor} = 0.8$$

$$\text{Capacity factor} = 0.5$$

$$\text{Utilization factor} = \frac{\text{Maximum demand}}{\text{Rated capacity}}$$

$$0.8 = \frac{40}{\text{Rated capacity}}$$

$$\text{Rated capacity} = \frac{40}{0.8} = 50 \text{ MW}$$

$$\text{Average load} = \text{Capacity factor} \times \text{Rated capacity}$$

$$= 0.5 \times 50 = 25 \text{ MW}$$

$$\text{Load factor} = \frac{\text{Average load}}{\text{Maximum load}} = \frac{25}{40} = 0.625$$

$$\text{Annual energy generated} = \text{Average load} \times 8760$$

$$= 25 \times 10^3 \times 8760$$

$$= 2.19 \times 10^9 \text{ kWh } \textbf{ Ans.}$$

EXERCISE

1. Define demand factor, load factor and diversity factor. Explain the effect of each on the cost of generation.
2. What is meant by load curve? Explain the importance in generation.
3. What do you mean by fixed cost and running cost of a power station?
4. What do you understand by power factor? Discuss the various method to improve power factor.
5. What are the advantages of power factor? Show how synchronous motor can be used for this purpose?
6. What is difference between base load and peak load of power stations?
7. What is interconnection of power stations?
8. What are the advantages of inter-connection of power station?

❑❑❑

3

Transmission Systems

INSIDE THIS CHAPTER

- Introduction
- Power System
- Layout of Power (Transmission) System
- Selection of Voltage for HT and LT Lines
- Advantages of High Voltage for Transmission
- Comparison between DC and AC Systems of Power Transmission
- High Voltage AC and DC Systems
- Electrical Power
- Comparison of Cost of Conductors Materials in Overhead Systems
- Results of Comparison of Systems
- Practical Working
- Economical Choice of Conductor Size
- Constructional Features of a Transmission Line
- Common Conductor Materials
- Main Components of Overhead Lines
- Types of Line Supports
- Insulators and their Properties
- Types of Insulators
- Failure of Insulators
- Earth wiring and Their Accessories
- Spacing of Conductors
- Length of the Span
- Sag
- Indian Electricity Rules Pertaining to Clearances
- Skin Effect
- Transposition of Conductors
- String Efficiency of Lines
- Bundle Conductors
- Electrical Features of a Line
- Inductance of an Transmission Line
- Concept of Corona
- HVDC Transmission Lines
- Salient Features
- Difference Between HVAC and HVDC Transmission
- Description of System to Block Diagram of HVDC Transmission Lines
- Ground Return in HVDC

3.1 INTRODUCTION

The system by which bulk power is delivered from power station to load centres is called transmission system.

As compared to other forms of power, electric power can be transmitted in bulk quantity over large distances at a high efficiency. Electric power can be obtained from different sources of power such as: (i) Fuel (coal and oil), (ii) Water, (iii) Nuclear disintegration. The energy obtained from these sources is used for running either steam turbines or water turbines. The generating stations using coal are known as *thermal power station* or *steam power station*. The generating stations using energy contained in water are called *hydro power stations*. Thermal power stations require huge quantity of coal, so it will be better if these power stations are located near the coal mines to cut down the transportation charges of coal.

Similarly hydro power plants which generate electric energy by harnessing the water power can be located only in mountaineous region, at very far distances from plains where energy is required for industrial purposes. So in the case of hydro power plants also long transmission lines will be required to transmit electrical energy from generating stations to industries.

3.2 POWER SYSTEM

The generation, transmission and distribution of electric power is called power system.

A power system has the following stages:

(i) Generation of electric power
(ii) Transmission of electric power
(iii) Distribution of electric power.

Electric power is produced at power stations which are located at favourable places, generally quite away from consumers. It is then transmitted to the centres of consumption with the help of conductors, called transmission lines. Finally, it is distributed to innumerable large and small electricity consumers.

It may not be out of place to mention here that electric power is exclusively generated, transmitted and distributed by three phase system employing 3-phase generators (also called *alternators*), transformers, transmission lines and distribution network. This is because three phase system has several advantages overall other systems.

3.3 LAYOUT OF POWER (TRANSMISSION) SYSTEM

Figure 3.1 shows a typical power system. It is convenient to consider the power system consisting of the following stages:

1. Power station or generating station
2. Primary transmission
3. Secondary transmission
4. Primary distribution
5. Secondary distribution.

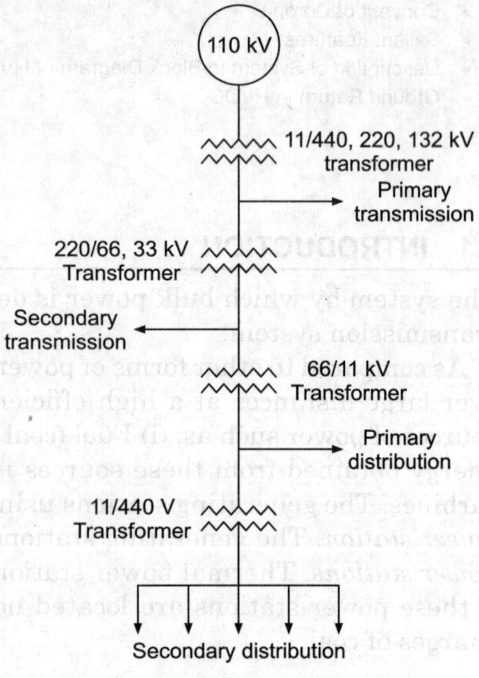

Fig. 3.1 Typical transmission system

1. **Power Station:** It is also called *generating station*. Here the power is generated at 11 kV, which is further stepped up to 400 kV or 220 kV or 132 kV for primary transmission.
2. **Primary transmission:** After stepping up power at 400 kV, 220 kV it is given to big consumers by 3-phase-3 wire overhead system. ACSR conductor runs over steel towers.
3. **Secondary transmission:** Power is stepped down to 66 kV/33 kV and is given to consumers. For this also 3-phase-3 wire overhead system is adopted.

4. **Primary distribution:** Power is stepped down again to 11 kV and 3-phase 3-wire lines runs along important roads of the city. This is given to big industries.
5. **Secondary Distribution:** Now the 11 kV voltage is further stepped down to 400 V and power is given by 3ph-4 wire system. The voltage between and two phases is 400 V which is given to small industries. The voltage between and phase and the neutral is 230 V and is given to domestic consumers.

3.4 SELECTION OF VOLTAGE FOR HT AND LT LINES

As we know that it is economical to transmit ac power at high voltages. But the high transmission voltage results in increase in transmission cost due to more insulation, higher towers and long cross-arms. The transmission cost also increases due to cost of transformers, switch gears and other apparatus such as lightning arrestors. Hence for the choice of proper transmission voltage economy is the essential factor. The transmission voltage for which the cost of transmission is minimum is called economical transmission voltage.

An approximate idea of commonly used transmission voltage for different lengths of transmission lines is given in Table 3.1.

Table 3.1 Commonly Used Voltages for Different Distances

Distance (km)	*Voltage (kV)*
15–30	11
30–60	33
60–100	66
100–200	132
200–300	220
300–400	400

The most economical voltage is given by the empirical formula

$$V_L = 5.5\sqrt{\frac{L}{1.6} + \frac{\text{Load in kVA}}{100}}\ \text{kV}$$

where V_L, Line voltage in kV and L is the length of line in km. At present, the most common transmission voltages used in our country are 33 kV, 66 kV, 220 kV and 400 kV. However, as a thumb rule 0.625 kV per km (i.e., 1 kV per mile) is very rough and useful guide for selecting the transmission voltage.

3.5 ADVANTAGES OF HIGH VOLTAGE FOR TRANSMISSION

It has been discussed above that if electrical power is transmitted at high voltage it has certain advantages such as:

(i) Efficiency of transmission is increased.
(ii) For the given power, the cost of conductor required is less.
(iii) Percentage line voltage drop is reduced. These advantages will be proved as below.

Let us assume that P be the power in kW transmitted by a three-phase transmission line and let the line voltage be V volts and $\cos\phi$ may be the power factor of the load.

As $$P = \sqrt{3}\, VI \cos\phi$$

So $$\text{Load current, } I = \frac{P \times 10^3}{\sqrt{3}\, VI \cos\phi} \quad \text{(As "}P\text{" is in kW)} \qquad \ldots(1)$$

Let "a" metre[2] be the cross-sectional area of conductor, L metre may be its length and ρ be the specific resistance of the conductor material used for transmission.

The resistance "R" of each conductor is given as

$$R = \frac{\rho . L}{a} \qquad \ldots(2)$$

Let "p" be the total power loss in three-phases of transmission line when I amp current flows through it.

Then $$p = 3I^2R$$

Substituting the value of "I" and "R" from equations (1) and (2) in (3), we get

$$p = 3\left[\frac{P \times 10^3}{\sqrt{3}\, V \cos\phi}\right]^2 \frac{\rho . L}{a} = \frac{3p^2 \times 10^6}{3V^2 \cos^2\phi} . \frac{\rho . L}{a} = \frac{p^2 \rho L \times 10^6}{V^2 . \cos^2\phi . a}$$

or $$\text{Area of conductor "}a\text{"} = \frac{p^2 \rho L \times 10^6}{V^2 . \cos^2\phi . p}$$

$$\text{The volume of conductor} = 3aL = 3\left[\frac{p^2 \rho L \times 10^6}{V^2 . \cos^2\phi . p}\right] L$$

The weight of conductor used is directly proportional to volume of the conductor.

$\therefore$ $$\text{Weight of conductor} = K \times 10^6 \left[\frac{3p^2 \rho L^2}{V^2 \cos^2\phi p}\right] \qquad \ldots(3)$$

As P, ρ, L and p are constant.

So from equation (3) it can be observed that increase in power factor and transmission voltage causes saving in the weight of conductor.

3.5.1 Efficiency of Transmission

$$\text{Input power} = \text{Output power} + \text{losses}$$

$$= 1000 \times P + 3I^2 R = 1000P + \frac{3I^2 \rho L}{a}$$

Let α be the current density, as $\alpha = \dfrac{I}{a}$

or $$a = \frac{I}{\alpha}$$

$$\text{Power input} = 1000 \times P + \frac{3I^2 \rho L}{I/\alpha} = 10^3 \times P + 3\rho L\, \alpha\, I$$

But with reference to equation (1)

$$I = \frac{P \times 10^3}{\sqrt{3}\, V \cos\phi}$$

So, $$\text{Power input} = P \times 10^3 + \frac{3\rho\, L\, \alpha\, P}{\sqrt{3} V \cos\phi} \times 10^3 = 10^3 \times P\left[1 + \frac{\sqrt{3}\rho\, L\, \alpha}{V \cos\phi}\right]$$

$\therefore$ $$\text{Efficiency of transmission} = \frac{\text{Power output}}{\text{Power input}} = \frac{1000\, P}{1000\, P\left[1 + \dfrac{\sqrt{3}\rho\, L\, \alpha}{V \cos\phi}\right]}$$

or $$\text{Efficiency of transmission} = \frac{1}{1 + \dfrac{\sqrt{3}\rho\, L\, \alpha}{V \cos\phi}} = \left(1 - \frac{\sqrt{3}\rho\, L\, \alpha}{V \cos\phi}\right) \text{approx.} \quad \text{...(4)}$$

From equation (4) it can be observed that higher the voltage of transmission and higher the power factor; higher will be the efficiency of transmission.

3.5.2 Percentage Line Voltage Drop

Total 3-phase line voltage drop = $3IR$

But $$I = \alpha \times a$$

and $$R = \frac{\rho L}{a}$$

So $$\text{3-phase voltage drop} = 3.\frac{\alpha.a.\rho.L}{a} = 3.\alpha.\rho.L$$

$$\text{Percentage voltage drop} = \frac{3\alpha\rho L}{V} \times 100$$

For constant current density, voltage drop remains constant but when transmission voltage is increase, percentage voltage drop in line will be decreased.

From the above arguments it is quite obvious that for long distance transmission very high voltages are essential and with ac system a high power factor is also desirable.

To summarized in brief the following points to preferred high voltage transmission.

(i) With increase in the transmission voltage the volume of conductor material decreases. This decreases the cost of the line.

(ii) If the voltage is high the current is reduced which reduces the line losses. Thus the efficiency of transmission is improved.

(iii) High voltage transmission also improves the regulation of the line.

Limitations of Increase in Transmission Voltage

The high transmission voltage has the following limitations:

1. **More Insulation:** For high transmission voltage, the insulation required between the conductors and the earthed tower is more.
2. **Higher Tower:** The clearance required between the conductors and ground depends upon the voltage of transmission line. For high transmission voltage, more clearance is required and hence, higher towers are used.
3. **Longer Cross-arms:** The clearance between the conductors also depends upon the transmission voltage. The greater the transmission voltage, the longer are the cross-arms required.

Generation voltages are 3.3, 6.6, 11 or 33 kV, most usual value adopted in practice is 11 kV. The primary transmission voltages are 110, 132, 220 or 400 kV depending upon the distance, the amount of power to be transmitted and the system stability. Secondary transmission voltage is normally of the order of 33 or 66 kV. The voltages for primary distribution are 11, 6.6 or 3.3 kV depending upon the requirements of the bulk consumers and for secondary distribution usable voltage is 400 volts.

In case of ac system the main advantage is that the voltage can be stepped up at generating end by means of step up transformers to the required value for transmission and then stepped down at distributing end by means of step down transformers for distribution with ease and efficiency. The other advantages of ac systems are that electrical power can be generated at high voltage easily and the maintenance of ac sub-stations is easier and cheaper. The disadvantages of ac systems are given below:

(i) In case of overhead lines spacing between the conductors is to be kept more in order to provide adequate insulation and to avoid corona loss.
(ii) More copper is required.
(iii) Greater the length of transmission line more is the capacitance of the line. There is a continuous loss on account of charging current even though the line is open.
(iv) The construction of transmission lines for ac systems is not so easy as for dc systems.
(v) The alternators are to be synchronised before putting them into parallel.
(vi) The variation in speeds of alternators are to be controlled within very low limits.

3.6 COMPARISON BETWEEN DC AND AC SYSTEMS OF POWER TRANSMISSION

Sr. No.	*DC transmission*	*AC transmission*
1.	It needs only 2 wires.	It needs 3 wires (3 phase system).
2.	Problem of inductance, and capacitance is not there.	Inductance and capacitance make voltage regulation poor.
3.	Skin effect is absent.	Skin effect reduces efficiency.
4.	It has better regulations.	Regulation is poor.
5.	DC lines need lesser insulation.	AC lines need higher insulation.
6.	There are less corona losses.	Carona creates interference problems.

(Contd....)

Sr. No.	DC transmission	AC transmission
7.	Power cannot be generated high voltages.	Power can be generated at high voltages.
8.	Underground cables can be used because of less potential.	Underground cables cannot used due more potential.
9.	Costly protective devices have to be employed.	Simple and low cost protective devices are employed.

3.7 HIGH VOLTAGE AC AND DC SYSTEMS

3.7.1 High Voltage AC (HVAC) System

(i) Single phase, a.c. two-wire system.
(ii) Single-phase, a.c. two-wire mid-point carthed system.
(iii) Two phase, a.c. three-wire system
(iv) Three phase, a.c. three-wire system
(v) Three phase, a.c. four-wire system

Advantages of HVAC System

(i) HVAC can be stepped-up by transformer.
(ii) It is possible to generate electrical energy at EHV very high voltage which is not possible with dc.
(iii) It is easier and cheaper to step down the voltage at the sub-station.
(iv) Maintenance of ac sub-station is cheaper and easier.

For generation : 6.6, 11, 13.2, 33 kV

For H.T. transmission: 110, 132, 220 or 400 kV

For L.T. transmission: 11, 33 or 66 kV

For H.T. distribution: 3.3, 6.6 or 11 kV

For L.T. distribution: 415 V, 3 phase, 230 V 1-phase

3.7.2 High Voltage DC (HVDC) System

(i) DC two-wire system
(ii) DC two-wire with mid-point earthed system
(iii) DC three wire system

Advantages of HVDC System

(i) In this system of transmission of electrical energy two conductors are required.
(ii) No stabilizers are required.
(iii) Effect of inductance, capacitance, surge and phase difference are not there.
(iv) Underground cables can be used safety.

3.8 ELECTRICAL POWER

Though in practice 3-phase, 3-wire ac system is universally used for transmission and 3-phase, 4-wire ac system is used for distribution of electric power but for special purposes other systems may also be used. The various systems of power transmission are:

(a) **DC Systems**
   (i) DC two-wire
   (ii) DC two-wire with mid-point earthed
   (iii) DC three wire-system

(b) **Single Phase ac Systems**
   (i) Single phase two-wire
   (ii) Single phase two-wire with mid-point earthed
   (iii) Single phase three-wire

(c) **Two-Phase ac Systems**
   (i) Two-phase four-wire
   (ii) Two-phase three-wire

(d) **Three-Phase ac Systems**
   (i) Three-phase 3-wire
   (ii) Three-phase 4-wire

From such a big list of possible systems of transmission it is difficult to decide the best system without making comparison. The basis for comparison between the various systems of power transmission is usually economy, i.e., volume of copper required. For comparing the amount of copper required for different systems two cases arise:

(i) **When Overhead System is Employed for Transmission of Power:** In overhead system the conductors are insulated from cross-arms and supporting towers and as the towers and cross-arms are earthed so the maximum voltage between each conductor and earth forms the basis of comparison of volume of conductor.

(ii) **When Underground Cables are Employed for Transmission of Power:** In underground cables the maximum disruptive stress is between the two conductors of the cable; so the maximum voltage between conductors forms the basis of comparison of volume of conductor.

3.9 COMPARISON OF COST OF CONDUCTORS MATERIALS IN OVERHEAD SYSTEMS

The assumptions made for comparison are:

(i) In all cases power to be transmitted is same (say, P watts),
(ii) The distance over which the power is to be transmitted is same (say l),
(iii) The line losses are same (say, p watts), and
(iv) The maximum voltage to earth is same (say, V_m volts).

3.9.1 D.C. Systems

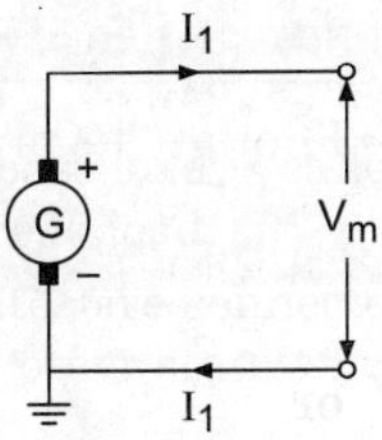

Fig. 3.2(a) D.C. Two wire system

(i) DC 2-wire System with One Conductor Earthed: Maximum voltage between conductors = V_m volts

Power transmitted, $p = VI$ watts

$$\text{Load current } I_1 = \frac{p}{V_m} \text{ Amps}$$

$$\text{Line losses, } p = 2I_1^2 R_1 \text{ watts}$$

$$= 2\left(\frac{P}{V_m}\right)^2 \rho \frac{l}{a_1}, \text{ since } R_1 = \rho \frac{l}{a_1} \text{ Ohms}$$

where l is the length of the line, P is the resistivity

$$\text{or} \qquad \text{Area of ×-section of, } a_1 = \frac{2\rho P^2 l}{pV_m^2}$$

$$\text{Volume of copper required} = 2a_1 l = \frac{2 \times 2P^2 \rho l^2}{V_m^2 p} = \frac{4\rho P^2 l^2}{pV_m^2} = K \text{ (say)}$$

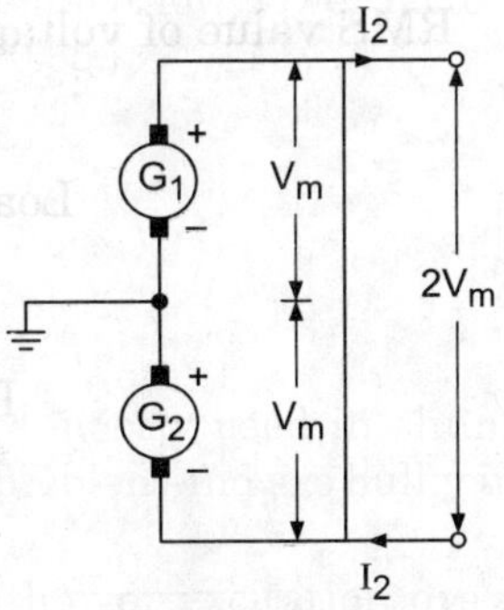

Fig. 3.2(b) DC two wire system with mid point earthed

(ii) DC Two Wire System with Mid-Point Earthed: Maximum voltage between conductors = $2V_m$ volts

$$\text{Load current, } I_2 = \frac{P}{2V_m}$$

$$\text{Line losses, } p = 2I_2^2 R_2$$

$$= 2\left(\frac{P}{2V_m}\right)^2 \rho \frac{l}{a_2} = \frac{P^2 \rho l}{2a_2 V_m^2}$$

$$\text{or} \qquad \text{Area of } X\text{-section, } a_2 = \frac{P^2 \rho l}{2pV_m^2}$$

$$\text{Volume of copper required} = 2a_2 l = 2\left(\frac{P^2 \rho l^2}{2pV_m^2}\right) l = \frac{P^2 \rho l^2}{pV_m^2}$$

$$= 0.25\,\text{K} \qquad \left[\because \; K = \frac{4P^2 \rho l^2}{pV_m^2}\right]$$

Hence copper required is one-fourth of that required in two-wire d.c. system with one conductor earthed.

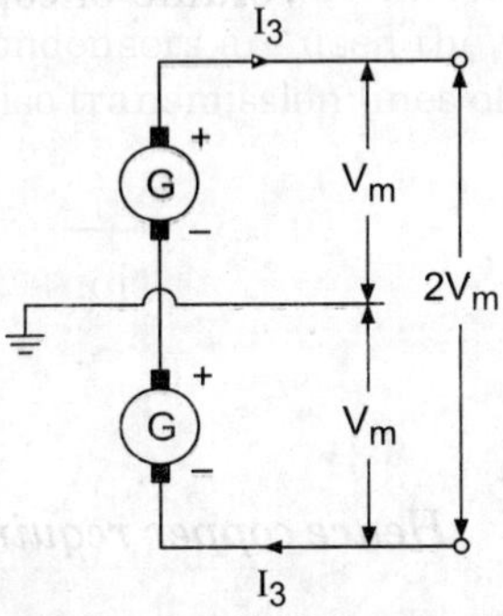

Fig. 3.2(c) DC three wire system

(iii) DC Three Wire System: Assuming load balanced. Maximum voltage between the outer and earth = V_m volts

$$\text{Load current, } I_3 = \frac{\frac{P}{2}}{V_m} = \frac{P}{2V_m}$$

$$\text{Line losses, } p = 2I_3^2 R_3$$

$$= 2\left(\frac{P}{2V_m}\right)^2 \frac{\rho l}{a_3} = \frac{P^2 \rho l}{2a_3 V_m^2}$$

(a_3 is the area of X-section of each outer wire)

or $$a_3 = \frac{P^2 \rho l}{2p V_m^2}$$

Assuming area of ×-section of neutral wire as half of any outer.

$$\text{Volume of copper required} = 2.5 a_3 l = \frac{2.5 P^2 \rho l^2}{2p V_m^2} = 0.3125\ \text{K}$$

Hence copper required is 0.3125 times of that required in two-wire dc system with one conductor earthed.

3.9.2 Single Phase ac System

(i) AC Single Phase Two Wire System with One Conductor Earthed:
Peak value of voltage between conductors = V_m volts.

RMS value of voltage between conductors = $\frac{V_m}{\sqrt{2}}$ volts

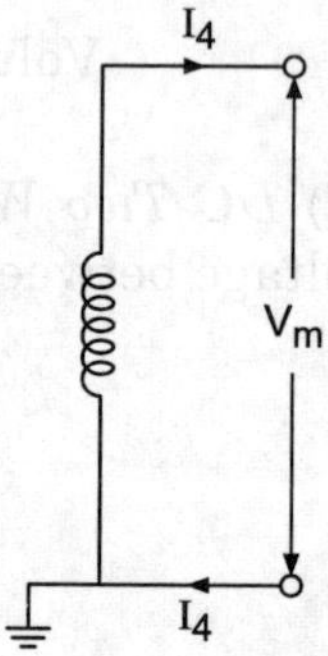

Fig. 3.2(d) Single phase ac system

$$\text{Load current, } I_4 = \frac{P}{\frac{V_m}{\sqrt{2}}\cos\phi} = \frac{\sqrt{2}P}{V_m \cos\phi}$$

$$\text{Line losses, } p = 2I_4^2 R_4$$

$$= 2\left(\frac{\sqrt{2}P}{V_m \cos\phi}\right)^2 \frac{\rho l}{a_4} = \frac{4P^2 \rho l}{a_4 V_m^2 \cos^2\phi}$$

or $$a_4 = \frac{4P^2 \rho l}{p V_m^2 \cos^2\phi}$$

$$\text{Volume of copper required} = 2a_4 l = 2\left(\frac{4P^2 \rho l}{p V_m^2 \cos^2\phi}\right) l$$

$$= \frac{2}{\cos^2\phi} \times \frac{4P^2 \rho l^2}{p V_m^2}$$

$$= \frac{2K}{\cos^2\phi} \qquad \left[\because K = \frac{4P^2 \rho l^2}{p V_m^2}\right]$$

Hence copper required in this system is $\frac{2}{\cos^2\phi}$ *times that of required in 2-wire dc system with one conductor earthed.*

(ii) AC Single Phase Two Wire System with Mid-Point Earthed:
Peak value of voltage between conductors = $2V_m$ volts

RMS value of voltage between conductors

$$= \frac{2V_m}{\sqrt{2}} = \sqrt{2}V_m \text{ volts}$$

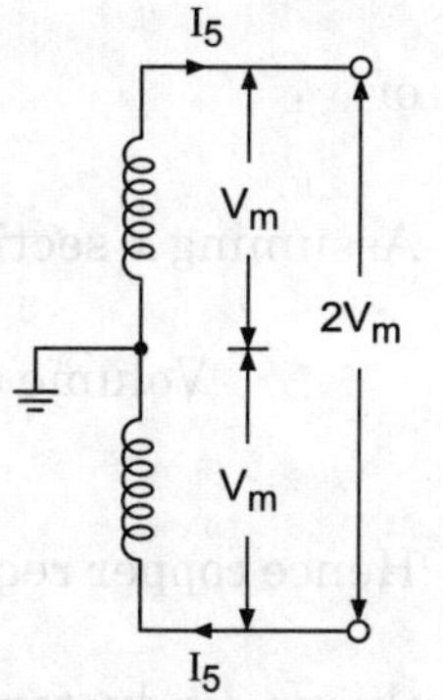

Fig. 3.2(e) AC single phase two wire system with mid point earthed

$$\text{Load current, } I_5 = \frac{P}{\sqrt{2}V_m \cos\phi}$$

$$\text{Line losses, } p = 2I_5^2 R_5$$

$$= 2\left(\frac{P}{\sqrt{2}V_m \cos\phi}\right)^2 \frac{\rho l}{a_5}$$

$$= \frac{P^2 \rho l}{a_5 V_m^2 \cos^2\phi}$$

or
$$a_5 = \frac{P^2 \rho l}{p V_m^2 \cos^2\phi}$$

$$\text{Volume of copper required} = 2a_5 l = \frac{2P^2 \rho l^2}{p V_m^2 \cos^2\phi}$$

$$= \frac{2}{\cos^2\phi} \times \frac{P^2 \rho l^2}{p V_m^2} \qquad \left[\because K = \frac{4P^2\rho l^2}{pV_m^2}\right]$$

$$= \frac{0.5}{\cos^2\phi}$$

Hence copper required in this system is $\frac{0.5}{\cos^2\phi}$ *times of that required in 2 wire dc system with one conductor earthed.*

(iii) AC Single Phase Three Wire System: RMS value of voltage between outer and earth = $\frac{V_m}{\sqrt{2}}$ volts

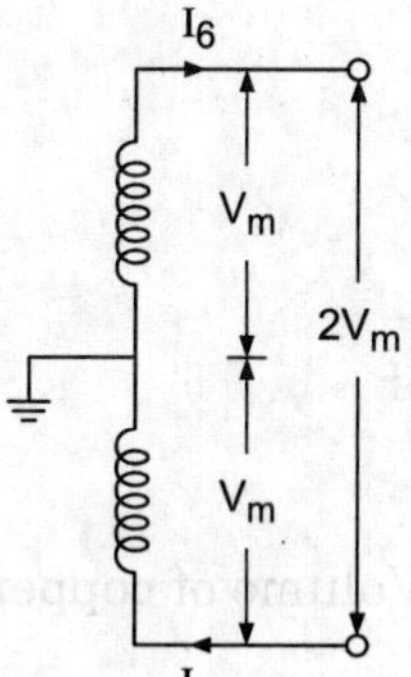

Fig. 3.2(f) AC single phase three wire system

$$\text{Load current, } I_6 = \frac{P/2}{\frac{V_m}{\sqrt{2}}\cos\phi} = \frac{P}{\sqrt{2}V_m \cos\phi}$$

Load being assumed balanced.

$$\text{Line losses, } p = 2I_6^2 R_6 = 2\left(\frac{P}{\sqrt{2}V_m \cos\phi}\right)^2 \frac{\rho l}{a_6}$$

$$= \frac{P^2 \rho l}{V_m^2 \cos^2\phi\, a_6}$$

or $$a_6 = \frac{P^2 \rho l}{pV_m^2 \cos^2 \phi a_6}$$

Assuming x-section of neutral wire half of that of any of the outers.

$$\text{Volume of copper required} = 2.5\, a_6 l = \frac{2.5P^2\rho l^2}{pV_m^2 \cos^2 \phi} = \frac{0.625K}{\cos^2 \phi} \quad \left[\because K = \frac{4P^2\rho l^2}{pV_m^2}\right]$$

Hence copper required in this system is $\frac{0.625}{\cos^2\phi}$ times of that required in 2-wire dc system with one conductor earthed.

3.9.3 Two-Phase AC Systems

(i) AC Two-Phase Four Wire System: RMS value of voltage between the outers

$$= \frac{2V_m}{\sqrt{2}} = \sqrt{2}V_m$$

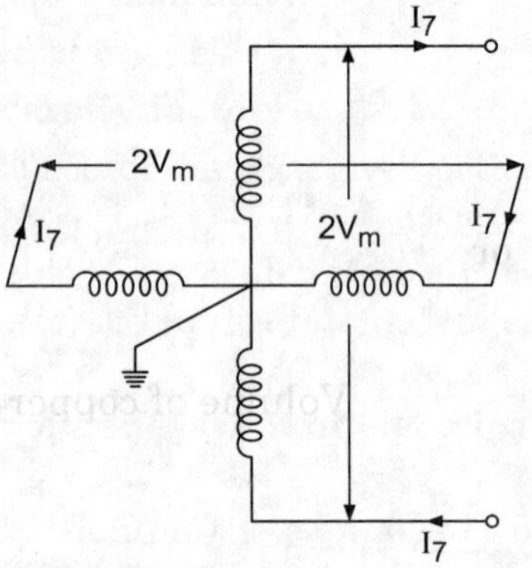

Fig. 3.2(g) AC two phase four wire system

$$\text{Load supplied by each phase} = \frac{P}{2}$$

$$\text{Load current per phase, } I_7 = \frac{P}{2\sqrt{2}V_m \cos\phi}$$

$$\text{Line losses, } p = 4I_7^2 R_7$$

$$= 4\left(\frac{P}{2\sqrt{2}V_m \cos\phi}\right)^2 \rho \frac{l}{a_7}$$

$$= \frac{P^2\rho l}{2V_m^2 a_7 \cos^2\phi}$$

or $$a_7 = \frac{P^2\rho l}{2V_m^2 p \cos^2\phi}$$

$$\text{Volume of copper required} = 4a_7 l = \frac{2P^2\rho l^2}{V_m^2 \cos^2 \phi p} = \frac{0.5K}{\cos^2\phi} \quad \left[\because K = \frac{4P^2\rho l^2}{pV_m^2}\right]$$

Hence copper required in this system is $\frac{0.5}{\cos^2\phi}$ *times of that required in two wire dc system with one conductor earthed.*

(ii) AC Two-Phase Three Wire System: Considering balanced load RMS value of voltage between outer and neutral

$$= \frac{V_m}{\sqrt{2}}.$$

Current in each of outer conductors,

$$I_8 = \frac{P/2}{\frac{V_m}{\sqrt{2}}\cos\phi} = \frac{P}{\sqrt{2}V_m\cos\phi}$$

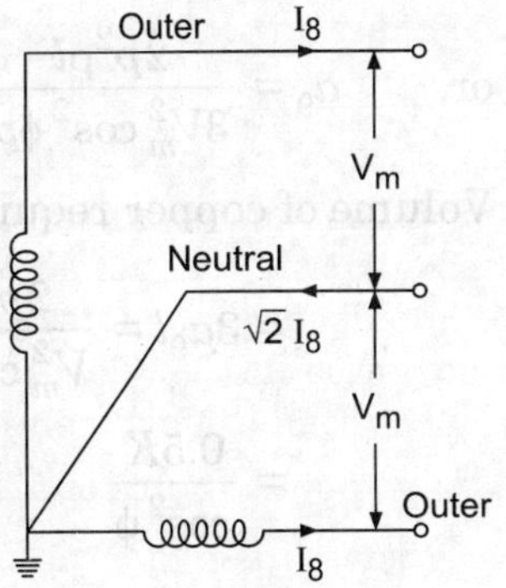

Fig. 3.2(h) AC two phase three wire system

Current in neutral wire $= \sqrt{(I_8^2 + I_8^2)} = \sqrt{2}I_8$

Assuming current density constant, area of *x*-section of neutral wire is $\sqrt{2}$ times of that of either of the outers.

So resistance of neutral wire $= \frac{R_8}{\sqrt{2}}$

$$= \frac{\rho l}{\sqrt{2}a_8} \text{ where } R_8 = \frac{\rho l}{a_8}$$

$$\text{Line losses, } p = 2I_8^2 R_8 + \left(\sqrt{2}I_8\right)^2 \frac{R_8}{\sqrt{2}}$$

$$= I_8^2 \frac{\rho l}{a_8}(2 + \sqrt{2}) = \frac{P^2 \rho l}{2V_m^2 \cos^2\phi a_8}(2 + \sqrt{2})$$

or
$$a_8 = \frac{P^2 \rho l}{2V_m^2 \cos^2\phi p}(2 + \sqrt{2})$$

$$\text{Volume of copper required} = 2a_8 l + \sqrt{2}\, a_8 l = a_8 l(2 + \sqrt{2})$$

$$= \frac{P^2 \rho l^2}{2V_m^2 \cos^2\phi p}(2 + \sqrt{2})$$

$$= \frac{P^2 \rho l^2}{V_m^2 \cos^2\phi p}(\sqrt{2} + 1)^2 = \frac{1.457}{\cos^2\phi}K$$

Hence copper required in this system is $\frac{1.457}{\cos^2\phi}$ *times of that required in 2-wire dc system with one conductor earthed.*

3.9.4 Three-Phase ac Systems

(i) AC Three-Phase Three-Wire System: RMS value of voltage per phase $= \frac{V_m}{\sqrt{2}}$

$$\text{Load current per phase, } I_9 = \frac{p/2}{\frac{V_m}{\sqrt{2}}\cos\phi} = \frac{\sqrt{2}p}{3V_m\cos\phi}$$

$$\text{Line losses, } p = 3I_9^2 R_9$$

$$= 3\left(\frac{\sqrt{2}p}{3V_m\cos\phi}\right)^2 \frac{\rho l}{a_9} = \frac{2p^2 \rho l}{2V_m^2 \cos^2\phi a_9}$$

or $$a_9 = \frac{2p^2 \rho l}{3V_m^2 \cos^2 \phi p}$$

Volume of copper required

$$= 3a_9 l = \frac{2p^2 \rho l^2}{V_m^2 \cos^2 \phi p}$$

$$= \frac{0.5K}{\cos^2 \phi}$$

Hence copper required in this system is $\frac{0.5}{\cos^2 \phi}$ *times of that required in two-wire dc system with one conductor earthed.*

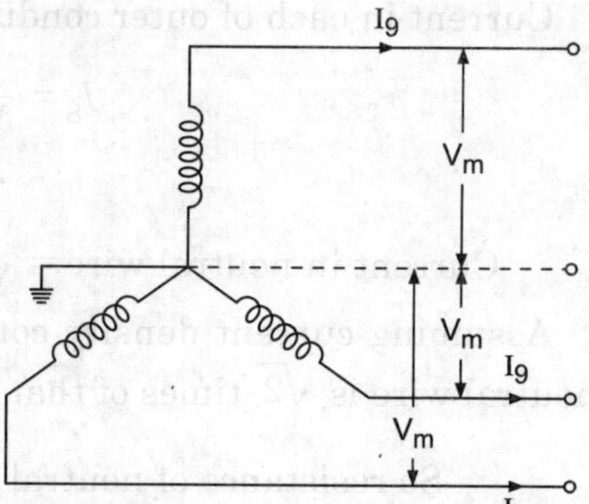

Fig. 3.2(i) Three phase ac system

(ii) A.C. Three-Phase Four-Wire System: Assuming balanced load, there will be no current in neutral wire and copper losses will be same as in three-phase three-wire system

i.e., $$p = \frac{2P^2 \rho l}{3V_m^2 \cos^2 \phi a_{10}}$$

or $$a_{10} = \frac{2P^2 \rho l}{3V_m^2 \cos^2 \phi p}$$

Taking x-section of neutral wire as half of either outer

Required volume of conductor material

$$= 3.5a_{10}l$$

$$= 3.5\left(\frac{2P^2 \rho l}{3pV_m^2 \cos \phi}\right) \times l$$

$$= \frac{7P^2 \rho l^2}{3V_m^2 \cos^2 \phi p}$$

$$= \frac{7}{3\cos^2 \phi} \times \frac{P^2 \rho l^2}{pV_m^2}$$

$$= \frac{0.583}{\cos^2 \phi} K$$

$$= \frac{7K}{12} \qquad \left[\because K = \frac{4P^2 \rho l^2}{pV_m^2}\right]$$

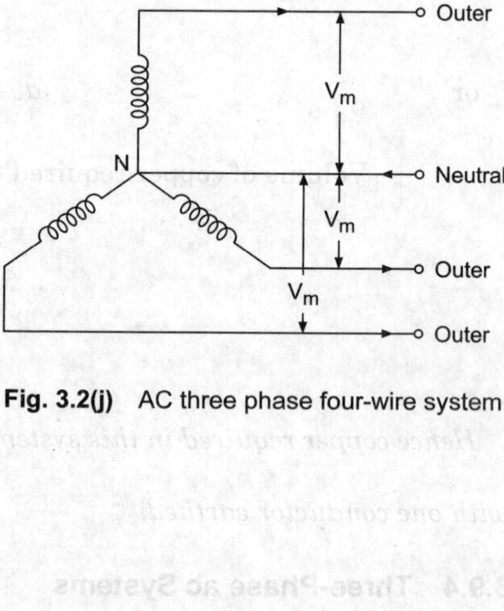

Fig. 3.2(j) AC three phase four-wire system

Hence copper required in this case is $\frac{0.583}{\cos^2 \phi}$ *times of copper required in case of two wire dc system with one conductor earthed.*

3.10 RESULTS OF COMPARISON OF SYSTEMS

The results obtained above are summarized as below:

Systems	*Volume of copper required on the basis of*	
	Maximum voltage between conductor and earth	***Maximum voltage between any two conductors***
(a) **DC Systems**		
(i) Two-wire	1	1
(ii) Two-wire with midpoint earthed	0.25	1
(iii) Three wire	0.3125	1.25
(b) **AC Single Phase Systems**		
(i) Two-wire	$\frac{2}{\cos^2\phi}$	$\frac{2}{\cos^2\phi}$
(ii) Two-wire with midpoint earthed	$\frac{0.5}{\cos^2\phi}$	$\frac{2}{\cos^2\phi}$
(iii) Three wire	$\frac{0.625}{\cos^2\phi}$	$\frac{2.5}{\cos^2\phi}$
(c) **AC Two Phase Systems**		
(i) Two-phase four wire	$\frac{2.5}{\cos^2\phi}$	$\frac{2}{\cos^2\phi}$
(ii) Two-phase three wire	$\frac{1.457}{\cos^2\phi}$	$\frac{2.914}{\cos^2\phi}$
(d) **AC Three Phase Systems**		
(i) Three-phase three wire	$\frac{0.5}{\cos^2\phi}$	$\frac{1.5}{\cos^2\phi}$
(ii) Three-phase four wire	$\frac{0.583}{\cos^2\phi}$	$\frac{1.75}{\cos^2\phi}$

From the above table, it is obvious that for transmission, dc system is an ideal one from economic point of view, particulary when it is remembered that the power factor of an ac system is usually considerably less than unity.

Two-phase three wire system is obviously quite unsuitable for long distance transmission and needs no further consideration.

Among the remaining a.c. systems for overhead systems there is no difference in single phase, two-wire and three phase three-wire systems and for underground systems there is a decided saving in copper with the three phase system. Considering other factors such as efficiency of operation and convenience three phase three wire system is usually adopted.

EXAMPLE 3.1 A 3-phase, 4-wire system is used for lighting. Compare the amount of copper required with that needed for a 2-wire direct current system with the same lamp voltage. Assume the same losses and balanced load. The neutral is one-half the ×-section of one of the respective outers.

Solution: Let the lighting load to be supplied be P watts at voltage V volts (between line and neutral in case of 3-phase, 4-wire system) and line losses be P watts in both of the cases:

(i) ***Two-Wire dc System***

$$\text{Load current, } I_1 = \frac{P}{V} \text{ amperes}$$

$$\text{Line losses, } p = 2I_1^2 R_1 = 2\frac{P^2}{V^2}\rho\frac{l}{a_1} = \frac{2P^2\rho l}{V^2 a_1}$$

where ρ is the resistivity of copper, l is the length of line, a_1 is the x-section of conductor in case of 2-wire dc system.

$$\text{or Area of } x\text{-section of conductor, } a_1 = \frac{2P^2\rho l}{V^2 p}$$

$$\text{Volume of copper required} = 2a_1 l = \frac{4P^2\rho l^2}{V^2 p}$$

(ii) ***Three-Phase Four-Wire System***

$$\text{Power supplied by each phase} = \frac{P}{3} \qquad (\because \text{ load is balanced})$$

RMS voltage between line and neutral = V volts

Power factor of lighting load be assumed unity

$$\text{Load current, } I_2 = \frac{P}{3V}$$

$$\text{Line losses, } p = 3I_2^2 R_2 = 3\left(\frac{P}{3V}\right)^2 \rho\frac{1}{a_2} = \frac{P^2\rho l}{3V^2 a_2}$$

where a_2 is the x-section of conductor in case of 3-phase 4-wire system.

$$\text{or} \qquad a_2 = \frac{P^2\rho l}{3V^2 p}$$

$$\text{Volume of copper required} = 3.5a_2 l = \frac{3.5P^2\rho l^2}{3V^2 p}$$

$$= \frac{3.5}{12} \times \frac{4P^2\rho l^2}{V^2 p} = 0.292 \times \frac{4P^2\rho l^2}{V^2 p}$$

Since the neutral is one-half of the ×-section of the outer.

i.e., in case of 3-phase 4-wire system copper required will be 0.292 times of that required in 2-wire d.c. system. **Ans.**

EXAMPLE 3.2 **An existing dc three wire system is to be converted into a 3-phase 4-wire system by adding a fourth wire equal in cross-section to each outer of the dc system. Assuming the same supply and load voltages to neutral and balanced condition find the extra power at unity power factor that can be supplied by the ac system.**

Solution: Let the supply and load voltages to neutral be V_s and V_L volts respectively and resistance of each conductor be R ohms.

$$\text{Line current in 3 wire dc system, } I_1 = \frac{V_s - V_L}{R}$$

$$\text{Power supplied, } P_1 = 2V_L I_1 = \frac{2V_L}{R} = (V_S - V_L) \qquad ...(i)$$

Line current in 3-phase 4-wire ac system,

$$I_2 = \frac{V_S - V_L}{R}$$

$$\text{Power supplied, } P_2 = 3V_L I_2 \cos\phi$$

$$= \frac{3V_L}{R}(V_S - V_L) \times 1 \qquad ...(ii)$$

Comparing expression (*i*) and (*ii*), we get

$$P_2 = 1.5P_1$$

i.e., 50 percent extra power can be supplied at unity pf by 3-phase, 4-wire ac system. **Ans**

EXAMPLE 3.3 **A 3-wire dc system is converted to a 4-wire 3-phase ac system by the addition of another wire equal in section to one of the outers. For the same effective voltage between outers and neutral at the consumer's terminals and the same percentage loss, find the percentage additional load that can be supplied. Assume balanced load and in the ac system a power factor of 0.9.**

Solution: Let the voltage between outers and neutral be V volts in both of the cases and currents in 3-wire dc system and 3-phase 4-wire system be I_1 and I_2 respectively.

3-wire dc System

$$\text{Power supplied, } P_1 = 2I_1 V$$

$$\text{Power loss} = 2I_1^2 R$$

$$\text{Percentage power loss} = \frac{2I_1^2 R}{2I_1 V} \times 100 = \frac{100 I_1 R}{V} \qquad ...(i)$$

3-Phase 4-wire ac System

$$\text{Power supplied, } P_2 = 3I_2 V \cos\phi = 3I_2 V \times 0.9 = 2.7 I_2 V$$

$$\text{Power loss} = 3I_2^2 R$$

$$\text{Percentage power loss} = \frac{3I_2^2 R}{2.7 I_2 V} \times 100 = \frac{100 I_2 R}{0.9V} \qquad ...(ii)$$

Since load is balanced, therefore, neutral wire will carry no current.

Since percentage loss is same, therefore, comparing expressions (*i*) and (*ii*), we get

$$\frac{100 I_1 R}{V} = \frac{100 I_2 R}{0.9V}$$

or

$$I_2 = 0.9 I_1$$

Hence power supplied in 3-phase 4-wire system,

$$P_2 = 2.7 \times 0.9\, I_1\, V + 2.43\, I_1\, V$$

$$\text{Percentage increase in load supplied} = \frac{P_2 - P_1}{P_1} \times 100$$

$$\frac{2.43 I_1 V - 2 I_1 V}{2 I_1 V} \times 100 = 21.5\% \textbf{ Ans.}$$

3.11 PRACTICAL WORKING

1. **Practical Working Voltage of Generation:** 11 kV
2. **Practical Working Voltage for Transmission**
   Primary Transmission: 66 kV, 132 kV, 220 V and 400 kV.
   Secondary Transmission Voltage: 33 kV
3. **Practical Working Voltage for Distribution**
   Primary Distribution Voltage: 11 kV, 3-phase, 3-wire.
   Secondary Distribution Voltage: 400 V between two phases (3-phase, 4-wire) and 230 V between any one phase and neutral.

3.12 ECONOMICAL CHOICE OF CONDUCTOR SIZE

The cost of conductor material is the major part of the total cost of the transmission lines. Therefore, it is very important to determine the proper size of the conductor.

3.12.1 Kelvin's Law

The most economical area of cross section of conductor is that for which annual cost of transmission line is minimum. This is known as Kelvin's law. This is used to calculate cross section of the conductor.

Explanation: The total annual cost of a line can be divided into:

(i) Annual Charges on Capital Outlay

They include the charges of annual interest and depreciation on capital cost of the conductors.

$$\text{Annual charges} = (P_1 + P_2 a) \qquad \text{...(i)}$$

where P_1 and P_2 are constants and '*a*' is the cross section of the conductor.

(ii) Annual Cost of Energy Wasted

This is the cost of energy lost in the conductor due to its resistance i.e., I^2R. losses.

$$\text{This is equal to } \frac{P_3}{a} \qquad \text{...(ii)}$$

where P_3 is a constant

Adding exp. (i) and (ii), we get,

$$\text{Total annual cost, } C = P_1 + P_2 a + \frac{P_3}{a} \quad \text{...(iii)}$$

The total annual cost will be minimum if the differentiation of exp. (iii) with respect to variable 'a' is zero.

i.e., $$\frac{d}{da}(C) = 0$$

or $$\frac{d}{da}\left(P_1 + P_2 a + \frac{P_3}{a}\right) = 0$$

or $$P_2 - \frac{P_3}{a^2} = 0$$

or $$P_2 = \frac{P_3}{a^2}$$

or $$P_2 a = \frac{P_3}{a}$$

i.e., Variable part of annual charges = Annual cost of energy wasted

or $$a = \sqrt{\frac{P_3}{P_2}}$$

Hence, the conductor size under this condition will be most economical.
Thus, Kelvin's law can also be stated as :

The most economical area of cross-section of conductor is that for which the variable part of annual charges are equal to the cost of energy wasted.

3.12.2 Practical Limitations to Applications of Kelvin's Law

Though theoretically Kelvin's law is true but in actual working an economical cross-section of the conductor determined by Kelvin's law may not suit because of the following factors:

(i) The assumption that the total annual cost on account of interest and depreciation on the capital outlay is of the form $P_1 + P_2 a$ is strictly speaking not true. For example, neither the cost of cable dielectric and sheath in underground cables very according to this simple law, nor the cost of laying.

(ii) The size of the conductor determined may be of such a small cross-section that it may cause too much voltage drop in the line.

(iii) The size of the conductor determined may be too weak or too strong from mechanical consideration. In case the size determined is too weak, it is advisable to go to the higher size irrespective to economy.

(iv) In case of cables the sizes of conductors determined by Kelvin's law usually gives higher current density thereby giving excessive heating. The only remedy is to decide the size of conductors in case of cables on the basis of current carrying capacity.

(v) The diameter of the conductor may be so small as to cause high corona loss.

(vi) Interest and depreciation on the capital outlay depends upon commercial conditions and estimated life of conductors and also the probable scrap value at the end of estimated life, which are not known with a fair degree of accuracy.

(vii) It is difficult to estimate the energy loss in the line without actual load curves, which are definitely not available at the time of estimation.

(viii) It is also difficult to estimate the cost per unit of the energy wasted in the line. The cost per unit of the energy wasted is not the same as that of cost of generation per unit since their cost per unit depends upon load factors which are different for the line losses and the generation.

(ix) In the case of cables there are sheath losses and with high voltages dielectric losses also. Dielectric loss occurs continuously, therefore, load factor of dielectric loss is 100%. Hence the cost per unit of energy lost as dielectric loss is less than cost per unit supplying the line loss.

It is impossible to drive an exact formula for the conductor x-section which will take into account all the above factors.

In case of overhead lines the question of temperature rise is of less importance and there are no losses other than I^2R loss so cross-sections derived from Kelvin's law have more chances of being acceptable.

EXAMPLE 3.4 A 2-conductor cable 1 km in length is required to supply a constant load of 200 A throughout the year. The cost of the cable is ₹ (100*a* + 40) per meter where *a* is the area of the cross-section of the conductor in cm². The cost of energy is 10 *P* per kWh and interest and depreciation charges amount to 10%. Specific resistivity of copper is 1.85 μΩ-cm. Find the cross-section area '*a*'.

Solution: Resistance of each conductor,

$$R = \frac{\rho l}{a} = \frac{1.83 \times 10^{-6} \times 1000 \times 100}{a} = \frac{0.185}{a}\,\Omega$$

$$\text{Energy lost per annum} = \frac{2I^2 R \times 8760}{1000}$$

$$= \frac{2 \times (200)^2 \times 0.185 \times 8760}{a \times 1000} = \frac{12964.8}{a}\,\text{kWh}$$

$$\text{Annual cost due to energy lost} = ₹\,\frac{10}{100} \times \frac{129648}{a} = ₹\,\frac{12964.8}{a}$$

Capital cost (variable) of the cable = ₹ 100 × a × 1000 = ₹ 100000 a

Annual charges on account of interest and depreciation on variable cost of cable

$$= ₹\,\frac{10}{100} \times 100000\,a = ₹\,10000\,a$$

For most economical ×-section of conductor

$$\frac{12964.8}{a} = 10000\,a$$

or

$$a = \sqrt{\frac{12964.8}{10000}} = 1.14\ \text{cm}^2 \quad \textbf{Ans.}$$

EXAMPLE 3.5 A 3-phase cable supplies an industry whose maximum demand is 1,000 kW and its total annual energy consumption is 5 × 10⁶ kWh at 0.85 p.f. The capital cost of the cable is ₹ (80,000 *a* + 20,000) per km where a is its cross-sectional area in cm²/core. The energy costs 5 paise per kWh. The rate of interest and depreciation is 10%. The specific resistance of copper = 1.72 × 10⁻⁶ Ω per cm cube. The voltage at which power is supplied to industry is 11 kV.

Loss load factor = 0.25 load factor + 0.75 (load factor)². Determine the most economical section of the conductor.

Solution: Let the length of the cable be L km.

$$\text{Maximum demand, MD} = 1000 \text{ kW}$$

$$\text{Annual energy consumption} = 5 \times 10^6 \text{ kWh}$$

$$\text{Annual load factor} = \frac{\text{Annual energy consumption}}{\text{MD} \times 8760}$$

$$= \frac{5 \times 10^6}{1000 \times 8760} = 0.57$$

$$\text{Loss load factor} = 0.25 \times 0.57 + 0.75(0.75)^2 = 0.387$$

Current corresponding to maximum demand.

$$I = \frac{1000 \times 1000}{\sqrt{3} \times 11000 \times 0.85} = 61.8\text{A}$$

Capital cost (variable) of the cable = ₹ 80000 aL

Annual cost on account of interest and depreciation on capital cost (variable) of cable

$$= ₹\, 80000\, a\, L \times \frac{10}{100} = ₹\, 8000\, aL$$

$$\text{Energy lost per annum} = 3 \times \frac{I^2 RT}{1000} \times \text{lost load factor}$$

$$= 3 \times (61.8)^2 \times \frac{1.72 \times 10^{-6} \times L \times 1000 \times 100}{a} \times \frac{8760}{1000} \times 0.387$$

$$= \frac{6681L}{a}$$

$$\text{Annual cost due to energy lost} = ₹\, \frac{5}{100} \times \frac{6681L}{a} = ₹\, 334.05 \frac{L}{a}$$

For most economical x-section of the conductor

$$8000aL = 334.05 \frac{L}{a}$$

or

$$a = \sqrt{\frac{334.05}{8000}} = 0.204 \text{ cm} \quad \textbf{Ans.}$$

EXAMPLE 3.6 Determine the most economical size of a 3-phase line which supplies the following loads at 10 kV.

(i) 1000 kW at 0.8 p.f. (lag) for 10 hours,

(ii) 500 kW at 0.9 p.f. (lag) for 8 hours, and

(ii) 100 kW at u.p.f. for 6 hours.

The above gives the daily load cycle. The cost per km of the completely erected line is ₹(8000 a + 1500) where a is the area of cross-section of each conductor in cm^2. The combined interest and depreciation is 10 percent per annum of capital cost. Cost of energy losses is 5 paise per kWh. Resistivity of conductor material = 1.72×10^{-6} Ω-cm.

Solution: Let the length of the line be L km

$$\text{Capital cost of line} = ₹\,(8000\,a + 1500) \times L$$

Annual cost on account of interest and depreciation on capital (variable) cost

$$= ₹\,\frac{10}{100} \times 8000\,aL = ₹\,800\,aL$$

The load currents:

(i) at 1000 kW, 0.8 p.f. (lag), $I = \dfrac{1000 \times 1000}{\sqrt{3} \times 10000 \times 0.8} = \dfrac{125}{\sqrt{3}}$ A

(ii) at 500 kW, 0.9 p.f. (lag), $I = \dfrac{500 \times 1000}{\sqrt{3} \times 10000 \times 0.9} = \dfrac{500}{9\sqrt{3}}$ A

(iii) at 100 kW, u.p.f., $I = \dfrac{100 \times 1000}{\sqrt{3} \times 10000 \times 1} = \dfrac{10}{\sqrt{3}}$ A

$$\text{Resistance of line conductor, } R = \frac{\rho l}{a} = \frac{1.72 \times 10^{-6} \times 1000 \times 100 \times L}{a} \text{ ohms}$$

$$= \frac{0.172L}{a} \text{ ohms}$$

$$\text{Energy lost per annum} = \frac{3I^2Rt}{1000} \text{ kWh}$$

$$= \frac{3 \times 0.172L}{a} \times \frac{365}{1000}\left[\left(\frac{125}{\sqrt{3}}\right)^2 \times 10 + \left(\frac{500}{9\sqrt{3}}\right)^2 \times 8 + \left(\frac{10}{\sqrt{3}}\right)^2 \times 6\right]$$

$$= \frac{11397}{a} \times L$$

$$\text{Cost of energy wasted per annum} = ₹\,\frac{5}{100} \times \frac{11397}{a} \times L = \frac{569.85L}{a}$$

For most economical cross-section of conductor,

$$800aL = \frac{569.85}{a} \times L$$

or $$a = \sqrt{\frac{569.85}{800}} = 0.844 \text{ cm}^2 \quad \textbf{Ans.}$$

3.13 CONSTRUCTIONAL FEATURES OF A TRANSMISSION LINE

Electric power can be transmitted either by overhead lines or by underground cables. When power is transmitted by bare conductors which are fixed on the insulators, insulators are further attached to line supports; then this system is called *overhead system*; on the other hand if power is transmitted by properly insulated conductors and properly burried in ground, then this system of transmission is called *underground system*. Generally overhead system is used for electric power transmission but underground system has got certain advantages overhead system. The comparison between the two systems has been given below:

1. **Public Safety:** Underground system is safer than overhead system; chances of accidents are also minimum in this system.
2. **Maintenance Cost:** Maintenance cost of underground system is minimum.
3. **Frequency of Faults:** There are very few chances of power failure in underground system, as the cables are laid underground and these are not easily accessible.
4. **Voltage Drop:** In underground system, because of less spacing between the conductors, the inductance of conductors is very low as compared to overhead system; therefore voltage drop is low in underground system.
5. **Damage Due to Thunder Storm and Lighting:** Underground system is free from interruption of service on account of lighting, thunderstorm and objects falling across the wires and thus causing short circuits.
6. **Interference to Communication Circuits:** In underground system there is no interference to communication circuits.
7. **Appearance:** Underground system is good looking, as no wiring is visible.

However, the underground system has the following disadvantages:

1. **Higher Initial Cost:** Underground system is more expensive. The cost of underground system is almost double the cost of overhead system for a particular amount of power to be transmitted at a given voltage.
2. **Fault Location and Repairs:** Though chances of occurring fault in underground system are rare, but if it occurs then location of the fault and its repair is difficult and expensive.
3. **Jointing:** Jointing of underground cables is very difficult and it requires specialized skill, so tapping of loads is not conveniently possible in underground system.
4. **Charging Current:** On account of less spacing between the conductors, the cables have more capacitance, so they draw higher charging current.

For low voltage distribution in thickly populated areas and posh localities, the underground cables are very useful. But due to initial cost limitations the transmission of power is carried out by overhead transmission lines.

3.14 COMMON CONDUCTOR MATERIALS

The conductors carry electric power from the sending station to the receiving station.

Usually the following materials are used for conductors:

(i) **Copper:** Hard Drawn Bare copper (HDBC) is usually used. It has high conductivity and tensile strength. Copper is ductile and reasonably good against atmospheric troubles. Copper is an ideal conductor for transmission but due to heavy cost and non-availability, it is rarely used.

(ii) **Aluminium:** Its conductivity and tensile strength is poor than copper. Due to less conductivity cross section of aluminium conductor is about 1.25 times to that of copper for the same load. Aluminium is lighter in weight therefore supports (poles) need not to be too heavy as in case of copper. Due to light in weight and cheaper in cost, aluminium is fast replacing copper nowadays.

(iii) **ACSR:** That is aluminium conductor with steel reinforcement has many advantages. It has less sag and therefore more suitable for larger spans. It has more tensile strength. The galvanized steel core in the centre makes it more stronger and at the same time cheaper than aluminium.

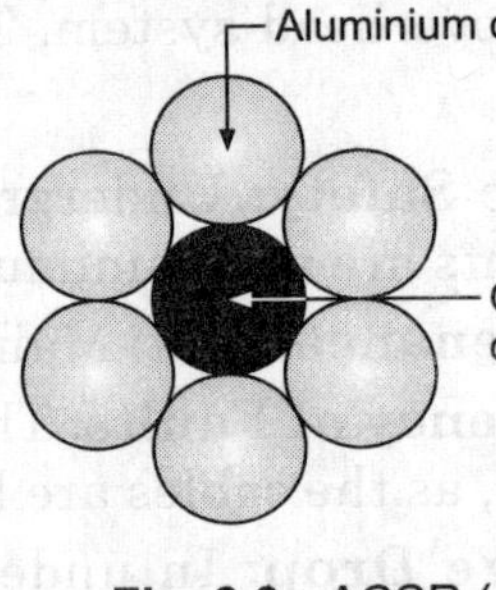

Fig. 3.3 ACSR (conductor)

3.15 MAIN COMPONENTS OF OVERHEAD LINES

The main components of an overhead line are enlisted as below:

(i) **The Supports:** Poles or towers depending upon the working voltage and the region where these are used.

(ii) **Cross Arms and Clamps:** These are either of wood or steel angle section and are used on pole structure to support the insulators.

(iii) **Insulators:** Pin, strain or suspension types, as the case may be, for supporting the conductors and taking strain or suspending the conductors respectively.

(iv) **Conductors:** Copper, aluminium or ACSR or of any other composition depending upon the current to be carried and the span of the line.

(v) **Guys and Stays:** Braces of cables are fastened to the pole at the termination or angle poles to resist lateral forces.

(vi) **Lightning Arrestors** to discharge excessive voltages built upon the line, to earth, due to lightning.

(vii) **Fuses and Insulating Switches** to isolate different parts of the overhead system.

(viii) **Continuous Earth Wire** is run on the top of the towers to protect the line against lightning discharges.

(ix) **Vee Guards** are often provided below bare overhead lines running along or across public streets to make the line safe if it should break.

(x) **Guard Wires** are provided above or below power lines while crossing telephone or telegraph lines. The guard wires and steel structures solidly connected to earth.

(xi) **Phase Plates** in order to distinguish the various phases.

(xii) **Bird Guards:** A stick of ebonite with rounded top is fixed near the insulator on the cross-arm to prevent flash over due to birds pecking on the conductors (on lines with pin insulators).

(xiii **Barbed Wire** over some portion of the pole as anti-climbing device.

(xiv) **Miscellaneous Items** such as danger plates, beads for jumpers, vibration dampers etc.

3.16 TYPES OF LINE SUPPORTS

The support used for transmission and distribution of electrical power must have the following characteristics:

(i) High mechanical strength
(ii) Change in cost
(iii) Light is weight
(iv) Low maintenance cost
(v) Longer life
(vi) Good looking
(vii) Easily accessible for painting and erection of line conductors.

The line supports are the various types including wood, steel, reinforced concrete poles and lattice steel towers.

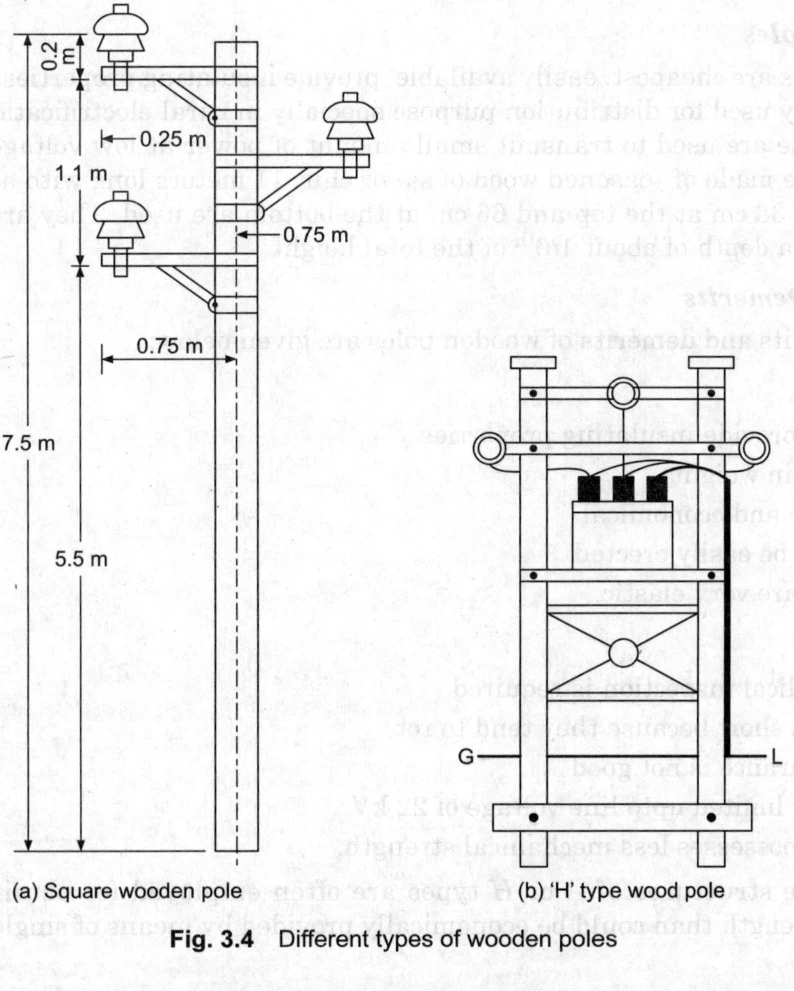

Fig. 3.4 Different types of wooden poles

The design of line supports depends upon the fact whether the support is rigid or has a certain amount of flexibility in the direction of the line. Wooden and some special type of steel structures are of lattice type and only the transverse wind pressure occurring upon the conductors and upon the support itself is usually considered in their design. The longitudinal pull of the conductors is normally balanced on either side of the support but in the event of breaking of one or more conductors on one side, there will be an unbalanced load which may be far in excess than transverse wind pressure. With flexible supports this unbalanced load is quickly absorbed by an increase in sag in undamaged span on account of bending of the supports on each side of the wrecked span towards the adjoining spans. After three or four spans the longitudinal pull becomes becomes negligible. A certain general rigidity in the longitudinal direction is provided for in practice by using rigid anchoring towers at an interval of 1.5 km or so. These anchoring towers are designed to withstand the breaking of one wire in three on one side as well as the transverse load.

In case of rigid supports such as the lattice-steel, broad-base structures equal strength is usually provided in both the longitudinal and transverse directions and every tower is designed to withstand the unbalanced load on account of breaking of one wire in three on the same side. In addition, anchor towers are often provided, in which the support is capable of withstanding the failure of two conductors out of three, or even of all conductors on one side.

1. Wooden Poles

These supports are cheapest, easily available, provide insulating properties and therefore, are extensively used for distribution purpose specially in rural electrification keeping the cost low. These are used to transmit small amount of power at low voltage, i.e., 440/220 volts. They are made of seasoned wood of sal or chir. 11 meters long with a minimum circumference of 38 cm at the top and 66 cm at the bottom are used. They are embedded in the ground to a depth of about 1/6th of the total height.

Merits and Demerits

The main merits and demerits of wooden poles are given below:

Merits

(i) They provide insulating properties
(ii) Light in weight
(iii) Cheap and economical
(vi) It can be easily erected
(v) They are very elastic.

Demerits

(i) Periodical inspection is required
(ii) Life is short because they tend to rot
(iii) Appearance is not good
(iv) Use is limited upto line voltage of 22 kV
(v) They possesses less mechanical strength.

Double pole structures of *A* or *H* types are often employed for obtaining a higher transverse strength than could be economically provided by means of single poles.

2. Steel Poles

The steel poles are of three types: (i) rail poles, (ii) tubular poles, and (iii) rolled steel joists. The rail poles are of the shape of track used for railways. Tubular poles are of round ×-section and rolled steel joists are of I-cross-section.

These poles possesses greater mechanical strength and so permit use of longer spans (50-80 metres) but cost is higher. Their life is longer than that of wooden poles and life is increased by regular painting. These poles are set in concrete muffs at the foundation in order to protect them from chemical action. Tubular poles in height of 9 to 11 metres are generally used for distribution purposes in cities to give good outlook, steel rail poles in height of 11 metres and 13 metres are used for transmission purposes at 11 kV and 33 kV respectively. The average life of steel poles is more than 40 years.

Fig. 3.5 Steel pole

Merits

The following are the main merits of steel poles:

(a) Longer life
(b) High mechanical strength
(c) Occupy less space
(d) Appearance is good.

Demerits

(a) High cost
(b) Regular painting is required to give nice outlook.
(c) High cost.

3. RCC Poles

These poles are of two types in shape. One type is of square cross-section from bottom to top but sides of square decreasing from bottom to top. The other type has rectangular bottom and square top with rectangular holes in it to facilitate the climbing of poles and reduce the weight of poles. These may be manufactured at site itself to avoid heavy cost of transportation.

The main merits and demerits of RCC poles are given below:

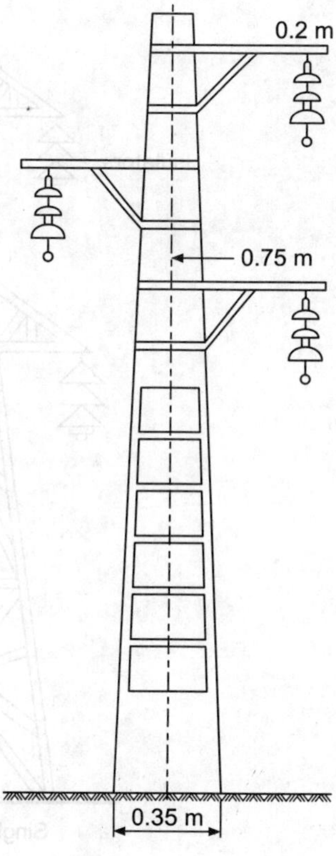

Fig. 3.6 R.C.C pole

Merits

(a) It requires no maintenance.
(b) It has good insulating property.
(c) Very long life.
(d) It can be used for longer span (80-200 metres)
(e) These give good outlook.

Demerits

(a) Initial cost is high.
(b) Transportation is difficult due to heavy weight.

4. Steel Towers

Narrow base towers are used for lines upto 33 kV. The brood base towers are used beyond 66 kV. They have greater mechanical strength and permit very long spans (more than 300 m). Hence they are very suitable for crossing railway lines, valleys, rivers etc. They may carry single sircuit as well as double circuit.

Comparison Between Single Circuit and Double Circuit Towers

	Single circuit design steel tower	*Double circuit design steel tower*
1.	Its structure is lighter in weight and requires lesser foundation because it is subjected to low wind pressure of conductors and structures.	Its structure is heavier in weight and of more height. It is subjected to more wind pressure.
2.	There is less danger at the time of repair.	There is always danger from the other line circuit.
3.	Reliability regarding continuity of supply is less.	Reliability regarding continuity of supply is more.
4.	Greater spacing of conductors is required.	Lesser spacing of conductors is required.
5.	High reactance due to greater spacing between conductors.	Low reactance due to lesser spacing between conductors.

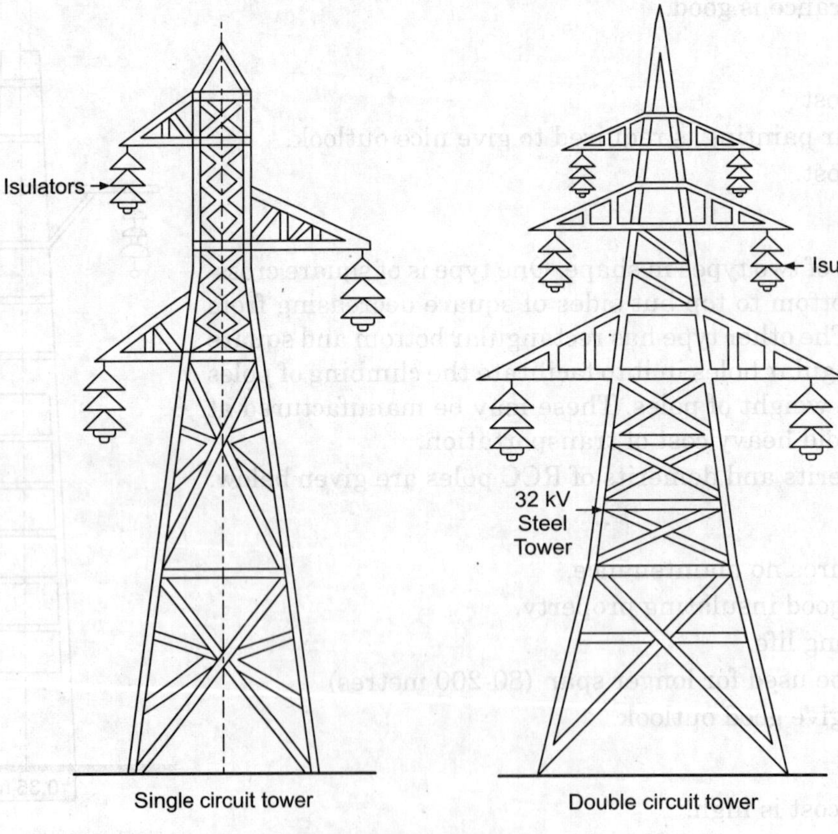

Fig. 3.7 Steel towers

3.17 INSULATORS AND THEIR PROPERTIES

3.17.1 Line Insulators

To prevent the flow of current from bare conductors to earth through line support; the conductors are secured to insulators. The insulators are usually placed on the cross arm which is clamped to the line support. Thus the successful operation of the transmission system depends to a great extent on the quality and maintenance of line insulators. The line insulators should have the following properties:

1. Their dielectric strength should be very high
2. Insulators should be robust and mechanically strong
3. They must be free from internal impurities
4. They should not be porous
5. They must provide high insulation resistance to the leakage current.

Insulators fail due to flash over or puncture. The flash over may occur between the line conductor and earth.

3.17.2 Materials for Insulators

The most practical insulator materials are porcelain and glass but steatite and special composition materials are also used.

1. Porcelain

Porcelain is produced by firing at a high temperature; a mixture which essentially consists of china clay; kaolin, feldspar and quartz in a kiln and the product thus obtained is mechanically strong. It gives less trouble from leakage and is less affected by changes of temperature. The porcelain should be ivory white, sound, free from defects, glazed and free from porosity. The dielectric strength of mechanically sound porcelain is of the order of 15000 volts to 17000 volts for every one fourth centimeter. Actually it is very difficult to manufacture perfectly homogeneous porcelain of required thickness and it is then necessary to adopt a two or three piece construction; the pieces are fixed and glazed separately and are cemented together. The compressive and tensile strength of porcelain insulators are 70000 kg/cm^2 and 500 kg/cm^2 respectively. Porcelain insulator has two advantages over glass insulator namely:

1. It can withstand great differences in temperature i.e., it will not crack when subjected to very high or very low temperatures.
2. It is not as brittle as glass and will not break easily in handling and during installation.

2. Glass

Very sound insulators are made from glass. The advantage of glass as insulator are:

1. It is mechanically stronger than porcelain under compression.
2. It possesses very high dielectric strength of the order of 140 kV per cm thickness and thus there is a possibility of one piece design.
3. Glass has lower coefficient of thermal expansion.
4. It has high resistivity when it is properly annealed.

5. Owing to its transparency, flaws in the material can be detected by visual examination.
6. Glass insulators are cheaper than porcelain insulators.

Its disadvantages are:

1. Moisture readily condenses on glass surface and facilitates the accumulation of dust thus giving a high surface leakage.
2. In large size the great mass of material, combined with the irregular shape may result in internal strains after cooling.

Glass insulators are often used up to 25 kV voltage applications.

3. Steatite

Steatite is magnesium silicate which is found combined with oxide. As compared to porcelain, it has much higher tensile and bending stress. Steatite insulators are used where insulators are in pure tension i.e., when transmission lines take sharp turns.

3.18 TYPES OF INSULATORS

The most commonly insulators used in the overhead lines are:

1. Pin type insulators
2. Suspension type insulators
3. Strain insulators
4. Shackle insulators

3.18.1 Pin Type Insulator

Pin type insulator is screwed on to a galvanise steel bolt which in turn is installed on the cross arm of the pole. Thes insulators are easily used upto 11 kV line but sometime upto 33 kV.

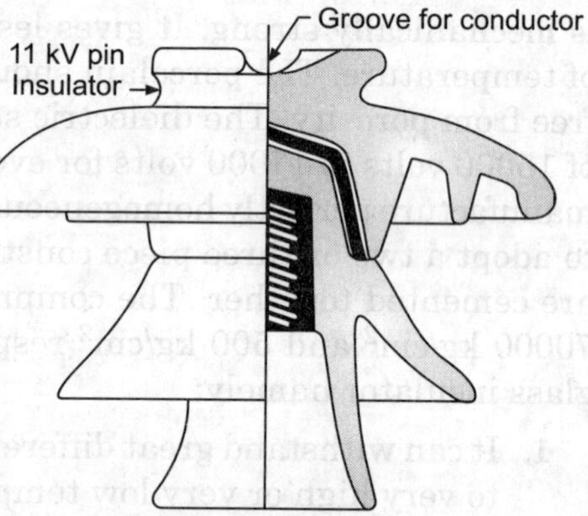

Fig. 3.8 Pin type insulator

Advantages of Pin Type Insulator

1. It is cheaper than suspension insulator.
2. Pin type insulator is placed on top of the pole to achieve more conductor clearance above the ground. Pin insulator raises the conductor above the cross arm while the suspension insulator suspends it below the cross arm.

Disadvantages

1. Beyond 33 kV, line voltage transmission, pin type insulator becomes too bulky and hence it is not economical.

3.18.2 Suspension Type

Above 33 kV, suspension type insulators are used. They consist of number of porcetain discs in series by metal links. Each disc is designed for 11 kV, hence by increasing number of discs very large voltage can be carried over. They are haned vertically down.

Several advantages of suspension insulators are:

1. Each insulator is designed for a comparatively low working voltage usually about 11 kV and the insulation for any required line voltage can be obtained by using a suitable number of such insulators in a string.
2. In the event of failure of an insulator, one unit, instead of the whole string has to be replaced.
3. The mechanical stresses are reduced, since the flexibility of line is more.
4. If in future, the operating voltage of the line has to be increased then this can be met by adding the requisite number of additional units to each string, instead of replacing all insulators as would be necessary with the pin type insulator.
5. Suspension type insulators placed on steel towers, also protect the line conductors partly from lightning, as the conductors run below the earthed cross arm.

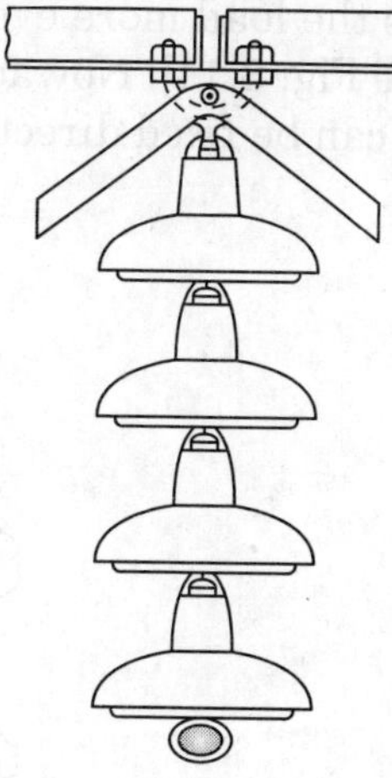

Fig. 3.9 Suspension type insulator

Disadvantages

1. It requires large spacing between the conductors.
2. It is costlier than pin type insulator and used below 33 kV transmission lines.

3.18.3 Strain Insulators

At dead ends, sharp turns and corners, where line is subjected to greater strains, strain insulators are used. Many number of discs (suspension) in series make a string which is put on pole horizontal to earth. Stain insulators are also used for stay wires, guard wires etc., when the tension is exceedingly high as at long river spans, two, three or four strings in parallel are used.

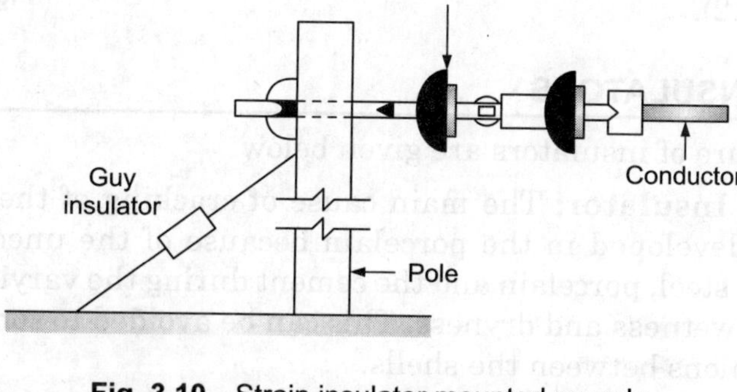

Fig. 3.10 Strain insulator mounted on pole

3.18.4 Spool or Shackle Insulator

These types of insulators along with single wire or rack assemblies for supporting low tension lines on the sides of poles and buildings both the low voltage distribution and house service wires are attached to the spool insulator. The insulator has tapered hole and thus distributes the load more evenly and minimizes the possibility of breakage when heavily loaded [See Fig. 3.11]. Nowadays shackle insulators are used all along the LT lines. These insulators can be fixed directly to the pole by a 175 mm × 16 mm bolts or to the cross-arm.

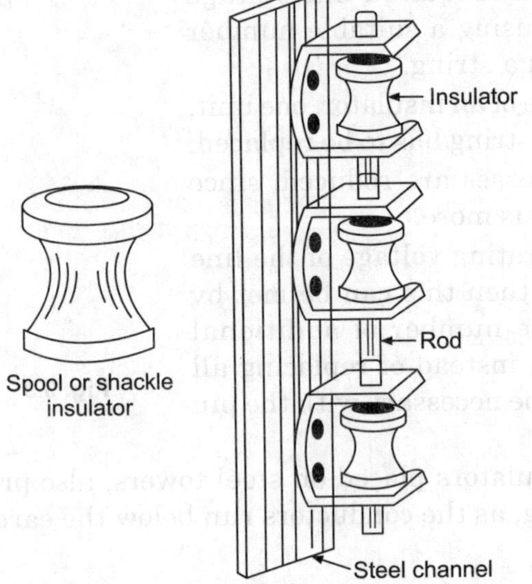

Fig. 3.11 Shackle insulator on clamp

3.18.5 Egg or Stay Insulators

Such insulators are of egg shape and are used in stay wire section to avoid flow of any leakage current to earth. Moreover, these are mounted at a height of 3 m from the ground level. The size of insulator depends upon the tensile strength of stay wire. These insulators are usually of porcelain. Those are so designed that in case of breakage of the insulator the guy wire will not fall to ground (Fig. 3.12).

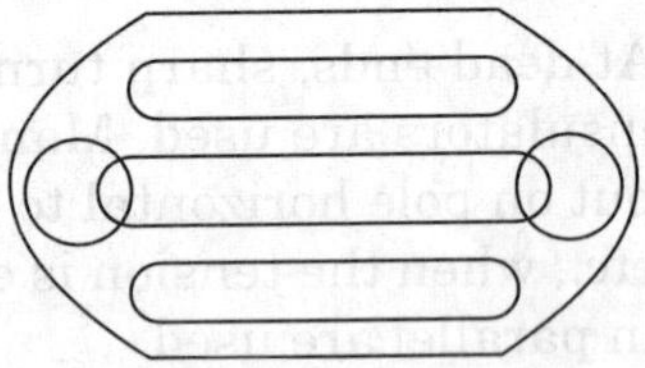

Fig. 3.12 Egg insulator

3.19 FAILURE OF INSULATORS

The causes of the failure of insulators are given below:

(i) **Cracking of Insulator:** The main cause of cracking of the insulator is due to the stresses developed in the porcelain because of the unequal expansion and contraction in steel, porcelain and the cement during the varying conditions of cold and heat and wetness and dryness. This can be avoided to some extent by the use of elastic cushions between the shells.

(ii) **Porosity of the Material:** This is usually caused by under firing of the china clay and leads to failure soon. The pores usually absorb moisture from air or from cement, thereby decreasing the insulation resistivity of the material. The current starts leaking through the insulator which may result into failure of the material. This failure is usually accomplished by puncture of the insulator and can be avoided by glazing the insulator, to some extent.

(iii) **Improper Vitrification:** This is another cause of the puncture of the material and it can be avoided by carrying out suitable routine tests during the course of manufacture.

(iv) **Flash-over:** The flash-overs on the insulators cause unequal expansion of the porcelain, thereby shattering the insulator with big cracks and causing interruptions of the supply. This can be avoided by providing arcing horns or rings which take up the arc and divert it away from the insulators.

(v) **Mechanical Stresses:** The pulling of the insulator may also sometimes cause mechanical stresses in the insulator (if its material is defective) due to which it may break. The most common check on this is to find out whether the material is up to the mark in tensile strength, before undertaking the manufacture, and this test should be included in the routine tests.

(vi) **Short Circuits:** In the case of pin insulators the large birds may also cause arc and thus may result in failure of the insulator. This can be avoided by providing bird guards near the insulator on the cross-arm.

(vii) **Deposition of Dust:** If the insulator material is not properly glazed, the water will stick over it resulting into deposition of dust etc., over it which is partially conducting and reduces the flash the flash-over distance. The deposits of dust and like matter e.g., salt, cement, dust etc., on the interior surfaces can actually cause much havoc under the condition of fog and mist. This can be easily avoided by cleaning the insulators periodically.

3.20 EARTH WIRING AND THEIR ACCESSORIES

In electrical engineering earthing is the reference point in an electrical circuit from which voltages are measured a common return path for electric current or a direct physical connection to the Earth.

Following are the accessories for earthing wire:

1. Earth wire vibration damper made of aluminium.
2. Earth wire pad clamp made of aluminium material.
3. Earth wire tension clamp also made of aluminium properly polished.
4. Earth wire suspension clamp made of aluminium alloys galvanised, chrome plated.
5. Flat earth wire cleat clamp.
6. Jointing sleeves.

3.21 SPACING OF CONDUCTORS

The spacing between conductors is determined by the voltage and span. As a thumb rule, spacing between conductors should be 1% of the maximum span for HT lines. A spacing of 20–30 cm is sufficient for LT lines. The lighter conductors should have more spacing than the heavier ones. The spacing of aluminium conductors is given by the formula.

$$\text{Spacing of conductors (in metres)} = \sqrt{S + \frac{V}{150}}$$

V = Voltage in kV, S = Sag in metres.

3.22 LENGTH OF THE SPAN

To keep the cost of transmission line minimum, the length of the span will have to be kept maximum possible. It will reduce the number of supporting poles, other fixtures and thus will reduce the overall cost of the transmission line. While deciding the length of the span various factors such as transmission voltage, maximum tension during any part of the year, public safety and Indian Electricity rules must be kept in mind. The usual length of spans with different types of supporting poles are as following:

Wooden poles	40–50 metres
Steel tubular poles	50–80 metres
RCC poles	80–100 metres
Steel towers	100–300 metres

It should also be kept in mind that

(i) The overhead conductor expands in summer season and contracts in the winter season. Thus in summer season the tension will be decreased and in winter season it will be increased.

(ii) The overhead conductor should be so erected that it is under safe tension. If conductors are too much tensioned in a bid to save the conductor material, the factor of safety against breaking of conductor will become too less and conductor may break due to excessive tension.

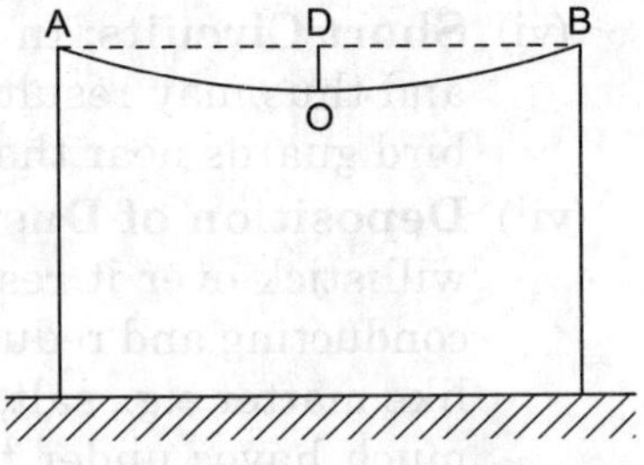

Fig. 3.13 Conductor suspended between two supports

3.23 SAG

Due to gravitation pull acting on the conductor, after some time a dip is produced in the transmission wire suspended between two supports. This dip is known as Sag. In other words the difference in level between the points of supports and the lower points on the conducrtor is called sag.

Figure 3.13 shows a conductor suspended between two supports A and B. The supports being on the same level. The conductor forms a catenary and is not fully stretched. The lowest point on the conductor is 'O', by definition:

$$\text{Sag or dip } `S' = OD$$

3.23.1 Calculation of Sag Formula

Consider a conductor suspended between two equilevel supports A and B in still air as shown. Where O is the lowest point on the conductor which happens to be in the middle of the span.

Let L = length of the span in metres

W = weight per metre length of conductor in kg

T = tension in the conductor in kg

Assume that the curvature is very small so that curved length of conductor AOB is equal to length of span.

Consider a point P on the conductor at a distance of x metres from the mid point O. The following two external forces are acting on the portion OP of the conductor:

(i) The weight of conductor of x metres i.e., wx kg is acting at $x/2$ meters from point P giving anticlockwise moment.

(ii) The tension T acting at point O at y metres from point P giving clockwise moment.

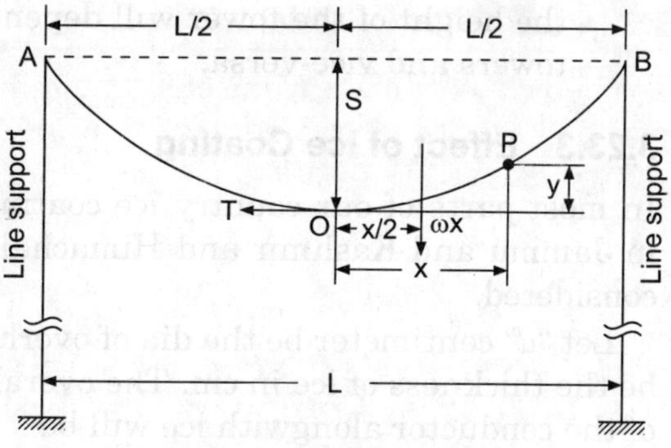

Fig. 3.14 Calculation of sag

Equating the two moments about point P,

$$T.y = wx\,\frac{x}{2}$$

or $$y = \frac{wx^2}{2T}$$

At point O ; $y = S$ (sag); and $$x = \frac{L}{2}$$

∴ $$\text{Sag, } S = w\frac{\left(\frac{L}{2}\right)^2}{2T}$$

or $$S = \frac{WL^2}{8T}$$

3.23.2 Importance of Sag

Sag has the following effects on the mechanical design of overhead lines:

1. **Tension of conductors:** When a conductor is stretched between the supports, sag is adjusted. If the conductors is stretched is more, the sag is small, thus sag determines the tension developed in the conductor. The smaller the sag, greater is the tension in the conductor and vice-vessa. Therefore, proper amount of sag must be provided to permit the safe tension in the overhead lines.
2. **Conductor material:** The conductor material required for overhead lines depends upon sag. If sag is large, more conductor length and hence more conductor material will be required and vice-versa.
3. **Temperature:** All metallic bodies expand with the rise in temperature and therefore, the length of the conductor increases with rise in temperature. Moreover due to fall in temperature there is strain in conductor and conductor is liable to break.
4. **Height of tower:** Appropriate clearance of the overhead conductors from ground depending upon the line voltage has to be maintain as per I.E.E rules. Obviously,

the height of the tower will depend upon the sag. Larger the sag. Taller will be the towers and vice-versa.

3.23.3 Effect of Ice Coating

In most parts of our country ice coating never occurs, yet at some mountaneous places in Jammu and Kashmir and Himachal Pradesh the effect of ice coating will have to be considered.

Let "d" centimeter be the dia of overhead conductor and "t" be the thickness of ice in cm. The overall cross-sectional area of the conductor alongwith ice will be

$$= \frac{\pi}{4}(d + 2t)^2 \text{ cm}^2$$

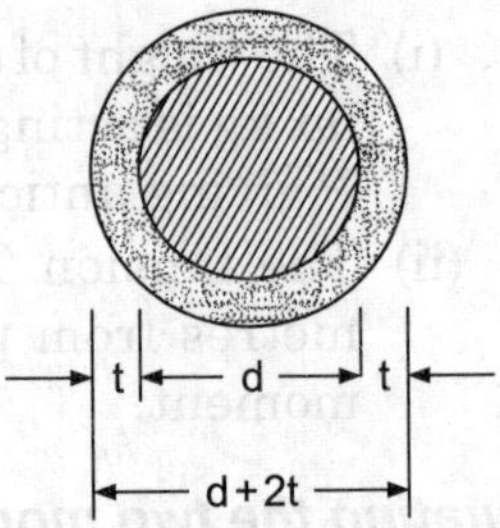

Fig. 3.15 Effect of ice coating

The cross-sectional area of ice is calculated by subtracting from the cross-sectional area of the conductor.

So, sectional area of ice $= \frac{\pi}{4}(d + 2t)^2 - \frac{\pi}{4}d^2$

$$= \pi t(d + t) \text{ cm}^2$$

Density of ice = 0.912 gm per c.c.

Volume of ice per meter length of conductor

$$= \pi t(d + t)\, 100 \text{ cm}^3$$

Weight of ice per meter length of the conductor

$$= \pi t(d + t)\, 100 \times 0.912 \times 10^{-3} \text{ kg-m}$$

$$W_i = 0.287\, t\,(d + t) \text{ kg.}$$

The weight of conductor having "t" cm thick ice on it will be $(W_c + W_r)$ kg as both of them are acting downward.

3.23.4 Effect of Wind Pressure

Let wind pressure be "p" kg per sq metre of the projected surface of the overhead conductor. If overhead conductor has a thickness of ice of "t" cm, then

The projected area of the surface per metre length of the conductor

$$= \frac{d+2t}{100} \times 1 \text{ sq metre}$$

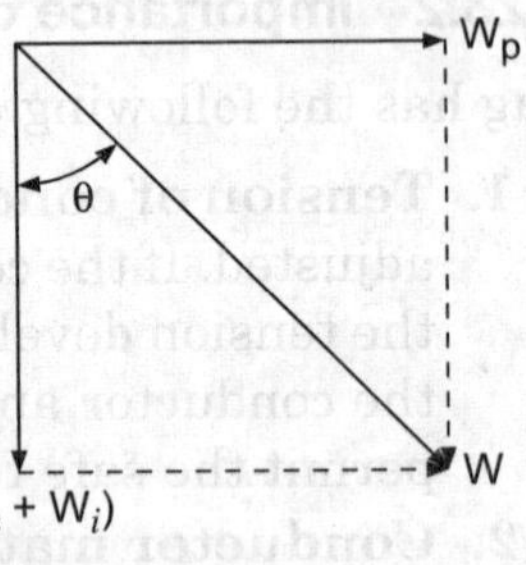

Fig. 3.16 Effect of wind pressure

Wind load per metre length

$$W_p = \left[p \times \frac{d+2t}{100}\right] \text{ kg-m.}$$

The resultant force "W" acting on the conductor when ice and wind pressure effect is considered per metre length will be

$$W = \sqrt{(W_C + W_i)^2 + W_p^2}$$

where W_c = weight of conductor per meter length

W_i = weight of ice loading per meter length

W_p = wind load per metre length.

EXAMPLE 3.7 A 220 kV transmission line uses ACSR conductors whose data is given as under:

The diameter of conductor = 20 mm

Weight = 844 kg/km, Breaking stress = 5000 kg per cm², Factor of safety = 2, Span length = 300 metres.

Calculate the sag. Also calculate the height above ground at which the conductor should be supported when ground clearance required is 7 metres.

Solution: Cross-sectional area of conductor

$$= \frac{\pi}{4} d^2 = \frac{22}{7 \times 4} (2 \times 2) = 3.14 \text{ cm}^2$$

$$\text{Ultimate strength} = \text{Breaking stress} \times \text{Cross-sectional area}$$
$$= 5000 \times 3.14 = 15700 \text{ kg}$$

$$\text{Factor of safety} = 2$$

$$\text{Allowable safe tension "}T\text{"} = \frac{15700}{2} = 7850 \text{ kg}$$

Weight of conductor per metre length

$$\text{"}W\text{"} = 0.844 \text{ kg}$$

$$\text{Span length } L = 300 \text{ metres}$$

$$\text{Sag "}S\text{"} = \frac{WL^2}{8T} = \frac{0.844 \times (300)^2}{8 \times 7850} = 1.21 \text{ metres}$$

Therefore, the conductor should be supported at a height of 7 + 1.21 = 8.21 metre above the ground level.

EXAMPLE 3.8 A transmission line has a span of 300 metres. If total sag is 8.484 metres and breaking stress is 5000 kg/cm², cross-sectional area 1 cm², weight of conductor 0.65 kg/metre, wind pressure 1 kg per metre, ice loading 0.35 kg/metre. Find the factor of safety.

Solution:

Weight of conductor per metre length "W_c" = 0.65 kg

Weight of ice coating per metre length "W_i" = 0.35 kg

Horizontal wind loading per metre length "W_p" = 1 kg

$$\text{Resultant force per metre length } W = \sqrt{(W_i + W_c)^2 + W_p^2}$$

$$= \sqrt{(0.65 + 0.35)^2 + (1)^2} = 1.414 \text{ kg/m}$$

Since

$$\text{Sag "}S\text{"} = 8.484 \text{ metre},$$

$$W = 1.414 \text{ kg/metre},$$

$$L = 300 \text{ meters}$$

$$T = ?$$

As $$S = \frac{WL^2}{8T}$$

So $$T = \frac{WL^2}{8S} = \frac{1.414 \times 300 \times 300}{8 \times 8.484} = 1875 \text{ kg}$$

$$\text{Allowable maximum stress} = \frac{\text{Allowable maximum tension}}{\text{Cross-sectional area of conductor}}$$

$$= \frac{1875}{1} = 1875 \text{ kg/cm}^2$$

$$\text{Factor of safety} = \frac{\text{Breaking stress}}{\text{Allowable maximum stress}}$$

$$= \frac{5000}{1875} = \mathbf{2.66} \quad \textbf{Ans.}$$

EXAMPLE 3.9 A transmission line has the following data: maximum span between level supports = 150 metres, cross-sectional area of conductor = 258 mm², wind load = 1.40 kg/per metre length, ultimate tensile strength = 42.2 kg per mm², specific gravity of the line conductor = 8.9, weight of conductor per meter length = 2.296 kgm.

If the sag is not to exceed 3.5 metres under the conditions specified what is the factor of safety for the line conductor.

Solution:

$$\text{Weight of conductor per metre length} = 258 \times 10^{-2} \times 1 \times 10^2 \times 8.9 \text{ gm}$$

$$W_c = 2.296 \text{ kg-m}$$

$$W_p = 1.4 \text{ kg}$$

$$W = \sqrt{W_c^2 + W_p^2} = \sqrt{(2.296)^2 + (1.4)^2} = 2.7 \text{ kg}$$

$$\text{Ultimate tensile strength} = 42.2 \times 258 \text{ kg}$$

$$\text{Span length, } L = 150 \text{ metres}$$

$$\text{Sag, } S = 3.5 \text{ metres}$$

Let safe tension be T kg, $$S = \frac{WL^2}{8S}$$

or $$\text{Safe tension } T = \frac{WL^2}{8S} = \frac{2.7 \times 150 \times 150}{8 \times 3.5} = 2170 \text{ kg}$$

$$\text{Factor of safety} = \frac{\text{Ultimate strength}}{\text{Safe tension}}$$

$$= \frac{42.2 \times 258}{2170} = \mathbf{5} \quad \textbf{Ans.}$$

Supports at different Levels

Consider an overhead line *AOB*, supported over the supports *A* and *B*, as shown in Fig. 3.17.

Let the difference in level between the two supports be *h* and lowest point *O* of the conductor be at a distance of *x* metres from the support at low level.

So, distance of *O* from higher level support = (*L* – *x*) metres

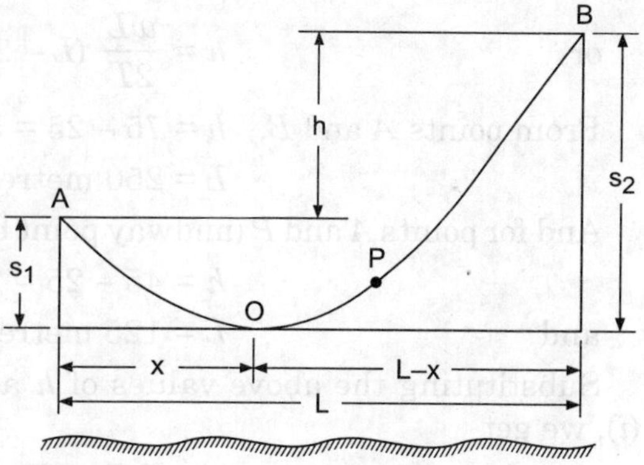

Fig. 3.17 Supports at different levels

From expression (*i*)

$$S_1 = \frac{wx^2}{2T} \quad \ldots(i)$$

and

$$S_2 = \frac{w(L-x)^2}{2T} \quad \ldots(ii)$$

Difference in level of two supports,

$$h = S_2 - S_1 = \frac{w(L-x)^2}{2T} - \frac{wx^2}{2T}$$

$$= \frac{wL^2 + wx^2 - 2wLx - wx^2}{2T} = \frac{wL^2 - 2wLx}{2T}$$

or

$$2Th = wL^2 - 2wLx$$

or

$$2wLx = wL^2 - 2Th$$

or

$$x = \frac{L}{2} - \frac{Th}{wL} \quad \ldots(iii)$$

From the above expressions (*i*), (*ii*) and (*iii*) location of point *O* and thus the values of S_1 and S_2 can be determined.

EXAMPLE 3.10 An overhead transmission line at a river crossing is supported from two towers at heights of 25 m and 75 m above the water level. The horizontal distance between the towers is 250 m. If the required clearance between the conductor and the water midway between the towers is 45 metres and if both of the towers are on the same side of the point of maximum sag of the parabolic configuration, find the stringing tension in the conductor. The Weight of the conductor is 0.70 kg-m.

Solution:

Span length, $L = 250$ metres

Weight of conductor per metre length, $w = 0.7$ kg

Difference in level between the two supports, $h = 75 - 25 = 50$ m

Let *T* be the stringing tension and *x* be the distance between the lowest point *O* of the conductor and the support at low level as shown in Fig. 3.18.

Since

$$h = S_2 - S_1$$

or

$$h = \frac{wx^2}{2T} - \frac{w(L-x)^2}{2T} = \frac{wL^2 - 2wLx}{2T}$$

or $$h = \frac{wL}{2T}(L - 2x) \quad ...(i)$$

From points A and B, $h = 75 - 25 = 50$ metres

$L = 250$ metres

And for points A and P (midway point between the towers)

$h = 45 - 25 = 20$ metres

and $L = 125$ metres

Substituting the above values of h and L in expression (*i*), we get

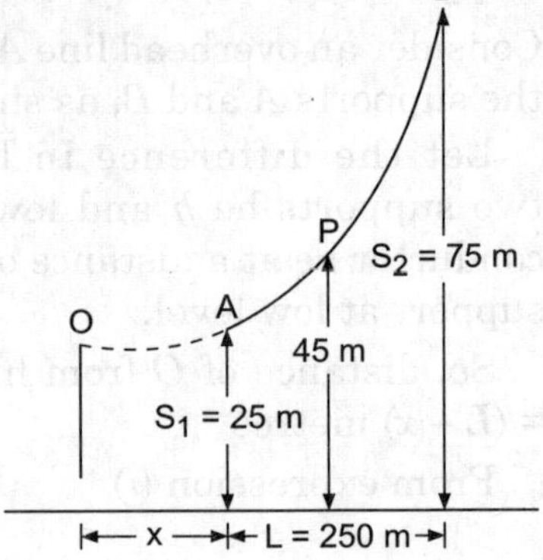

Fig. 3.18

$$50 = \frac{0.7 \times 250}{2T}(250 - 2x) \quad ...(ii)$$

and $$20 = \frac{0.7 \times 125}{2T}(125 - 2x) \quad ...(iii)$$

Dividing expression (*ii*) by expression (*iii*), we get

$$2.5 = 2 \times \frac{250 - 2x}{125 - 2x}$$

or $$2.5\,(125 - 2x) = 500 - 4x$$

or $$x = -500 + 312.5 = -187.5 \text{ metres}$$

Substituting $x = -187.5$ in expression (*ii*), we get

$$50 = \frac{0.7 \times 250}{2T}[250 - 2 \times (-187.5)]$$

or $$T = \frac{0.7 \times 250}{2 \times 50}(250 + 375) = \mathbf{1{,}093.75\ kg}\ \textbf{Ans.}$$

EXAMPLE 3.11 An overhead line with stranded copper conductors is supported on two towers 250 metres apart having a difference in level of 10 metres. The conductor diameter is 2.0 cm and weights 2.3 kg per metre length. Determine the sag at the lower support when the line is subjected to wind pressure of 57.5 kg per square metre of projected area. The maximum tensile strength of copper is 4,220 kg/cm². Take a factor of safety 4.

Solution: Span length, $L = 250$ metres

Weight of conductor per metre length,

$$w_c = 2.3 \text{ kg/m}$$

Horizontal wind force per metre length,

$$w_w = \text{Wind pressure} \times \text{Projected area of the conductor}$$
$$= 57.5 \times 0.02 = 1.15 \text{ kg/m}$$

Resultant pressure, $$w_r = \sqrt{w_c^2 + w_w^2} = \sqrt{(2.3)^2 + (1.15)^2} = 2.57 \text{ kg/m}$$

Difference in level of two supports,

$$h = 10 \text{ metres}$$

$$\text{Area of ×-section of conductor, } a = \frac{\pi}{4}d^2 = \frac{\pi}{4} \times (2.0)^2 = 3.14 \text{ cm}^2$$

$$\text{Allowable tension, } T = \frac{4220 \times 3.14}{4} = 3312 \text{ kg}$$

Distance of lowest point of the conductor, O (Fig. 3.14) from the support at low level.

$$x = \frac{L}{2} - \frac{Th}{wL} = \frac{250}{2} - \frac{3312 \times 10}{2.57 \times 250} = 73.45$$

$$\text{Slant sag, } S = \frac{wx^2}{2T} = \frac{2.57 \times (73.45)^2}{2 \times 3312} = \mathbf{2.09 \text{ metres}} \quad \textbf{Ans.}$$

$$\cos\theta = \frac{w_c}{w_r} = \frac{2.3}{2.57} = 0.895$$

$$\text{Vertical sag} = S\cos\theta = 2.09 \times 0.895 = \mathbf{1.87 \text{ metres}} \quad \textbf{Ans.}$$

3.24 INDIAN ELECTRICITY RULES PERTAINING TO CLEARANCES

Government of India has farmed certain rules so that all electric works are executed in a systematic and safe way. These rules were framed and passed by Indian Parliament as Indian Electricity Act, 1956. The rules under this act are called Indian Electricity Rules. Indian Electricity rules pertaining to clearances are incorporated in Rules 77, 79, 80 and 81.

Rule 77 Minimum Ground Clearance of the Lowest Conductor Along and Across Street.

Class of voltage	*Along street*	*Across street*
Low and medium voltage	5.791 metres (19')	5.496 metres (18')
High voltage	6.095 metres (20')	5.791 metres (19')
Extra high voltage	6.095 metres (20')	6.095 metres (20')

Minimum Ground Clearance of Service Lines Else where than the Above Locations

Low, medium and high voltage lines up to 11 kV (Bare)

= 4.572 metres (15')

Low, medium and high voltage lines up to 11 kV (insulated)

= 3.963 metres (13')

High voltage lines above 11 kV = 5.182 metres (17')

Extra high voltage lines = 5.182 plus 0.305 metre (1') for every 33 kV or part there of by which the voltage of the line exceeds 33 kV.

Rule 79, Minimum Clearance from Building

Vertical clearance from flat roofs, open balconies, verandahs, roofs etc., a vertical clearance of 2.439 metres (8') and a horizontal clearance of 1.219 metres from the nearest point should be provided in case of low and medium voltage.

For high voltage lines up to 33 kV, the corresponding vertical clearance will be 3.658 metres and in case of extra high voltage lines equal to 3.658 metres plus 0.305 metres for every additional 33 kV or part thereof.

Horizontal Clearance

For voltage lines up to and including 11 kV = 1.219 metres (4')

For voltage lines above 11 kV but upto 33 kV = 1.829 metres (6')

For extra high voltage lines – 1.829 metres plus 0.305 metre for every 33 kV or part thereof that the voltage exceeds 33 kV.

Clearance Between Power and Communication Lines

Low and medium voltage lines = 1.380 metres (4' 6")

H.V. lines upto and including 7.2 kV lines = 1.525 metres (5')

H.V. lines up to 12 kV – 2.130 metres (7')

Clearance between communication and ground wires will not be less than 1070 mm (3' 6").

The minimum clearance between the guard wires and the communication lines shall be 60 cm. If the guards are fastened to the same supports as the power line, then the minimum distance will be 90 cm.

Clearance Over Rivers

There must be a minimum clearance of 3 metres over the maximum flood level in the case of rivers where there is no navigation.

Clearance Over Rail Tracks

The minimum height above rail level of the lowest portion of any conductor under conditions of maximum sag shall be as follows:

Clearance over rail tracks

Voltage Gauge 33 kV	*Upto 650 volt and including*	*Above 650 volt upto 66 kV*	*Above 33 kV and upto 110 kV*	*Above 66 kV and upto*
Broad gauge outside station in limits	7.16 metres	7.6 (25') metres	7.92 (26') metres	8.23 (27') metres
Inside station limits	7.16 metres	10.06 metres (33')	10.36 metres (34')	10.66 metres (35')
Metre gauge outside station limits	6.1 metres (20')	6.40 metres (21')	6.71 metres (22')	7.01 metres (23')
Inside station limits	6.1 metres (20')	8.84 metres (29')	9.15 metres (30')	9.45 metres (31')

Clearances from Buildings of High and Extra High Voltage Lines

Where a high or extra-high voltage overhead line passes above or adjacent to any building or part of a building it shall have on the basis of maximum sag as vertical clearance above the highest part of the building immediately under such line, of not less than:

(a) For high voltage lines upto load including 11,000 volts 1.219 metre (4 ft).
(b) For high voltage lines above 11,000 volts and upto and including 33,000 volts 1.829 metre (6 ft).
(c) For extra high voltage lines 1.829 metre (6 ft) plus 0.303 metre (1 ft) for every additional 33,000 volts or part thereof.

Conductors at Different Voltage on Some Supports

Where conductors forming parts of systems at different voltages are erected on the same supports, the owner shall make adequate provision to guard against danger to linesmen and other from the lower voltage system being charged above its normal working voltage by leakage from or contact with the higher voltage system, and the methods of construction and clearances between the conductors of the two systems shall be subjected to the prior approval of the Inspector.

Lines Crossing or Approaching Each Other

1. Where an overhead line, crosses or is in proximity to any telecommunication line, the owner of the overhead line shall project it in a manner laid down in the code of practice of the power and telecommunication coordination committee.
2. When it is intended to erect a telecommunication line which will cross or be in proximity to an overhead line, the person proposing to erect such communication line shall give notice in writing of his intention to the owner of the overhead line and the owner of the overhead line shall within twenty one days of receiving such notice, provide the protection referred to in sub-rule (1).
3. Where an overhead line crosses or is in proximity to an overhead line belonging to another person, the owner of the line which was last erected shall so protect it as to guard against the possibility of its coming into contact with the other overhead line.
4. A person erecting or proposing to erect an overhead line may require the owner of the other overhead line to provide the protection referred to in sub-rule (3). Within twenty-one days of the receipt of the notice in that behalf.
5. In all cases referred to in the preceding sub-rules, the expenses of making the guarding arrangement shall be borne by the person whose line was last erected.
6. Where two lines cross the crossing shall be made as nearly as right angles as the nature of case admits.

3.25 SKIN EFFECT

The direct current flowing through a conductor is uniformly distributed over the whole cross section of the conductor. But alternating current does not distribute uniformly but it tends to concentrate near the surface of the conductor. This is known as *skin effect*. It increases the resistance of the conductor.

Skin Effect may be defined as the tendency of AC to concentrate near the surface of the conductor.

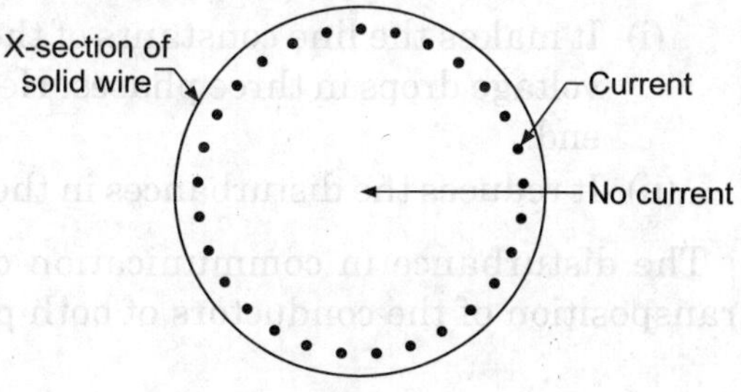

Fig. 3.19 Skin effect

Generally a stranded conductor is used and each strand carries a small part of the current. The inductance of each strand, near the centre are surrounded by a grater magnetic flux and hence have larger inductance than that strand near the surface. The high reactance (opposition) of inner strands restricts the flow of current in the centre and cause it to flow near the surface of the conductor which produces skin effect.

Proximity Effect

The flux set up by the nearly current carrying conductor affects the distribution current in the conductor.

Factors Affecting Skin Effect

The skin effect depends upon the following factors.

(i) Nature of material
(ii) Diameter of wire–increase with diameter of wire
(iii) Shape of wire–less for stranded conductor than solid conductor
(iv) Frequency–increase with increase in frequency.

3.26 TRANSPOSITION OF CONDUCTORS

The unbalancing effect on account of irregular spacing of conductors can be avoided by changing the positions of the conductors at regular distances. This is called *transposition of conductor*.

The process of changing the position of conductors spaced unsymmetrically of a three phase overhead line at regular distances in order to make the line constants (Resistance, Inductance and Capacitance) of the line symmetrical is called Transposition of conductors.

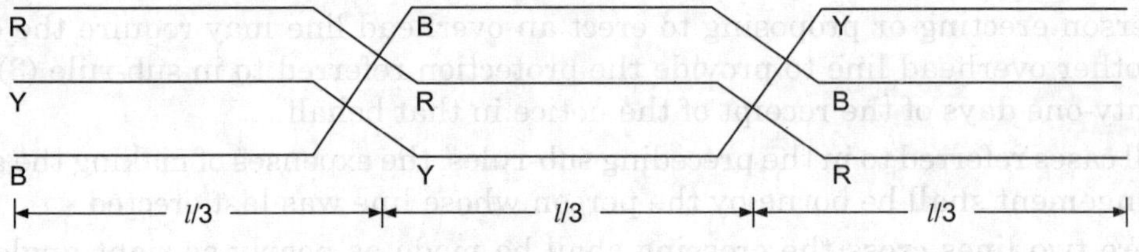

Fig. 3.20 Transposition of conductors

Advantages of Transposing Conductors

Transposition of overhead conductors of an unsymmetrical line has the following advantages:

(i) It makes the line constants of the three phases symmetrical which results in equal voltage drops in three phases. Hence equal line voltage are available at the receiving end.
(ii) It reduces the disturbances in the neighbouring communication (telephone) circuits.

The disturbance in communication circuit can be kept down by means of a through transposition of the conductors of both power line and telephone lines.

3.27 STRING EFFICIENCY OF LINES

String efficiency is defined as the ratio of voltage across the whole string to the product of number of discs in the string and voltage across the disc nearest to the conductor.

$$\text{String efficiency} = \frac{\text{Voltage across the string}}{n \times \text{voltage across disc nearest to conductor}}$$

or
$$\text{String efficiency} = \frac{V}{n \times V_n}$$

where V = voltage across the whole string

n = number of discs

V_n = voltage across the disc nearest to the conductor

The greater the value of string efficiency, the more uniform is the voltage distribution along the string. If the string efficiency is 100% then voltage across each disc is same although it is almost impossible to achieve 100% string efficiency due to presence of shunt capacitance.

3.27.1 Mathematical Expression for String Efficiency

Figure 3.21 shows the equivalent circuit for a three disc string.

Let mutual capacitance between links = C

Shunt capacitance between links and earth = C_1

Voltage across the first unit = V_1

Voltage across the second unit = V_2

Applying Kirchhoff's current law to node A, we get

$$I_2 = I_1 + i_1$$

$$\frac{V_2}{X_c} = \frac{V_1}{X_c} + \frac{V_1}{X_{C_1}}$$

or
$$V_2\omega C = V_1\omega C + V_1\omega C_1$$

or
$$V_2\omega C = V_1\omega C + V_1\omega KC$$

or
$$V_2 = V_1 (1 + K)$$

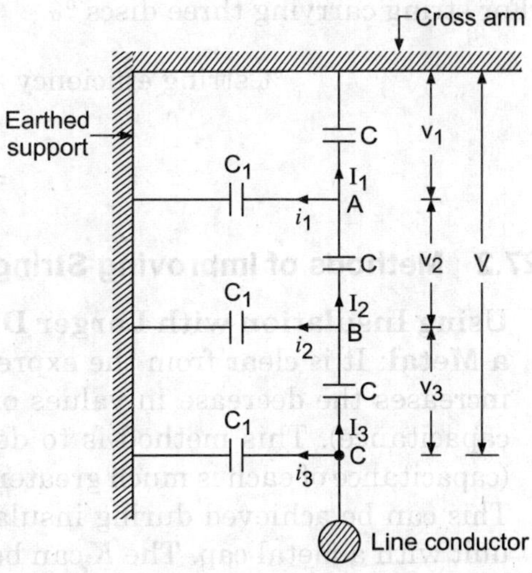

Fig. 3.21 Equivalent circuit of three disc string

Applying Kirchhoff's law to node B, we get

$$I_3 = I_2 + i_2$$

$$\frac{V_3}{X_C} = \frac{V_2}{X_C} + \frac{V_2 - V_1}{X_{C_1}}$$

or
$$V_3\omega C = V_2\omega C + (V_1 + V_2)\omega C_1$$

or
$$V_3\omega C = V_2\omega C + (V_1 + V_2)\omega KC$$

$$V_3 = V_2 (V_1 + V_2)K$$

$$V_3 = KV_1 + V_2 (1 + K)$$

$$V_3 = KV_1 + V_1 (1 + K)$$

$$V_3 = KV_1 + V_1 (1 + K^2 + 2K) \qquad [\because V_2 = V_1 (1 + K)]$$

$$V_3 = V_1 (1 + 3K + K^2) \qquad ...(ii)$$

Voltage between conductor and earth (i.e., tower is)

$$V = V_1 + V_2 + V_3 = V_1 + V_1 (1 + K) + V_1 (1 + 3K + K^2) = V_1 (3 + 4K + K^2)$$

$$V = V_1 (1 + K)(3 + K)$$

From expression (*i*), (*ii*) and (*iii*), we get

$$V_1 = \frac{V_2}{1+K} = \frac{V_3}{1+3K+K^2} = \frac{V}{(1+K)(3+K)} \qquad ...(iv)$$

$\therefore$ Voltage across top unit, $V_1 = \dfrac{V}{(1+K)(3+K)}$ ...(*v*)

Voltage across middle unit, $V_2 = \dfrac{V(1+K)}{(1+K)(3+K)} = \dfrac{V}{(3+K)}$ ...(*vi*)

Voltage across bottom unit, $V_3 = \dfrac{V_1(1+3K+K^2)}{(1+K)(3+K)}$ ...(*vii*)

$$\% \text{ String efficiency} = \frac{\text{Voltage across string}}{n\times \text{ voltage across disc nearst to conductor}} \times 100$$

For string carrying three discs %

$$\% \text{ string efficiency} = \frac{V}{3V_3} = 100 = \frac{(1+K)(3+K)}{3V(1+3K+K^2)} \times 100$$

$$= \frac{(1+K)(3+K)}{3(1+3K+K^2)} \times 100$$

3.27.2 Methods of Improving String Efficiency

1. **Using Insulation with Larger Discs or by Providing Each Insulator Unit with a Metal**: It is clear from the expression of string efficiency that the string efficiency increases the decrease in values of K (i.e., the ratio of shunt capacitance to mutual capacitance). This method is to design the units such that the mutual capacitance (capacitance of each is much greater than the shunt capacitance (capacitance to earth)). This can be achieved during insulators with larger discs or providing each insulator unit with a metal cap. The K can be made 1/6 to 1/10 by this method.
2. **Using Longer Cross-arm:** The ratio of shunt capacitance to mutual capacitance, K can alternatively be reduced by using longer cross-arms so that the horizontal distance from line support (pole or tower) is increased thereby decreasing the shunt capacitance. But the limitations of cost and mechanical strength of line supports do not allow the

cross-arms to be long and it has been found that in practice it is not possible to obtain the value of K than 0.1.

3. **Capacitance Grading:** It is seen that non-uniform distribution of voltage across an insulator string is due to leakage current from the insulator pin to the supporting structure. The current cannot be eliminated. However, it is possible that discs of different capacities are used such that the product of their capacitive reactance and the current flowing through respective unit is same. This can be achieved by grading the mutual capacitance of the insulator units, i.e., by having lower units of more capacitance–maximum at the line unit and minimum at the top unit, nearest to the cross-arm. It can be shown that by this method complete equality of voltage across the units of an insulator string can be obtained but this method needs a large number of different-sized insulator units. This involves maintaining spares of all varieties of insulator discs which is contrary to the tendency of standardization. So this method is not used in practice below 200 kV.
4. **By Static Shielding:** In case of capacitance grading, insulator units of different capacitances are used so that the flow of different currents through the respective units produce equal voltage drop. In static shielding, pin to supporting structure charging currents are exactly cancelled so that the same current flows through the identical insulator units and produce equal voltage drops across each insulator unit. In this method a guard or grading ring, which usually takes the form of a large metal ring surrounding the bottom unit and electrically connected to the metal work at the bottom of this unit, and therefore to the line conductor. The guard ring screens the lower units, reduce their earth capacitance and introduces a number of capacitance between the line conductor and various insulator unit capacitors.

EXAMPLE 3.12 In a 33 kV overhead transmission line, there are 3 units in the string of insulators. If the capacitance between each insulator pin and earth is 11% of self capacitance of each insulator, find: (a) the distribution of voltage over 3 insulators and (*b*) string efficiency.

Solution: Figure 3.22 shows the equivalent circuit of the string insulators. Let V_1, V_2 and V_3 be the voltage across top, middle and bottom unit respectively. If C is the self conductance of each unit, then K_C will be the shunt capacitance.

$$K = \frac{\text{Shunt capacitance}}{\text{Self capacitance}} = 0.11$$

Voltage across string, $V = \dfrac{33}{\sqrt{3}} = 19.05\ kV$

At Junction A, $\quad I_2 = I_1 + i_1$

or $\quad V_2\omega C = V_1\omega C + V_1 K\omega C$

or $\quad V_2 = V_1 (1 + K) = V_1 (1 + 0.11)$

$$V_2 = 1.11\ V_1 \quad ...(i)$$

At Junction B, $\quad I_3 = I_2 + i_2$

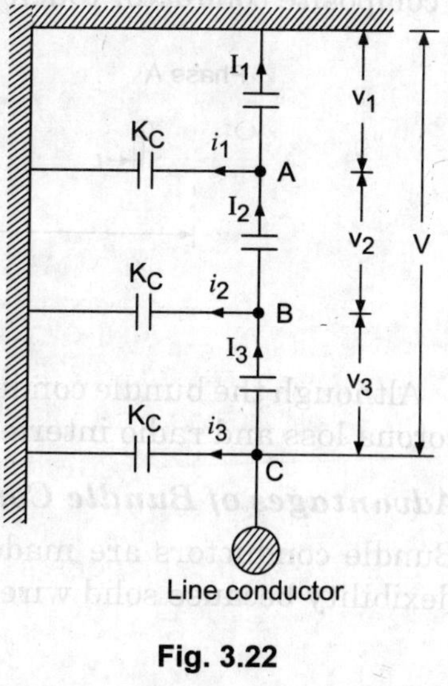

Fig. 3.22

or $$V_3\omega C = V_2\omega C + (V_1 + V_2)\ K\omega C$$

or $$V_3 = V_2\ (V_1+V_2)K$$

$$= 1.11\ V_1 + (V_1 + 1.11\ V_1)\ 0.11$$

$$V_3 = 1.342\ V_1$$

Voltage across the whole string

$$V = V_1 + V_2 + V_3 = V_1 + 1.11\ V_1 + 1.342V = 3.452V_1$$

or $$19.05 = 3.452\ V$$

$$\text{Voltage across top unit, } V_1 = \frac{19.05}{3.452} = 5.52 \text{ kV}$$

$$\text{Voltage across middle unit, } V_2 = 1.11 \times V_1 = 1.11 \times 5.52 = 6.13 \text{ kV}$$

$$\text{Voltage across bottom unit, } V_3 = 1.342 \times V_1 = 1.342 \times 5.52 = 7.4 \text{ kV}$$

(b) $$\text{String efficiency} = \frac{\text{Voltage across string} \times 100}{\text{No. of insulators} \times V_3}$$

$$= \frac{19.05}{3 \times 7.4} \times 100 = \mathbf{85.8\%\ Ans.}$$

3.28 BUNDLE CONDUCTORS

A bundle conductor is a conductor made up of two or more conductors called the *subconductors,* per phase in close proximity compared with the spacing between phases (Fig. 3.23). The basic difference between a composite conductor and bundle conductor is that the sub-conductors of a bundle conductor are separated from each other by a constant distance varying from 0.2 m to 0.6 m depending upon designed voltage and surrounding conditions throughout the length of the line with the help of spacers whereas the wires of a composite conductor touch each other.

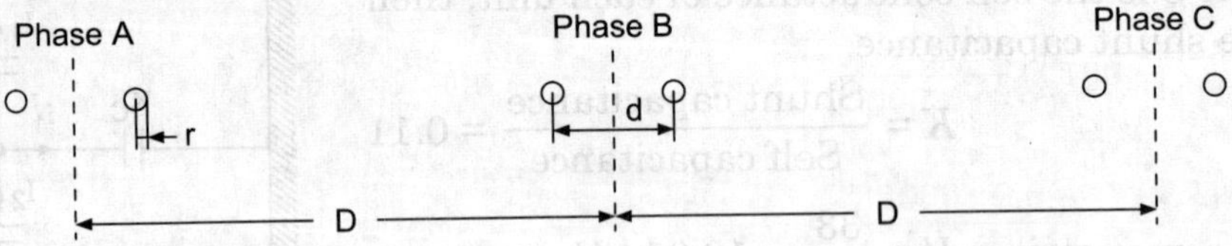

Fig. 3.23 Bundle conductors

Although the bundle conductors are used on EHV transmission lines primarily to reduce corona loss and radio interference.

Advantages of Bundle Conductors

Bundle conductors are made of number of solid wires without insulation. They provide flexibility because solid wires slip over each other while bending.

Advantages

1. **High conductivity:** Higher the conductivity, smaller is the area of cross-section. Thus, it reduces the cost of supporting structure.
2. **Low cost**: Being low cost it can be used for long distances.
3. **Low specific gravity:** Lower the specific gravity, smaller is the weight of conductor which is to be taken by the supporting structure. Thus supporting with smaller strength will be required.
4. **High tensile strength:** The tensile strength used for bundle conductor must bear the high mechanical stresses with this property larger span reduces the number of supports and thus reduces the cost of overhead lines.
5. **High ductility:** The wire used for bundle conductor must have high ductility.

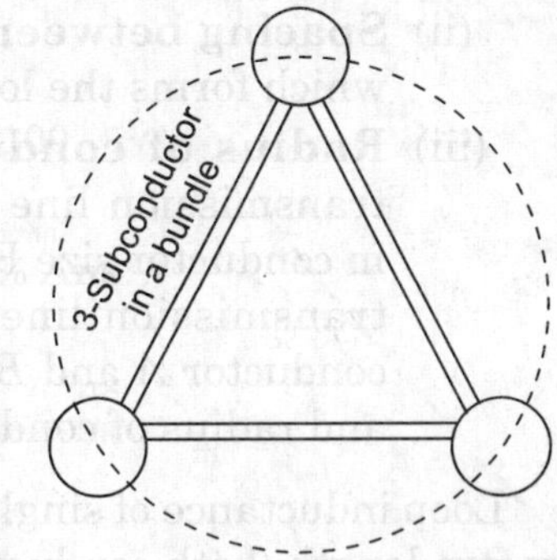

Fig. 3.24

3.29 ELECTRICAL FEATURES OF A LINE

A transmission line possesses three constants of parameters such as resistance, inductance and capacitance. The performance of such a line mainly depends on these parameters. Due to the presence of these parameters, the current, voltage and power factor are different at receiving end and at sending end. Therefore it becomes very important to know the concept of resistance, inductance and capacitance in AC transmission lines and the factors on which these depend.

3.29.1 Concept of Resistance, Inductance and Concept of Transmission Lines

Transmission lines are basically electrical circuits having distributed constants. These constants are resistance, inductance and capacitance these parameters are uniformly distributed along the entire length of line. Performance of transmission line depend upon these constants.

Resistance: In a single phase line the loop resistance is taken as double of resistance either conductor but in three phase system, the resistance per phase is the resistance of either conductor. The resistance '*R*' of a conducting material having length '*l*' cross-section '*a*' and specific resistance *p* is given by $R = p\,\dfrac{l}{a}$.

3.30 INDUCTANCE OF AN TRANSMISSION LINE

A current carrying conductor is surrounded concentric circles of magnetic lines of force. In an ac transmission, when alternating current flows through a conductor, changing flux is set up around it. This flux links with the same conductor as well as with other conductors. Due to these flux linkages the line possesses inductance. Inductance depends upon the following factors:

(i) **Length of the transmission line:** Inductance of line increases with increase in length of transmission lines.

(ii) **Spacing between conductors:** If the distance between two parallel conductors which forms the loop is more then the inductance if the line will be more.

(iii) **Radius of conductor:** The inductance of a transmission line decrease with the increases in conductor size Fig. 3.25 shows a single phase transmission line consisting of two overhead conductor A and B having spacing of 'd' metres and radius of conductor 'r' metre.

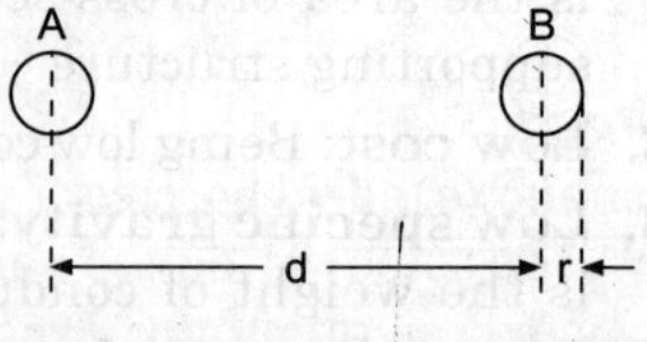

Fig. 3.25 Single phase transmission line with two overhead conductors.

Loop inductance of single phase transmission line per metre length (both conductors)

$$L = (1 + 9.212 \log_{10} \frac{d}{r}) \times 10^{-7} \text{ Henry/metre}$$

Inductance of each conductor per meter length,

$$L = (0.05 + 4.606 \log_{10} \frac{d}{r}) \times 10^{-7} \text{ henry/metre}$$

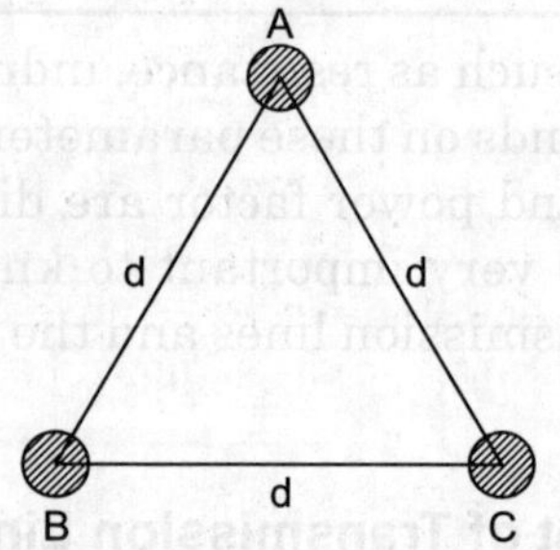

Fig. 3.26 Conductors speed symmetrically

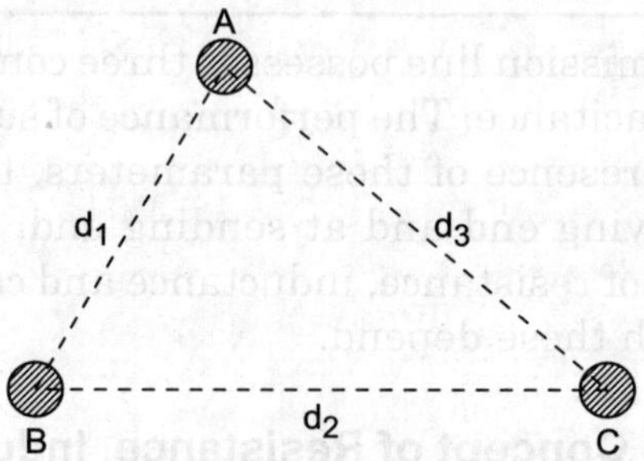

Fig. 3.27 Conductors speed unsymmetrically

However, if the conductors are placed unsymmetrically as shown in Fig. 3.27, then the inductance per conductor is determined from the following expression.

$$L = \left(0.05 + 4.606 \log_{10} \frac{\sqrt[3]{d_1 d_2 d_3}}{r}\right) \times 10^{-7} \text{ henry/metre}$$

3.30.1 Capacitance of a Transmission Line

Any two conductors separated by an insulating medium constitute condenser or a capacitor if a potential difference is maintained between these two conductors. The conductors of an overhead transmission line fulfill these conditions and when an alternating potential difference is applied across this line, then the line draws a leading current; even when supplying no load. This leading current is in quadrature with the applied voltage and it is termed as charging current. The capacitance of the line, frequency of ac supply and transmission voltage determine the strength of charging current.

Capacitance of single phase line is given by the following expression.

$$C = \frac{\pi K_0}{2.303 \log_{10} \frac{d}{r}} \text{ Farad/m}$$

But $$K_0 = \frac{1}{36\pi \times 10^9}$$

or $$C = \frac{0.0121}{\log_{10} \frac{d}{r}} \ \mu F/\text{km}$$

3.30.2 Capacitance of 3-Phase Transmission Line

In a three-phase transmission line, the capacitance of each conductor is considered. If the three conductors are symmetrically spaced then

$$C = \frac{0.0242}{\log_{10} \frac{d}{r}} \ \mu\text{F/km}$$

In case of unsymmetrically spaced conductors,

$$C = \frac{0.0242}{\log_{10} \frac{\sqrt[3]{d_1 d_2 d_3}}{r}} \ \mu\text{F/km}$$

EXAMPLE 3.13 A single phase line has two parallel conductors 3.5 metres apart, diameter of each conductor is 1.5 cm. Calculate the loop inductance in milli henry of the line per km.

Solution: Conductor radius $(r) = \frac{1.5}{2} = 0.75$ cm

Spacing of conductors (d) = 3.5 metres = 350 cm

$$\text{Loop inductance of line per km} = \left(1 + 9.212 \log_{10} \frac{d}{r}\right) \times 10^{-7} \text{ henry/metre}$$

$$= \left(1 + 9.212 \log_{10} \frac{3.50}{0.75}\right) \times 10^{-7} \times 10^3 \times 10 \text{ milli henry}$$

= **(0.1 + 2.46) mH or 2.56 mH Ans.**

EXAMPLE 3.14 Calculate the capacitance of a single phase line, having two parallel conductors placed 2.5 metres apart, diameter of each conductor being 2 cm. The length of line being 100 km.

Solution: Radius of conductor (r) = 1 cm

Spacing of conductor (d) = 2.5 metres = 250 cm

$$\text{Capacitance of single phase line } C = \frac{0.0121}{\log_{10} \frac{d}{r}} \ \mu\text{F/km}$$

$$C = \frac{0.0121 \times 100}{\log_{10} \frac{250}{1}} = \frac{0.0121 \times 10^2}{2.3979} \ \mu\text{F}$$

= **0.504 μF Ans.**

3.30.3 Classification of Transmission Line

The overhead transmission lines can be classified as:

(i) Short transmission line
(ii) Medium transmission line
(iii) Long transmission line.

1. Short Transmission Line

When the length of an overhead transmission line is about 50 to 60 km and the transmission voltage is upto 33 kV, then the transmission line is called *short transmission line.*

In short transmission line the effect of the capacitance is too small as the length of the line and the line voltage is small. So, for short transmission line calculations, the effect of capacitance is ignored and only resistance and inductance of the transmission line are considered.

As discussed above, in a short transmission line, the effect of capacitance is not considered. Figure 3.28 shows the equivalent circuit of a short transmission line. R is the total resistance of the line and X_L is the inductive reactance of the transmission line lumped at one place. If the effect of transformers and alternator is to be taken into consideration, the same can be done by adding their impedances to the impedance of the line. In case of single phase circuits the total loop resistance and inductance is considered but in case of 3-phase circuits resistance and inductance per phase are considered.

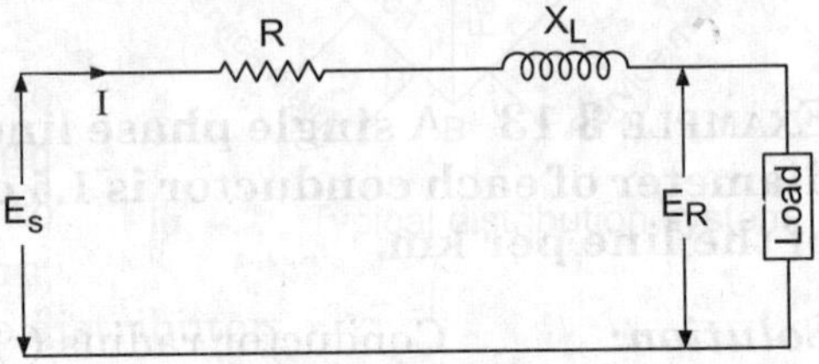

Fig. 3.28 Short transmission line

2. Medium Transmission Line

When the length of an overhead transmission line is about 80 to 150 km and the transmission voltage is upto 132 kV, it is considered as *medium transmission line.* In this line the effect of capacitance will be taken into account. The capacitance of the line is uniformly distributed over the entire length of transmission line but to simplify the calculations, in medium transmission lines, the capacitance effect is considered as lumped either at both receiving and sending ends or at the centre of the transmission line.

3. Long Transmission Line

When the length of transmission line is more than 150 km and line voltage is very high, then the transmission line is considered as *long transmission line.* In this case the capacitance effect can not be considered as lumped, but it is considered as distributed and for the solution of these lines rigorous methods of calculations are used.

3.30.4 Voltage Regulation of a Transmission Line

The rise in voltage at receiving end, when full load is thrown off and the sending end voltage remaining the same is called voltage regulation. It is expressed as a percentage of receiving end voltage. When whole of the load is thrown off i.e., when the line is supplying no load the receiving end voltage becomes equal to the sending end voltage mathematically.

$$\% \text{ Regulation} = \frac{V_S - V_R}{V_S} \times 100$$

where V_S = Sending end voltage

V_R = Receiving end voltage

It is desirable that regulation of a transmission line should be low.

3.30.5 Expression for Voltage Regulation

Figure 3.29(a) shows the equivalent circuit of a short transmission line. The load is drawing. I ampere current a lagging power factor $\cos \phi_R$.

V_R and V_S are receiving end and sending end voltage $\cos \phi_s$ may be sending end power factor.

R is the loop resistance of the line.

X_L is the loop reactance of the line.

Figure 3.29(b) shows the vector diagram. Current is taken as a reference vector.

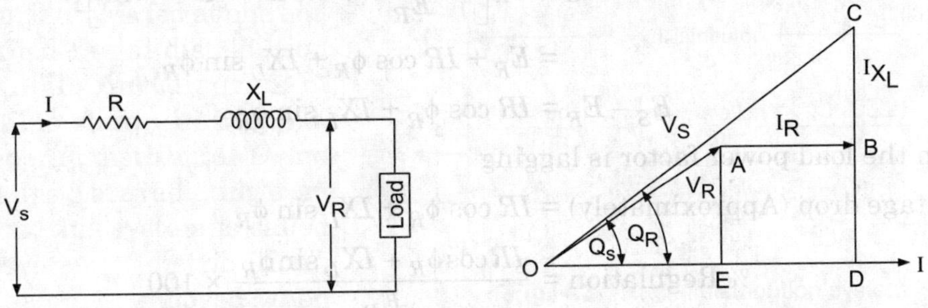

(a) Circuit diagram (b) Vector diagram

Fig. 3.29

OA represents the receiving end voltage V_R, leading the current vector by an angle ϕ_R. AB represents the voltage drop in the resistance R of line. It is in phase with current vector BC represents the voltage drop IX_L in the inductance X_L of line. It leads the current vector by 90°. OC represents the sending end voltage V_S leading the current vector by an angle ϕ_s.

Extend CB to cut reference line at D. Draw AE on the reference line OD from Fig. 3.29(*b*)

$$OC^2 = (CD)^2 + (OD)^2 = (CB + BD)^2 + (OD + ED)^2$$

$$BD = AE = E_R \sin \phi_R$$

$$OE = E_R \cos \phi_R$$

$$ED = AB = IR$$

$$E_S^2 = (IX_L + E_R \sin \phi_R)^2 + (E_R \cos \phi_R + IR)^2$$

$$E_S^2 = (I^2 X_L^2 + E_R^2 \sin^2 \phi_R + 2IX_L E_R \sin \phi_R + I^2 R^2 + E_R^2 \cos^2 \phi_R + 2IR \cos \phi_R)$$

$$= [E_R^2 (\cos^2 \phi_R + \sin^2 \phi_R) + 2E_R \text{I} (R \cos\phi_R + X_L \sin \phi_R) + I^2 (R^2 + X_L^2)]$$

or $$E_S^2 = E_R^2 + 2E_R I (R \cos \phi_R + X_L \sin \phi_R) + I^2 (R^2 + X_L^2)]$$

or $$E_S = E_R\left[1+2\frac{IR\cos\phi_R}{E_R}+2\frac{IX_L\sin\phi_R}{E_R}+\frac{I^2(R^2+X_L^2)}{E_R}\right]^{1/2} \quad \text{...(i)}$$

The voltage drops I_R and IX_L are small, their squares will be still smaller, so the last term of equation (1) can be neglected.

So approximately

$$E_S = E_R\left[1+2\frac{IR\cos\phi_R}{E_R}+2\frac{IX_L\sin\phi_R}{E_R}\right]^{1/2}$$

$$= E_R\left[1+2\frac{I}{E_R}\{R\cos\phi_R+X_L\sin\phi_R\}\right]^{1/2}$$

Taking Binomial approximation

$$E_S = E_R\left[1+\frac{I}{E_R}(R\cos\phi_R+X_L\sin\phi_R\}\right]$$

$$= E_R + IR \cos \phi_R + IX_L \sin \phi_R$$

or $$E_S - E_R = IR \cos \phi_R + IX_L \sin \phi_R$$

So when the load power factor is lagging

$$\text{Voltage drop (Approximately)} = IR \cos \phi_R + IX_L \sin \phi_R \quad \text{...(2)}$$

$$\%\ \text{Regulation} = \frac{IR\cos\phi_R + IX_L\sin\phi_R}{E_R} \times 100$$

$$\text{Power delivered} = E_R I \cos \phi_R$$

$$\text{In this case line losses} = 2I^2R$$

$$\text{Power sent out} = E_R I \cos \phi_R + 2I^2R$$

Efficiency of transmission line

$$\eta_R = \frac{E_R IR\cos\phi_R}{E_S I_S\cos\phi_R + 2I^2R}$$

When Load Power Factor is Leading

In this case the vector diagram has been represented in Fig. 3.30. In this case also current vector has been taken as reference.

The receiving end voltage V_R lags behind the current vector by angle ϕ_R and has been represented by vector OA. The voltage drop in line resistance has been represented by vector AB in phase with current vector. The voltage drop in line reactance leads the current vector by 90° and has been represented by vector BC.

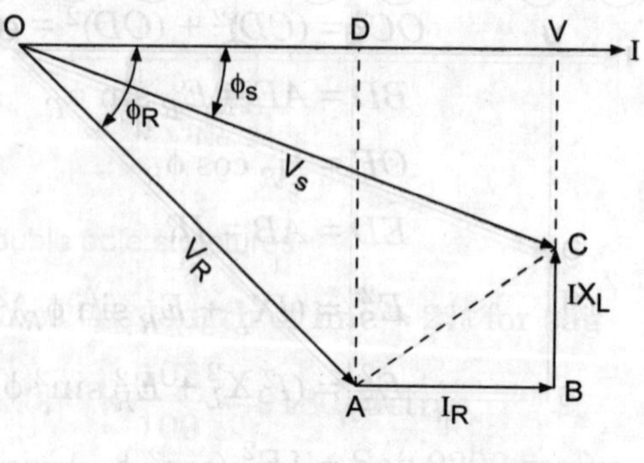

Fig. 3.30 Leading PF

OC represents the sending end voltage E_S lagging behind current vector by ϕ_R.

Extend the line BC to cut reference line at V and draw AD perpendicular on the reference line.

From Fig. 3.27.

$$OC^2 = OV^2 + VC^2 = (OD + DE)^2 + (BE - BC)^2$$

But $\quad BE = AD$ and $DE = AB$

So $\quad OC^2 = (OD + AB)^2 + (AD - BC)^2$

$$OD = V_R \cos \phi_r$$

$$AD = V_R \sin \phi_r$$

$$\therefore \quad V_S^2 = [V_R \cos \phi_r + IR]^2 + [V_R \sin \phi_r - IX_L]^2 = V_R^2\left[\left(\cos \phi_R + \frac{IR}{V_R}\right)^2 + \left(\sin \phi_R - \frac{IX_L}{V_R}\right)^2\right]$$

$$V_S^2 = V_R^2\left[\cos^2 \phi_R + \sin^2 \phi_R + 2\frac{IR}{E_R}\cos\phi_R - 2\frac{IX_L}{E_R}\sin\phi_r + \frac{I^2}{V_R^2}(R^2 + X_L)^2\right] \quad \text{...(3)}$$

As discussed earlier the last term can be neglected as the voltage drops are too small as compared to E_R, Equation (3) can be written as

$$V_S^2 = V_R^2\left[1 + 2\frac{I_R}{V_R}\cos\phi_R - 2\frac{IX_L}{V_R}\sin\phi_R\right]$$

or

$$V_S = V_R\left[1 + 2\frac{I}{V_R}(R\cos\phi_R - IX_L\sin\phi_R)\right]^{1/2}$$

or Approximately

$$V_S = V_R\left[1 - \frac{IR\cos\phi_R}{V_R} - \frac{IX_L\sin\phi_R}{V_R}\right]$$

or

$$V_S = V_R + IR\cos\phi_R - IX_L\sin\phi_R$$

or $\quad$ Voltage drop $(V_S - V_R) = IR\cos\phi_r - IX_L\sin\phi_r$ $\quad$ ...(4)

Hence generalizing the expansion for voltage drop from equation (2) and (4).

$$\text{Voltage drop} = IR\cos\phi_R \pm IX_L\sin\phi_R$$

Plus sign is to be used for lagging power factor and minus sign is to be used for leading power factor.

$$\%\ \text{Regulation (for leading power factor)} = \frac{IR\cos\phi_R - IX_L\sin\phi_R}{V_R} \times 100$$

The expression for efficiency of transmission remains the same as in lagging p.f.

3.30.6 Efficiency of a Transmission Line

The ratio of receiving end power to the sending end power of a transmission line is called the transmission efficiency.

Mathematically,

$$\text{Transmission efficiency, } \eta = \frac{\text{Receiving end power}}{\text{Sending end power}} \times 100$$

$$= \frac{V_R I \cos \phi_R}{V_S I \cos \phi_S} \times 100$$

where V_R = Receiving end voltage (phase)

I = Current flowing through each conductor

$\cos \phi_R$ = Receiving power factor

V_S = Sending end voltage (phase)

$\cos \phi_S$ = Sending end power factor

EXAMPLE 3.15 A single phase transmission line has a loop resistance of 0.2 Ω and loop inductive reactance of 0.4 Ω. Find the voltage at the sending end, if a load of 550 kW at 11 kV and unity power factor is delivered by this transmission line.

Solution: Loop resistance (go and return, i.e., for both conductors)

$$R = 0.2\,\Omega$$

$$X_L = 0.4\,\Omega$$

$$\text{Receiving end voltage } E_R = 11 \text{ kV}$$

$$\text{Load current} = \frac{550 \times 1000}{11 \times 1000 \times 1} = 50 \text{ amps}$$

$$\cos \phi_R = 1$$

∴ $$\sin \phi_R = \text{zero}$$

Voltage at sending end

$$E_S^2 = (E_R \cos \phi_R + IR)^2 + (E_R \sin \phi_R + IX_L)^2$$

$$= (11000 + 50 \times 0.2)^2 + (0 + 50 \times 0.4)^2$$

$$= (11000 + 10)^2 + (20)^2$$

or $$E_S = \sqrt{(11010)^2 + (20)^2}$$

$$= \mathbf{11015 \text{ volts or } 11.015 \text{ kV Ans.}}$$

EXAMPLE 3.16 A short line of 3-phase circuit delivers a balanced load of 200 amperes at 0.8 p.f. lagging. The impedance per conductor is (0.75 + *j* 1) ohm. Calculate the sending end voltage necessary to maintain the efficiency of transmission at 91 percent.

Solution: Resistance per conductor = 0.75 Ω

Load current = 200 amp.

$$\cos \phi_R = 0.8$$

Let the receiving end voltage/phase may be E_R (volts)

$$\text{Load received} = 3E_R I \cos \phi_R = 3E_R \times 200 \times 0.8 = 480E_R \text{ (watts)}$$

Total losses in the 3-phase line = $3I^2R = 3 \times 200 \times 200 \times 0.75 = 90000$ watts

Sending end power = $(480E_R + 90000)$ watts

Transmission efficiency = 91%

So
$$\frac{91}{100} = \frac{480E_R}{480E_R + 90000}$$

$$91\,(480E_R + 90000) = 48000E_R$$

or
$$48000E_R - 480 \times 91E_R = 91 \times 90000$$

or
$$48000E_R - 43680E_R = 8190000$$

or
$$4320E_R = 8190000$$

or
$$E_R = 1896 \text{ volts}$$

Voltage drop per phase = $IR \cos\phi + IX_L \sin\phi = 200\,[0.75 \times 0.8 + 1 \times 0.6]$

$= 200\,[0.6 + 0.6] = 240$ volts

Phase $E_S = E_R$ + voltage drop = 1896 + 240 = 2136 volts

Sending end line voltage = $\sqrt{3} \times (2136)$ = **3700 volts Ans.**

EXAMPLE 3.17 A single phase 11 kV line with a length of 15 km is to transmit 500 kVA. The inductive reactance of the line is 0.5 ohm per km and the resistance 0.3 ohm per km. Calculate the efficiency and regulation for:

(i) Unity power factor

(ii) Power factor 0.8 lagging

(iii) Power factor 0.8 leading. What conclusion you draw from the result?

Solution: Receiving end voltage E_R = 11000 volts

Loop resistance of line $R = 0.3 \times 15 = 4.5\ \Omega$

Loop inductive reactance of line $X_L = 0.5 \times 15 = 7.5\ \Omega$

$$\text{Load current} = \frac{P(VA)}{V} = \frac{500000}{11000} = 45.5 \text{ amperes}$$

(i) When Power Factor is one

$\cos\phi = 1$

$\sin\phi = 0$

Voltage drop = $IR \cos\phi + IX_L \sin\phi$

$= 45.5 \times 4.5 \times 1 + 45.5 \times 7.5 \times 0 = 204.75$ volts

$$\text{Voltage regulation} = \frac{\text{Voltage drop}}{E_R} \times 100 = \frac{204.75}{11000} \times 100$$

Voltage regulation = **1.86% Ans.**

Power factor $\cos\phi = 1$

Power received = $500 \times 1 = 500$ kW

Line losses = $I^2 R = (45.5)^2 \times 4.5 = 9.3$ kW

$$\text{Power sent} = \text{Power received} + \text{line losses}$$
$$= 500 + 9.3 = 509.3 \text{ kW}$$

$$\text{Transmission efficiency} = \frac{\text{Power received}}{\text{Power sent}} \times 100$$
$$= \frac{500}{509.3} \times 100 = \mathbf{98\%\ Ans.}$$

(ii) When Power Factor is 0.8 lagging

$$\cos \phi = 0.8; \sin \phi = 0.6$$
$$\text{Voltage drop} = IR \cos \phi + IX \sin \phi$$
$$= 45.5 \times 4.5 \times 0.8 + 45.5 \times 7.5 \times 0.6$$
$$= 163.800 + 204.75 = 368.55 \text{ volts}$$
$$\text{Voltage regulation} = \frac{368.55}{11000} \times 100 = 3.3\%$$

Transmission efficiency

$$\text{Power received} = 500 \times 0.8 = 400 \text{ kW}$$
$$\text{Line losses} = I^2 R = (45.5)^2 \times 4.5 = 9.3 \text{ kW}$$
$$\text{Power sent} = 400 + 9.3 = 409.3 \text{ kW}$$
$$\text{Transmission efficiency} = \frac{400}{409.3} \times 100$$
$$= \mathbf{97.6\%\ Ans.}$$

(iii) When Power Factor is 0.8 leading

$$\cos \phi = 0.8; \sin \phi = 0.6$$
$$\text{Voltage drop} = IR \cos \phi - IX \sin \phi$$
$$= 45.5 \times 4.5 \times 0.8 - 45.5 \times 7.5 \times 0.6$$
$$= 163.8 \times 205.8 = -42 \text{ volts}$$

Voltage at sending end is less than voltage at receiving end

$$\text{Voltage regulation} = \frac{-42}{11000} \times 100$$
$$= \mathbf{0.382\%\ (-ve)\ Ans.}$$

Transmission efficiency remains the same as in *(ii)*.

Conclusion: When power factor increases the voltage regulation decreases.

EXAMPLE 3.18 A three-phase 50 Hz transmission line 30 km long has the following line constants:

Resistance per km per conductor = 0.2 Ω

Inductance per km per conductor 1.8 mH.

Load at receiving end is 3000 kVA at 33 kV. Find out the p.f. of load if sending end voltage is also 33 kV.

Solution: Total resistance per conductor = $0.2 \times 30.6\ \Omega$

$$\text{Total inductance per conductor} = 2 \times 3.14 \times 50 \times 1.8 \times 10^{-3} \times 10 = 10.96\ \Omega$$

$$\text{Load} = 3000\ \text{kVA}$$

$$\text{Load current} = \frac{3000}{\sqrt{3} \times 33} = 52.5\ \text{amperes}$$

Receiving end voltage and sending end voltage are equal and each is equal to 33 kV line voltage or 19.052 kV phase voltage. So the power factor is such that the voltage drop in the line is zero.

$$\text{Voltage drop} = IR \cos\phi \pm IX \sin\phi$$

or
$$IR \cos\phi = IX \sin\phi$$

or
$$R \cos\phi = X \sin\phi$$

or
$$\tan\phi = \frac{R}{X} = \frac{6}{16.96} = 0.3538$$

Moreover this condition is possible when ($IX \sin\phi$) is –ve; viz. the power factor should be leading.

$$\text{Leading power factor of load} = \cos(\tan^{-1} 0.3538)$$

$$= \mathbf{0.9424\ leading\ Ans.}$$

EXAMPLE 3.19 An overhead single phase line delivers 1100 kW at 33 kV at 0.9 p.f, lagging. The total resistance of the line is 10 Ω and total inductive reactance is 15 Ω. Determine: (i) Regulation, (ii) Power factor, (iii) Efficiency of the line.

Solution: Power to be transmitted,

$$P = 1100\ \text{kW}$$

$$= 1100 \times 10^3\text{W}$$

$$\text{Receiving end voltage, } V_R = 33\ \text{kV} = 33 \times 10^3\text{V}$$

$$\text{Load power factor, } \cos\phi_R = 0.8\ \text{lagging}$$

$$\text{Resistance of the line, } R = 10\ \Omega$$

$$\text{Inductive reactance of the line, } X_L = 15\ \Omega$$

$$\text{Line current, } I = \frac{P}{V_R \cos\phi_R} = \frac{1100 \times 10^3}{33 \times 10^3 \times 0.8} = 41.67\text{A}$$

$$\text{Load p.f. } \cos\phi_R = 0.8\ \sin\phi_R, = \sin\cos^{-1} 0.8 = 0.6$$

$$\text{Sending end voltage } V_S = V_R + I_R \cos\phi_R + IX_L \sin\phi_R$$

$$= 33000 + 41.67 \times 10 \times 0.8 + 41.67 \times 15 \times 0.6$$

$$= 33708.33V$$

$$\%\text{Regulation} = \frac{V_S - V_R}{V_S} \times 100 = \frac{33708.33 - 33000}{33000} \times 100$$

$$= \mathbf{2.146\%\ Ans.}$$

$$\text{Sending end power factor, } \cos\phi_S = \frac{V_R \cos\phi_R + I_R}{V_S} = \frac{33000 \times 0.8 + 41.67 \times 10}{33000.33}$$

$$= 0.7956 \text{ lagging } \textbf{Ans.}$$

$$\text{Losses in the line} = I^2R = (41.67)^2 \times 10 = 17361\text{W} = 17.631 \text{ kW}$$

$$\text{Receiving end power} = 1100 \text{ kW}$$

$$\text{Sending end power} = \text{Receiving end power} + \text{losses in the line}$$

$$= 1100 + 17.361 = 1117.361 \text{ kW}$$

$$\text{Efficiency of the line, } \eta = \frac{\text{Receiving end power}}{\text{Sending end power}} \times 100$$

$$= \frac{1100}{1117.361} \times 100 = \mathbf{98.45 \ Ans.}$$

3.31 CONCEPT OF CORONA

The phenomenon of hissing noise with violet glow and production of ozone gas (O_3) in an overhead transmission lines is known as corona.

When ac is applied across two line conductors whose spacing is large as compared to their diameter and the potential difference between the conductors is increased, the air around the conductors become conducting and a stage is reached when flash occurs between the conductors along with hissing noise and production of ozone gas.

Factors Affecting Corona

1. Irregular shape conductors. If the diameter, shape (stranded or smooth) and surface in dirty or clean of conductor, the corona is considerably effected i.e., give rise to more corona.
2. Corona will be effected by the physical state of the atmosphere. In stormy weather, corona occurs at much less voltage as compared fair weather.
3. If the spacing between the conductor is more corona effect is reduced.
4. If the potential difference is more, the corona effect is increased.

Advantages of Corona

1. Due to the formation of corona, the air surrounding the conductor become conducting hence virtual diameter of conductor increases.
2. Since diameter of conductor increases for same current thus reduces the probability of flash over.
3. It is reduces the effect of transient produced by lighting.

Disadvantages of Corona

1. It results in loss of energy which is dissipated in the form of heat, light, sound and chemical action.
2. Corona produces ozone gas which is harmful.
3. The current drawn by the line due to corona loss is non-sinusoidal and non-sinusoidal voltage drop occurs in the line. Due to this it increases the interference to nearby communication lines.

Methods to Reduce Corona

1. Corona effect can be reduced by increasing the conductor size.
2. Corona effect can be reduced by increasing the spacing between conductors.
3. Corona effect can also be reduced by using conductors made of regular shape.

3.32 HVDC TRANSMISSION LINES

A high voltage, direct current HVDC electric power transmission system uses direct current for bulk transmission of electric power over a long distances by overhead transmission lines. It is also used to interconnect separate power systems, where alternating current connections cannot be used.

In an HVDC system, electric power is taken from one point in a three-phase AC network, converted to DC in a converter station. Typically an HVDC transmission has rated power of more than 100 MW. HVDC system may only need a few skilled staff for operation and maintenance. The cost of an HVDC transmission depends on many factors, such as power capacity to be transmitted, environmental conditions and other safety.

3.33 SALIENT FEATURES

3.33.1 Advantages of HVDC Transmission

1. **Cheaper in cost:** Cost of transmission is less, since only two conductors are used for transmission.
2. **Low transmission losses:** Due to high transmission voltage, for the same power current is less. So I^2R loss is very less.
3. **No Skin Effect:** Because of DC transmission, there is no skin effect. So thin conductors can be used. In case of HVDC, the thick conductors must be used to climate skin effect.
4. **Tower size and cost:** The phase to phase clearness and phase to ground clearance are smaller for DC transmission as compared to equivalent AC transmission line for same power and distance.
5. **Voltage regulation:** There is no inductance, hence the voltage drop due to inductive reactance does not exist in dc transmission lines. Thus voltage regulation is better in case of dc transmission.
6. **Installation cost:** Installation cost is less. Due to only two conductors and smaller towers required for HVDC.
7. **Improve transient stability:** HVDC uses electronic converters. So protection, fault clearance can be faster than HVAC. Therefore DC transmission system have improved transient stability.
8. **Greater reliability:** A two conductor dc line is more reliable than 3-wire-3 phase ac line because it can be used with ground return.
9. **Dielectric loss:** HVDC transmission does not have any dielectric loss heating problem in the insulation of the conductor.
10. **Less interference:** HVDC has minimum audible noise as well as minimum radio, TV interference.
11. **Ground return:** Ground return can be used as a return conductor in case of dc system.

3.33.2 Disadvantages of HVDC Transmission

1. **Costly terminal equipment:** High cost of converting and inverting equipments are required for HVDC transmission. So it is uneconomical for low power supply for short distances.
2. **More maintenance of line insulators:** Maintenance of insulators in HVDC transmission line is more.
3. **Complex converter control:** Converter control is quite complex.
4. **Voltage regulation:** Voltage regulation is not easier in case of dc and hence it can be done on ac side of the system.

3.34 DIFFERENCE BETWEEN HVAC AND HVDC TRANSMISSION

1. DC transmission requires fewer conductors than AC transmission. Moreover two conductors per DC circuit where as three conductors per phase AC circuit.
2. Skin effect is absent in DC. Also, corona losses are lower in the case of DC. However an HVDC line has considerably lower losses compared to HVAC over longer distances.
3. Interference with nearby communication lines is lesser in case of HVDC overhead line than that for an HVAC line.
4. Voltage control in HVAC is difficult for long lines due to series and shunt capacitance.
5. Short circuit current level in longer distance HVAC at receiving system is high. An HVDC system does not contribute to the short circuit current of the interconnected. AC system.

3.35 DESCRIPTION OF SYSTEM TO BLOCK DIAGRAM OF HVDC TRANSMISSION LINES

The block diagram of HVDC transmission system is shown below:

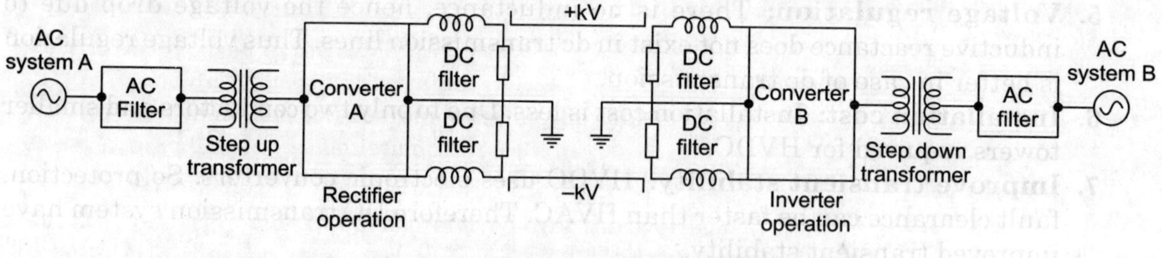

Fig. 3.31 Block diagram of HVDC transmission line

1. As shown two AC systems *A* and *B* are interconnected by DC line.
2. From the system — A three phase AC supply is first passed through a AC filter.
3. The AC filters reduced the current harmonic generated by the converters from entering into the AC systems.
4. Then the supply stepped up through the step-up transformer.

5. This gives high AC voltage which is ready for transmission.
6. The high voltage AC is converted into high voltage DC by the converters that are connected in series.

If power flows from system *A* to *B*, then converter-*A* operates as rectifier and converter-*B* operates as an inverter.

If the power flows in reverse manner i.e., *B* to *A*, then converter-*B* acts as a rectifier and converter-*A* acts as an inverter.

The DC output of the converter is filtered by DC filters and smoothing inductors to eliminate the DC ripples. Thus ripple free high voltage DC is obtained this high voltage DC is then transmitted over the DC transmission lines.

The DC line has +kV and –kV with respect to ground. This is done to balance the voltage of two transmission lines with respect to earth.

At the receiving station, the high voltage dc is again filtered and passed to converter *B* which act as an inverters. This inverter output is stepped down, passed through AC filters. Thus three phase supply is obtained at the receiving end.

3.36 GROUND RETURN IN HVDC

Most dc transmission lines use a return path through the ground or sea water or both, either continuously or for a short time. Such return paths are called ground returns. Most of the dc transmission lines use ground return path for reason of economy and reliability. The ground path has a very low resistance and low power loss.

For the same length of transmission the resistance offered by the ground in case of dc is much less than that in case of ac transmission. This is because the direct current in the earth, unlike alternating current does not allow closely the router of the line but spreads over a large cross-sectional area in both depth and width. The resistance of the ground return path in case of dc is independent of length of the lines.

There are two main advantages of using ground return the first advantage is that a dc line can be built in two stages – the line can be built as a monopolar line with ground return in first stage and may be converted into a bipolar line on later stage when load requirement increases.

Ground return have problems also. The main problems are designing of ground electrodes for low resistance and low cost of installation and maintenance and location etc.

SUMMARY

1. **Power system:** The generation, transmission and distribution of electric power is called power system.
2. **Advantages of high voltage for transmission**
   (i) Efficiency is increased
   (ii) Cost of conductor is less
   (iii) Percentage line voltage drop is reduced.
3. **Comparison between dc and ac system for transmission**
   (i) It requires only two conductor
   (ii) No inductance, capacitance and phase displacement.

(iii) No skin effect
(iv) A dc line has less corona loss
(v) Less interference with communication lines
(vi) Better voltage regulation.

4. Various systems of transmission of electric power

(a) DC system
 (i) DC two wire
 (ii) DC two wire with mid-point earthed
 (iii) DC three wire system.
(b) Single phase ac system
 (i) Single phase ac system.
 (ii) Single phase two wire with mid-point earthed
 (iii) Single phase three-wire
(c) Two phase ac system
 (i) Two phase four wire
 (ii) Two phase three wire
(d) Three phase ac system
 (i) Three phase three wire
 (ii) Three phase four wire

5. Kelvin's law: According to Kelvin's law the most economical x-section of a conductor is that which makes the annual cost of electrical energy wasted in the conductor equal to the annual cost of interest and depreciation of capital cost of the conductor.

6. Types of line support
(i) Wooden poles
(ii) Steel poles
(iii) RCC poles, lattice steel towers

7. Conductor materials: Copper, aluminimum, steel, galvanized steel conductors.

8. Line insulator are
(i) Pin type
(ii) Suspension type insulators
(iii) Strain type insulators
(iv) Shackle type insulators
(v) Egg insulators

9. Materials for insulators
(i) Porcelain
(ii) Glass
(iii) Steatite

10. Causes of failure of insulators
(i) Cracking insulators
(ii) Porosity of materials
(iii) Improper vitrification
(iv) Flash over
(v) Short circuits
(vi) Deposition of dust.

11. Factors affecting sag

(i) Weight of the conductor
(ii) Length of the conductor
(iii) Working tensile strength
(iv) Temperature

12. Sag: Sag in overhead transmission line conductor refers to the difference in level between the point of support and the lowest point on the conductor. It is also called dip.

$$S = \frac{WL^2}{8T}$$

where W = weight of conductor in kg/m
L = length of span
T = working tensile strength.

13. String efficiency $= \frac{\text{Flash-over voltage of the string}}{n \times \text{Flash-over voltage of one unit}} \times 100$

$$\eta_s = \frac{V}{nv} \times 100$$

where n = number of discs in string
V = voltage across string
v = voltage across disc nearest to conductor

14. Inductance of the line depends upon

(i) Length of transmission line
(ii) Spacing between conductors
(iii) Radius of conductor

15. Capacitance of transmission line

$$C = \frac{0.0121}{\log_{10}\frac{d}{r}}\ \mu\text{F/km}$$

16. Resistance of transmission line

$$R = \rho\frac{l}{a}$$

17. Skin effect: When a conductor is carrying steady direct current, the current is uniformly distributed over the whole of the cross-section of the conductor. But an alternating current flowing through the conductor does not distribute uniformly, rather it has the tendency to concentrate near the surface of the conductor as shown in Fig. 3.32. This is known as *skin effect*. *The tendency of alternating current to concentrate near the surface of the conductor is known as skin effect.*

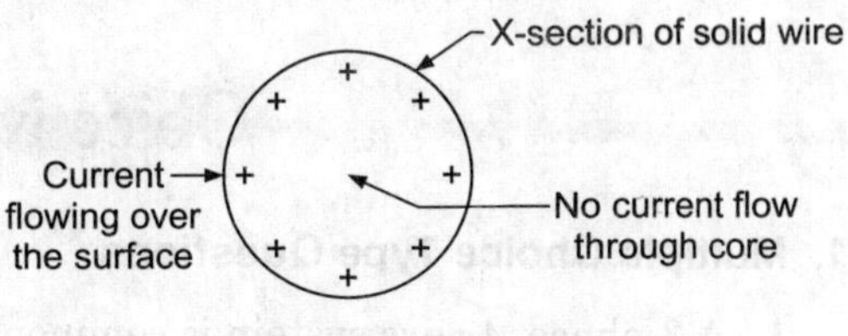

Fig. 3.32 Skin effect

As a result of skin effect, the resistance of the conductor is slightly increased when carrying an alternating current. The skin effect depends upon the following factors:

(i) Nature of material
(ii) Diameter of wire–increase with diameter of wire.

(iii) Shape of wire–less for stranded conductor than solid conductor.
(iv) Frequency–increase with increase in frequency.

18. **Transposition of conductors:** The unbalancing effect on account of irregular spacing of conductors can be avoided by changing the position of the conductors at regular distances. This is called transposition of conductors.

19. **Classification of transmission lines**
(i) Short transmission lines (50 to 60 km)
(ii) Medium transmission lines (80 to 150 km)
(iii) Long transmission lines (above 150 km)

20. **Regulation of transmission line**

$$\% \text{ Regulation} = \frac{V_S - V_R}{V_S} \times 100$$

where V_S = Sending end voltage/phase
V_S = Receiving end voltage/phase

21. **Efficiency of a transmission line**

$$\text{Transmission efficiency, } \eta = \frac{\text{Receiving end power}}{\text{Sending end power}} \times 100$$

22. **Corona:** The phenomenon of hissing noise with violet glow and production of ozone gas in an overhead transmission line is known as corona.

23. **Factors affecting corona**
(i) Atmosphere
(ii) Size and shape of conductor
(iii) Spacing between conductors
(iv) Line voltage

24. **Advantage of corona**
(i) Reduces electrostatic stresses between the conductors
(ii) Reduces effects of transients produced by lightning.

Disadvantages of corona
(i) Causes loss of energy
(ii) Due to ozone gas reaction with conductor causing correction
(iii) The current drawn by the line due to corona loss in non-sinusoidal causes interfere with the neighbouring communication lines.

Objective Type Questions

1. Multiple Choice Type Questions

1. A 3-phase, 4 wire system is commonly used for
(a) Primary distribution (b) Secondary distribution
(c) Primary transmission

2. The highest transmission voltage in India is
(a) 750 kV (b) 400 kV
(c) 132 kV

3. The electric power can be transmitted by
   (a) Overhead system (b) Underground system
   (c) Either (a) or (b) (d) None of the above
4. Wooden poles are used as line supports for voltage upto
   (a) 11 kV (b) 22 kV
   (c) 66 kV
5. RCC poles usually have the span of
   (a) 250–400 m (b) 80–150 m
   (c) 50–80 m
6. In transmission line cross-arms are made of
   (a) aluminium (b) copper
   (c) RCC (d) steel
7. In overhead lines, we generally use
   (a) Copper conductors (b) ACSR conductors
   (c) None of the above
8. In transmission line sag depends upon
   (a) conductor material (b) length of span
   (c) the tension in conductor (d) all of the above
9. HV transmission line uses
   (a) pin type insulators (b) suspension type insulators
   (c) both (a) and (b)
10. Strain type insulators are used
    (a) at dead ends (b) on straight curve
    (c) any of (a) and (b)
11. Corona is accompanied by
    (a) violet visible discharge (b) hissing sound
    (c) radio interference (d) all of the above
12. The usual generation voltage in India is:
    (a) 11 kV (b) 20 kV
    (c) 66 kV (d) 400 kV
13. The economic size of the conductor is determined by
    (a) Ohm's law (b) Kirchhoffs law
    (c) Kelvin's law (d) Faradays law.
14. The ac resistance of conductor is more than dc resistance due to.
    (a) Skin effect (b) Proximity effect
    (c) Both (a) and (b) (d) None of the above
15. Efficiency of a transmission line.
    (a) Increase with the increase
    (b) Is independent of load p.f.
    (c) Increase with the decrees in load p.f.
    (d) Decreases with the increase in load p.f.

16. What kind of insulator will be used if the direction of the transmission line is changed.
(a) pin-type insulator
(b) strain insulator
(c) suspension insulator
(d) all of the above

17. If the height of the transmission tower is decreased, the induction of the line
(a) Decrease
(b) Increase
(c) Increase proportionately
(d) Remain same

ANSWERS

1. (b)	**2.** (b)	**3.** (c)	**4.** (b)	**5.** (b)	**6.** (c)	**7.** (b)	**8.** (d)	**9.** (c)
10. (c)	**11.** (d)	**12.** (a)	**13.** (c)	**14.** (c)	**15.** (a)	**16.** (b)	**17.** (d)	

2. Fill in the Blanks

1. Generation of electrical energy is usually at __________ voltage.
2. HVDC transmission stands for __________
3. The cost of aluminium is __________ than that of copper.
4. Wooden poles are used for __________
5. RCC pole are used in __________ area.
6. Skin effect is __________ in DC supply than AC supply.
7. Corona effect is __________ in stranded conductors as compare to solid conductor.
8. Shacle insulators are used on __________ lines.
9. Expand ACSR __________
10. The egg insulator is used in the __________ wire.
11. The phenomenon of hissing and production of ozone in high tension line is called __________
12. The corona can be reduced by __________ space between lines.
13. The skin effect depends upon __________
14. The highest transmission voltage in India is __________
15. Transmission is done by phase system.

ANSWERS

1. 11 kV **2.** high voltage direct current transmission **3.** less
4. distribution **5.** urban **6.** less **7.** more **8.** low voltage
9. aluminium cored steel reinforcement **10.** stay **11.** corona
12. increasing **13.**frequency **14.** 400 kV **15.** three

3. True-False Type Questions

1. Transmission is done by single phase system.
2. Electric power is used at 220 V in our country.
3. Step up sub-stations are installed near the generating stations.
4. In India overhead system is adopted for transmission of electric power.
5. The skin effect is less for stranded conductor than the solid conductor.
6. AC resistance is more than DC resistance.
7. The economic size of conductor is determined by Kelvins law.

8. If the length of the transmission is increase, their capacitances will increase.
9. Corona loss can be minimized if the size of conductor is increased.
10. Cross-arms are used on pole to provide support to the insulator.
11. DC transmission is inferier to ac transmission.
12. The skin effect is independent of the supply frequency.
13. In short transmission lines, the effect of inductance and capacitance are neglected.
14. There is no skin effect in dc transmission line.
15. Corona loss in transmission lines is more in winter season than the summer.

ANSWERS

1. (F)	2. (T)	3. (T)	4. (T)	5. (T)	6. (T)	7. (T)	8. (T)	9. (T)
10. (T)	11. (F)	12. (F)	13. (F)	14. (T)	15. (T)			

SHORT ANSWER TYPE QUESTIONS

Q.1 What is power system?

Ans. The generation transmission and distribution of electric power constitute a power system.

Q.2 Define the term transmission.

Ans. The system by which bulk power is delivered from power station to load centers is called transmission.

Q.3 What are the various components of overhead lines?

Ans. The main components of overhead lines are tower cross-arm, conductors, guys and stays, lighting arresters, earth wire, V-guards, guard wires, phase plates, bird guards, danger plates, anti-climbing devices, vibration dampers etc.

Q.4 What is the function of line support?

Ans. The function of a line support is to support the line conductors and keep them at a safe distance from the ground.

Q.5 What are the main requirements of line supports?

Ans. The main requirements of line supports are high mechanical strength, lighter in weight, low maintenance cost, longer life, cheaper in cost, good appearance, easy accessibility for painting and erection of line conductors and immune to damage from lightning and fire.

Q.6 What are four types of line supports?

Ans. The four types of line supports are wooden poles, RCC poles, rail poles and steel structures or towers.

Q.7 What are the drawbacks of wooden poles?

Ans. The main drawbacks of wooden poles are comparatively smaller life, poor mechanical strength, tendency to rot below the ground level and requirement of periodical inspection.

Q.8 What are the main requirement of good conductor material used for overhead lines?

Ans. Main requirements of good conductor material used for overhead lines are high electrical conductivity, high tensile strength, low specific gravity, low cost, easy availability, free from brittleness and the material should not react with atmospheric condition.

Q.9 What for ACSR conductor stands?

Ans. ACSR conductor stands for aluminium conductor steel reinforced conductor.

Q.10 Why are conductor for transmission line stranded?

Ans. All conductors used for overhead transmission lines are stranded so as to increase the flexibility. Solid wires, except of smaller sizes, are difficult to handle when used for long spans and tend to crystallize at the points of supports because of swinging in winds.

Q.11 Why is galvanized steel wire not suitable for EHT lines for the purpose of transmitting large amounts of power over a long distance?

Ans. The galvanized steel wire is not suitable for EHT lines for the purpose of transmitting large amounts of power over a long distance because of poor conductivity, high internal reactance and eddy current and hysteresis.

Q.12 What is the function of cross-arms?

Ans. The function of cross-arms is to keep the line conductors at a safe distance from each other and from the pole.

Q.13 What are the factors on which conductor spacings and ground clearance depend?

Ans. Factor affecting conductor spacings is voltage while factors affecting ground clearance are voltage and area (living or non-living, urban or suburban, along the streets or across the streets, river crossings/hill crossings, railway track/bridge etc.)

Q.14 What is sag?

Ans. The difference in level between the points of line supports and the lowest point on the conductor is known as sag.

Q.15 What are the factors affecting the sag in a transmission line?

Ans. Factors affecting the sag in transmission line are weight of conductor, span length (distance between the poles), working tensile strength, ice coating, wind pressure and temperature.

Q.16 What are the important properties that an overhead line insulator must possess?

Ans. The most important properties that an overhead line insulator must process are: High mechanical strength, high relative permittivity, high insulation resistance, high ratio of rupturing strength to flash-over voltage and capability of withstanding temperature variations.

Q.17 What types of insulators are used for overhead transmission and distribution lines?

Ans. The insulators used for overhead line are pin type, suspension type, strain type and shackle insulators.

Q.18 What are the causes of failure of insulators?

Ans. The insulators failure may occur due to cracking of porcelain, porosity, puncture, mechanical stresses, flash-over etc.

Q.19 How do the insulators fail?

Ans. Electric failure of insulators may occur either by puncture of flash-over. In the case of puncture the arc passes through the insulator body while flash-over is caused by an arc discharge between the line conductor and earth through air surrounding the insulator.

Q.20 How are insulators tested to determine flash-over voltages?

Ans. For determination of flash-over voltage of a given insulator high voltage supply terminals are connected to the pin and insulator and the test voltage is gradually raised to a specified value in approximate 10 seconds and is maintained for one minute. The voltage is then gradually raised till a flash-over takes place. The flash-over voltage depends upon barometric pressure, temperature, humidity etc.

Q.21 What is meant by birdage?

Ans. Birdage means the short-circuiting of the line conductor to earth through the large birds or similar objects.

Q.22 On what factors does the skin effect depend?

Ans. The skin effect depends upon the type of material, frequency of current, diameter of conductor and shape of conductor. It increases with the increase of cross-section permeability and supply frequency.

Q.23 List the factors effecting the inductance of line.

Ans. (i) Greater the line length, greater the inductance and vice-versa.

(ii) Decrease with increase in conductor diameter and vice-versa.

(iii) More the spacing between conductors, higher the inductance and vice-versa.

Q.24 List the factors effecting the capacitance of line.

Ans. (i) Greater the line length, greater the capacitance of the line and vice-versa.

(ii) Increase with increase in conductor diameter and vice-versa.

(iii) More the spacing between the conductor, smaller the capacitance and vice-versa.

MEDIUM ANSWER TYPE QUESTIONS

Q.1 List the advantages of high voltage transmission and their limitations.

Ans. Following are the advantages of high voltage transmission:

(i) At higher voltage, current is reduced. Hence with increase in voltage, volume of conductor required to transmit same power is reduced. The results in decreases the cost of transmission line.

(ii) Since required less conductor volume hence reduces the strength of supporting structures.

(iii) Less current result in less copper lossed and hence high efficiency.

(iv) Reduces current result in less voltage drop and leads to better voltage regulation.

Q.2 Limitations to select high transmission voltage?

Ans. (i) At high voltage, more insulation is required between conductor and earth.

(ii) At high voltage, more clearance is required between conductors.

(iii) High voltage demand greater height of tower.

Q.3 List the advantages and disadvantages of HVDC transmission over HVAC transmission system.

Ans. Advantages:

(i) It requires only two conductors for transmission.

(ii) There is no inductance, capacitance and phase displacement problem.

(iii) There is no skin effect.

(iv) Since no inductance and capacitance, hence less voltage drops that leads to better voltage regulation.

(v) In such system less insulation is required.

(vi) There is less corona losses.

(vii) In such system, there is no stability and synchronizing problems.

(viii) It does not interference to nearby communication.

Q.4 Name the most commonly employed conductor materials. Explain ACSR.

Ans. The most commonly employed conductor materials are following:

(i) Copper

(ii) Aluminium
(iii) ACSR
(iv) Galvanised steel.

ACSR: ACSR stand for alluminium conductor steel reinforced. Since aluminium conductors having large sag because of low tensile strength. Hence, can't be used for longer span.

In order to make it suitable for longer span, a Galvanised steel conductor is placed in centre of aluminium conductor as shown in Fig. 3.33. This composite conductor is known as *aluminium conductor* steel reinforced.

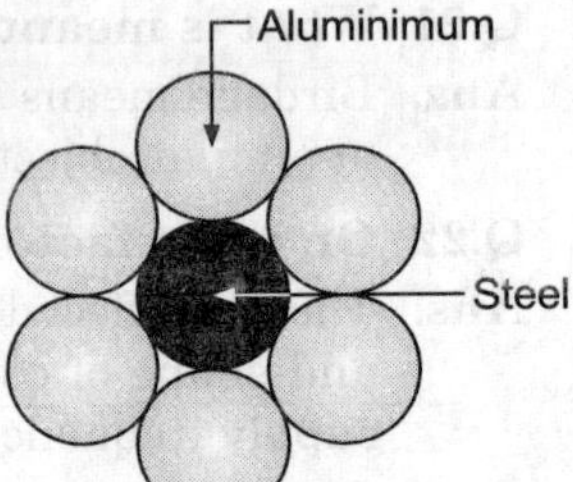

Fig. 3.33 ACRS conductor

Advantages:
(i) High tensile strength
(ii) High conductivity

Q.5 Mention the various types of line supports.

Ans. Line Supports: The various types of poles and towers used to keep the bare conductor at a suitable height above the ground is known as line supports.

Properties:
(i) High mechanical strength
(ii) Light in weight
(iii) Low cost
(iv) Long life
(v) Low maintenance.

Types of Line Supports:

(i) **Wooden Poles:** Wooden poles are made of seasoned wood and suitable for shorter spans, say upto 60 metres. They have general height upto 11 metres with minimum circumference of 38 cm at top and 66 cm at bottom.

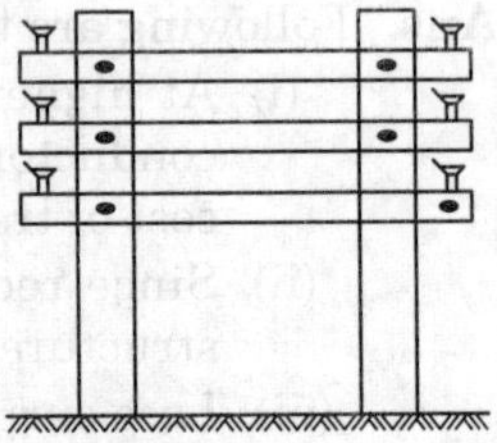
Fig. 3.34 Wooden pole

Advantages:
(a) Low cost
(b) Easily available
(c) Provide insulating properties.

Disadvantages:
(a) Can't used for long span.
(b) Smaller life span.
(c) Can't used for high voltage.

(ii) **Steel Poles:** Steel poles are used as substitute for wooden poles, as they posses greater mechanical strength and can be used for longer span at high voltage. But these poles are costly and require painting.

(iii) **RCC Pole:** RCC pole stands for reinforced cement concrete poles. These poles replace steel poles in recent days.

Advantages:
(a) Greater mechanical strength
(b) Longer life
(c) Can be used for longer span
(d) Little maintenance requirement
(e) Better insulation properties.

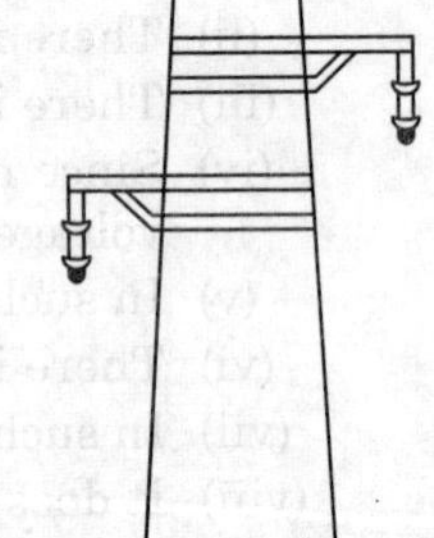
Fig. 3.35 RCC pole

Q.6 Explain various types of insulators.

Ans. **(i) Pin Type Insulator:** These insulators are installed on the corss-area of pole with the help of galvanised steel bolt. The conductor is placed on the job of insulator and tied down with wire of same conductor as that of conductor. These insulators are used upto 33 kV.

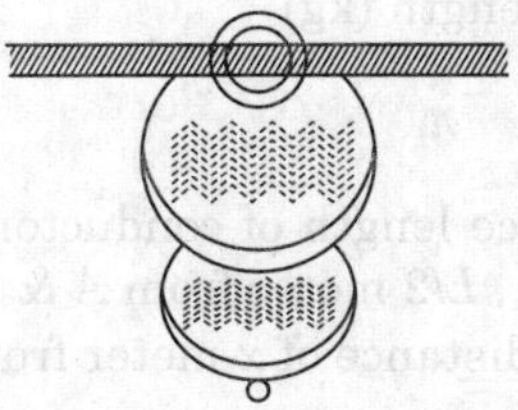

Fig. 3.36 Pin type insulator

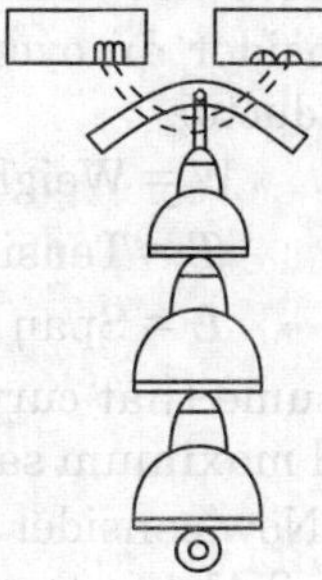

Fig. 3.37 Suspension type insulator

(ii) Suspension type insulator: For voltage above 33 kV, pin type insulator become costly and bulky in construction. For voltage above 33 kV, suspension type insulator are employed. The consists of number of discs connected in series in the form of string.

(iii) Strain insulator: Strain insulators are used where lines is subjected to greater strain. For example, at sharp turns, river crossing, at corner end etc. These insulators are used for voltage above 11 kV.

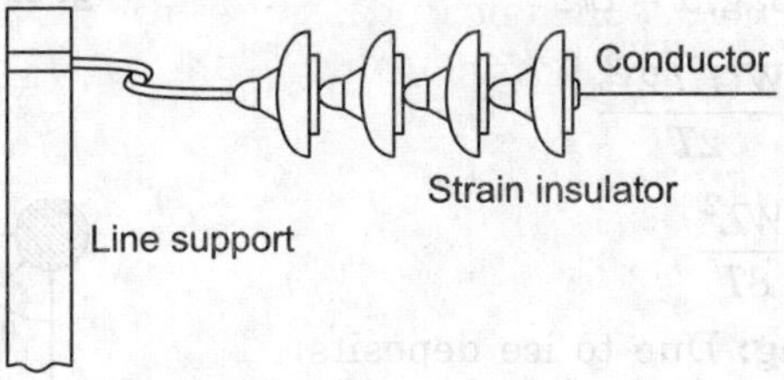

Fig. 3.38 Strain insulator

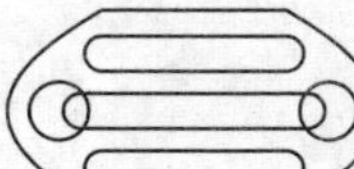

Fig. 3.39 Egg insulator

(iv) Egg insulator: These insulators are also known as *stay insulators* and employed at dead end, in the guy wire above 3 meter from ground.

Q.7 Define sag. Give its importance also.

Ans. Sag is defined as the difference in level between the point of support and lowest point on conductor as shown in Fig. 3.40.

$$\text{Sag} = OC$$

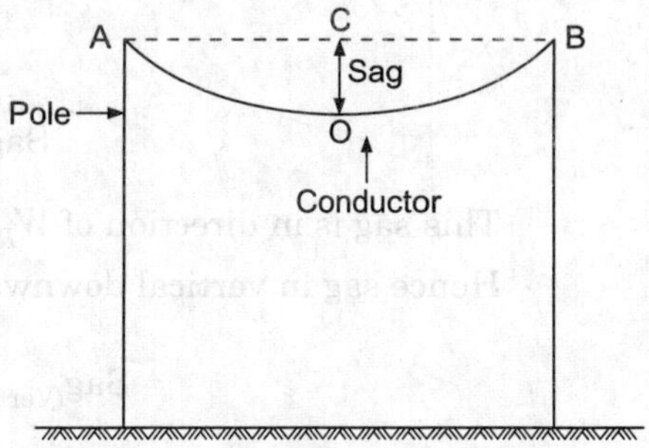

Fig. 3.40 Sag in the transmission line

Importance:

(i) The tension provided to conductor depends upon the sag. Greater the tension, smaller the sag and vice-versa.

(ii) Height of tower or pole depends upon the sag. Greater the sag, greater the height of tower is required from safety point of view.

(iii) More the sag, greater the length of conductor is required for same span. Hence high material cost.

Q.8 Derive the formula of sag.

Ans. Consider an overhead conductor supported at point *AB*. Point *O* is the lowest point of conductor.

Let W = Weight of conductor per meter length (kg)

T = Tension

L = Span length (meter)

Assume that curve *AOB* is very small, hence length of conductor is equal to span length and maximum sag occurs at mid of span i.e., $L/2$ meter from *A* & *B*.

Now consider a point *P* on conductor at distance of x-meter from mid point as shown in Fig. 3.41.

Two external forces acting on point *P*.

(i) T at a point *O*.

(ii) Wx at $x/2$ meters from point *P*.

Equate these external forces at point *P*.

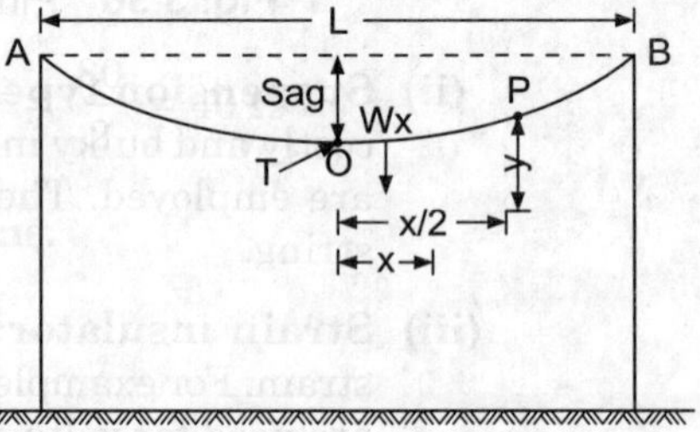

Fig. 3.41

$$T.y = Wx.\, x/2$$

$$y = \frac{Wx^2}{2T}$$

At Point *O*

$$y = \text{Sag},\ x = L/2$$

$$\text{Sag} = \frac{W(L/2)^2}{2T}$$

$$\text{Sag} = \frac{WL^2}{8T}$$

Effect of Ice and Wind Loading: Due to ice deposits and wind pressure, the mechanical stress increases in the conductor. The ice load say Wi acting downward in the same direction of conductor weight say w. where wind pressure say Ww acting horizontal as shown in Fig. 3.42.

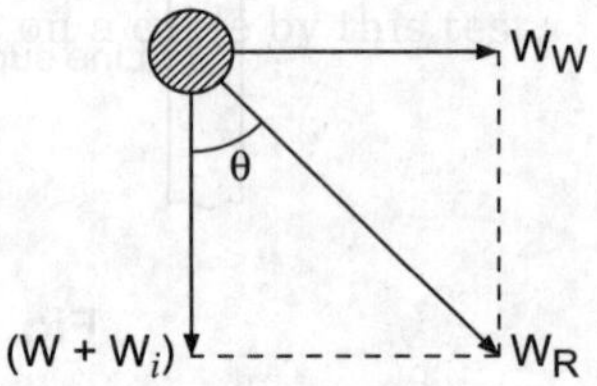

Fig. 3.42

The resultant weight of conductor per unit length is given by

$$W_R = \sqrt{(W+W_i)^2 (W_W)^2}$$

$$\text{Sag(s)} = \frac{W_R L^2}{8T}$$

This sag is in direction of W_R making an angle θ with vertical axis.

Hence sag in vertical downward

$$\text{Sag}_{(\text{Vertical})} = \int \cos\theta = \int \frac{(W+W_i)}{W_R}$$

Q.9 Define skin effect and factor effecting it.

Ans. Skin Effect: Skin effect is defined as the tendency of an alternator current (ac) to concentrate near the surface of conductor. Therefore, effective area of conductor is reduced through which current flows, hence increase the conductor resistance.

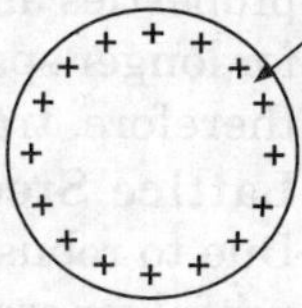

Fig. 3.43 Skin effect

Factors Effecting Skin Effect:

(i) Nature of material

(ii) Skin effect increases with increase in diameter of conductor.

(iii) Irregular the shape of conductor, more the skin effect.

(iv) Skin effect increases with increase in frequency.

Q.10 What do you understand from transposition of conductors? List its advantages.

Ans. Transposition of conductor: It is the process of changing the position of three phase conductors on regular interval in order to make the line constants symmetrical.

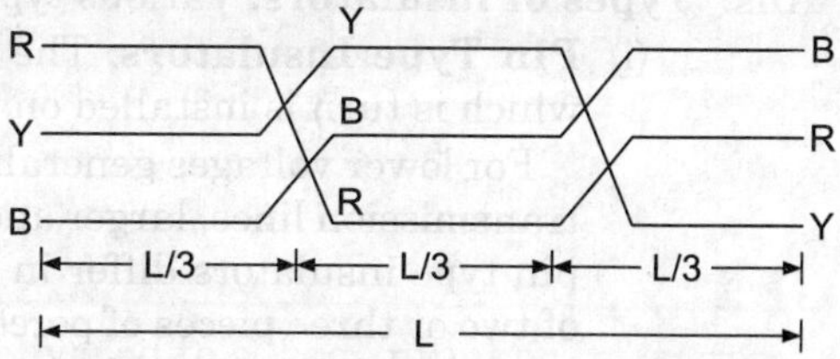

Fig. 3.44 Transposition of conductors

Advantages:

(i) It makes the line parameter symmetrical hence equal voltages received at receiving end.

(ii) It reduces the interference to near by communication.

Q.11 What is the purpose of transposition of conductors?

Ans. Due to mechanical considerations, conductors are spaced irregularly. Hence they have different inductance and capacitance. The apparent resistance is also effected due to mutual induction.

Thus line constants are different in three-phases of line that result in different voltage drop and leads to different line voltages at receiving end. This can be avoided by transposition of conductors at regular interval.

LONG ANSWER TYPE QUESTIONS

Q.1 Discuss in brief the various types of line supports used in transmission of electricity.

Ans. The line supports are of various types including wood, steel, reinforced concrete poles and lattice steel towers.

(i) **Wooden Poles:** These are cheapest, easily available, providing insulating properties and therefore, are extensively used for distribution purposes, specially in rural areas, keeping the cost low. Their use is usually limited to low pressures (upto 22 kV) and for short spans (upto 60 m). The wooden poles, well impregnated with preservative compound have life from 25 to 30 years. The disadvantage of such supports is that these need periodical inspection because they tend to rot and their life is short.

(ii) **Steel Poles:** The steel poles are of three types: (a) Rail poles, (b) Tubular poles and (c) Rolled steel joists.

These poles possess greater mechanical strength and so permit use of longer spans (50–80 m) but cost is higher. The average life of steel poles is more than 40 years.

(iii) **RCC Poles:** These give good outlook, need no maintenance, have good insulating properties and resistance against chemical action. They very strong and can be used for longer spans (80–200 m) and have very long life. Since these poles are very heavy, therefore, transportation cost is heavy and require care in handling and erection.

(iv) **Lattice Steel Towers:** These are mechanically stronger and have got longer life. Due to robust construction long spans (300 m and above) can be used and are much useful for crossing fields, valleys, railway lines, rivers etc. Even though these are two to four times costlier than wooden poles, yet for tall supports and longer span these prove economical. These towers need periodical painting or galvanizing for protection against corrosion. Narrow-base lattice steel towers are used for transmission at 66 kV and broad-base lattice steel towers are used for transmission at 66 kV and above.

Q.2 Discuss various types of insulators used in transmission lines.

Ans. Types of insulators: Various types of insulators are briefly described below:

(i) **Pin Type Insulators:** The pin type insulator is designed to be mounted on a pin which is turn is installed on the cross-arm of the pole.

For lower voltages generally one piece type of insulators are used. For high-voltage transmission lines, larger and stronger pin type insulators are used. The high voltage pin type insulators differ in construction from low voltage type in that they consist of two or three pieces of porcelain cemented together. These pieces from what we call petti-coats. These are designed to shed rain and sleet easily. These are available for use upto 50,000 volts.

(ii) **Suspension type Insulators:** With the increase in operating voltage, the insulation required increases. Transmission lines use extremely high voltage, 220 kV or 400 kV for example. At these voltages the pin type insulators become bulky, cumbersome and costly. Besides, the pin which must hold it would have to be in ordinarily long and large. In order to meet the problem of insulators for these high voltages, the suspension insulator was developed.

The suspension insulator hangs from the cross arm, as opposed to the pin insulator which sits on the top of it. The line conductor is attached to its lower end. Because there is no pin problem we can put any distance between the suspension insulator and the conductor just by adding more insulators to the "string". The entire unit of suspension insulators is called a string.

(iii) **Strain Insulators:** Some times a line is to withstand great strain, for instance at a dead end or at a corner or on sharp turns. In such a circumstance for LT (low tension) lines shackle insulators are used but for H T (high tension) transmission lines strain insulators consisting of an assembly of suspension type insulators are used. Because of its peculiarly important job, a strain insulator must have considerable strength as well as the necessary electrical properties. Two or more strings of suspension insulators are used in parallel when the tension is exceedingly high. The discs of strain insulators are employed in a vertical plane where as the suspension insulators are used in horizontal plane.

(iv) **Shackle insulators:** The shackle or spool-type insulator, which is easily identified by its shape, is usually used on LT lines. Both the low voltage conductors and the house service wires are attached to the shackle insulator.

(v) **Stay Insulator:** Such insulators are of egg shaped and are used in guy cables, where it is necessary to insulate the lower part of the guy cable from the pole for the safety of the people on the ground. These are provided at a height of about 3 m from the ground level.

Q.3 Define string efficiency. Discuss methods to improve string efficiency.

Ans. The voltage impressed on a string of suspension insulators does not distribute itself uniformly across the individual discs owing to the proximity of supporting structure (which is at earth potential). The line unit (unit nearest to the conductor) shall have to withstand the maximum percentage of voltage, to which progressively decreases as the unit nearest the tower is approached. The inequality of voltage distribution between individual units is all the more pronounced with a larger number of insulator units and also depends on the ratio of capacity of insulator of capacity to earth. The ratio of flash over voltage of n units to n times of flash-over voltage of one unit is called the string efficiency.

$$\text{i.e., String efficiency} = \frac{\text{Flash-over voltage of the string}}{n \times \text{Flash-over voltage of one unit}} \times 100 = \frac{V}{nv} \times 100$$

When the insulators are wet mutual capacitance increases while shunt capacitance remains constant (except for the unit nearest to the cross-arm), therefore the ratio of shunt capacitance to mutual capacitance decreases, and more uniform potential distribution is obtained and the string efficiency improves.

Methods of Improving String Efficiency: The string efficiency or voltage distribution across different units of a string can be improved by following methods.

(a) Long cross-arm method
(b) Capacitance grading method
(c) Static shielding

(a) The limitations of cost and strength of supports does not allow the used of very long cross arms.

(b) In capacitance grading, the insulators of different dimensions are selected so that different capacitors should have different capacitance and are assembled together in such a way that top unit has minimum capacitance and the bottom unit has maximum capacitance. It is not convenient to make all the insulators of different size. Usually the lower most unit which is placed near the conductor is of larger size.

(c) Static shielding in achieved by connecting a metallic guard ring electrically with the conductor. The ring surrounds the lower most insulator. It introduces capacitance which further improve the uniformily of voltage among units of string.

Q.4 What are the most commonly used conductor materials for transmission lines?

Ans. Most commonly used conductors are of copper, aluminium and steel. Conductors used for overhead lines are stranded to increase the flexibility. Started conductors have a central wire around which there are successive ACSR conductors have high tensile strength and less weight. This property enables us to use ACSR conductors for longer spans. Steel-cored aluminum conductors consist of a core of galvanized steel stand surrounded by number of aluminum strands. Galvanization is done of steel conductors in order to avoid rusting and corrosion. The steel core withstands large portion of mechanical stresses and aluminium carries much of the current. The diameter of ACSR conductor is larger than diameter of any other type of conductor having same resistance. This results in reduced carona losses.

Galvanised steel conductor are most widely used in rural areas where cost is the main consideration. These conductors find application where very-very large spans are required. These are most suitable for small power transmission over short distance.

Due to its properties, galvanized steel is most commonly used as stay wire and earth wire.

Q.5 What are the advantages of high voltage transmission?

Ans. Following are the advantages of high voltage transmission:

1. **Reduction in volume (size) of conductor material:** It is found that the volume of conductor required is inversely proportional to square of transmission voltage i.e.,

by increasing the transmission voltage to n times, the size of conductor can be reduced to $\frac{1}{n^2}$ times for supplying a given power with same % of voltage drop in feeder.

2. **Higher transmission efficiency:** With the increase is transmission voltage, the line current is reduced. The reduced current reduces the line losses which results in increase in efficiency.
3. **Better voltage regulation:** As the line current decreases with increase in transmission voltage, the voltage drop in the line gets reduced. Hence it leads to better regulation of line.

Q.6 What are the advantages and disadvantages high voltage DC transmission?

Ans. Transmission of electric power by high voltage dc system is superior to that by high voltage ac system in many respects.

(i) It requires only two conductors for transmission and it is also possible to transmit the power through one conductor only by using earth as returning conductor, hence much copper is saved.

(ii) No inductance, capacitance, phase displacement and surge problem.

(iii) There is no skin effect.

(iv) The potential stress on the insulation in case of dc system is $\frac{1}{\sqrt{2}}$ times on that in ac system for the same working voltage. Hence for same working voltage, less insulation is required.

(v) There is no charging current.

(vi) Underground cables can be used because of less potential stress and negligible dielectric loss.

(vii) For the same load and sending end voltage, voltage regulation for dc transmission is better.

(viii) No stabilizer is required for transmission over long distances.

Disadvantages: The only difficulty is of obtaining the necessary high voltage required for transmission as electrical power can be not generated at high voltage because of commutating difficulties. Also voltage can not be stepped up.

Q.7 What are the advantages and disadvantages of AC transmission?

Ans. Following are the advantages of AC system.

(i) In ac system voltage can be stepped up at generating end by means of transformer to the required value for transmission and then stepped down at the receiving end by step down transformer for distribution with ease and efficiency.

(ii) Voltage can be generated at high voltage easily.

(iii) Maintenance of AC substation is easier and cheaper in comparison to DC substation.

Disadvantages: The disadvantages of AC system are:

(i) In case of overhead lines spacing between the conductors is to be kept more in order to provide adequate insulation and to avoid corona loss.

(ii) More copper is required.

(iii) Greater the length of transmission line more is the capacitance of the line. There is a continuous loss on account of charging current even though the line is open.

(iv) The alternators are to be synchronised before putting them into parallel.

(v) The variation in speed of alternators are to be controlled within very low limits.

PROBLEMS

1. A 2-conductor cable one km in length is required to supply a constant load of 200 A throughout the year. The cost of the cable is ₹ (50a + 25) per metre where 'a' is the area of cross-section of the conductor in sq cm. The cost of energy is 6 paisa per kWh and interest and depreciation charges amount to 10%. Specific resistance of copper is 1.73 μ ohm-cm. Find the cross-sectional area 'a'. **(Ans.** $a = 1.2\ \text{cm}^2$**)**
2. An overhead line has a span of 100 m, the line conductor is weighing 420 kg per 1000 m. Calculate the maximum sag in the line, if the maximum allowable tension in the line is 500 kg. **(Ans.** $S = 1.05$ m**)**
3. An overhead single-phase line delivers 1100 kW at 33 kV at 0.9 p.f lagging. The total resistance of the line is 10 ohms and the total inductive reactance is 15 ohms. Determine:
   (i) Percentage voltage regulation.
   (ii) Sending end power factor.
   (iii) Transmission efficiency. **(Ans.** (i) 2.146%, (ii) 0.7956 lagging, (iii) 98.45%**)**
4. Three disc insulators are employed in the string of a three phase, 33 kv overhead line. If the capacitance between the pin of each insulator and earth is 10% of self-capacitance of each insulator, find: (i) the distribution of voltage over 3 insulators, (ii) string efficiency. **(Ans.** (i) 5.586, 6.146 kV, 7.318 kV; (ii) 86.77%**)**
5. An overhead line has a span of 150 m between two level supports. The conductor weighs 0.62 kg per metre length. The allowable tension is 586 kg. Calculate the sag of the wind pressure is 0.3685 kg per metre length. **(Ans.** 3.46 m**)**

Solution of Problems

1. Length of the cable, $e = 1\text{km} = 1 \times 10^5$ cm

Load current, $I = 200\ A$

Cost of cable/m = ₹ (50 a + 25)

Cost of energy/kWh = $6P$ = ₹ 0.06

Interest and depreciation = 10%

Resistivity of copper, $\rho = 1.73 \times 10^{-6}\ \Omega$-cm

$$\text{Resistance of each conductor, } R = \rho\frac{l}{a} = \frac{1.73\times10^{-6}\times l\times10^5}{a} = \frac{0.173}{a}\ \text{ohm}$$

$$\text{Energy lost per annum} = \frac{2I^2R\times24\times365}{1000}$$

$$= 2\times(200)^2\times\frac{0.173\times24\times365}{a\times1000} = \frac{121238}{a}\ \text{kWh}$$

$$\text{Annual cost of energy lost} = \frac{0.06\times121238}{a} = ₹\ \frac{7274.3}{a}$$

Capital cost of the cable = ₹ 50 a × 1000 = ₹ 50,000 a

$$\text{Annual charge on account of interest and depreciation } ₹\ \frac{10}{100}\times 50000\ a$$

$$= ₹\ 50{,}000\ a$$

For most economical section of conductor

$$\frac{7274.3}{a} = 50{,}000\,a$$

$$a = \sqrt{\frac{7274.3}{5000}} = 1.2 \text{ cm}^2 \quad \textbf{Ans.}$$

2. Length of span, $L = 100$ m

Weight of conductor, $w = 420$ kg/1000 m

Working tension, $T = 500$ kg

$$\text{Weight of conductor, } w = \frac{420}{1000} = 0.42 \text{ kg}$$

$$\text{Sag, } S = \frac{WL^2}{8T} = \frac{0.42 \times 100 \times 100}{8 \times 500} = 1.05 \text{ m} \quad \textbf{Ans.}$$

3. Power to be transmitted, $P = 1100$ kW $= 1100 \times 10^3$

Receiving end voltage, $V_R = 33$ kV $= 33 \times 10^3 V^W$

Load power factor, $\cos\phi_R = 0.8$ lagging

Resistance of the line, $R = 10\ \Omega$

Inductive reactance of the line,

$$X_L = 15\ \Omega$$

$$\text{Line current, } I = \frac{P}{V_R \cos\phi_R} = \frac{1100 \times 10^3}{33 \times 10^3 \times 0.8} = 41.67\ A$$

Load p.f., $\cos\phi_R = 0.8$; $\sin\phi_R = \sin\cos^{-1} 0.8 = 0.6$

$$\text{Sending end voltage, } V_S = V_R + I_R \cos\phi_R + IX_L \cos\phi_R$$

$$= 33000 + 41.67 \times 10 \times 0.8 + 41.67 \times 15 \times 0.6$$

$$= 33708.33 \text{ V}$$

(*i*)

$$\%\ \text{Regulation} = \frac{V_S - V_R}{V_R} = \frac{33708 - 33000}{33000} \times 100$$

$$= 2.146\% \textbf{ Ans}$$

(*ii*) Sending end power factor,

$$\cos\phi_S = \frac{V_R \cos\phi_R + IR}{V_S} = \frac{33000 \times 0.8 + 41.67 \times 10}{33000.33}$$

$$= 0.7956 \text{ lagging } \textbf{Ans}$$

$$\text{Losses in the line} = I^2R = (41.67)^2 \times 10 = 17361 \text{ W}$$

$$= 17.361 \text{ kW}$$

Receiving end power = 1100 kW

Sending end power = Receiving end power + losses in the line

$$= 1100 + 17.361 = 1117.361 \text{ kW}$$

(*iii*) Efficiency of transmission line,

$$\eta = \frac{\text{Receiving end power}}{\text{Sending end power}} \times 100$$

$$\eta = \frac{1100}{1117.361} \times 100 = 98.45\% \textbf{ Ans}$$

4. Line voltage, $V_L = 33$ kV

Self capacitance = C

Shunt capacitance = C_1

$$K = \frac{\text{Shunt capacitance}}{\text{Self capacitance}} = \frac{C_1}{C}$$

$$= 10\% = 0.1 \text{ (given)}$$

Voltage across the string

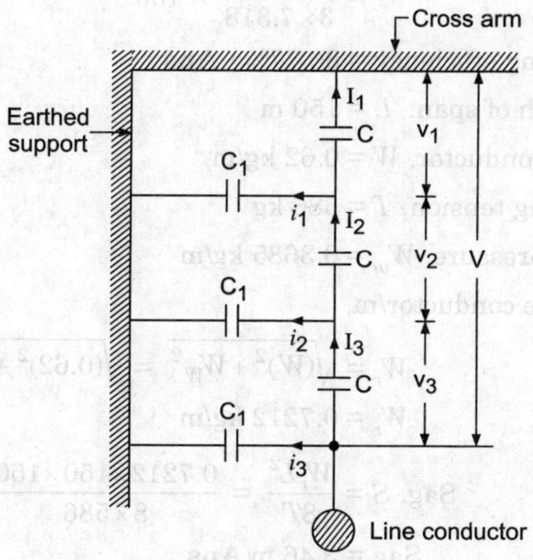

Fig. 3.45 Equivalent circuit of string

$$V = \frac{V_L}{\sqrt{3}} = \frac{33}{\sqrt{3}} = 19.05 \text{ kV}$$

Applying Kirchhoff's current law at node *X*, we get

$$I_2 = I_1 + i_1$$

$$= V_2\, WC = V_1\, WC + V_1\, WC_1$$

$$= V_2\, WC = V_1\, WC + V_1\, W\, KC$$

$$V_2 = V_1\,(1 + K)$$

$$V_2 = (1 + 0.1)V_1 + 1.1V_1$$

Applying Kirchhoff's current law at node, *Y* we get

$$I_3 = I_2 + i_2$$

$$V_3WC = V_2\, WC + (V_1 + V_2)WC$$

$$V_3WC = V_2\,WC + (V_1 + V_2)WKC$$

$$V_3 = V_2 + (V_1 + V_2)\,K$$

$$V_3 = 1.1\,V_1 + (V_1 + 1.1V_1)\,0.1 = 1.31V_1$$

(i) Voltage across the string, $V = V_1 + V_2 + V_3$

$$= 19.05 = V_1 + 1.1V_1 + 1.31\,V_1$$

$$V_1 = \frac{19.05}{3.41} = 5.586 \text{ kV } \textbf{Ans}$$

$$V_2 = 1.1V_1 = 1.1 \times 5.586 = 6.146 \text{ kV } \textbf{Ans}$$

$$V_3 = 1.31V_1 = 1.31 \times 5.586 = 7.318 \text{ kV } \textbf{Ans}$$

(ii) String efficiency $= \dfrac{\text{Voltage across the string}}{\text{No. of units} \times \text{Voltage across lower most unit}} \times 100$

$$= \frac{19.05}{3 \times 7.318} \times 100$$

String efficiency = 86.77% **Ans**

5. Length of span, $L = 150$ m

Weight of conductor, $W = 0.62$ kg/m

Working tension, $T = 586$ kg

Wind pressure, $W_w = 0.3685$ kg/m

Resultant weight of the conductor/m,

$$W_r = \sqrt{(W)^2 + W_W{}^2} = \sqrt{(0.62)^2 + (0.3685)^2}$$

$$W_r = 0.7212 \text{ kg/m}$$

$$\text{Sag, } S = \frac{W_r L^2}{8T} = \frac{0.7212 \times 150 \times 150}{8 \times 586}$$

Sag = 3.46 m **Ans**

EXERCISE

1. Draw a single line representation of a power system for transmission and distribution. Explain in brief.
2. List the various advantages of using high voltage for transmission and what are its limitations?
3. What are the various types of support used for transmission of electric power? Explain with suitable diagram.
4. What is voltage regulation? On what factors does the regulation of transmission line depend?
5. What is corona effect? How it can be reduced?
6. What is ACSR conductor and why it is preferred over copper conductor for transmission lines?
7. What is transposition of transmission line? What is its purpose?

❑❑❑

Distribution System

4

INSIDE THIS CHAPTER

- Introduction
- Design Considerations in Distribution System
- Distributors
- Underground Cable
- Laying of Underground Cables
- Components of an Overhead 400/230 (L.T.) Line
- Classification of Distribution Systems
- Erection of Supports
- Requirements of a Distribution System
- Construction of 11 kV HT and LT Power Cable
- Overhead Versus Underground System

4.1 INTRODUCTION

Distribution of electric power is an important part of power system. In the more specialized form it is refers to the lines and circuits over which electrical energy passes along streets of the city. The distribution system in general is the electrical system between the stepdown substation fed by transmission system and the consumers meters. The most important requirement for such distribution system is that electrical power should be distributed to the consumers efficiently and economically. The electrical energy is also made available for a use in a factory.

Energy transmitted at the voltage which used is called secondary distribution, for example, 230 volts is given to the residence and 400 V is given to the factory. The lines supplying energy to the secondary distribution at a higher voltage such as 6.6 kV or 3.3 kV. The connecting link between primary and secondary distribution system is the distribution transformer.

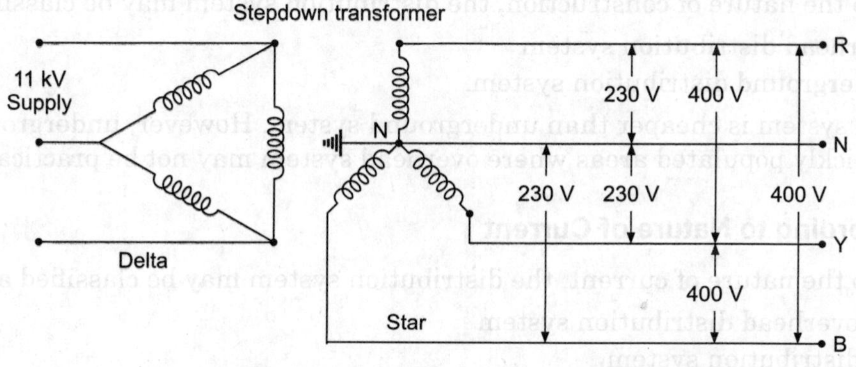

Fig. 4.1 Scheme for primary and secondary distribution

The high-voltage primary distribution network is usually–three-phase, three wire system and inter converts a required number of substation by overhead lines. The low voltage network is three phase four wire system. The scheme for primary and secondary distribution is shown in Fig. 4.1.

4.1.1 Feeder, Distributor and Service Mains

The LT (low tension) distribution system i.e., not including the transmission lines can be sub-divided into:

1. Feeders, 2. Distributors and 3. Service mains

1. **Feeders:** A feeder is a conductor which connects sub-station to area where the power is to be distributed. In Fig. 4.2 '*S*' is the substation and *SA*, *SB* and *SD* are the feeders *A*, *B* and *D* are the feeding point. No tappings are taken from the feeders. The carry same current throughout their length.
2. **Distributor:** A distributor is a conductor to which various consumers are connected through services mains is known as distributor. It is to distribute electric power to various consumers, thus a number of tappings are taken from the distributor. Hence, it carries different current along its length. In Fig *AB*, *BCD* and *DA* are the distributors.
3. **Service Mains:** A line conductor which connects the consumer to the distributor is known as service mains. It is designed as per the connected load of the consumers.

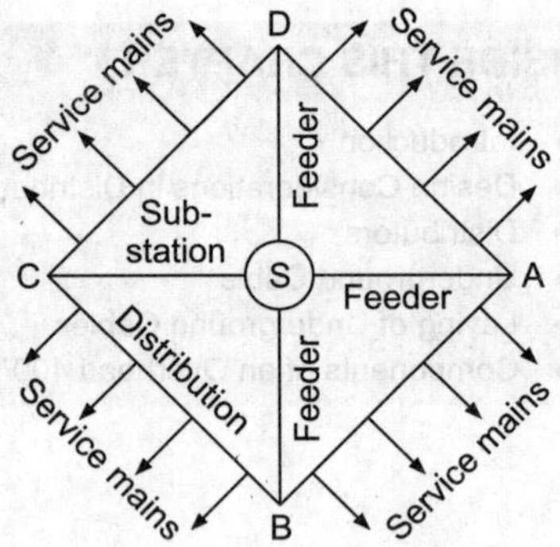

Fig. 4.2 Typical distribution system

4.2 CLASSIFICATION OF DISTRIBUTION SYSTEMS

The distribution system may be classified in the following ways:

4.2.1 According to Nature of Construction

According to the nature of construction, the distribution system may be classified as:

(i) Overhead distribution system

(ii) Underground distribution system.

Overhead system is cheaper than underground system. However, underground system is used in thickly populated areas where overhead system may not be practicable.

4.2.2 According to Nature of Current

According to the nature of current, the distribution system may be classified as:

(i) DC overhead distribution system

(ii) AC distribution system.

AC distribution is universally adopted due to many advantages of ac power over dc power.

4.2.3 According to Number of Wires

According to the number of wires, distribution system may be classified as:

(i) 2-wire dc system
(ii) 3-wire dc system
(iii) Single phase, 2-wire, ac system
(iv) 3-phase, 3-wire, ac system
(v) 3-phase, 4-wire, ac system.

4.2.4 According to the Scheme of Connection

According to the scheme of connections, the distribution system may be classified as :

(i) Radial system
(ii) Ring main system
(iii) Interconnected system.

4.2.4.1 Radial System

When the distributor is fed at one end only, it is called radial distribution system. A single line diagram of radial system is shown in Fig. 4.3. Since the feeder *F*, distributor *D* and the service mains *S* are radiating from the substation, this system is called the "Radial system of distribution". This system is only employed when power is generated at low voltage and the substation is located at the centre of the load. Due to the following reasons, radial system of distribution is not used in general.

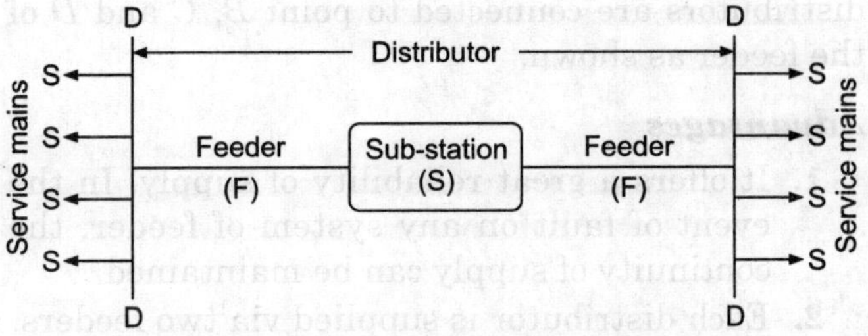

Fig. 4.3 Radial distribution system

(i) The consumers are dependents on a single feeder and a single distributor and a fault on either of them causes interruption of supply to all the consumers away from the fault.
(ii) The end nearest to the supply point of the distributor is heavily loaded.
(iii) Consumers located at the far end of the system experience severe voltage fluctuations associated with changing load.
(iv) Low reliability of supply. In case of fault occurring anywhere on the distributor, those consumers beyond the fault point undergo disconnection of power supply till the fault is rectified.

Advantages

1. This system is simplest
2. Its initial cost is minimum
3. This system is employed when electrical energy is generated at low voltage and the power station is situated at the center of load.

Disadvantages

1. The end of the distributor nearest to the supply end would be heavily loaded.
2. The consumers are dependent on a single feeder and a single distributor. Therefore, any fault on the feeder or distributor cuts off supply to the consumers who are on the side of the fault away from the substation.
3. The consumers at the distant end of the distributor would be subjected to serious voltage variations when the load on the distributor changes.

Due to these disadvantages, this system is not used.

4.2.4.2 *Ring Main System*

When the distributor is supplied by two feeders, it is called a *ring main distribution system*. In this system the feeder closes on itself, *i.e.*, it forms a complete ring and hence the name ring mains. Figure 4.4 shows a ring system where the substation S supplies to the closed feeder $ABCDA$. The distributors are connected to point B, C and D of the feeder as shown.

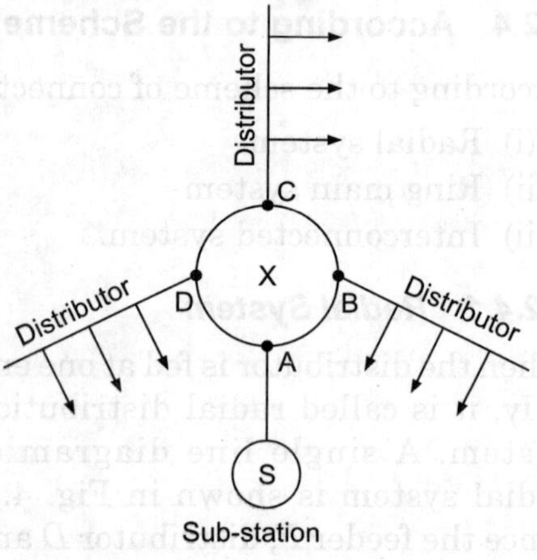

Fig. 4.4 Ring main distribution system

Advantages

1. It offers a great reliability of supply. In the event of fault on any system of feeder, the continuity of supply can be maintained.
2. Each distributor is supplied via two feeders, for example, the distributor connected at point D is fed via feeder AD and $ABCD$. This reduces the fluctuations in voltage at the consumers terminals.

Difference between Radial System and Ring System

S.No.	*Radial system*	*Ring system*
1.	It is used for low voltage. It feeds the distributor at one end only.	It is used for high voltage. It feeds the distributor with two feeders.
2.	Its initial cost is minimum	Initial cost is high.
3.	It is less reliable.	It increases the reliability of supply.
4.	The consumers are dependent on single feeder. In case of failure of supply, all the consumers suffer.	There are two feeders for the distributor so if one fails other can be used for continuing the supply.
5.	The consumers near to the feeder are heavily loaded and consumers at far end of distributor would be subjected to serious voltage fluctuation.	There is uniform voltage distribution near to feeder and at far end.
6.	More copper is needed because it carries more current.	Less copper is needed as each part of the ring carries less current than radial system.

Advantages of Ring Main System over Radial System

(i) Less copper is needed as each part of the ring carries less current than in radial system.

(ii) Each distributor is supplied via two feeders. Thus, the distributor from point *D* is supplied by the feeders *AD* and *ABCD*.

(iii) Less voltage fluctuations. The voltage level is also improved.

(iv) The system is very reliable. In the event of a fault on any section of the feeder, the continuity of supply can be maintained. This is the greatest advantage of this system. Suppose fault occurs at any point *X* of section *AD* of the feeder. Then section AD of the feeder can be isolated for repairs and at the same time continuity of supply is maintained to all consumers.

4.2.4.3 *Interconnected System*

In an "interconnected system the feeder ring is energized by two or more than two generating stations or sub-stations. Figure 4.5, shows the single line diagram of an inter-connected system. The closed feeder ring *ABCDA* is supplied by four stations S_1, S_2, S_3 and S_4 at points *D*, *A*, *B* and *C* respectively. Distributors are connected to points *E*, *F*, *G* and *H*.

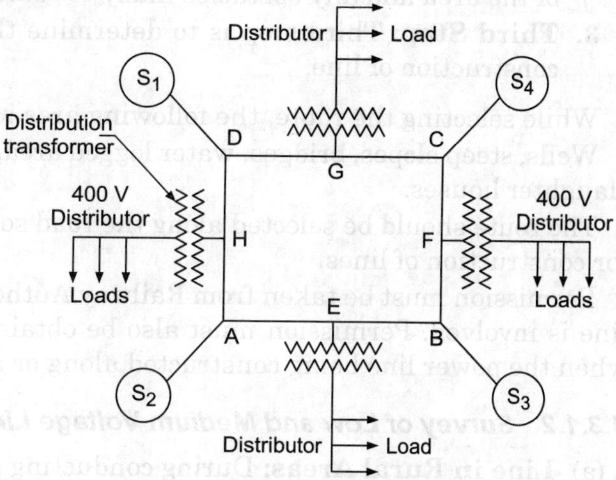

Fig. 4.5 Interconnected system

Advantages

The advantages of this system are:

(i) In the event of fault on any section of the feeder, the continuity of supply to all consumers can be maintained by isolating the faulty section.

(ii) If any area is being fed from one generating station then during peak hours of load it can be fed from the other generating station. Thus it reduces the reserved power capacity and increases the efficiency of the power system.

4.3 DESIGN CONSIDERATIONS IN DISTRIBUTION SYSTEM

The main elements of a distribution network are the feeders and distributors. To maintain a required voltage at the terminals of a consumer, proper care has to be taken while designing these elements.

(i) **Feeder:** While designing a feeder, the main consideration is on its current carrying capacity. The voltage drop consideration is relatively unimportant. The reason is that the voltage drop in a feeder can be compensated by means of voltage regulating equipment placed at the sub-stations.

(ii) **Distributor:** While designing a distributor, the main consideration is the voltage drop in it. The carrying capacity consideration is not that much important. The reason is that the distributor supplies power to the consumers and there is a statutory limit to the voltage fluctuations at the consumers terminals. This limit is 6% of the rated value (as per India Electricity Rules). Hence the size and length of the distributor is designed in such a way that the voltage at the consumer's terminals is within the permissible limits.

4.3.1 Construction Features of Overhead Distribution Lines and their Erection

4.3.1.1 Survey of Line

In order to determine the route along which the line is laid. Survey of area must be done:

1. **First Step:** First step is to select the shortest route and plot it with larger scale.
2. **Second Step:** Second step is to conduct a walk over survey to determine topography of the area and any obstacles likely to come across.
3. **Third Step:** Third step is to determine the quantity of material required for the construction of line.

While selecting the route, the following area should be avoided:

Wells, steep slopes, bridges, water logged area, gardens, trees, proximity of aerodromes, slaughter houses.

The route should be selected along the road so that the material can be delivered easily for construction of lines.

Permission must be taken from Railway Authorities where ever a crossing over railway line is involved. Permission must also be obtained from Telecommunication Authorities when the power line being constructed along or across the telephone lines.

4.3.1.2 Survey of Low and Medium Voltage Lines (240 to 440 V)

(a) **Line in Rural Areas:** During conducting survey of distribution lines in village, the map of village is taken and following are marked on the map:

1. The nearest HT lines from which the tapping will be taken.
2. Load
3. Layout of line.

(b) **Lines in Urban Areas:** The power lines should be plotted on map of the city after consulation with the municipal authorities. The following should be considered: Road crossing, Private land, Railway track crossing, Telephone line crossing.

(c) **Agricultural Area:** In case of the agricultural loads the transformers should be installed in the centre of load so as to reduce the length of lines and voltage drop.

4.3.1.3 Survey of HT Lines (11 kV to 33 kV)

Points to be Considered

1. The HT lines should be run along a road if possible. This will help in construction and maintenance of lines.
2. The number of angle pole should be minimum.
3. An intersection of highway and railway tracks and telephone lines should be avoided.

4.3.1.4 Planning of Construction Work

1. **Preparation of Estimate:** After the completion of survey work and working-out the length of the line detail of material is prepared and estimate the cost and purchase and then site offices should be built.
2. **Transport tion:** The poles should be arranged and unloaded at different places. Great care should be taken in loading and unloading of RCC poles because they are liable to damage. Conductor drums should be loaded at different places. Other materials such as cross-arm, insulators, nuts, bolts, channel, earthing pipe, barbed wire, cement should be stored at the site.
3. **Staff:** The number of field staff such as line superintendents, foreman, surveyer, draftman, lineman, unskilled labour should be arranged to watch the construction schedule.
4. **Tools and Plant (T&P):** These should also be arranged well in time to start the work with safety and efficiency.
5. **Marking of Trees for Falling:** A good method of marking of trees is to put a right around the tree to be fallen at a level when falling is required. If looping (branches of trees) only is required, a cross should be put on the site to be looped.

4.4 ERECTION OF SUPPORTS

After the collection and transportation of material, pole foundation, excavation work is commended. A hole is drilled in ground with crowbars (Shovels) etc. In rocky area blasting is done with gun powder to make the foundation of pile.
1/6th part of pole should be inserted in the ground.

Poles: A steel tubular pole, RCC pole etc. A suitable pad of cement concrete steel is provided at the bottom of pit before the pole is erected.

To avoid corrosion and better grounting a cement concrete muff is shown in Fig. 4.6 is provided.

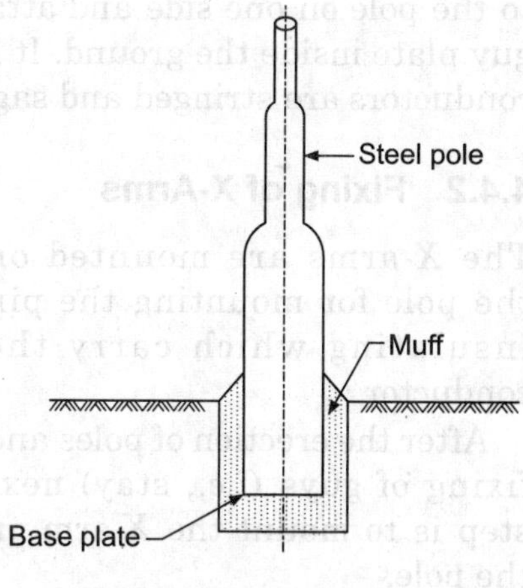

Fig. 4.6 Steel pole with muff

4.4.1 Raising and Setting of Poles

To carryout pole erection with maximum safety and efficiently, there should be erection squad of one Lineman, one Assistant Lineman and six trade mates along with required tools and plants.

Method of Erecting Poles

1. Dead-man method
2. Derrick pole method

The dead man is a temporary *X*-shaped structure made of two wooden *X*-arms shown in Fig. 4.7. The pole is laid down along the line route. A wooden board is placed vertically at the back of foundation pit and pole is moved till rests against the board. The pole is then raised manually and is supported on the dead-man. The guy ropes of diameter 2.5 cm are attached on the upper part in the three different directions and winch rope of 3.2 cm diameter is attached in the fourth direction.

The pole is raised and dead-man is moved forward until it can be replaced by 3 metre ladder. The ladder is now removed till the pole is pushed upto the vertical position. The pole is then carefully plumbed with the help of guy ropes. The pit is then filled in earth and rammed.

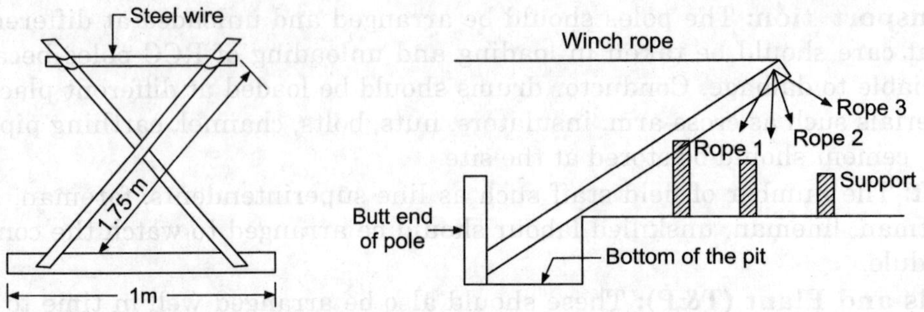

(a) Dead man structure (b) Dead-man method of erection of pole

Fig. 4.7

Derrick Pole Method: It is used for heavy concrete pole erection as these are liable to cracks.

H-pole Structure: One H-pole is provided after every one kilometer to make the line stable.

Guy: It is also called stay wire and consists of stranded galvanized steel wire clamped to the pole on one side and attached to guy rod on other. The guy rod is further fixed to guy plate inside the ground. It is not used before the line conductor erected on the pole if conductors are stringed and sagged first, the poles would be pulled out of position.

4.4.2 Fixing of X-Arms

The *X*-arms are mounted on the pole for mounting the pin insulating which carry the conductor.

After the erection of poles and fixing of guys (*i.e.*, stay) next step is to mount the *X*-arm on the pole.

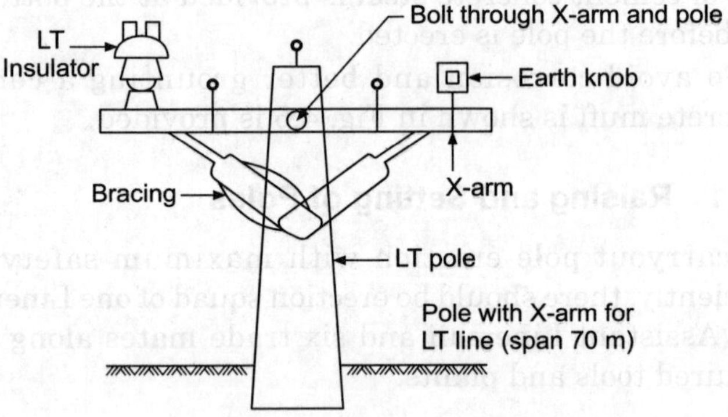

Fig. 4.8 Fixing of cross arms

In some cases the *X*-arms are fixed prior to the erection of poles. If the *X*-arm is fixed after the erection of pole then the line man will have to climb the pole to fix the *X*-arm.

4.4.3 Fixing of Insulators

In case of pole for 11 kV and 33 kV lines for straight runs, the pin insulators are used because they are under compression. The pin for mounting the pin insulators are fixed in the holes provided on the *X*-arm and at the top of pole. The insulators are then mounted in their places and tightened as shown in Fig. 4.9.

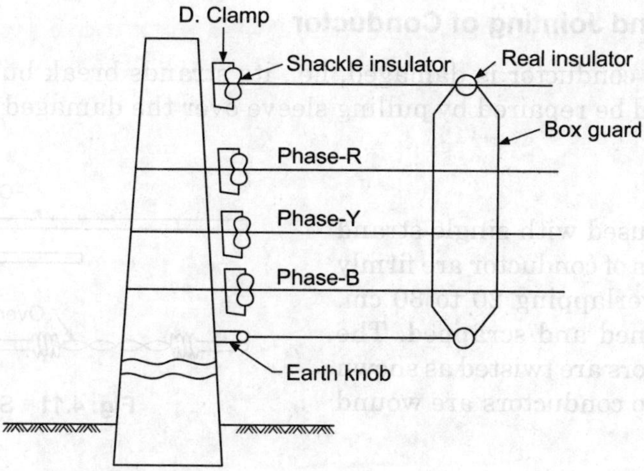

Fig. 4.9 Fixing of insulators

In LT poles the insulators are attached directly to the poles with the help of D-clamp.

4.4.4 Erection of Conductors

ACSR conductors received from manufacture wound on wooden drums. The conductor drum should never be dropped while unloading.

To mount the conductor on the poles is called stringing of conductors. An aluminimum roller block is used as shown in Fig. 4.10. During the conductor is running out of drum is should be simultaneously raised to level of *X*-arm of pole.

One drum contains 5 km length of conductor. For 1 km generally 10 number of poles are convered. Figure 4.10 shows how the conductor is strung on the poles. The conductor is started to string at point *A* and finished upto point *B* with 1 km apart. The pole *B* is called terminal.

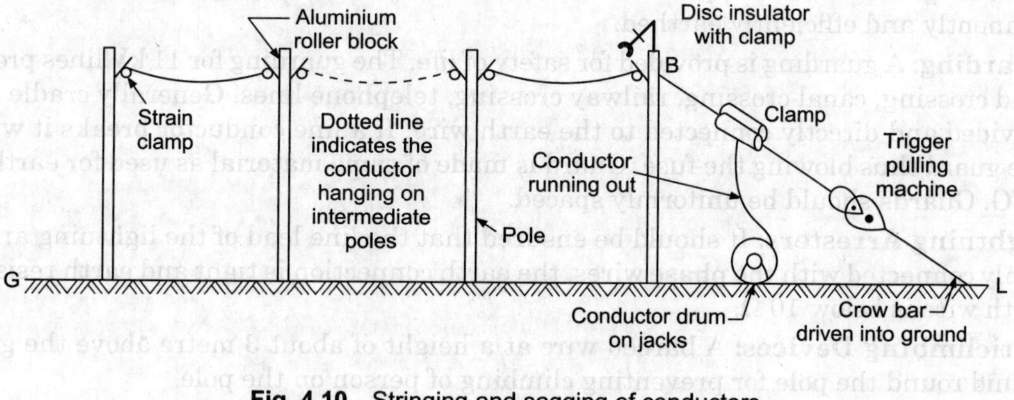

Fig. 4.10 Stringing and sagging of conductors

At terminal *B* disc insulator is provided because at end the insulator comes under tension. The pulling of conductor with Trifer pulling m/c keep the necessary sag in the line of 1 km.

4.4.5 Repairing and Jointing of Conductor

Wherever an ACSR conductor is damaged, i.e., its strands break but whole conductor is not broken, it should be repaired by pulling sleeve over the damaged part of conductor.

4.4.6 Jointing

Splice Joint: It is used with single strand conductors. The ends of conductor are firmly held together by overlapping 20 to 30 cm. The surface is cleaned and scrapped. The overlapping conductors are twisted as shown in Fig. 4.11. The two conductors are wound around each other.

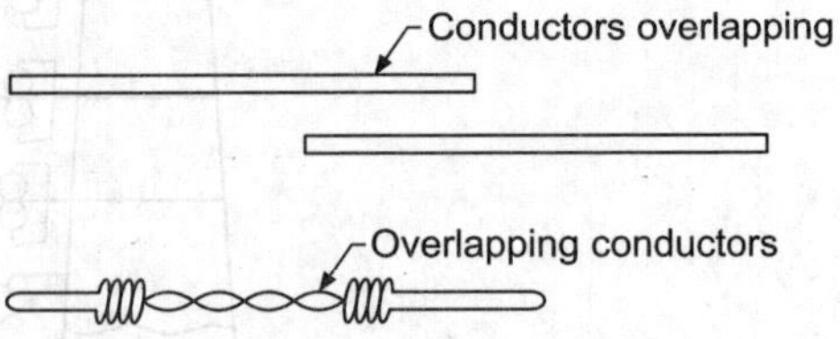

Fig. 4.11 Splice joint

4.4.7 Positioning of Conductor and Binding with Insulator

The conductor is put in the grove of pin insulator. The conductor is then fastened to the insulators by means of aluminium binding wire on LT lines.

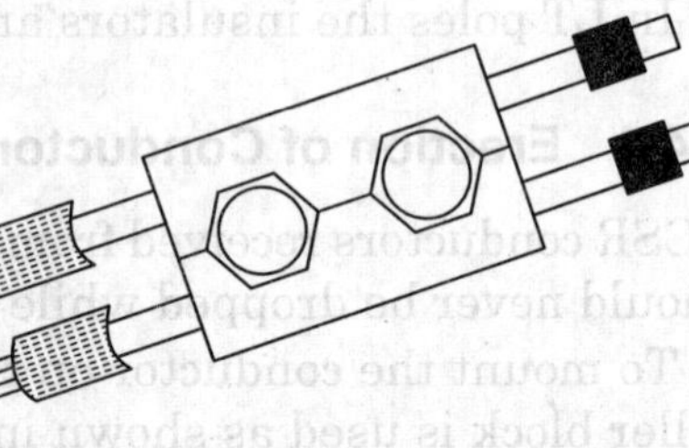

Fig. 4.12 Clamp with two bolts

Jumpers: It is the short length of conductor used to connect the line pole (dead end) to the line conductor on the other side of the terminal pole is known as *Jumper*. Jumper is made of the same material and current carrying capacity as that of line conductor. It is fixed with line conductor with suitable line conductor. Sometimes the pin insulator is used supporting jumper on 11 kV line.

Tee-off: Tee off is only taken from pole and in the middle of span. The connection from main line to the feed line may be made by using parallel groove (PG) clamps.

Earthing: All metal supports of overhead lines metal fittings attached should be permanently and efficiently earthed.

Guarding: A guarding is provided for safety of life. The guarding for 11 kV lines provided at road crossing, canal crossing, railway crossing, telephone lines. Generally cradle guard is provided and directly connected to the earth wire. If a line conductor breaks it will fall on the guard thus blowing the fuse. Guard is made of same material as used for earth wire 8.5 WG. Guards should be uniformly spaced.

Lightning Arresters: It should be ensured that the line lead of the lightning arroster is firmly connected with the phase wires, the earth connection is tight and earth resistance of earth wire is below 10 Ω.

Anticlimbing Devices: A barbed wire at a height of about 3 metre above the ground is wound round the pole for preventing climbing of person on the pole.

Testing of Lines: After the erection of 11 kV and LT lines is completed, the tests should be carried out.

1. **Conductor Continuing test:** The objective of this test to verify that each conductor is electrically properly connected. The electrical continuity is checked with meggar.

2. **Insulation Resistance Test:** LT lines 440/230 V between phase and neutral tested with meggar for leakage. It should not be less than 2 10 Ω.
3. **11 kV Line:** Between each phase – 50 10 Ω.
4. **Earth Resistance Test:** It is carried out with an earth resistance tester on earth wire on metallic fitting, stags. It should not be more than 10 Ω.

4.5 DISTRIBUTORS

A number of tappings are taken from the distributor along its length to provide supply to the various consumers. The voltage along the length of the distributor will vary according to the resistance and actual value of the load currents carried by the various sections of the distributor at a particular time. Since the voltage at the consumer's terminals must remain within specified limits as laid down by the Indian Electricity Rules, (a voltage variation of $\pm$ 5% is permissible) the main basis of distributor design is the drop in volts and means must be available for determining the voltage at any point under any anticipated loading conditions.

In case of dc distribution the voltage drop will be due to conductor resistance, but in the ac distributor the resistance, inductance and capacitance of the conductor and the power factor of the load must also be taken into account.

Classification of Distribution System

A distribution system may be classified according to:

(i) **Nature of Current:** According to nature of current distribution system may be classified as *(a)* dc distribution system, *(b)* ac distribution system. Now a days ac system is universally adopted for distribution of electric power as it is simples and more economical than direct current method.

(ii) **Type of Construction:** According to type of construction, distribution system may be classified as *(a)* overhead system, *(b)* underground system. The overhead system is generally employed for distribution as it is 5 to 10 times cheaper than the equivalent underground system. In general, the underground system is used at places where overhead construction is impracticable or prohibited by the local laws.

(iii) **Scheme of Connection:** According to scheme of connection, the distribution system may be classified as *(a)* radial system, *(b)* ring main system, *(c)* interconnected system. Each scheme has its own advantages and disadvantages.

4.5.1 DC Distribution

It is a common knowledge that electric power is almost exclusively generated, transmitted and distributed as ac. However, for certain applications dc supply is absolutely necessary. For instance, d.c. supply is required for the operation of variable speed machinery (i.e., dc motors), for electrochemical work and for congested areas where storage battery reserves are necessary. For this purpose, ac power is converted into dc power at the substation by using converting machinery, e.g., mercury arc rectifiers, rotary converters and motor-generator sets. The dc supply from the substation may be obtained in the form of (*i*) 2-wire or (*ii*) 3-wire for distribution.

4.5.1.1 *Types of dc Distributors*

The following are the types of dc distributors:

1. Distributors fed at one end.
2. Distributors fed at both ends.
3. Distributors fed at the centre.
4. Ring mains distributors.

1. Distributors Fed at One End

In this type, the distributor is connected to supply mains at one end and loads are tapped at different points along the path of the distributor. Fig. 4.13 shows the single line diagram of a distributor *AB* fed at point *A*.

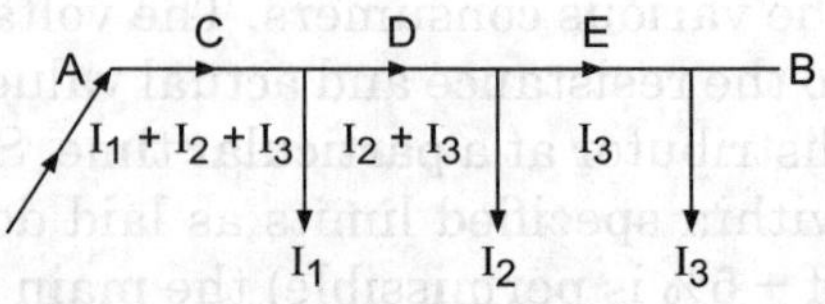

Fig. 4.13 Distributors fed at one end

The various loads are shown along the path at *C*, *D* and *E* respectively. The direction and magnitude of current in different section is shown in Fig. 4.13.

Important points regarding singly fed distributor are given below:

(i) The current away from feeding point and voltage across the loads away from feeding point goes on decreasing.

(ii) In case of any fault occurs in any section of distributor. The whole distributor is required to be disconnected from the supply for repair for continuity.

2. Distributors Fed at Both Ends

In this type of feeding, the distributor is connected to the supply mains at both ends i.e., at *A* and *B* respectively and the loads I_1, I_2, and I_3 are tapped along the length of the distributor at *C*, *D* and *E* respectively. (see Fig. 4.14)

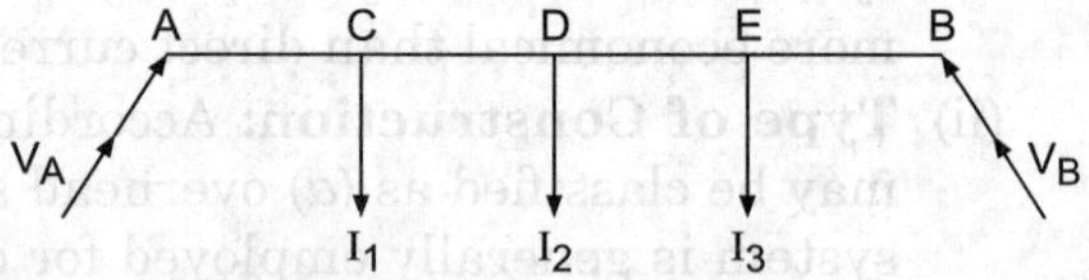

Fig. 4.14 Distributors fed at both ends

The voltage at terminals *A* and *B* is V_A and V_B. The voltage at both ends may be equal or different.

In this case load voltage first goes on decreasing at *A*, reaches the minimum value, then starts increasing and reaches the maximum value when reaching the other feeding point *B*. The point of minimum voltage is never fixed and shifts with the variation of load on the different sections of the distributor.

Advantages

The following are the advantages of the doubly fed distributor.

(i) If fault occurs on any feeding point of the distributor, the continuity of supply is maintained from the other feeding end.

(ii) In case of fault on any section of distributor, the faulty section can be disconnected and supply can be maintained to the remaining section.

(iii) Since area of cross section required for doubly fed distributor is much less than singly fed distributor hence it is economical.

3. Distributor Fed at the Centre

In this type, the centre of the distributor is connected to the supply mains as shown in Fig. 4.15. It is equivalent to two singly fed distributors, each distributor having common feeding point and length equal to half of the total length.

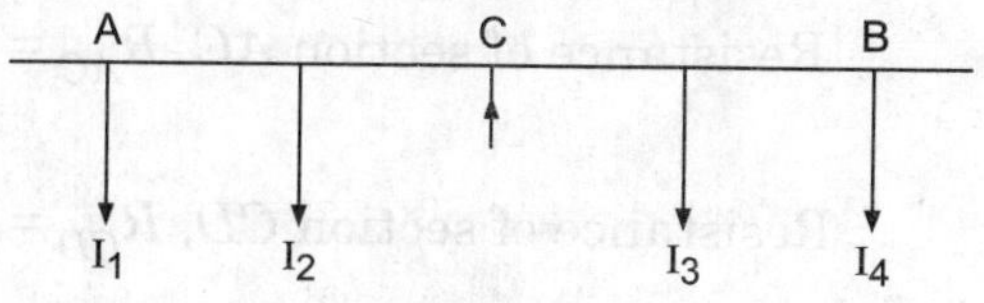

Fig. 4.15 Distributors fed at the centre

4. Ring Mains Distributor

In this type, the distributor is in the form of a closed ring as shown in Fig. 4.16. It is just a doubly fed distributor fed at equal voltage at both ends, the two ends being brought together to form a closed ring.

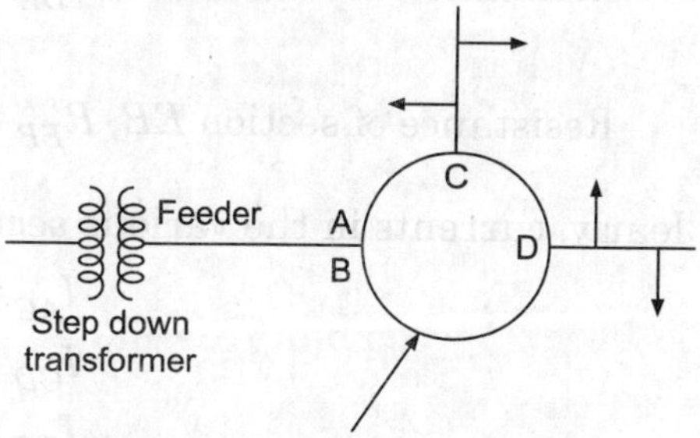

Fig. 4.16 Ring mains distributor

4.5.1.2 Calculation for DC Distribution

1. 2-Wire DC Distributor Fed at One End (Concentrated Loading)

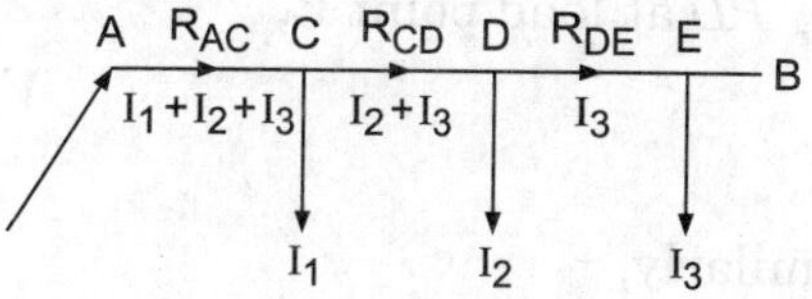

Fig. 4.17 Distributor fed at one end (Concentrated loading)

Figure 4.17 shows the single line diagram of a 2-wire dc distributor *AB* fed at one end *A* and having concentrated loads I_1, I_2, and I_3 at points *C*, *D*, and *E* respectively.

Let R_{AC}, R_{CD} and R_{DE} be the resistance of both wires (go and return) of the sections *AC*, *CD*, and *DE* of the distributor respectively.

Current in section, $AC = I_1 + I_2 + I_3$

Current in section, $CD = I_2 + I_3$

Current in section, $DE = I_3 + I_4$

$\therefore$ Voltage drop in section $AC = R_{AC}\,(I_1 + I_2 + I_3)$

Voltage drop in section $CD = R_{AC}\,(I_2 + I_3)$

Voltage drop in section $DE = R_{DE}\,I_3$

$\therefore$ Total voltage drop in the distributor $= (I_1 + I_2 + I_3)\,R_{AC} + (I_2 + I_3)\,R_{CD}\,I_3\,R_{DE}$

EXAMPLE 4.1 A 2-wire dc distributor cable *AB* is 2 km long and supplies loads of 100 *A*, 150 *A*, 200 *A* and 50 *A* situated 500 metres, 1000 metres, 1600 metres and 2000 metres respectively from the feeding point *A*. Each conductor has a resistance of 0.01 Ω per 1000 metres. Calculate potential at each load point if a pd of 300 V is maintained at point *A*.

Solution: Figure 4.18 shows the distributor with concentrated loads.

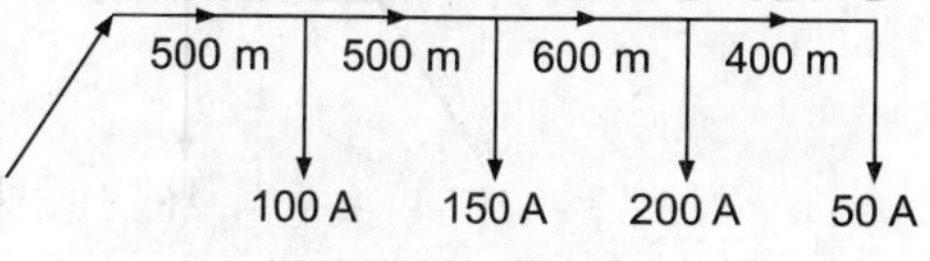

Fig. 4.18 Distributor fed at one end

Resistance per 1000 m of the distributor

= 2 × resistance per 1000 m of each conductor

= 2 × 0.01 = 0.02 Ω

$$\text{Resistance of section } AC, R_{AC} = \frac{500}{1000} \times 0.02 = 0.01\ \Omega$$

$$\text{Resistance of section } CD, R_{CD} = \frac{500}{1000} \times 0.02 = 0.01\ \Omega$$

$$\text{Resistance of section } DE, R_{DE} = \frac{600}{1000} \times 0.02 = 0.012\ \Omega$$

$$\text{Resistance of section } EB, R_{EB} = \frac{400}{1000} \times 0.02 = 0.008\ \Omega$$

Clearly, currents in the various sections of the distributor are:

$$I_{AC} = 500\ A,$$
$$I_{CD} = 400\ A,$$
$$I_{DE} = 250\ A,$$
$$I_{EB} = 50\ A$$

$\therefore$ *PD* at load point C,

$$V_C = \text{Volume at point } A - \text{Voltage drop in section } AC$$
$$= V_A - I_{AC} \times R_{AC} = 300 - 500 \times 0.01 = \textbf{295 V Ans.}$$

Similarly,

$$P.D. \text{ at load point } D, V_D = V_C - I_{CD} \times R_{CD} = 295 - 400 \times 0.01 = \textbf{291 V Ans.}$$
$$P.D. \text{ at load point } E, V_E = V_D - I_{DE} \times R_{DE} = 291 - 250 \times 0.012 = \textbf{288 V Ans.}$$
$$P.D. \text{ at load point } B, V_B = V_E - I_{EB} \times R_{EB} = 288 - 50 \times 0.008 = \textbf{287.6 V Ans.}$$

2. *2-wire DC Distributor Fed at Both Ends (Concentrated Loading)*

In this type of feeding, the distributor is fed at both ends. The two ends of the distributor may be supplied with:

(i) Equal voltages.
(ii) Unequal voltages.

(i) Two Ends Fed with Equal Voltages

Consider a distributor *AB* supplied at both ends with equal voltage *V* volts and having concentrated loaps I_1, I_2, I_3, I_4 and I_5 at points *C*, *D*, *E*, *F* and *G* respectively as shown in Fig. 4.19. As we move away from feeding point *A*, *p.d.* goes on decreasing till it reaches the minimum value at some load point say *E* and then again starts rising and becomes *V* volts as we reach the other feeding point *B*. The following points can be noted.

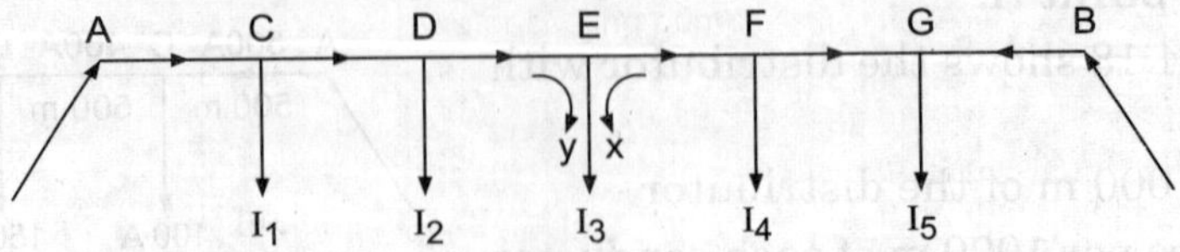

Fig. 4.19 Two ends fed with equal voltages

(i) All the currents tapped off between A and E (minimum p.d. point) are supplied from A whereas the currents tapped off between B and E are supplied from the feeding point B.

(ii) The current tapped at the minimum p.d. point E is supplied partly by feeding point A and partly by feeding point B.

Current tapped at point E = Current supplied by B + Current supplied by A

or $$I_3 = x + y$$

Voltage drop from A to E = Voltage drop from B to E

(ii) Two Ends Fed with Unequal Voltages

Figure 4.20 shows the distributor AB fed with unequal voltages, end A being fed at V_1 volts and end B fed at V_2 volts.

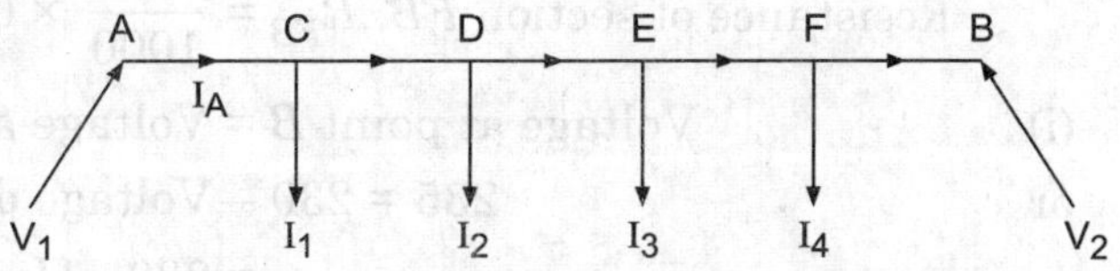

Fig. 4.20 Two ends fed with unequal voltages

Point of Minimum Potential

In order to find the point of minimum potential, suppose x amperes is supplied by point A.

$\therefore$ *P.D.* between AB = Voltage drop over AB

or $$V_1 - V_2 = I_A R_{AC} + (I_A - I_1)R_{CD} + (I_A - I_1 - I_2)\, R_{DE}$$
$$+ (I_A - I_1 - I_2 - I_3)R_{EF} + (I_A - I_1 - I_2 - I_3 - I_4)R_{FB}$$

From this equation, the unknown I_A can be calculated as other quantities are generally given. Then, indicate the actual direction of currents in the various sections of the distribution. The load point where the currents are coming from both sides of the distribution is the *point of minimum potential.*

EXAMPLE 4.2 A distribution *AB* is fed from both ends. At feeding point *A*, the voltage is maintained at 230 *V* and at *B* 235 *V*. The total length of the feeder is 200 metres and loads are tapped as under :

25 *A* at 50 metres from *A*; 50 *A* at 75 metres from *A*, 30 *A* at 100 metres from A and 40 *A* at 150 metres from *A*.

The resistance per 1000 metres of the conductor is 0.3 Ω. Calculate:

(i) Current in various sections of the distributor,

(ii) Minimum voltage and the point at which it occurs in the system.

Solution: Figure 4.21 shows the distributor with various loads. Let I_A amperes be the current supplied from the feeding end A. Then the currents in the various sections of the distributor are as shown in Fig. 4.21.

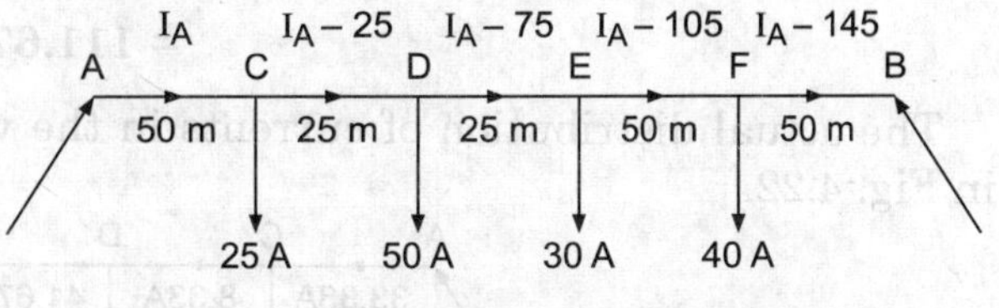

Fig. 4.21 Distributor fed from both ends

Resistance per 1000 m of the distributor

$= 2 \times$ resistance per 1000 metres of one conductor

$= 2 \times 0.3 = 0.6\ \Omega$

$\therefore$ Resistance of section AC, $R_{AC} = \frac{50}{1000} \times 0.6 = 0.03\ \Omega$

Resistance of section CD, $R_{CD} = \frac{25}{1000} \times 0.6 = 0.015\ \Omega$

Resistance of section DE, $R_{DE} = \frac{25}{1000} \times 0.6 = 0.015\ \Omega$

Resistance of section EF, $R_{EF} = \frac{50}{1000} \times 0.6 = 0.3\ \Omega$

Resistance of section FB, $R_{FB} = \frac{50}{1000} \times 0.6 = 0.03\ \Omega$

(i) Voltage at point B = Voltage at point A – Voltage drop over AB

or 235 = 230 – Voltage drop in section AC, CD, DE, EF and FB

$$= 230 - [I_A \times 0.03 + (I_A - 25) \times 0.015 + (I_A - 75)\ 0.015 + (I_A - 105)\ 0.03 + (I_A - 145)\ 0.03]$$

$$= 230 - 0.03I_A - 0.015\ I_A + 0.375 - 0.015\ I_A + 1.125 - 0.03I_A + 3.15 - 0.03\ I_A + 4.35$$

or $235 = 239 - 0.12\ I_A$

$$\therefore \quad I_A = \frac{239 - 235}{0.12} = \frac{4}{0.12} = 33.33\ A$$

Current in section AC, $I_{AC} = I_A$ – **33.3 A Ans.** from C to C

Current in section CD, $I_{CD} = I_A - 25 = 33.33 - 25 =$ **8.33 *A* Ans.** from C to D

Current in section DE, $I_{DE} = I_A - 75 = 33.33 - 75$

$= -41.67\ A$ from D to E

= 41.67 *A* Ans. from E to D

Current in section EF, $I_{EF} = I_A - 105 = 33.33 - 105$

$= -71.67\ A$ from E to F

= 71.67 *A* Ans. from F to E

Current in section FB, $I_{FB} = I_A - 145 = 33.33 - 145$

$= -111.67$ from F to B

= 111.67 *A* Ans. from B to F

The actual distribution of currents in the various sections of the distributor is shown in Fig. 4.22.

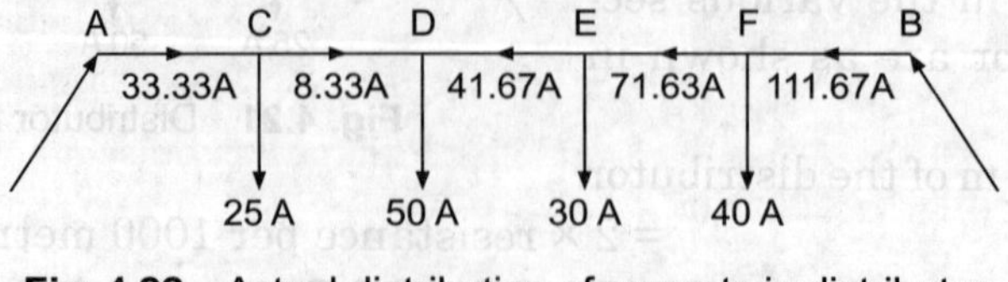

Fig. 4.22 Actual distribution of currents in distributor

(ii) The currents are coming to load point D from both sides of the distributor, i.e., from point C and point E.

∴ *D is the point of minimum potential.* **Ans.**

$$\begin{aligned} \text{Voltage at point } D,\ V_D &= \text{Voltage at point } A - \text{Voltage drop over } AD \\ &= V_A - \text{Voltage drop in sections } AC \text{ and } CD \\ &= 230 - [(33.33 \times 0.03) + 8.33 \times 0.015)] \\ &= 230 - 1.0 - 0.125 = \mathbf{228.875\ V\ Ans.} \end{aligned}$$

Ring Main Distributor

A distributor arranged to form a closed loop and fed at one or more point is called ring distributor. Such a distributor is starts from one point, makes a loop through the area to be served, and returns to the original point. The main advantage of ring main distributor is that in case of some fault on any section of the distributor, the faulty section can be isolated from both side and supply is maintained. For the purpose of calculations, it is equivalent to a straight distributor fed at both ends with equal voltage.

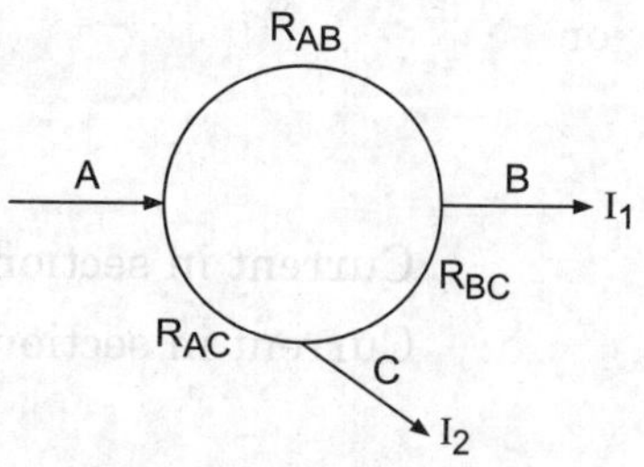

Fig. 4.23 Ring distributor

Fig. 4.23 shows the ring distributor. The distributor is being fed at only one feeding point A and tapping of current I_1 and I_2 are taken from point B and C respectively.

EXAMPLE 4.3 A two wire ring distributor is 300 metres long and is fed at 240 *V* at point *A*. At point *B*, 150 metres from *A*, there is a load of 120 *A* and at *C* 100 metres in the opposite direction, there is load of 80 *A*. The resistance per 100 metres of single conductor is 0.03 ohm. Find :

(i) Current in each section of the distributor

(ii) P.D. at points *B* and *C*.

Solution: Resistance per 100 m of distributor = 2 × resistance per 100 of each conductor

$$= 2 \times 0.03 = 0.06\ \Omega$$

$$\text{Resistance of section } AB,\ R_{AB} = \frac{0.06}{100} \times 150 = 0.09\ \Omega$$

$$\text{Resistance of section } BC,\ R_{BC} = \frac{0.06}{100} \times 50 = 0.03\ \Omega$$

$$\text{Resistance of section } CA,\ R_{CA} = \frac{0.06}{100} \times 100 = 0.06\ \Omega$$

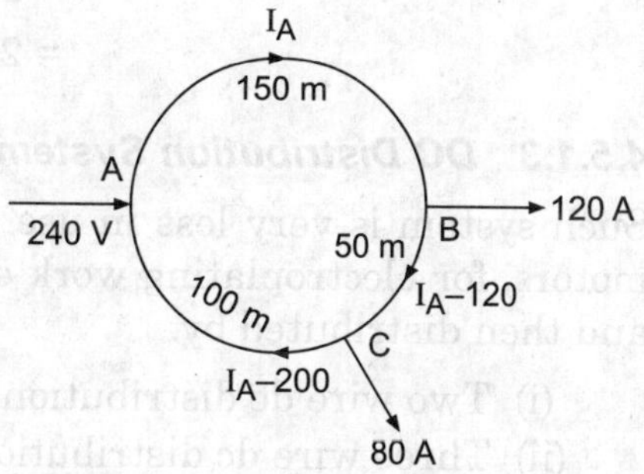

Fig. 4.24 Two wire ring distributor

(i) Let I_A amperes be the current supplied by the feeding point A in the section AB of the distributor as shown in Fig. 4.24.

Current in section AB, $I_{AB} = I_A$

Current in section BC, $I_{BC} = I_A - 120$

Current in section CA, $I_{CA} = I_A - 200$

Applying Kirchhoff's second law to the closed loop $ABCA$,
Algebraic sum of voltage drops in the loop = 0

or $$I_{AB} R_{AB} + I_{BC} R_{BC} + I_{CA} R_{CA} = 0$$

or $$I_a \times 0.09 + (I_A - 120) \times 0.03 + (I_A - 200)\ 0.06 = 0$$

or $$0.09\ I_A + 0.03\ I_A - 3.6 + 0.06\ I_A - 12 = 0$$

or $$0.18\ I_A = 15.6$$

$$I_A = \frac{15.6}{0.18} = 86.67\text{ A}$$

Current in section AB, $I_{AB} = I_A = 86.67$ A **Ans.** from A to B

Current in section BC, $I_{BC} = I_A - 120 = 86.67 - 120$

$= -33.33\ A$ from B to C

= 33.33 *A* Ans. from C to B

Current in section CA, $I_{CA} = I_A - 200 = 86.67 - 200$

$= -113.33\ A$ from C to A

= 113.33 A Ans. from A to C

The actual distribution of currents in the various sections of the distributor is shown in Fig. 4.25

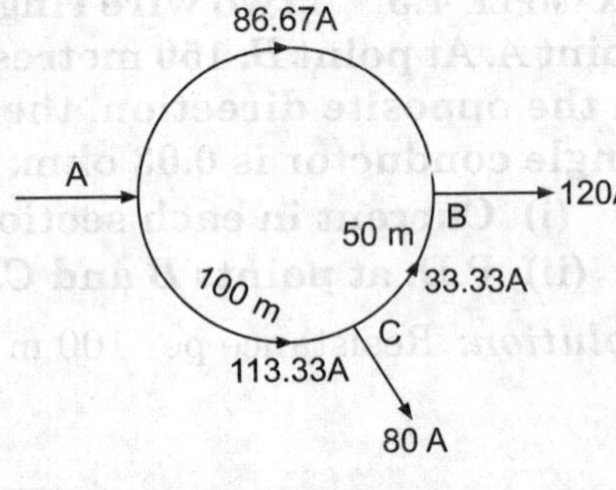

Fig. 4.25 Actual distribution of currents

(ii) Voltage at point B = Voltage at point A – voltage drop over AB

or $$V_B = V_A - I_{AB} R_{AB}$$

or $$= 240 - 86.67 \times 0.09$$

$$= 240 - 7.8$$

$$= \mathbf{232.2\ V\ Ans.}$$

Voltage at point C, $V_C = V_B + I_{CB} R_{BC}$

$$= 232.2 + 33.33 \times 0.03$$

$$= 232.2 + 1 = \mathbf{233.2\ V\ Ans.}$$

4.5.1.3 DC Distribution System

Such system is very less in use. But for certain applications such as for operation of dc motors, for electroplating work etc. For this purpose ac is converted in dc at sub-station and then distributed by.

(i) Two wire dc distribution system

(ii) Three wire dc distribution system

(i) **Two wire d.c. distribution system:** Such system use two conductors, one as positive and other is negative conductor. The loads such as lamps, motors etc., are connected in parallel between these two conductors shown in Fig. 4.26.

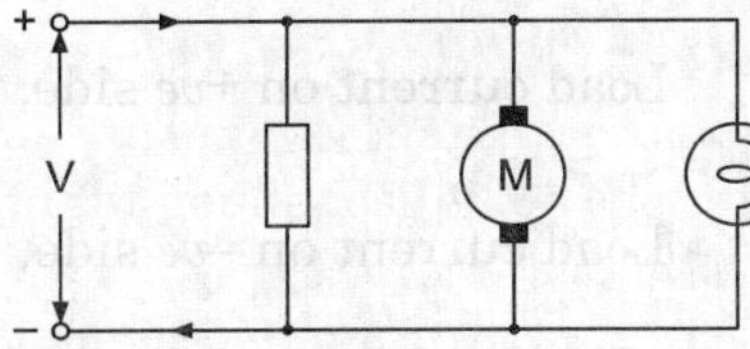

Fig. 4.26 Two-wire dc distribution system

(ii) **Three wire d.c distribution system:** Such systems use three conductors, two outer conductor (one positive and other negative) and one middle conductor (neutral). The voltage between outer conductor is 2*V* and heavy loads are connected.

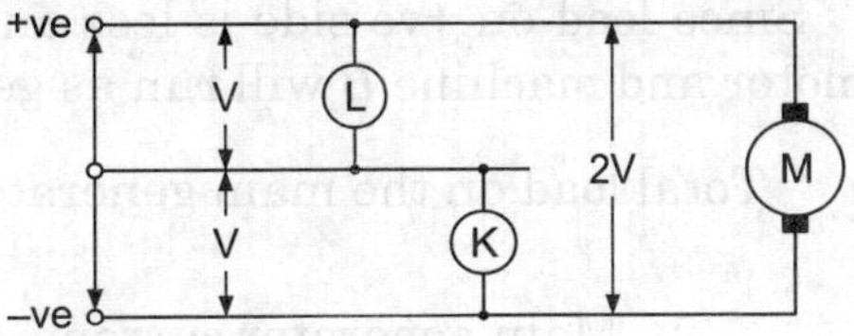

Fig. 4.27 Three-wire dc distribution system

The voltage between one outer and middle conductor is *V* volts and light loads are connected as shown in Fig. 4.27.

Advantages of 3-wire dc Distribution

(i) Two different voltages are available, high voltage across outer for power load and low voltage across neutral and one of the outer for domestic and light load.

(ii) With the same volume of copper, 3-wire dc distribution is able to deliver twice of that with two wire distribution system with out affecting the efficiency.

Disadvantages

(i) In three wire system, third wire is required.

(ii) The safety is partially reduced.

(iii) In overhead system, the cross-arm of greater length is required.

(iv) A balancer is required, cost is therefore increased

EXAMPLE 4.4 A d.c. 3 wire system with 500 V between outers supplier 300 kW on the +ve side and 500 kW at the *–ve* side. Calculate:

(i) Current in each balance armature

(ii) Current in middle wire

(iii) Total current supplied by the generator.

Solution: The connections are shown in Fig. 4.28

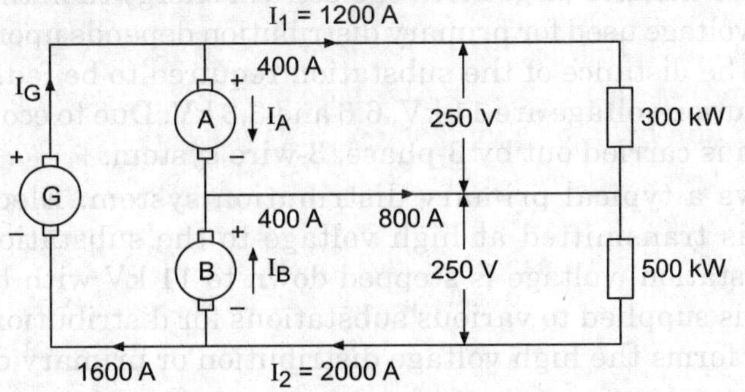

Fig. 4.28 DC 3 wire system

$$\text{Load current on } +ve \text{ side, } I_1 = \frac{300 \times 1000}{250} = 1200 \text{ V}$$

$$\text{Load current on } -ve \text{ side, } I_2 = \frac{500 \times 1000}{250} = 2000 \text{ A}$$

$$\text{Current in neutral wire, } I_N = I_2 - I_1$$

$$= 2000 - 1200 = 800 \text{ A}$$

Since load on +ve side is less and on *–ve* side is more, therefore, machine *A* is run as motor and machine *B* will run as generator.

Total load on the main generator = 300 + 500 = 800 kW

$$\text{Main generator current, } I_G = \frac{800 \times 1000}{500} = 1600 \text{ A} \quad \textbf{Ans.}$$

$$\text{Current in machine } A,\ I_A = I_G - I_1 = 1600 - 1200 = 400\ A \quad \textbf{Ans.}$$

$$\text{Current in machine } B,\ I_B = I_2 - I_G = 2000 - 1600 = 400\ A \quad \textbf{Ans.}$$

4.5.2 AC Distribution

Nowadays electrical energy is generated, transmitted and distributed in the form of alternating current. One important reason for the widespread use of alternating current in preference to direct current is the fact that alternating voltage can be conveniently changed in magnitude by means of a transformer. Transformer has made it possible to transmit ac power at high voltage and utilise it at a safe potential. High transmission and distribution voltages have greatly reduced the current in the conductors and the resulting line losses.

There is no definite line between transmission and distribution according to voltage or bulk capacity. However, in general, the ac distribution system is the electrical system between the step-down substation fed by the transmission system and the consumers' metres. The ac distribution system is classified into: (*i*) primary distribution system and (*ii*) secondary distribution system.

4.5.2.1 Primary Distribution System

It is that part of ac distribution system which operates at voltage somewhat higher than general utilization and handles large block of electrical energy than the average low-voltage consumer uses. The voltage used for primary distribution depends upon the amount of power to be conveyed and the distance of the substation required to be fed. The most commonly used primary distribution voltage are 11 kV, 6.6 and 3.3 kV. Due to economic considerations, primary distribution is carried out by 3-phase, 3-wire system.

Figure 4.29 shows a typical primary distribution system. Electric power from the generating station is transmitted at high voltage to the substation located in or near the city. At this substation, voltage is stepped down to 11 kV with the help of step-down transformer. Power is supplied to various substations for distribution or to big consumers at this voltage. This forms the high voltage distribution or primary distribution.

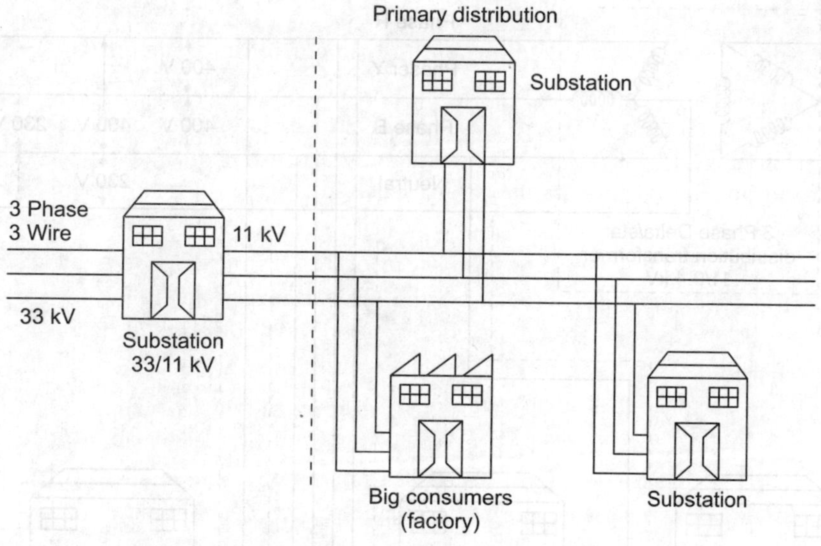

Fig. 4.29 Primary distribution system

4.5.2.2 Secondary Distribution System

It is that part of a.c. distribution system which includes the range of voltages at which the ultimate consumer utilizes the electrical energy delivered to him. The secondary distribution employs 400/230 V, 3-phase, 4-wire system.

Figure 4.30 shows a typical secondary distribution system. The primary distribution circuit delivers power to various substations, called distribution substations. The substations are situated near the consumer's localities and contain step-down transformers. At each distribution substation, the voltage is stepped down to 400 V and power is delivered by 3-phase, 4-wire ac system. The voltage between any two phases is 400 V and between any phase and neutral is 230 V. The single phase domestic loads are connected between any one phase and the neutral whereas 3-phase 400 V motor loads are connected across 3-phase lines directly.

4.5.3 Difference Between AC Distribution and DC Distribution

An ac distribution differs from d.c. distribution in the following respects:

(i) In dc system, the voltage drop is due to resistance alone but in case of ac system, voltage drops are due to the combined effects of resistance, inductance and capacitance.

(ii) In dc system, additions and subtractions of currents are done arithmetically, but in case of ac system, additions and subtractions are done vectorially. Therefore, in ac system voltages and currents are expressed in symbolic notation.

(iii) All methods used for dc distributors also hold good for ac distributors, the only difference being that in ac system all impedances, currents and voltages are expressed symbolically with voltage or current as the reference vector.

(iv) At load points, the phase angle between voltage and current has to be taken into account, i.e., power factor plays an important part. There are two ways of referring power factor namely:

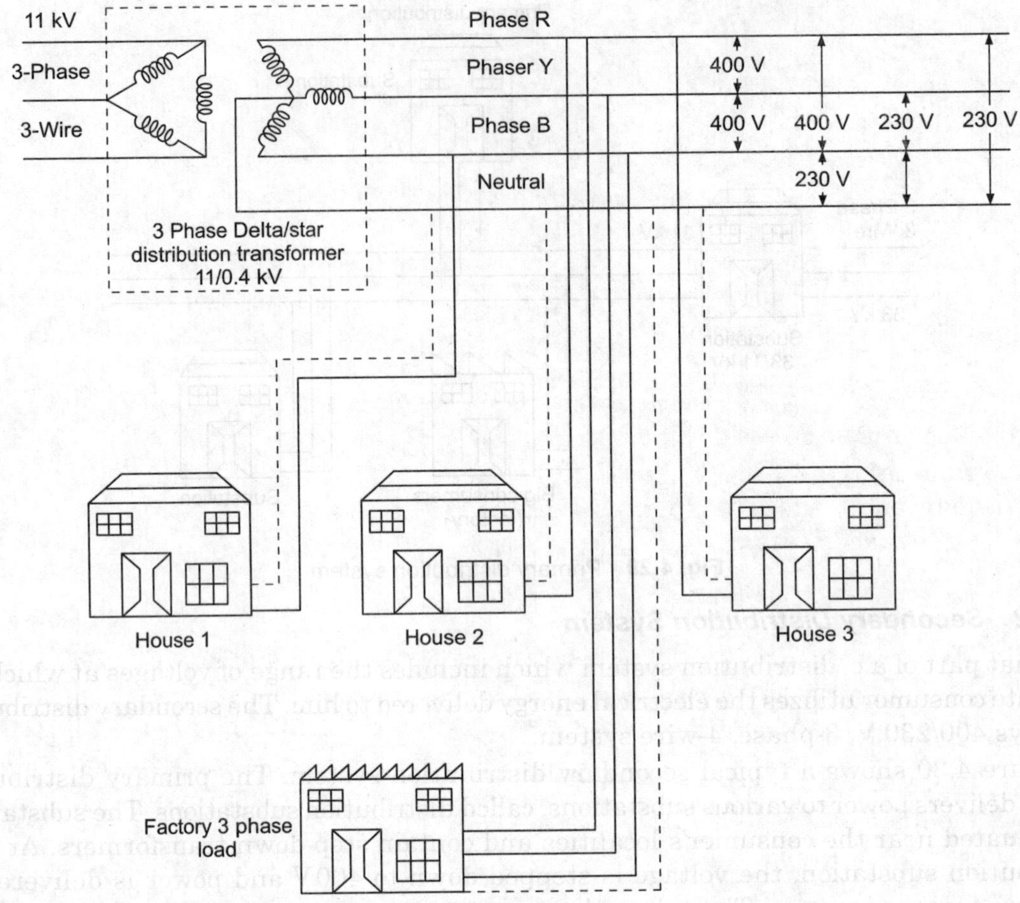

Fig. 4.30 Secondary distribution system

(a) It may be referred to supply voltage or receiving end voltage which is the reference vector.

(b) It may be referred to the voltage at the load point itself.

Solution of AC Distributors

AC distribution with Concentrated Loads

In the solution of ac distributors, power factors at load points play very important part. There are two ways of referring power factor, namely:

1. Power factors referred to receiving end (or sending end) voltage.
2. Power factors referred to various load points.

1. Power Factor Referred to Receiving End (or Sending End) Voltage

Consider an ac distributor *AB* with concentrated loads I_1 and I_2 at points *C* and *B* as shown in Fig. 4.31. Calling V_B as the receiving end voltage and taking it to be reference vector, let the power factors of loads at points *C* and *B* be $\cos \phi_1$ and $\cos \phi_2$ *lagging* respectively as referred to V_B. Let R_1, X_1 and R_2, X_2 be the resistance and reactance of sections *AC* and *CB* of the distributor.

Load current at point C,

$$I_1 = I_1\,(\cos\phi_1 - j\sin\phi_1)$$

Load current at point B,

$$I_2 = I_2\,(\cos\phi_2 - j\sin\phi_2)$$

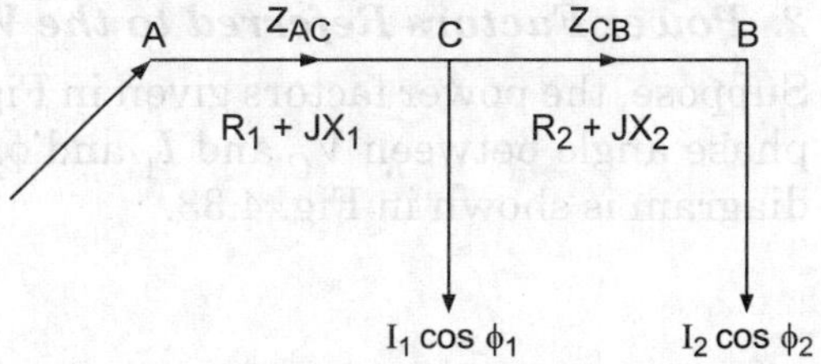

Fig. 4.31 Power factor referred to receiving end voltage

Impedance of section AC, $Z_{AC} = R_1 + jX_1$

Impedance of section CB, $Z_{CB} = R_2 + jX_2$

$\therefore$ Voltage drop in section CB, $V_{CB} = I_2\,Z_{CB}$

$$= I_2\,(\cos\phi_2 - j\sin\phi_2)\,(R_2 + jX_2)$$

Current in section $AC = I_1 + I_2$

$$= I_1\,(\cos\phi_1 - j\sin\phi_1) + I_2\,(\cos\phi_2 - j\sin\phi_2)$$

$\therefore$ Voltage drop in section AC, $V_{AC} = (I_1 + I_2)Z_{AC}$

$$= [I_1\,(\cos\phi_1 - j\sin\phi_1) + I_2\,(\cos\phi_2 - j\sin\phi_2)]\,[R_1 + jX_1]$$

Sending end voltage, $V_A = V_B + V_{CB} + V_{AC}$

Sending end current, $I_S = I_1 + I_2 = I_1\,(\cos\phi_1 - j\sin\phi_1) + I_2\,(\cos\phi_2 - j\sin\phi_2)$

Sending end power factor $= \cos\phi_s$

Phasor Diagram

Figure 4.32 shows the phasor diagram of the a.c. distributor under reference. Here, receiving end voltage V_B is taken as the reference vector. Since power factors are referred to V_B, therefore, I_1 lag behind V_B by ϕ_1 and ϕ_2 respectively.

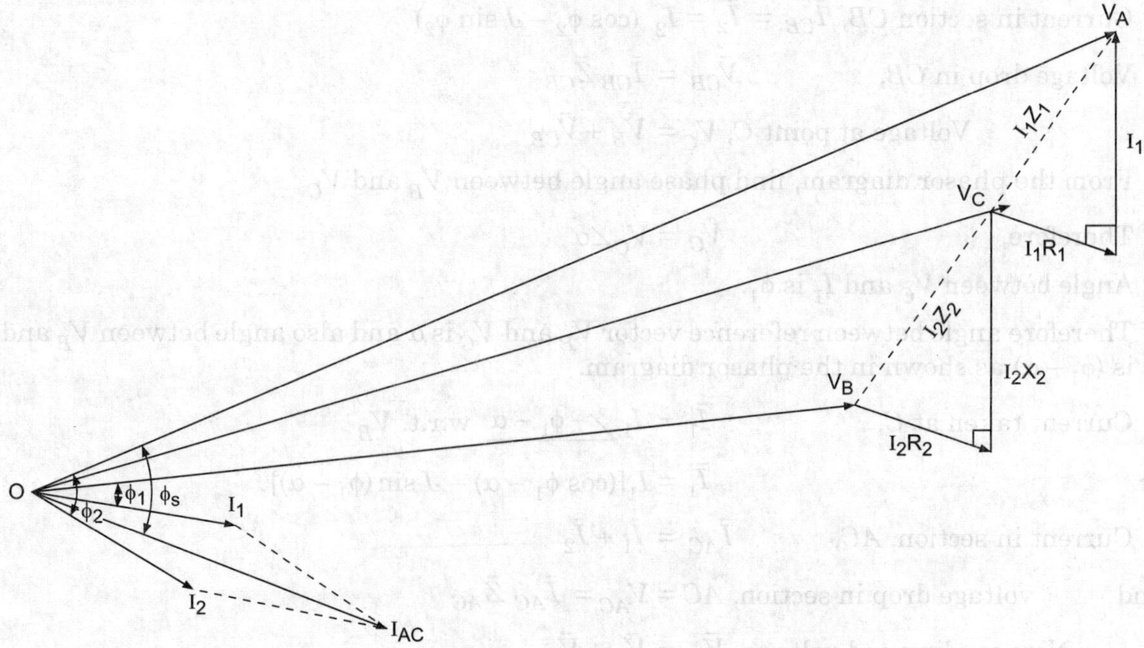

Fig. 4.32 Phasor diagram

2. Power Factors Referred to the Various Load Voltages

Suppose, the power factors given in Fig. 4.33 are referred to the load points. Then, ϕ_1 is the phase angle between V_C and I_1 and ϕ_2 is the phase angle between V_B and I_2. The phasor diagram is shown in Fig. 4.33.

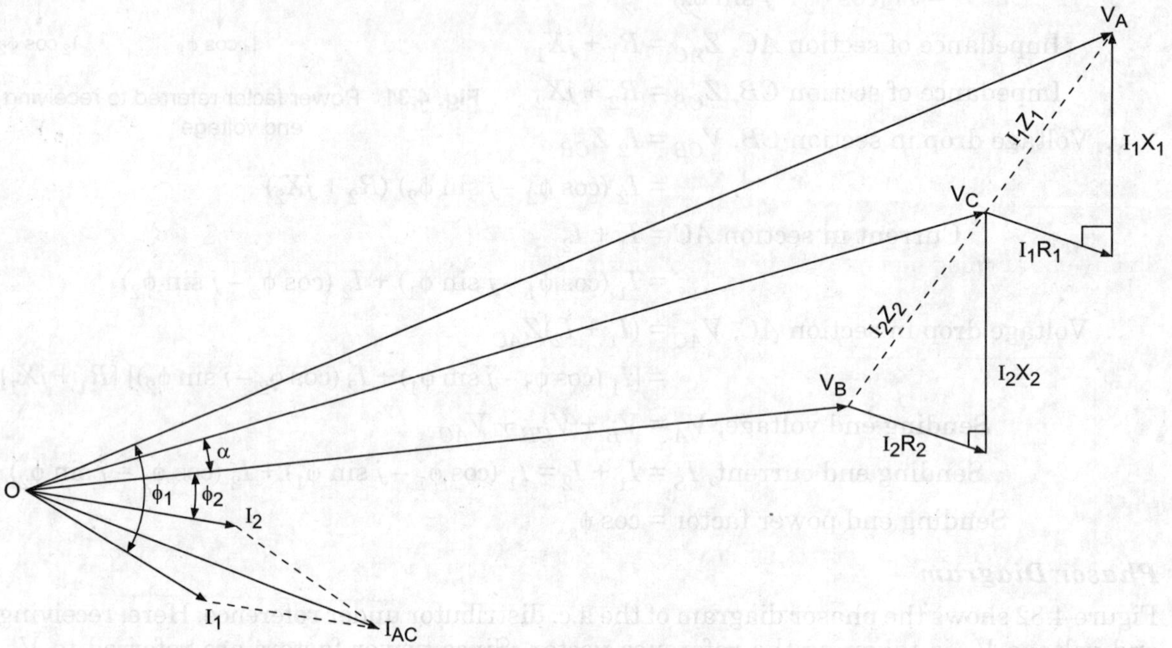

Fig. 4.33 Phasor diagram

Current in section CB, $\vec{I}_{CB} = \vec{I}_2 = I_2\ (\cos\phi_2 - J\sin\phi_2)$

Voltage drop in CB, $\vec{V}_{CB} = \vec{I}_{CB}\,\vec{Z}_{CB}$

$\therefore$ Voltage at point C, $V_C = \vec{V}_B + \vec{V}_{CB}$

From the phasor diagram, find phase angle between V_B and V_C

Therefore, $\vec{V}_C = V_C \angle \alpha$

Angle between V_C and I_1 is ϕ_1.

Therefore angle between reference vector V_B and V_C is α and also angle between V_B and I_1 is $(\phi_1 - \alpha)$ as shown in the phasor diagram.

Current taken at C, $\vec{I}_1 = I_1 \underline{\angle -\phi_1 - \alpha}$ w.r.t. V_B

or $\vec{I}_1 = I_1[(\cos\phi_1 - \alpha) - J\sin(\phi_1 - \alpha)]$

Current in section, AC, $\vec{I}_{AC} = \vec{I}_1 + \vec{I}_2$

and voltage drop in section, $AC = V_{AC} = \vec{I}_{AC}\,\vec{Z}_{AC}$

Now sending end voltage, $\vec{V}_A = \vec{V}_C + \vec{V}_{AC}$

EXAMPLE 4.5 A single phase a.c. distributor *AB* cable 300 metres long supplies a load of 100 A at 0.707 p.f. lagging and 200 A at 0.8 p.f. lagging at a distance of 200 metres and 300 metres respectively from the feeding point *A*. The total resistance and reactance of the cable is 0.2 Ω and 0.1 Ω per kilometer. Calculate the total voltage drop in the cable. The load power factors refer to the voltage at the far end.

Solution: Impedance of cable per km run,

$$Z = R + jX_L = (0.2 + j\,0.1)\ \Omega$$

$$\text{Impedance of section } AC,\ Z_{AC} = \frac{(0.2 + j0.1)}{1000} \times 200 = (0.04 + j\,0.02)\ \Omega$$

$$\text{Impedance of section } CB,\ Z_{CB} = \frac{(0.2 + j0.1)}{1000} = 100 = (0.02 + j\,0.01)\ \Omega$$

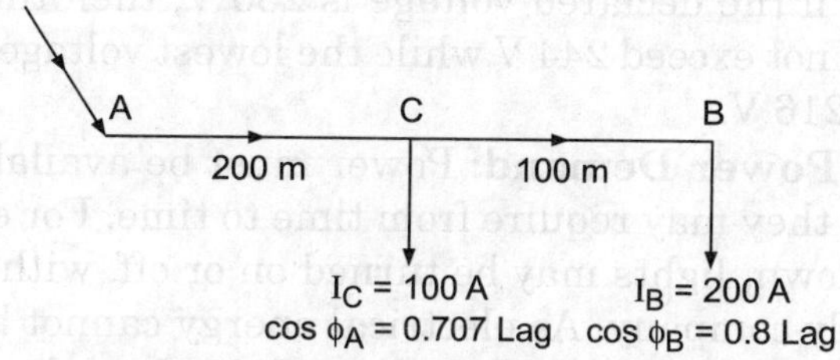

Fig. 4.34 Single phase ac distributor

Taking voltage at the far end point *B* as the reference vector,

$$\text{Load current at point } B,\ I_B = I_B\,(\cos\phi_B - j\sin\phi_B)$$

$$= 200\,(0.8 - j\,0.6) = (160 - j\,120)\ A$$

$$\text{Load current at point } C,\ I_C = I_C\,(\cos\phi_A - j\sin\phi_A)$$

$$= 100\,(0.707 - j\,0.707) = (70.7 - j\,70.7)\ A$$

$$\text{Current in section } CB,\ I_{CB} = I_B = (160 - j\,120)\ A$$

$$\text{Current in section } AC,\ I_{AC} = I_B + I_C = (70.7 - j\,70.7) + (160 - j\,120)$$

$$= (230.7 - j\,190.7)\ A$$

$$\text{Voltage drop in section } CB,\ V_{CB} = I_{CB} + Z_{CB}$$

$$= (160 - j\,120)\,(0.02 + j\,0.01) = (4.4 - j\,0.8)\ \text{volts}$$

$$\text{Voltage drop in section } AC,\ V_{AC} \times Z_{AC}$$

$$= (230.7 - j\,190.7)\,(0.04 + j\,0.02)$$

$$= (13.04 - j\,3.01)\ \text{volts}$$

$$\text{Total voltage drop in the cable} = V_{AC} + V_{CB} = (13.04 - j\,3.01) + (4.4 - j0.8)$$

$$= (17.44 - j\,3.81)\ \text{volts}$$

$$\text{Magnitude of total voltage drop} = \sqrt{(17.44)^2 + (3.81)^2} = \sqrt{304 + 14.5} = \mathbf{17.73\ V} \quad \textbf{Ans.}$$

4.6 REQUIREMENTS OF A DISTRIBUTION SYSTEM

A considerable amount of effort is necessary to maintain an electric power supply within the requirements of various types of consumers. Some of the requirements of a good distribution system are : proper voltage, availability of power on demand and reliability.

(i) **Proper Voltage:** One important requirement of a distribution system is that voltage variations at consumer's terminals should be as low as possible. The changes in voltage are generally caused due to the variation of load on the system. Low voltage causes loss of revenue, insufficient lighting and possible burning out of motors. High voltage causes lamps to burn out permanently and may cause failure of other appliances. Therefore, a good distribution system should ensure that the voltage variations at consumers terminal are within permissible limits. The statutory limit of voltage variations is ±6% of the rated value at the consumers terminals. Thus, if the declared voltage is 230 V, then the highest voltage of the consumer should not exceed 244 V while the lowest voltage of the consumer should not be less than 216 V.

(ii) **Availability of Power Demand:** Power must be available to the consumers in any amount that they may require from time to time. For example, motors may be started or shut down, lights may be turned on or off, without advance warning to the electric supply company. As electrical energy cannot be stored, therefore, the distribution system must be capable of supplying load demands of the consumers. This necessitates that operating staff must continuously study load patterns to predict in advance those major load changes that follow the known schedules.

(iii) **Reliability:** Modern industry is almost dependent on electric power for its operation. Homes of ice buildings are lighted, heated, cooled and ventilated by electric power. This calls for reliable service. Unfortunately electric power, like everything else that is man-made, can never be absolutely reliable. However, the reliability can be improved to a considerable extent by: (*a*) interconnected system, (*b*) reliable automatic control system, (*c*) providing additional reserve facilities.

4.6.1 Determination of Size of Conductor for a Distribution System

It is known that power to consumers comes from the generating station via transmission and distribution lines. These lines have resistances, inductances and capacitances, resulting in a voltage drop in the line so that the voltage at the receiving end is reduced.

Good voltage regulation of a distribution network is probably the most important factor for delivering good service to the consumers.

The following are the factors taken into consideration for determining the size of conductor for the distribution system:

1. Permissible voltage drop in the line
2. Current carrying capacity
3. Tensile strength of the conductor.

While considering the current carrying capacity of the conductor, the maximum safe temperature is taken into consideration. For aluminimum conductors this temperature is 75°C. If the temperature is more beyond the limit during peak hours, then conductor tensile strength is reduced and it may melt. Therefore, while selecting the conductor size, the officially declare ambient temperature of the area is considered. From that temperature permissible temperature rise is calculated.

After the conductor size has been selected on the basis of permissible voltage drop and current carrying capacity, tensile strength of the selected conductor size should be sufficient to withstand the mechanical force acting during fog weather.

The feeder is designed from the point of view of its current carrying capacity while the distributor is designed from the point of view of the voltage drop in it.

4.7 UNDERGROUND CABLE

An underground cable essentially consists of one or more conductors covered with suitable insulation surrounded by a protecting cover. The cable is laid underground to transmit electric power.

The underground cables are mostly used for distribution of electric power in urban areas. Underground cables are used for transmission and distribution of power where it becomes impracticable to make use of overhead construction.

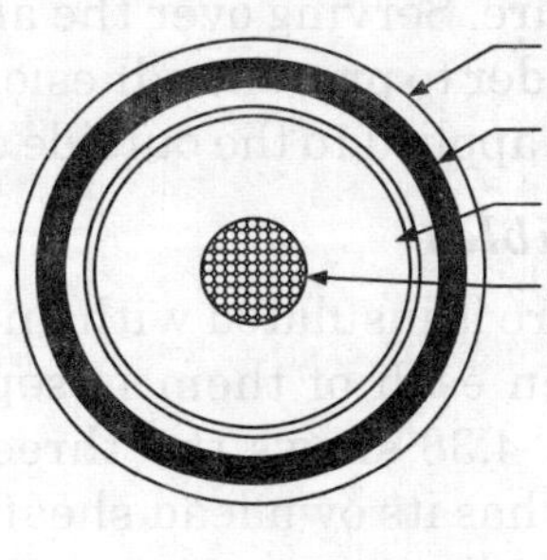

Fig. 4.35 Single core LT cable

4.7.1 Classification of Cables

Cables are usually classified according to the voltage for which these are manufactured. According to voltage, these are classified as:

(i) Low voltage (or LT) cables for operating voltage up to 1,000 V.
(ii) High voltage (or HT) cables for operating voltage up to 11,000 V.
(iii) Super tension (or ST) cables for operating voltage up to 33,000 V.
(iv) Extra high tension (or EHT) cables for operating voltage upto 66,000 V.
(v) Extra super voltage power cables for operating voltage beyond 1,32,000 volts.

1. Low Voltage Cables

These cables are meant for use upto 6,600 volts. For voltage upto 6,600 volts the electrostatic stresses developed in cables are very small and the thermal conductivity is also of not much importance so no special construction is required.

The cables are of two types viz. single-core and multicore cables. The former types has the advantages of simplicity of construction.

2. Single Core Cables

Single core LT cable consists of one circular core of tinned stranded copper or aluminium insulated by layer of impregnated paper as shown in Fig. 4.36.

Single core cables are not usually provided with armouring in order to avoid excessive loss in the armour.

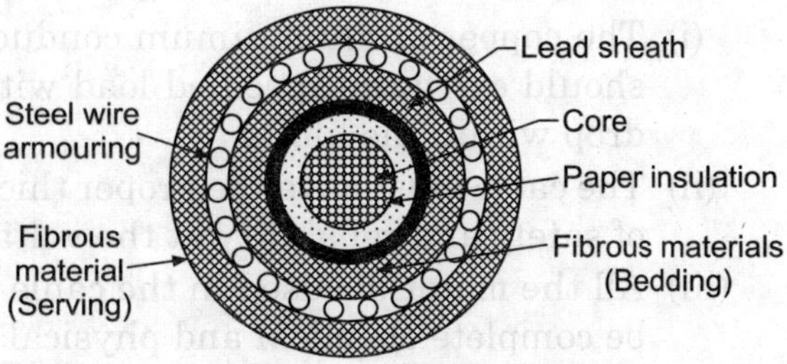

Fig. 4.36 Single core cable

3. Multicore Cables

Multicore cables for use upto 11000 volts are of belt type. The belt type cable consists of either circular shaped or oval shaped core of stranded conductors wrapped around by impregnated paper and then warmed together. The interstics are filled with packing to make the cable of circular cross-section. A lead sheath enclosed the whole is provided for its protection against entry of moisture. Serving over the armouring is provided. In order to prevent adhesion, a coating of lime wash is applied to the outside of the cable.

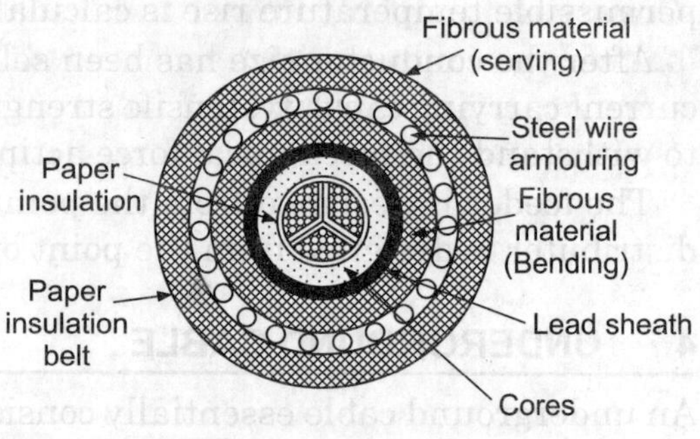

Fig. 4.37 3-core cable (belted)

4. SL Type Cables

Firstly each core is insulated with an impregnated paper and then each of them is separately lead sheathed. Fig. 4.38 shows the three core cables. The three core has its own lead sheath and laid up with fillers in ordinary way, armoured and served overall with impregnated hessian tape as usual.

The disadvantage of S.L. type cable is that the manufacturing is difficult because of thinner lead sheaths. S.L. type cables can be used upto 66 kV.

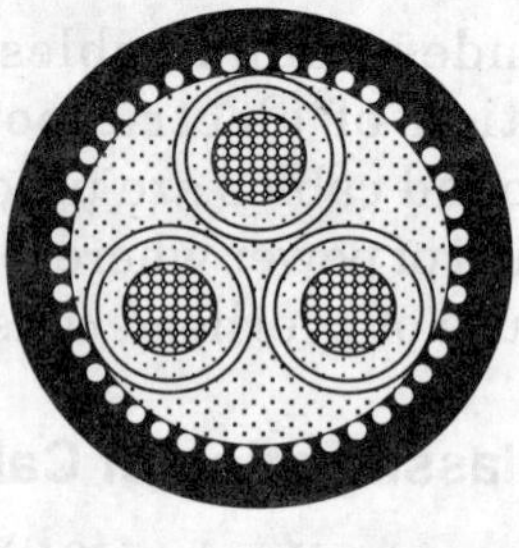

Fig. 3.38 SL type cable (33 kV three core)

Advantages of SL Type Cables Over H-type Cables

1. Less tendency for oil drainage on hilly routes owing to eliminator of filler spaces contained compound.
2. Bending of cable becomes possible owing to no overall lead sheath.

The main disadvantages of SL type cable is that the manufacturing is difficult because of thinner lead sheath. SL type cable can be used upto 66 kV.

5. HSL Type Cables

Such type of cable is a combination of H-type and SL type cables. In HSL type cables each conductor is insulated sheathed with metalized paper and then covered with lead sheath. The three cores are then laid up and provided with filler braided armoured and finally served.

Requirement of Cables

The following are the necessary requirements of the cables:

(i) The copper or aluminimum conductor used should be of such size that the cable should carry the specified load without over heating and should cause a voltage drop within the limits.

(ii) The cable must have the proper thickness of the insulation so as to give high degree of safety and reliability at the voltage for which it is designed.

(iii) All the materials used in the cable manufacture should be such that there should be complete chemical and physical stability throughout.

(iv) The cable must be provided with a mechanical protection so as to withstand the rough use in laying it.

4.8 CONSTRUCTION OF 11 kV HT AND LT POWER CABLE

Construction of HT Power Cables: High tension (HT) cables are used upto 11 kV. A 3-core balted type cable is generally employed at 11 kV. It consists of the following main parts:

1. **Core of Conductor:** A three-core cable has three conductors as shown in Fig. 4.39. These conductors are made of copper or aluminimum and usually stranded to make the cable flexible. The copper conductors are always tinned to protect cable to react with compound used for insulation.

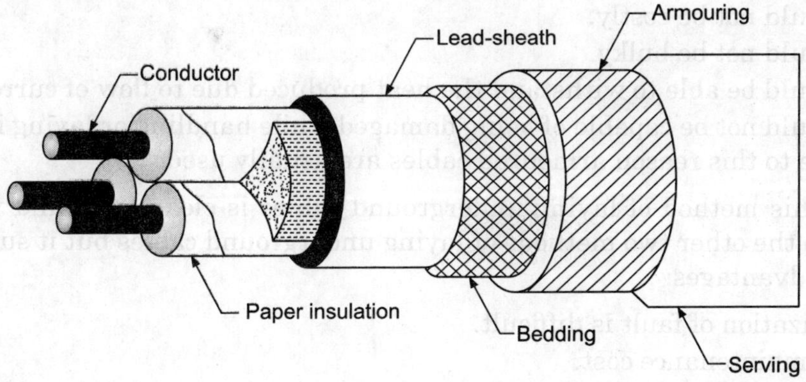

Fig. 4.39 Parts of three conductor cable

2. **Insulation:** The different insulations used to insulate the conductors are paper, varnished cambric and volcanised bitumen. But impregnated paper is mostly used when varnished cambric is used as insulation, petroleum jelly is applied between the layers of the cambric tape which prevents damage to the insulating tape due to friction when the cables are handled. Fig. 4.39 shows the various parts of cable.
3. **Metallic Sheath:** In order to protect the cable from moistures, gases or other damaging liquids (acids, alkalies) in the soil and atmosphere, a metallic sheath of lead or aluminium is provided over the insulation. Figure 4.40. shows the ×-section of the cable.
4. **Bedding:** In order to protect the metallic sheath against corrosion and from mechanical injury due to armouring, a layer of bedding is provided over the sheath. The bedding consists of a fibrous material like jute or hessian tape.

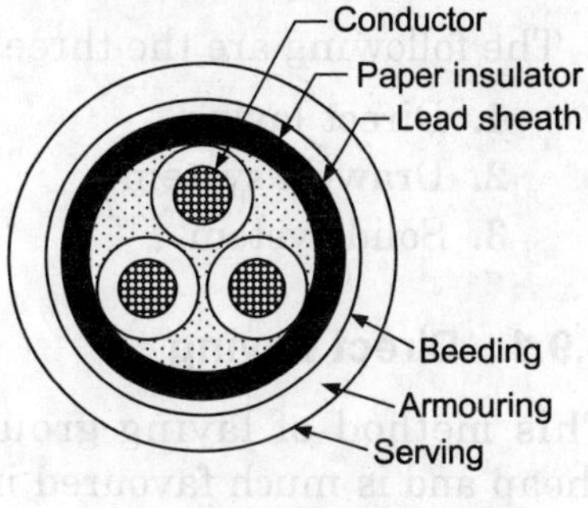

Fig. 4.40 x-section of cable

5. **Armouring:** Over the bedding, armouring is provided to protect the cable from mechanical injury while laying it and during the course of handling. Armouring usually consists of one or two layers of galvanized steel wire or steel tape.
6. **Serving:** To protect the armouring from atmospheric conditions, a layer of fibrous material similar to bedding is provided over the armouring. This is known as *serving*.

It may not be out of place to mention here that bedding, armouring and serving are only applied to the cables for protection of conductor insulation and to protect the metallic sheath from mechanical injury.

4.9 LAYING OF UNDERGROUND CABLES

Before laying cable under the ground, its route should be surveyed and the position of water mains of drains etc., should be ascertained. The cable to be buried underground must have the following properties:

(i) The moisture of the soil should not entre the core of the cable.
(ii) It must have high insulation resistance.
(iii) It should be sufficiently flexible.
(iv) It should not be costly.
(v) It should not be bulky.
(vi) It should be able to withstand the heat produced due to flow of current.
(vii) It should not be capable of being damaged while handling or laying in the ground; so due to this reason armoured cables are usually used.

Although this method of laying underground cables is clean, safe and very cheap in comparison to the other two methods of laying underground cables but it suffers from the following disadvantages:

(i) Localization of fault is difficult.
(ii) High maintenance cost.
(iii) High cost.
(iv) The cable sheath may sometimes undergo chemical changes and get damaged due to impurities in the soil.
(v) There is always a risk of the cable being damaged during a subsequent excavation work carried out for expansion or repair work.
(vi) Increasing in the load needs completely new excavation costing as much as the original laying.

The following are the three methods of laying underground cables:

1. Direct laying
2. Draw-in system
3. Solid system.

4.9.1 Direct Laying

This method of laying ground cables is simple and cheap and is much favoured in modern practice. In this method of laying, a trench about 1.5 metres deep and 45 cm wide is dug. The cable is laid in the trench over a sand bedding which is then covered with soil. The cable maybe protected by planks, bricks, tiles or concrete slabs. In most of the cases, digging and trenching are done manually, but in place free from obstruction, machine methods can be used.

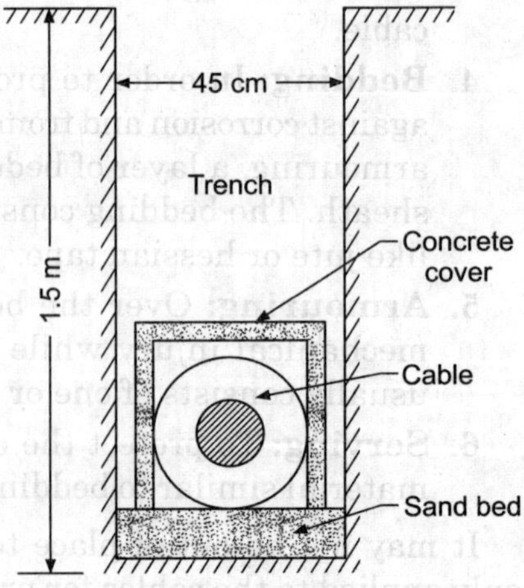

Fig. 4.41 Direct lying method

The Fig. 4.41 shows a cable in a trench with concrete cover for protection. When more than one cable is to be laid in the same trench, a horizontal or vertical inter-axial spacing of at least 30 cm is admissible in order to reduce the effect of mutual heating, and also to ensure that a fault occurring on one cable does not damage the adjacent cable.

4.9.2 Draw-in-System

In this system a line of conduits, ducts or tubes is laid in a trench. The conduits or ducts are to glazed stone ware, cement or concrete. After laying conduits or ducts, the cables are drawn into position from manholes or brick pits spaced at regular intervals.

Cable intended for drawing into ducts need not be provided with armouring but must be provided with serving of hessian tape and jute in order to product them when being drawn in.

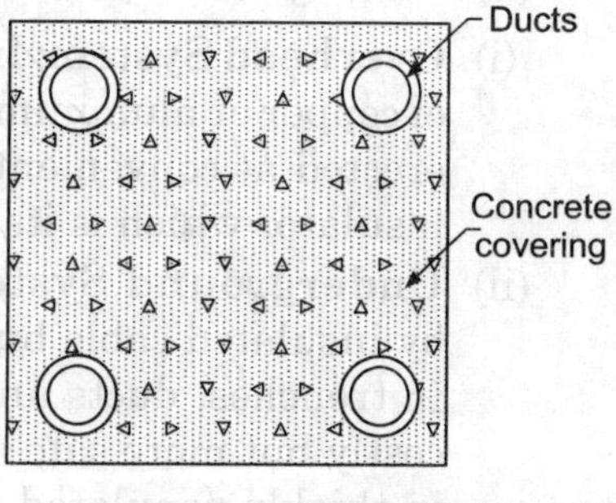

Fig. 4.42 Draw-in system

The initial cost of this system is rather high and the current carrying capacity of the cable is reduced due to close grouping of cables because dissipation of heat is restricted. Any how, if fault occurs that can be repaired very easily. This method is often used in congested city areas where excavation is expensive and inconvenient. This method of cable laying is most suitable for short length cable routes such as in workshops, railway bridge crossing, road crossing, where frequent digging is costlier or impossible.

4.9.3 Solid System

In this system the trench all along the route is made as in the direct laying system. Then troughs of china clay, treated wood, earthen ware, cast iron, stone ware or asphalt are placed in a row and the cable is laid out in these troughs. Cables laid in this manner are usually plain lead covered as the troughing affords good mechanical protection.

Glazed earthen ware through is largely employed and has the advantage over wood that it is not liable to rot. A large number of joints are inevitable since glazed earthen ware troughs are not obtained in lengths more than 90 cm.

After placing the cable in position, the troughs are then filled with bitumen compound in liquid state and then troughs covered over with bricks, tiles or wood. When the bitumen compound solidifies, it seals the cable throughout its length.

Advantages

(i) The cables are protected mechanically and from chemical reaction due to impurities in the soil if any.

(ii) The cables are protected from breakdown due to electrolysis and corrosion.

Disadvantages

(i) It is more expensive than direct laying system.

(ii) Laying and repair require more time.

(iii) Laying and repair cannot be carried out in rainy season.

(iv) Skilled supervision is essential.

Due to the above mentioned disadvantages, this method is rarely used now-a-days.

4.10 OVERHEAD VERSUS UNDERGROUND SYSTEM

Electric power may be transmitted or distributed by the following two methods :

(i) Overhead system

(ii) Underground system

(i) **Overhead System:** In overhead system, electric power is carried by bare conductors of copper or aluminimum which are strung between line supports (poles or towers) erected at convenient distances along a route. The bare conductor is fixed to an insulator which is itself fixed on a cross-arm on the line support.

(ii) **Underground System:** In the underground system, electric power is conveyed by insulated cable buried in the ground. In this system the cables are being laid in trenches, ducts and pipes under the surface of earth. Underground system is costly but more safe and reliable than overhead system. This system is employed in thickly populated area, on the crossing of roads and bridges and in important localities.

Comparison between overhead and underground system is given below in the tubular from:

4.10.1 Comparison between Overhead and Underground System

S.No.	*Particular*	*Overhead system*	*Underground system*
1.	Public safety	It is less safe.	It is more safe.
2.	Initial cost	It is less expensive.	It is more expensive.
3.	Maintenance	It has high maintenance cost.	It has low maintenance cost.
4.	Appearance	It gives shabby look.	It gives good look as the wires are not visible.
5.	Frequency of faults	Faults occur frequently.	Very little chances of faults.
6.	Location of faults	Faulty point can be easily located.	Faulty point cannot be easily located.
7.	Repair	Overhead lines can be easily repaired.	Underground lines cannot be easily repaird.
8.	Frequency of accidents	It has more chances of accidents.	Very little chances of accidents.
9.	Flexibility	It is more flexible as new conductors can be laid along the existing ones for load expansion.	It is not flexible. New conductors are to be laid in new channels.
10.	Supply interruption	It has more chances of supply interruption.	It has very little chance of interruption.

(Contd...)

S.No.	*Particular*	*Overhead system*	*Underground system*
11.	Interference with communication system	It interferes with communication system.	No interference with communication system.
12.	Working voltage	It can be worked up to 400 kV.	It cannot be worked above 66 kV due to insulation difficulties.
13.	Lightning thunder	More chances of being subjected to lightning.	Very little chance of being subjected to lightning.
14.	Erection along zigzag routes	Difficult.	Easy.

4.10.2 Erection and Estimation of an LT and HT Overhead Line

Introduction

It is very important for the engineering students to be conversant with the erection and estimation of an overhead line because many of them will be employed by the State Electricity Board, where they are likely to work as junior engineers, line superintendents to supervise the erection of overhead lines. It is hot possible to deal with the erection of LT and HT overhead line as this would entail another volume but the estimate of material for LT and HT overhead lines will be dealt in details. The students are advised to refer any book on overhead line practice for erection procedure.

4.10.3 Components of Overhead 11 kV/(HT) Line

Electrical power can be transmitted and distributed by either ac or dc but in practice 3-phase, 3-wire a.c. system is universally adopted for transmission of bulk of power and three-phase, 4 wire a.c. system is usually adopted for distribution of electrical power. The voltage for primary distribution are 11, 6.6 or 3.3 kV depending upon the requirement of the bulk consumers and for secondary distribution usable voltage is 400 volts. The various components of 3-phase, 3-wire primary distribution i.e., 11 kV overhead line numbered in the Fig. 4.43 are given below.

1. **RCC Poles:** 10.973 metres (36') Poles made of RCC are used to support the conductor system. Normally $1/6^{th}$ of the pole length is embedded in the ground. The span between two poles is usually 55 metres to 60 metres and can go upto 100 metres.
2. **Pin Type Insulators:** Three pin type insulators are placed on individual pole; two are fixed on wooden cross-arms and one at the top of hamper which is fixed to the top of the pole. These insulators are used to support the phase (i.e., *R*, *Y*, *B*) conductors and insulate them from the supporting structure.
3. **Top Hampers:** These are used to fix the pin-type insulators at the top of the pole.
4. **Bird Guards:** The pin-type insulators are fitted over wooden pieces known as Bird Guards. These are used to avoid short circuit or earth fault due to sitting of birds,

which may short circuit two live conductors or may earth one of the line conductors. These are just fitted on the top of the Hamper.

5. **Line Conductors:** There are three-phase conductors usually of ACSR conductors, which are named as Red, Yellow and Blue (RYB).
6. **Earth Wires:** Two galvanized iron (GSL 8) earth wires are run in parallel below the line conductors and are supported on hooks fixed to the cross-arm attached to the pole.
7. **Hooks for Earth Wires or Eye Screw Bolt:** Two hooks or eye screw bolt are used on each cross arm to support the earth wires.
8. **Knee Bracing Set:** One knee bracing set is fixed on each pole to support the cross arm on which two pin type insulators and two eye screw bolts are fixed for supporting the phase wires and earth wires.
9. **Stay Wire:** GI standard stay wire is used with the end pole to take up the strain of the line and transverse load acting on the line.
10. **Egg Insulator:** Egg type insulators are used in the stay to avoid flow of any leakage current to earth. Normally stay insulators are provided at a height of 3 metres from the ground level. These are generally made of porcelain.

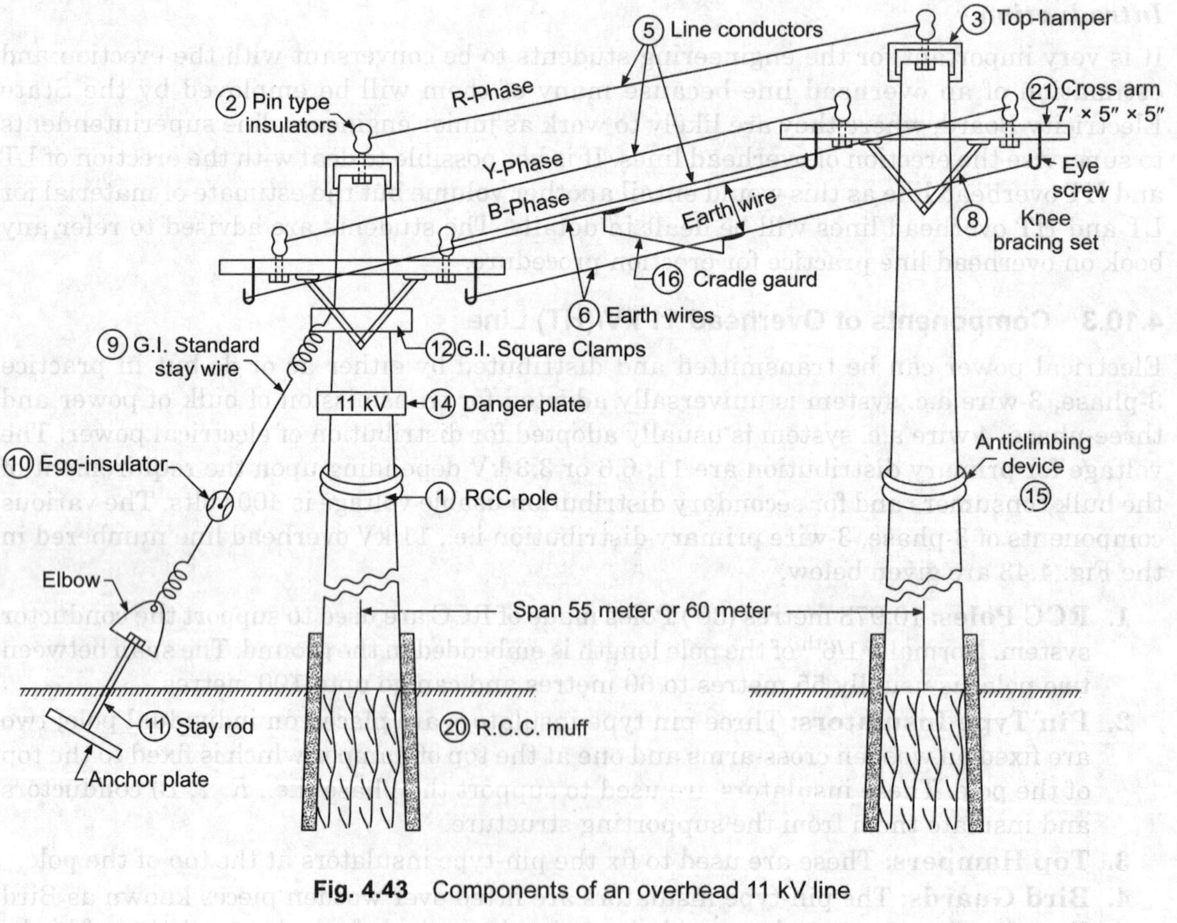

Fig. 4.43 Components of an overhead 11 kV line

11. **Stay or Anchor Rod:** Stay rod is used to tighten the stay wire.
12. **GI Square Clamp:** Clamp is made of galvanized iron (GI) and is used for fixing or holding stay wire.
13. **PG Clamps:** The jumper connections to the line conductors is made through PG (Parallel grooved) clamps. The PG clamps are not shown in the Fig.
14. **Danger Plates:** On each pole or tower of HT line a danger plate indicating the working voltage of the line and word "Danger" is provided at a height of 2.5 metres from the ground level.
15. **Anticlimbing Devices:** GI barbed wire is placed around the poles at a height of 2.3 metres from the ground level to safeguard against the climbing by unauthorized persons.
16. **Cradle Guard:** A cradle guard is a small piece of GI wire and is connected between two earth wires. Its function is to earth the phase conductor, if the phase conductor is accidentally broken.
17. **Earthing:** After every 1 km length of the line the earth wires are connected to earth.
18. **Lightning Arrester:** To prevent line against lightening a lightning arrester is provided on each phase after every 3 km of the line.
19. **Binding Wire:** Binding wire of aluminium is used to bind the aluminium conductors with pin type insulators.
20. **RCC Muffs:** These are used for concreting the poles.
21. **Cross-arms:** On each 7′ × 5″ 5″ wooden cross arm is fixed to support the pin type insulator and eye screw bolts or hooks for earth wires.

4.10.4 Estimate of Material for 3 km, 11 kV, Overhead Line

Let us assume that there is an existing 11 kV overhead line having span between two supports equal to 60 meters. The estimate of the material required for the assumed line of 3 km length is given below:

Length of the line = 3,000 meter (Given)

Span between two poles = 60 meter (Given)

$$\text{No. of spans} = \frac{3000}{60} = 50 \text{ Nos.}$$

i.e., No. of poles = 50 Nos,

To sectionalize the OH line, double pole structures as shown in Fig. 4.45 will be erected after every 1.02 kilometer length of line.

The arrangement of poles and double pole structures (DPS) is shown in Fig. 4.45.

Assume one double pole structure already exists for taking connections at the starting of the line.

1. ∴ No. of Double pole structure = 2 Nos.
2. (i) No. of RCC Poles 10.973 meters (36 ft) long, 800 1b
   = 50 – 2 = 48 Nos.

   (ii) No. of RCC Poles 10.973 meters long 800 lbs for
   Double pole structure = 2 + 2 = 4 Nos.

   (iii) ∴ Total No. of RCC Poles = 48 + 4 = 52 Nos.

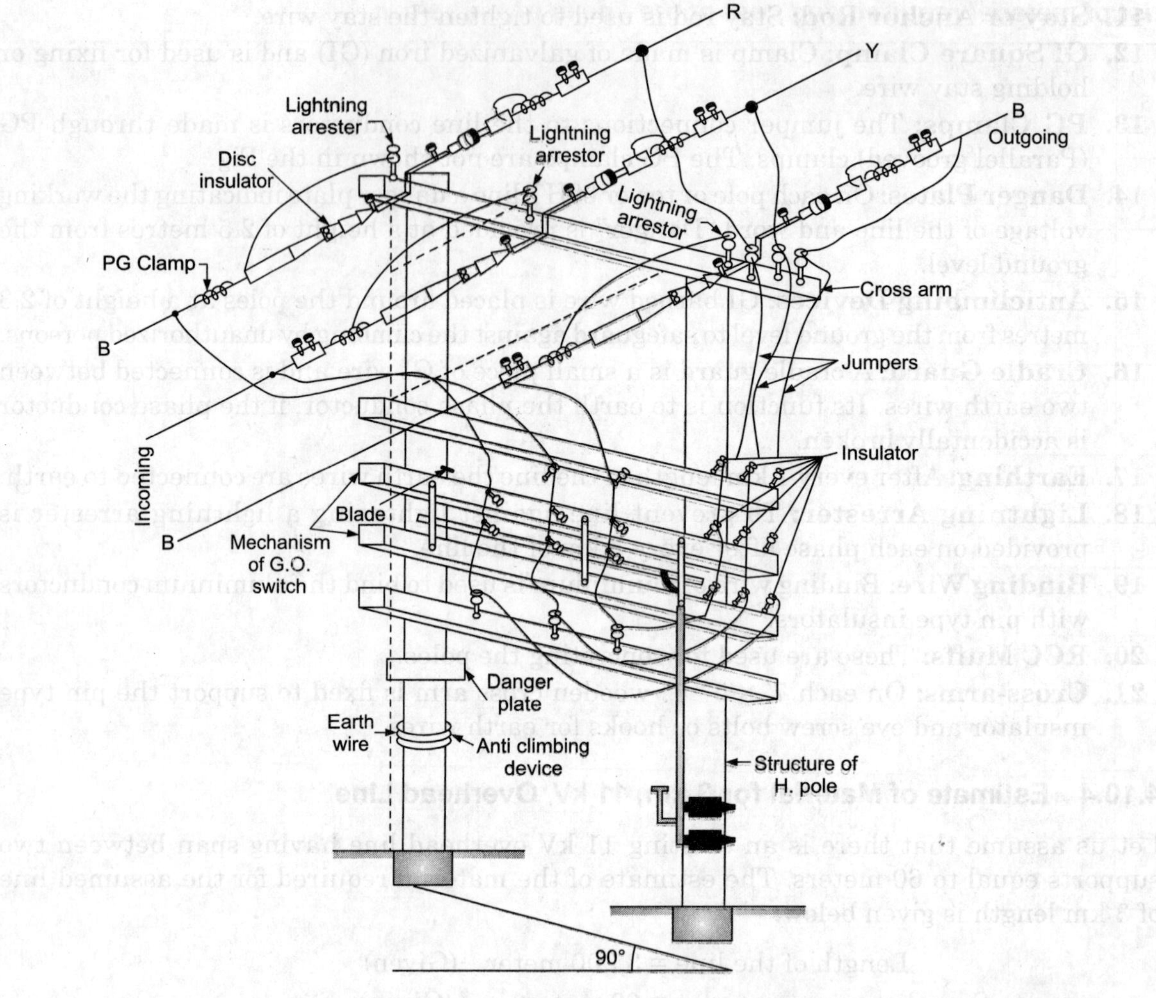

Fig. 4.44 Structure of H-pole 11 kV line

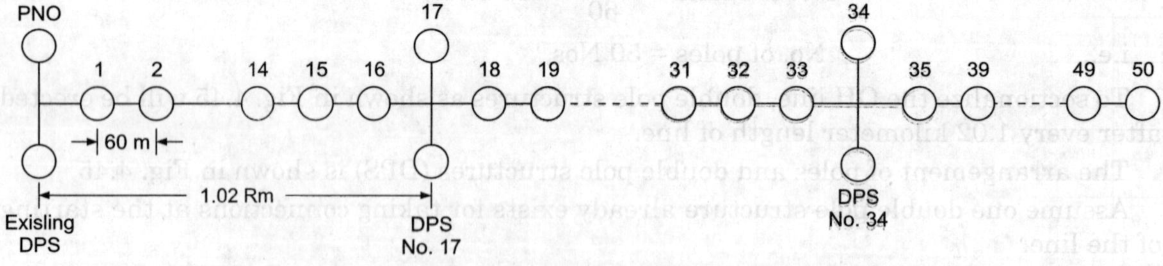

Fig. 4.45 Arrangement of poles and double pole structures

3. Length of 7/2 11 mm AGSR conductor = 3 times the length of line + 2% for sag

$$= 3 \times 3000 \times \frac{102}{100} = 9180 \text{ metres}$$

Say 9200 metres

List of material required and cost of the line is given below:

(1) S. No.	(2) Description of Material with complete specification	Quantity required		Rate			Amount		(10) Remarks
		(3) Qnty	(4) Units	(5) ₹	(6) P.	(7) Per	(8) ₹	(9) P.	
1.	10.973 meters (36') long RCC poles	52	Nos.	2000	00	each	104000	00	
2.	(*i*) 11 kV pin insulators complete with pins.	150	do	150	00	do	22500	00	3 (No. of single pole structure + DPS) = 3 × (48 + 2) = 150 Nos.
	(*ii*) Strain or disc insulators complete with fittings	12	do	200	00	do	2400	00	6 on each double pole structure = 6 × 2 = 12 Nos,
3.	Top hampers.	52	do	30	00	do	1560	00	No. of single pole + 2 × No. of DPS = 48 + 2 × 2 = 52 Nos.
4.	Bird gaurds (wooden)	52	do	20	00	do	1040	00	Do
5.	7/2 11 mm ACSR line conductor	9180	meters	6	00	meter	55080	00	
6.	GI earth wire 8 SWG	6000	metre	5	40	do	30,000	00	No. of earth wires × length of line = 2 × 3000 = 6000 metre.
7.	Hooks on eye bolt for earth wire	102	Nos.	10	00	each	1.20	00	2 × Total No. of poles = 2 × 51 = 102 Nos.
8.	Ring braking set	48	Nos.	50	00	each	2400	= 00	1 × No. of single poles = 1 × 48 = 48 to support the X–arms.
9, 10.	Stay sets complete with Anchor rod								Stay wires = 4 × No. of DPS = 4 × 3 = 12 Nos.
11.	RCC base plate, Tension screw etc. Stay insulator including stay wire (SWG GI wire)								Stay insulators = No. of stay wires = 12 Anchor rods = No. of stay wire = 12
12	GI dead end clamps	12	Nos.	150	00	do	1800	00	6 × No. of DPS = 6 × 2 = 12 Nos.
13.	PG clamp	12	Nos.	20	00	each	240	00	6 × No. of DPS = 6 × 2 = 12 Nos.
14.	11 kV Danger plates with clamp	52	Nos.	10	00	do	520	00	Total No. poles = 52
15.	Barbed wire (Anti climbing devices)	70	kg	20	00	kg	1400	00	52 No. anticlimbing devices is taken = 70 kg. appr.
16.	Cradle guard	68	Nos.	10	00	each	680	00	4 Nos. in each span = 17 × 4 = 68 Nos.
17.	Earthing sets complete	3	Nos.	1000	00	each	3000	00	
18.	11 kV lightning arrestor sets complete	3	Nos.	1500	00	do	4500	00	
19.	14 SWG copper or aluminium binding wire	5	kg.	100	00	kg	500	00	

(Contd...)

(1) S. No.	(2) Description of Material with complete specification	Quantity required		Rate			Amount		(10) Remarks
		(3) Qnty	(4) Units	(5) ₹	(6) P.	(7) Per	(8) ₹	(9) P.	
20.	Cross Arms of Teak wood 7' × 5" × 5" (2.6 m × 13 cm × 13 cm)	50	No.	120	00	each	6000	00	Used on the poles to support the insulators.
21.	Sundries to complete the job such is Nuts, Bolts & Thimbles etc.						2400	00	
	Total						241280		
	Transportation and Storage						10000		
	Labour charges						30000		
	Contingencies 1%						2412		
	Inspection fee						3000		
	Grand Total						**2,86,692**		

4.11 COMPONENTS OF AN OVERHEAD 400/230 (L.T.) LINE

AC Secondary distribution usually consists of a three phase four wire system. Two voltages line voltages (V_L) and phase voltage (V_{ph}) are obtainable, simultaneously in this system. The voltage between any two lines is 400 volts and between any one line and neutral is 230 volt. This 3-phase, 4-wire, 400/230 volt constitutes an overhead LT system. The main components of an overhead 400/230 volts (LT) line numbered in Fig. 4.46 are given below:

1. **RCC Poles.** 30′ or 32′ high RCC poles are used to support the Conductor System. Normally $1/6^{th}$ of the pole height is embedded in the ground. The span of 50 meter is usually fixed between two poles.
2. **Egg type strain Insulators:** These insulators are used at the dead ends to insulate the pole from the line.
3. **Shackle insulators:** Nowadays shackle insulators are used all along the LT lines. These insulators are fixed to the poles with D-straps. The D-straps are fixed directly to the poles by a $8'' \times \frac{5''}{8}$ bolts.
4. **D-Straps:** Single D-strap is fixed to the pole with nut and bolt to accommodate single shackle insulator.
5. **M.S. Bolts and Nuts** $8'' \times \frac{5''}{8}$: These are used to fix the D-straps on the poles.
6. **M.S. Nuts and Bolt** $2''\frac{5''}{8}$: These are used to fix the clamps on dead end poles.
7. **Stay Clamps:** For making clamps, M.S. Flat 50 × 6.3 mm is used for fixing or holding service line, stay wires, earth wire and for fixing the street light bracket.
8. **M.S. Eye Screw Bolt** $5'' \times \frac{5''}{8}$: This is used for fixing the earth wire on the pole.

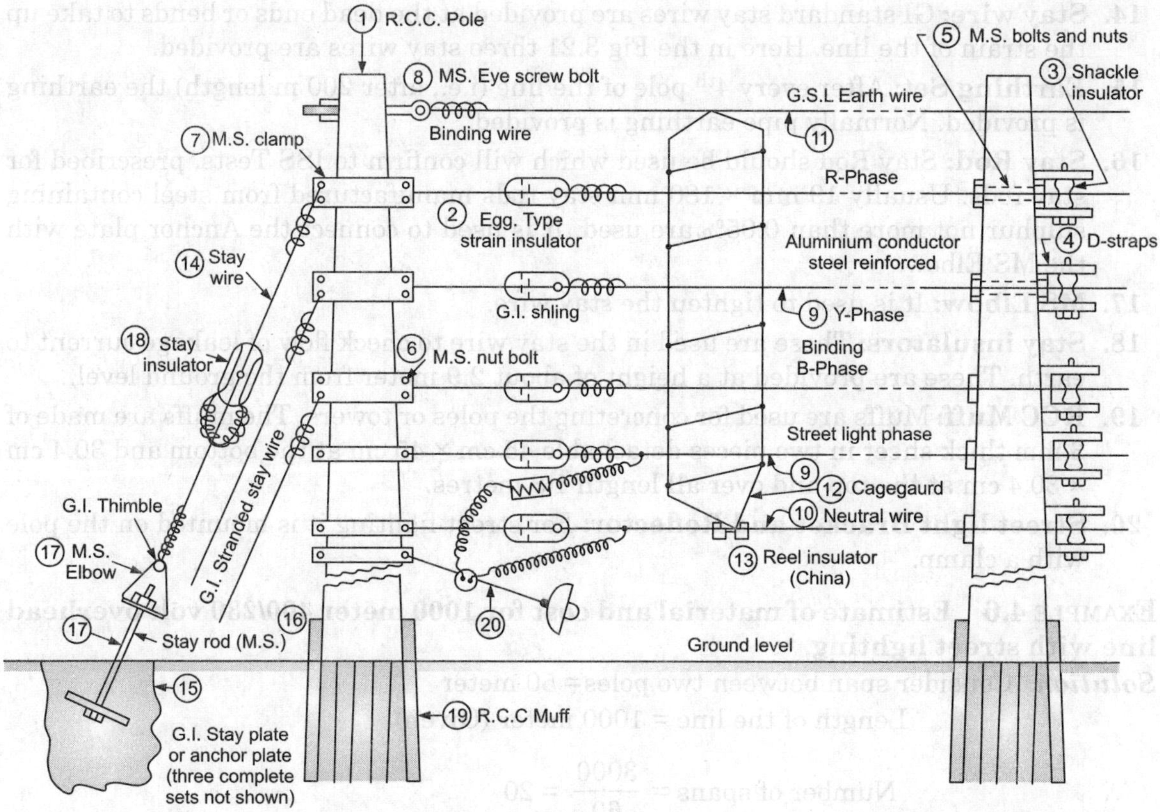

Fig. 4.46 Components of an overhead LT line (400/230 V)

9. **Phase and Street Light Wire:** Three ACSR No.-8 wires are used for three phases i.e., red, yellow and blue (R, Y, B) and one ACSR conductor (Fifth from top) is used for street light only and is controlled from the sub-station. The voltage between any two phases will be 400 volts and between one phase and neutral will be 230 volts.
10. **Neutral wire:** At the bottom on ACSR conductor runs which is usually at a zero potential and is known as neutral wire.
11. **Earth wire:** 7/16 SWG Galvanised iron wire suitable as earth wire is run over the top of the poles. The wire should be uniform X-section, smooth and free from defect. It shall also conform to ISS in all aspects.
12. **Cage-Guard:** Two cage type guards are provided in each span. Approximately the length of one guard is usually taken 5 meter. It is either made of small pice of GI wire or ACSR conductor wire. These cage guards are provided from pole to pole so that in the event of breakage of one of the phase conductors, the broken conductor will make contact with the earth wire there by will operate the earth leakage relay at the substation and consequently the circuit breaker will trip off, cutting the faulty section.
13. **Reel Insulators:** The reel insulators of China are provided along each span of line in order to insulate the neutral from earth wire. The Cage Guard Connection is made to the neutral through reel insulator.

14. **Stay wire:** GI standard stay wires are provided at the dead ends or bends to take up the strain of the line. Here in the Fig 3.21 three stay wires are provided.
15. **Earthing Set:** After every 4th pole of the line (i.e., after 200 m length) the earthing is provided. Normally pipe earthing is provided.
16. **Stay Rod:** Stay Rod should be used which will confirm to ISS Tests, prescribed for stay rods. Usually 19 mm × 180 mm stay rods manufactured from steel containing sulphur not more than 0.05% are used. It is used to connect the Anchor plate with the MS Elbow.
17. **MS Elbow:** It is used to tighten the stay wire.
18. **Stay insulators:** These are used in the stay wire to check flow of leakage current to earth. These are provided at a height of about 2.9 meter from the ground level.
19. **RCC Muff:** Muffs are used for concreting the poles or towers. The muffs are made of 3 mm thick sheet in two pieces detachable 45 cm × 45 cm at the bottom and 30.4 cm × 30.4 cm at the top and over all length 1.8 metres.
20. **Street light Bracket and Reflector:** For street lighting it is mounted on the pole with a clamp.

EXAMPLE 4.6 Estimate of material and cost for 1000 meter 400/230 volt overhead line with street lighting.

Solution: Consider span between two poles= 50 meter

Length of the line = 1000 meter (Given)

$$\therefore \quad \text{Number of spans} = \frac{3000}{60} = 20$$

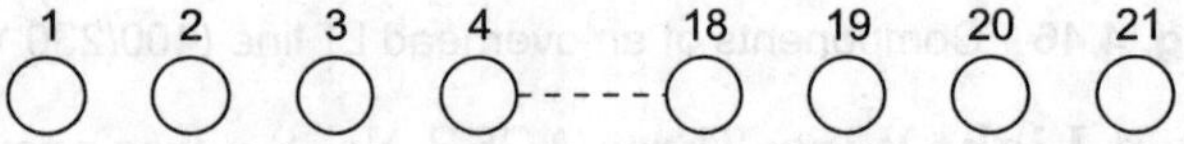

Fig. 4.47 400/230 V overhead line with street lighting

No. of RCC Poles = No. of spans + 1 = 20 + 1 = 21

(1) S. No	*(2) Description of material complete specification*	*(3) Quantity*	*(4) Required unit*	*(5) Rate*		*(6) Amount*	*(7) Remarks*
				₹	***P.***		
1.	No. of RCC poles (i.e. No. Of spans + 1)	21	no	2000	00 each	42000 = 00	$\frac{30}{32'}$ high RCC poles are used.
2.	Egg type strain insulators	5	no.	5	00 each	250	To insulate the pole
3.	Shackle insulators (or Bobin)						
	(a) For line conductors	80	no.	50	00 each	4000 = 00	Four on each pole i.e., 20 × 4 = 80

(Contd...)

(1) S. No	*(2) Description of material complete specification*	*(3) Quantity*	*(4) Required unit*	*(5) Rate*		*(6) Amount*	*(7) Remarks*
				₹	*P.*		
	(b) For Neutral conductors	20	no.	50	00 each	1000 = 00	One on each pole.
4.	D-straps (M.S)	100	nos.	75	00 each	7500 = 00	Five on each pole.
5.	MS Bolts and Nuts 8" × 5″/8	35	kg	30	00 kg	1050 = 00	To fix the D-straps on the poles.
6.	MS Bolts & Nuts 2" × 5″/8	2	kg	2	00 kg	40 = 00	To fix the clamps on dead end pole.
7.	MS Flate 2" × 5″/8	12	kg	40	kg	480 = 00	MS Flate is used for making Dead end clamps.
8.	MS eye screw Bolt 5" × 5″/8	21	No.	20	00 each	420 = 00	For earth wire, to be fixed on pole.
9.	ACSR No. 8	4000	metre	10	00 per metre	40, 000	For 4-phases i.e., 1000 × 4 = 4000 meter
10.	ACSR No. 8	1000	meter	10	00	10,000	For neutral wire length 1000 metre.
11.	ACSR No. 8	50	meter	10	00	500 = 00	Allowing 4% for sag and wastage in phase wires and neutral.
12.	GSL No. 8, (Galvanized steel wire,	125	kg	20	00	250 = 00	100 metre earth wire of GSL No. 8. Allowing 4% wastage i.e., 40 meter Total earth wire = 1040 metre
13.	ACSR No. 8 for making the Guard.	210	meter	1	00 per meter	4200	Two guards are in each span No. of span is 21 Length of one guard to be taken 5 metre so total length = 21 × 2 × 5 = 210 metre
14.	Reel insulators	42	Nos	10	each	420 = 00	Two in each span
15.	GI Standard stay wires	175	kg	15	00 per kg	2625 = 00	3-stay wires for end pole and 4 number stay wires in whole of the length No. of spans $\frac{20}{5} = \frac{20}{5} = 4$ Total 7 stay wires = 175 kg

(Contd...)

(1) S. No	(2) Description of material complete specification	(3) Quantity	(4) Required unit	(5) Rate		(6) Amount	(7) Remarks
				₹	P.		
16.	Earthing sets	5	Nos.	500	00 per set	2500 = 00	After every 4-poles (i.e., 200 meter) pipe earthing done i.e., $\frac{\text{length of the line in meter}}{200}$ $= \frac{1000}{200} = 5$ Nos.
17.	Stay set complete	7	Nos.	300	00 each set	2100 = 00	Stay set complete in all respects but excluding stay wires. 3-stay set at end pole and remaining 4-sets after the distance of 250 meters.
18.	RCC Muff	21	No.	100	00 each	2100 = 00	One for each pole
19.	Street light bracket complete in all respect- 2 core	21	Nos	50	00 each	1050	Once for each pole for street lighting
20.	PVC wire 2.5 mm^2	105	metre	5	00 metre	515 = 00	5 m for each lighting point at each pole i.e., 21 × 5 = 105 metre
		Storage and transport atom 5% = 6.287 = 00 Labour charges 10% = 12.575 = 00 Contingencies 10% = 12575 = 00 Electrical inspection fee = 3000 = 00 Grand Total = 153,900 = 00 Total = 241280 = 00					

SUMMARY

1. **Distributor:** The part of the power system by which electric power distributed among consumers for their use of *A* line or conductor to which various consumers are connected through service main is called distributor.
2. **Feeder:** This is the conductor that connects the local substations to the distributor.
3. **Radial system:** Here separate feeders radiate from a single substation and fed the distributors at one end.
4. **Ring main system:** When the distributor is supplied by two feeders, it is called ring main system.
5. **Method of erecting the poles**

   (i) Dead man method (ii) Derrick pole method

6. **Types of dc distributors**
   (i) Distributor fed at one end
   (ii) Distributor fed at both ends
   (iii) Ring mains distributors
   (iv) Distributor fed at the centre.
7. **Requirements of distribution system**
   (i) Proper voltage
   (ii) Availability of power demand
   (iii) Reliability
8. **Underground cable:** The cable which are buried in the ground is called underground cable.
9. **Classification of cables**
   (i) Low voltage LT cables upto 1000 V
   (ii) High voltage HT cables upto 11000 V
   (iii) Super tension ST cables upto 33000 V
   (iv) Extra high tension EHT cables upto 66 kV.
10. **Main parts of cable**
    (i) Core or conductor
    (ii) Insulator
    (iii) Metallic sheath
    (iv) Bedding
    (v) Armouring
    (vi) Serving
11. **Method of lying of cables**
    (i) Direct lying
    (ii) Draw in system
    (iii) Solid system
12. **Interconnected system:** In an interconnected system the feeder ring is energised two or more than two substation.
13. **Service mains:** It is the small conductor which connects the distributor to consumer terminals.
14. **Factors to determine the size of conductor for distribution system:**
    (i) Permissible voltage drop in the time
    (ii) Current carrying capacity
    (iii) Tensile strength of the conductor.
15. **Purpose of armouring in power cables:** To protect the cable from mechanical injury while lying.
16. **Stay wire:** Stay wire takes up the strain of the line. These are galvanised steel stranded wires.
17. **AC distribution:** It is mostly adopted since AC can be generated at high voltage and can be easily step up or step down.
18. **DC distribution:** It is rarely used such system is used for operation of dc motors, electroplating etc.

Objective Type Questions

1. Multiple Choice Type Questions

1. A line which connects to a consumer to the distributor is called
   (a) feeder
   (b) distributor
   (c) service main
2. In a transmission system feeder supplies power to
   (a) service main
   (b) distributor
   (c) all of the above

3. Feeder is mainly designed from the point of view of
(a) its current carrying capacity (b) operating voltage
(c) frequency

4. The underground system cannot be operated above
(a) 220 kV (b) 66 kV
(c) 33 kV (a) 11 kV

5. Which of the following distribution system is most economical?
(a) DC system (b) single phase ac system
(c) 3-ϕ, 3 wire ac system

6. Which of the following dc distribution system is the cheapest
(a) radial (b) ring system
(c) interconnected

7. A line from which number of tapping are taken is called
(a) feeder (b) distributor
(c) service main

8. The bulk power consumers are supplied at
(a) 11 kV (b) 66 kV
(c) 400 kV (d) 1230 V

9. A line from which number of tappings are taken is called
(a) feeder (b) distributor
(c) service main (d) none of these

10. The most reliable distribution system is
(a) Radial system (b) Ring main system
(c) Interconnected system (d) All of the above

11. The distribution transformer is generally connected is
(a) delta/delta (b) star/delta
(c) star/star (d) delta/star

12. Distributors are designed from the point of view of
(a) its current carrying capacity (b) operating voltage
(c) voltage drop in it (d) operating frequency

13. Sheath is used in the cables to
(a) provide strength to the cable
(b) present the moisture from entering the cable
(c) provide proper insulation
(d) all of the above

14. The underground system is preferred over the overhead system because
(a) it is cheaper (b) easy to detect fault
(c) safer (d) all of the above

15. The voltages drop as the main consideration while designing a
(a) distributor (b) feeder
(c) service main (d) none of these

16. In underground system, the earth fault is located by
(a) blavier test (b) murray loop text
(c) varley loop test (d) all (a), (b) and (c)

ANSWERS

1. (c)	2. (c)	3. (a)	4. (b)	5. (a)	6. (a)	7. (b)	8. (a)	9. (b)
10. (c)	11. (d)	12. (b)	13. (b)	14. (c)	15. (a)	16. (d)		

2. Fill in the Blanks

1. ________ distribution is done by 3-phase 4-wire system.
2. A distributor is designed from ________ consideration.
3. ________ insulators are used for LT lines.
4. A feeder is designed from the point of view of its ________
5. The limit for the variation of voltage at any point of a distributor is ________
6. Feeders are the conductors which carry ________ to the feeding points.
7. A ring man distributor is equivalent to ________
8. Service main connects ________ and ________
9. ________ system is cheaper than ________ system.
10. Armouring of cable is done to protect the cable from ________
11. Pin type insulators are used for ________ line conductors.
12. The underground system has ________ initial cost than the overhead system.
13. A ring main system of distribution is ________ reliable than the radial system.
14. The distribution transformer links the primary and distribution systems ________.
15. The most common system for secondary distribution is ________ 3-phase, ________ wire system.
16. The statutory limit for voltage variations at the consumer's terminals is ________ % of rated value.
17. The service mains connect the ________ and the ________
18. The overhead system is ________ flexible than underground system.
19. The main consideration in the design of a feeder is the ________
20. A 3-wire dc distribution makes available ________ voltages.
21. Nowadays ________ system is used for distribution.
22. The interconnected system ________ the reserve capacity of the systems.
23. The major part of investment of secondary distribution is made on ________
24. The chances of faults in underground system are ________ as compared to overhead system.
25. The frequency of faults in underground cable system is ________ the overhead system.

ANSWERS

1. Secondary 2. voltage drop 3. Shackle 4. current carrying capacity
5. ±6% 6. large currents 7. doubly fed distributor at equal voltages
8. Distributor, consumer 9. Overhead, underground
10. mechanical injuries 11. kV 12. more 13. more
14. secondary 15. 400/230 V 16. 6%
17. distributor, consumer terminals 18. more
19. current carrying capacity 20. two 21. ac
22. Increases 23. distribution transformers, 24. less

3. True-False Type Questions

1. Electric power is distributed among consumers by transmission.
2. In 11 kV overhead lines earth wires are run below the line conductors.
3. The three elements of distribution system are: feeder, distributor and service mains.
4. Feeder is line which connects distributor to substation.
5. The line from which tappings are taken is called feeder.
6. Bulk power consumers are supplied at 11 kV.
7. DC two wire distribution system is more economical the dc three-wire system.
8. In singly fed distributor is fault occurs on any section the supply to all consumers has to be shut off.
9. In a 3-wire dc system if load is balanced the current in neutral is zero.
10. The guy wire is used at the dead end poles to taken mechanical load of the line.
11. Underground system is rafer.
12. Underground system is cheaper than overhead system.
13. The most common distribution system is radial.
14. The distributor transformer is generally connected in star-star.
15. The sheath on the cable does not allowed moisture to entire into the cable.
16. It is easier to locate the fault in overhead system since the conductors are naked.

ANSWERS

1. True	2. True	3. True	4. True	5. False	6. True	7. False	8. True
9. True	10. False	11. True	12. False	13. True	14. False	15. True	16. True

SHORT ANSWER TYPE QUESTIONS

Q.1 For what purpose metallic sheath is provided in underground cables?

Ans. The metallic sheath is provided around the insulation to protect it against ingress of moisture, gas or other demaging liquids (acid or alkalies) from the soil and atmosphere.

Q.2 Why is a layer of bedding provided over the metallic sheath in underground cables?

Ans. A layer of bedding is provided over the metallic sheath for the protection of metallic sheath against corrosion and from mechanical injury.

Q.3 Why are copper conductors not used in power cables?

Ans. Cooper conductors are not used in power cables because of scarcity of copper.

Q.4 What are the main requirements of insulating materials used for underground cables?

Ans. The main requirements of the insulating materials used for underground cables are high insulation resistivity, high dielectric strength, good mechanical properties, non-hydroscopic, non-inflammable, immune to attacks by acids and alkalies.

Q.5 Why is it necessary to keep voltage variation at the consumer's terminals as low as possible?

Ans. All the appliances and motors are designed to be operated at a particular or declared value of voltage. Large voltage variation means either a too high or a too low voltage. Low voltage will cause not only is burning of motors/appliances/equipment and insufficient lighting but also loss of revenue to the supplier. On the other hand high voltage will cause the lamps to burn out permanently and also may cause failure of other appliances. So the primary requirement of a distribution system is that voltage variations at the consumer's terminals should be the lowest possible (not more than ±6% of the rated value).

Q.6 What is a feeder?

Ans. Feeder is a line which supplies a point of distribution network without being tapped at any intermediate point. In simple terms, the feeder may be defined as the line carrying current from the secondary substation to the distribution substations or as a primary distribution line.

Q.7 What is a distributor?

Ans. Distributor is a line from which tappings are taken along its length for providing supply to the consumers.

Q.8 Why dc 2-wire system is never employed for transmission purpose?

Ans. Because of poor efficiency.

Q.9 Why is radial system of distribution is not generally used?

Ans. Because of poorest service reliability.

Q.10 What are the advantages of ring main distributor?

Ans. Better flexibility, greater reliability, better voltage regulation and less power losses.

Q.11 What is service mains?

Ans. It is the small conductor which connects the distributor to consumer terminals.

Q.12 What is an interconnected system?

Ans. In a interconnected system the feeder ring is energized by two or more than two generating stations.

Q.13 State the factors which are taken for determining the size of conductor for distribution system?

Ans. *(i)* Current carrying capacity

(ii) Permissible voltage drop in the line

(iii) Tensile strength of the conductor.

Q.14 What is an LT cable?

Ans. The cable used for operating voltages upto 1000 V are called LT cables.

Q.15 What is an HT cable?

Ans. The cable used for operating voltage upto 11000 V are called HT cable.

Q.16 What is the purpose of stay wires in distribution system?

Ans. Poles are provided with stay wires at the dead end in a line. Stay wire takes up strain of the line.

Q.17 What is booster?

Ans. Booster is a low-voltage, high-current series wound dc generator inserted in to a dc circuit to add or inject a certain voltage proportional to circuit current.

Q.18 What are the transmission voltages that are used in India?

Ans. 33, 66, 110, 132, 220 ans 440 kV. 765/800 kV is also in used in India.

Q.19 What are the advantages of adopting extra high voltage/ultra high voltage for transmission of ac electric power.

Ans. Advantages of adopting of EHV/UHV for transmission of ac electric power are reduced line losses, high transmission efficiency, improved voltage regulation, reduced conductor material requirement, flexibility for future system growth, increase in transmission capacity of the line, increase of SIL and reduction in ROW.

Q.20 On what basis the conductor size is determined for transmission lines upto 220 kV?

Ans. For overhead transmission lines operating at voltages upto 220 kV, the conductor size is determined on the basis of its current carrying capacity.

Q.21 What material is universally imployed for overhead transmission lines?

Ans. ACSR conductors.

MEDIUM ANSWER TYPE QUESTIONS

Q.1 What is radial system of distribution?

Ans. Radial system : When the distributor is fed at one end only, it is called radial distribution system. A single line diagram of radial system is shown in Fig. 4.48. Since the feeder *F*, distributor *D* and the service mains *S* are radiating from the sub-station, this system is called the "Radial system of distribution". This system is only employed when power is generated at low voltage and the sub-station is located at the centre of load.

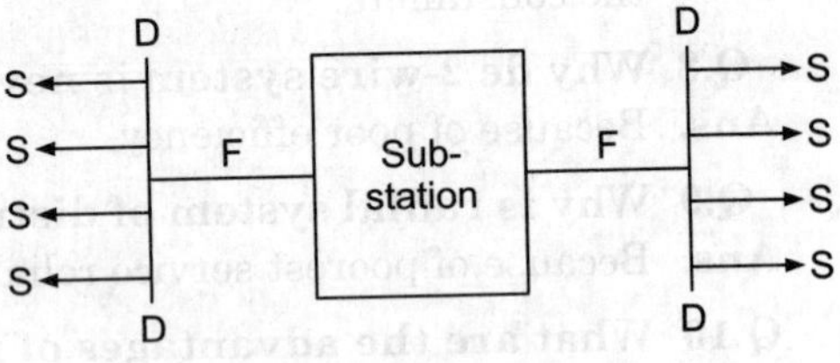

Fig. 4.48 Radial system

Q.2 What are advantages and disadvantages of radial system of distribution?

Ans. Advantages:

(i) The system is simplest

(ii) Its initial cost is minimum

(iii) This system is employed when electrical energy is generated at low low voltage and the power station is situated at the centre of load.

Disadvantages: Radial system has following disadvantages.

(i) The end of the distributor nearest to the supply end would be heavily loaded.

(iii) The consumers are dependent on a single feeder and a single distributor. Therefore, any fault on the feeder on distributor cuts off supply to the consumers who are on the side of the fault away from the sub-station.

(iii) The consumers at the distant end of the distributor would be subjected to serious voltage variations when the load on the distributer changes.

Q.3 What is ring main system of distribution?

Ans. Ring main system: When the distributor is supplied by two feeders, it is called a ring main distribution system. In this system the feeder closes on itself i.e., it forms a complete ring and hence the name ring mains. Fig. 4.49 shows a ring system where the sub-station *S* supplies to the closed feeder *ABCEA*. The distributors are connected to point *B*, *C*, *D* and *E* of the feeder as shown.

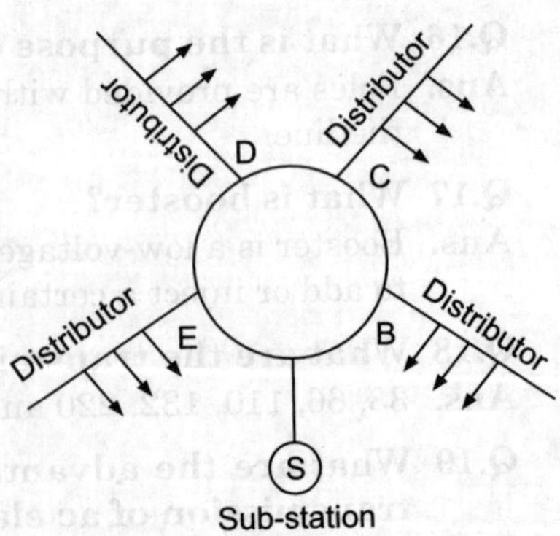

Fig. 4.49 Ring main system of distribution

Q.4 Mention advantages of ring system over radial system distribution.

Ans. 1. Radial System: In radial system, separate feeders radiate from a single sub-station and feed the distributors at one end only. A single line diagram of a radial system for ac distribution is shown in Fig. 4.50.

Here sub-station (*S*) supplies power to a distributor *AB* at end *A* through feeder *SC*. This system is only employed when power is generated at low voltage and the sub-station is located at the centre of the load.

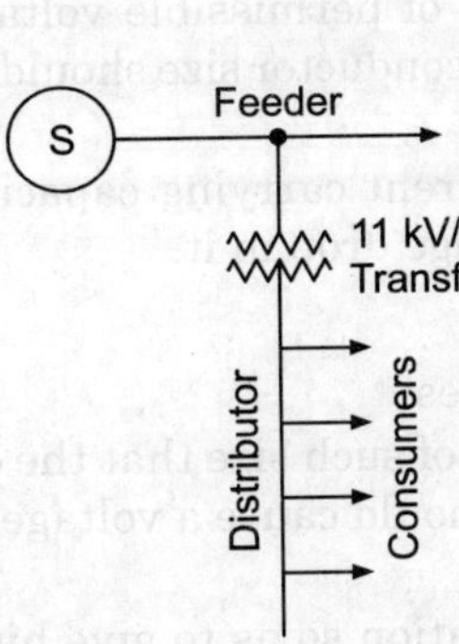

Fig. 4.50 Radial system

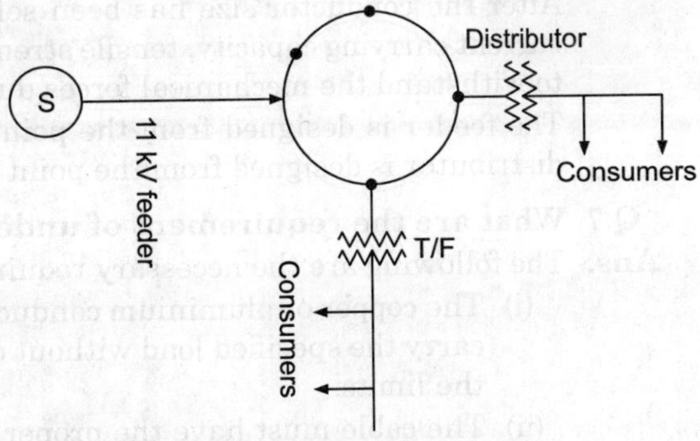

Fig. 4.51 Ring main system

2. Ring main system: In this system, the feeder closes on itself forms a complete ring and hence the name ring main system. Fig. 4.51 a.c. ring main system, where *ABCDA* is the closed feeder supplied by the sub-station *S* at point *A*. The various distributors are connected to points *BC* and of the feeder as shown in Fig. 6.51.

Advantages of Ring main system

(i) Each distributor is supplied via two feeders, for example, the distributor connected at point *C* is fed via feeder *ABC* and *ADC*. This reduces the voltage fluctuations at the consumers' terminals to some extent.

(ii) The system is more reliable since each distributor is fed via two feders. In the event of fault on any section of feeder, the continuity of supply can be maintained. For instance, suppose fault occurs at any point of section *CD* of the feeder. Then section *CD* of the feeder can be isolated for repairs and at the same time continuity of supply is maintained to all the consumers.

Q.5 Explain 3-phase 4-wire *AC* distribution (secondary distribution) system.

Ans. 3-phase 4-wire Distribution System: This system is suitable for small consumers. It employs 400/230 V where 400 V is the voltage between any two phases and 230 V is voltage between any phase and the neutral.

A typical secondary distribution system is shown. The primary distributor delivers power to a distribution sub-station, where a 3-phase, delta/star, distribution transformer steps-down the voltage from 11 kV to 400 V. The low voltage secondary distributor (3-phase, 4-phase is run along the streets of the area to be fed by it. The single phase domestic loads are connected between any one phase and the neutral where as 3-phase, 400 V motor loads are connected across 3-phase lines.

Q.6 How the size of conductor in distribution system is determined?

Ans. The following are the factors taken into consideration for determining the size of conductor for the distribution system.

(i) Permissible voltage drop in the line
(ii) Current carrying capacity
(iii) Tensile strength of the conductor.

While considering the current carrying capacity of the conductor, the maximum safe temperature is taken into consideration. For aluminium conductors this temperature is 75°C. If the temperature is more beyond the limit during peak hours, then conductor tensile strength is reduced and it may melt. Therefore, while selecting the conductor size. The officially declared ambient temperature of the area is considered. From that temperature, permissible temperature rise is calculated.

After the conductor size has been selected on the basis of permissible voltage drop and current carrying capacity, tensile strength of the selected conductor size should be sufficient to withstand the mechanical forces during foul weather.

The feeder is designed from the point of view of its current carrying capacity while the distributor is designed from the point of view of the voltage drop in it.

Q.7 What are the requirement of underground cables?

Ans. The following are the necessary requirements of the cables:

(i) The copper or aluminium conductor used should be of such size that the cable should carry the specified load without over heating and should cause a voltage drop within the limits.

(ii) The cable must have the proper thickness of insulation so as to give high degree of safety and reliability at the voltage for which it is designed.

(iii) All the materials used in the cable manufacture should be such that there should be complete chemical and physical stability throughout.

(iv) The cable must be provided with a mechanical protection so as to withstand the rough use in laying it.

Q.8 Give the various systems of "distribution".

Ans. The distribution system, may be classified as:

1. According to the nature of current

(i) dc system – (a) Two wire dc system
(b) Three wire dc system

(ii) ac system – (a) Primary distribution
(b) Secondary distribution

2. According to the nature of construction

(i) Overhead system
(ii) Underground system

3. According to the connection scheme

(i) Radial system
(ii) Ring main system
(iii) Interconnected system

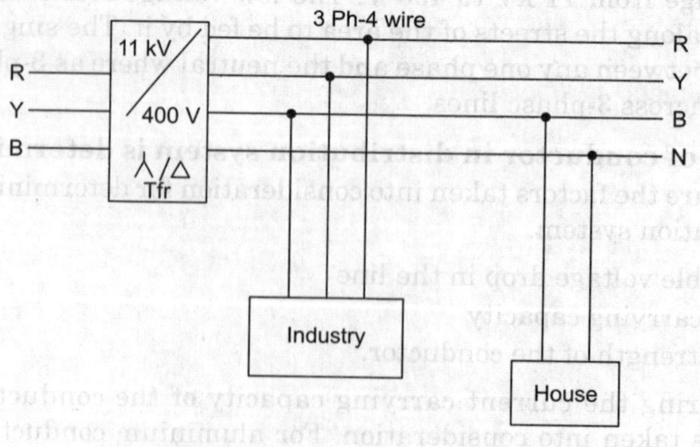

Fig. 4.52 Various types of distribution

Q.9 Draw a neat sketch of a LT pole and label the important components.

Ans. The Fig. 4.53 shows a pole of a LT 400/230 V line. The various components are:

1. Pole
2. Insulators
3. Clamp
4. Phase wire
5. Street wire
6. Earth wire
7. Guard wire
8. Real insulator
9. Stay wire
10. Pole clamp
11. Stay insulator

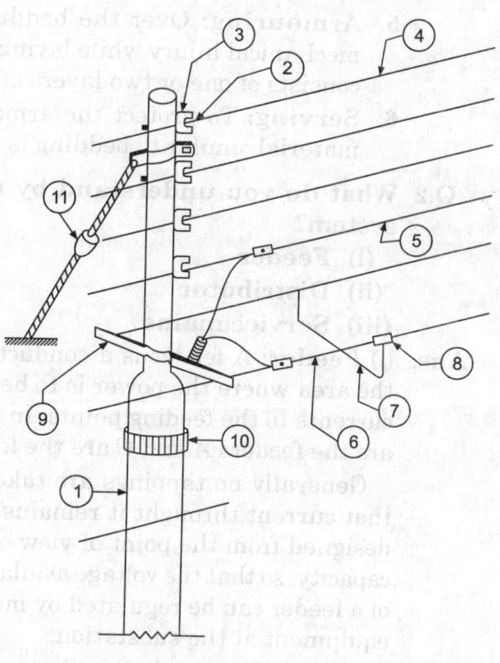

Fig. 4.53 LT pole

LONG ANSWER TYPE QUESTIONS

Q.1 Explain with the help of a heat sketch the construction of multicore 11kV underground cable.

Ans. 1. **Core or conductors:** A three-core cable has three conductors as shown in Fig. 4.54. These conductors are made of copper or aluminium and are usually stranded to make the cables flexible. The copper conductors are always tinned otherwise they may react with the chemical compounds used in the insulation placed around them.

2. **Insulation:** Each core or conductor is provided with a suitable thickness of insulating material. The thickness of layer of the insulation depends upon the voltage to be withstand by the cable. Generally used material for insulation of 11 kV cable is impregnated paper tape.

3. **Sheath:** In order to protect the cable from moistures, gases or other damaging liquids (acids, alkalies) in the soil and atmosphere, a metallic sheath of lead or aluminium is provided ever the insulation.

4. **Bedding:** In order to protect the metallic sheath against corrosion and from mechanical injury due to armouring, a layer of bedding is provided over the sheath. The bedding consists of a fibrous material like jute or hessian tape.

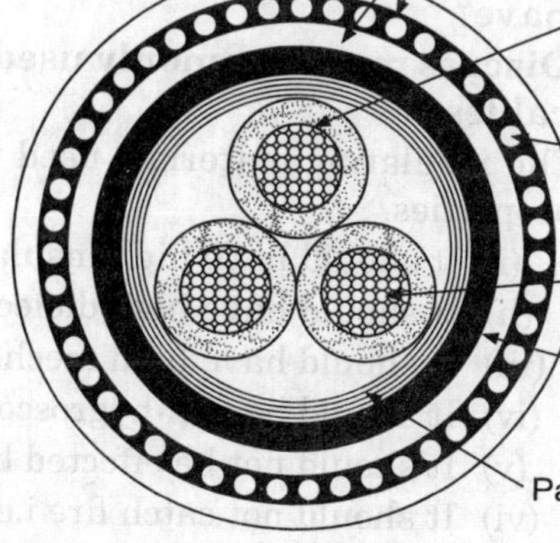

Fig. 4.54 Multi core 11 kV underground cable

5. **Armouring:** Over the bedding, armouring is provided to protect the cable from mechanical injury while laying it and during the course of banding. Armouring usually consists of one or two layers of galvanized steel wire or steel tap.
6. **Serving:** To protect the armouring from atmospheric conditions, a layer of fibrous material similar to bedding is provided over the armouring. This is known as serving.

Q.2 What do you understand by the following terms connected with distribution system?
(i) Feeder
(ii) Distributor
(iii) Service mains

Ans. (i) **Feeder:** A feeder is a conductor which connects substation (or generating station) to the area where the power is to be distributed. These are the conductors which carry large currents to the feeding points. In the following. Figure *S* is the sub-station and *SA* and *SC* are the feeders *A* and *C* are the feeding point.

Generally no tappings are taken from the feeder so that current throught it remains the same A feeder is designed from the point of view of its current carrying capacity, so that the voltage available at the farthest end of a feeder can be regulated by means of the regulating equipment at the substation.

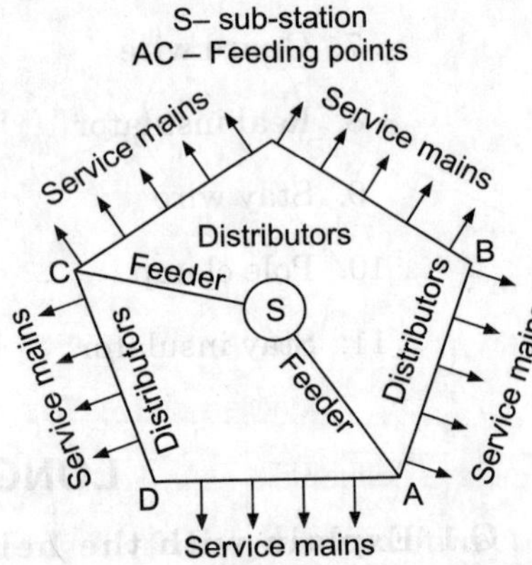

Fig. 4.55 Feeder and distributor

(ii) **Distributor:** A distributor is a conductor from which tappings are taken for supply to the consumer or it is the conductor which carries current to the service mains from the feeding points. The current loading of a distributor varies along its length. Distributor is designed from the point of view of the voltage drop in it because the voltage drop in the distributor is solely dependent on the loading done on it by the consumers. There is a limit for the variation of voltage at any point of a distributor. It should not vary more than + 5% of the declared voltage. Thus if the declated voltage is 230 V, the maximum values of voltages are 242 V and 218 V. The former value should not be exceeded when the distributor is lightly loaded and the latter value should not be reached when the distributor is loaded maximum.

(iii) **Service Mains:** A service main is generally a small cable which connects the distributor to the consumer terminals.

Q.3 (*a*) State the properties that the insulation used in underground cables should have?
(*b*) Discuss most commonly used insulating materials employed for underground cables.

Ans. (a) The insulating materials used in the underground cables should have the following properties.

(i) It should have high insulation resistance.
(ii) It should have high dielectric strength.
(iii) It should have high mechanical strength.
(iv) It should be non-hygroscopic i.e., it should not absorb water.
(v) It should not be effected by acids and alkalies.
(vi) It should not catch fire i.e., it should be non-inflammable.

(b) The most commonly used insulating materials in underground cables are:

(i) Impregneted paper
(ii) Varnished cambric
(iii) Vulcanised Indian Rubber

(i) **Impregnated Paper:** It has high dielectric strength and high insulation resistance. But paper is hygroscopic i.e., absorbs water even after impregnated. Its working temperature is 100°C and dielectric strength in 25 kV/mm.

(ii) **Varnished Cambric:** This consists of cotton cloth impreganated with varnish. It is also hygroscopic therefore such cables are provided with metallic sheath. The dielectric strength of cambric is 4 kV/mm.

(iii) **Vulcanised Indian Rubber (VIR):** This is prepared by mixing rubber with sulphur. The process is called vulcanization since sulphur reacts quickly with copper therefore the copper conductor is tinned before vulcanization. This has higher mechanical strength. Its working temperature is 150°C.

PROBLEMS

Q.1 A 2-wire dc distributor *OB* is fed at *O*. The cross-sectional area of each copper conductor is 3.4 sq. cm and resistivity of copper is 1.7×10^{-8} ohm-m. The distributor supplies 200 A at point *B*. If length of distributor is 500 metres. Calculate the voltage at the feeding end of the distributor if voltage at *B* is 230 V. ***(Ans. 241 V)***

Q.2 A 2-wires distributor *AB* 400 m long is fed at *A* and *B* at 250 volts. It is loaded as under :

70 *A*-100 metres from *A*:

80 *A*-250 metres from *A*:

50 *A*-300 metres from *A*:

If each line conductor has area of cross-section of 1 cm^2 and its material has a resistivity of 1.7 ohm-cm. Find the point of minimum potential and voltage at this point.

(Ans. 245.495 V)

Q.3 A 2-wires dc distributor cable *AB* is 2 km long supplies load of 100 *A*, 150*A* and 50 *A* situated 500 m, 1000 m, 1600 m and 2000 m from the feeding point *A*. Each conductor has a resistance of 0.01 Ω per 1000 m. Calculate p.d. at each load if p.d. of 300 V is maintained at point *A*. ***(Ans. 295 V, 291 V, 288 V, 287.6 V)***

Q.4 2-conductor ring main 500 metres long is fed at point *A* at 250 volts loads of 50 *A*, 60 *A*, 40 *A* and 30 are tapped at distance of 100 m 250 m, 350 m and 400 m from *A* are clockwise direction respectively. If the cross-section of the conductors be 1 cm^2 and specific resistance of the material of conductors is 1.7 ohm cm, determine the minimum consumer voltage. ***(Ans. 245.07 V)***

Q.5 A single phase ac distributor *AB* 300 metres long is fed from end *A* and is loaded as under, 100 *A* at 0.707 p.f. lagging 200 m from point *A*. 200 *A* at 0.707 p.f. lagging 300 m from point *A*.

The total resistance and reactance of the distributor is 0.2 Ω and 0.1 Ω per kilometer. Calculate the total voltage drop in the distributor. ***(Ans. 17.85 V)***

Solution of Problems

Solution 1: The distributor is shown in the Fig. 4.56.

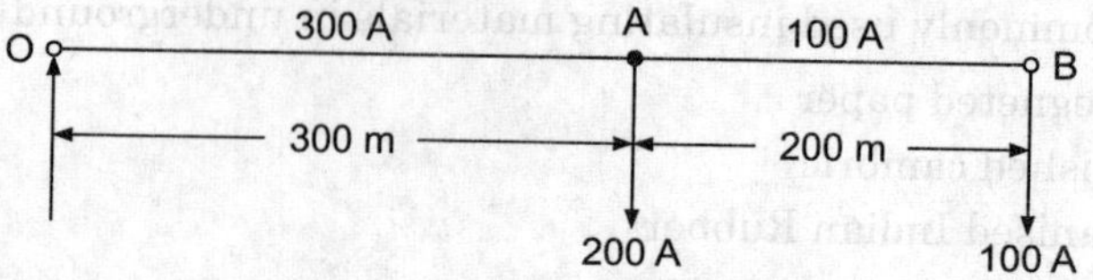

Fig. 4.56 2-wire dc distributor

Resistance of various sections:

$$R_{OA} = \rho\frac{l}{a} = \frac{1.7\times10^{-8}\times300\times2}{3.4\times10^{-4}} = 0.03 \text{ ohm}$$

$$R_{AB} = \frac{1.7\times10^{-8}\times200\times2}{3.4\times10^{-4}} = 0.02 \text{ ohm}$$

Current in various section :

$$I_{AB} = 100 \text{ A}$$

$$I_A\ 100 + 200 = 300 \text{ A}$$

Voltage drop in various sections :

$$V_{OA}\ I_{OA}\ R_{OA} = 300 \times 0.03 = 9\text{V}$$

$$V_{AB} = I_{AB}\ R_{AB} = 100 \times 0.02 = 2 \text{ V}$$

Voltage at far end, $V_B = 230$ V

Voltage at load point A, $V_A = V_B + V_{AB}$

$= 230 + 2 = 232$ V

Voltage at feeding end O, $V_o = V_B + V_{OA}$

$= 232 + 9 = 241$ V **(Ans.)**

Solution 2: The distributor is shown in the Fig. 4.57.

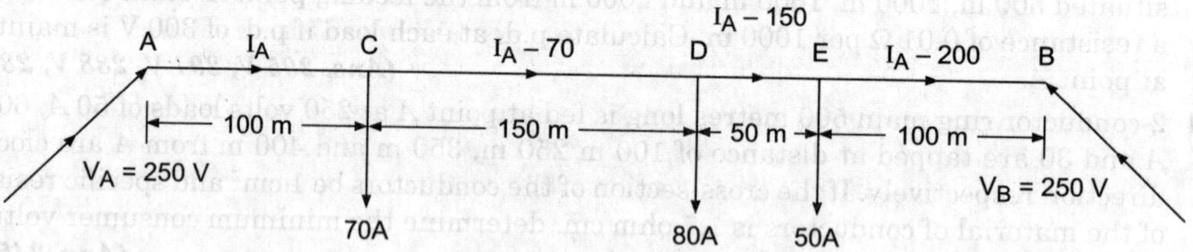

Fig. 4.57 2-wire distributor

Resistance of various sections of the distributor :

$$R_{AC} = \frac{\rho l}{a} = \frac{1.7\times10^{-6}\times100\times100\times2}{1}$$

$$= 0.034 \text{ ohm}$$

$$R_{CD} = \frac{1.7\times10^{-6}\times150\times100\times2}{1} = 0.051 \text{ ohm}$$

$$R_{DE} = 0.017 \text{ ohm}$$
$$R_{EB} = 0.034 \text{ ohm}$$

Let the current fed at point A be I_A. Then current flowing through various section:

$$I_{AC} = I_A \text{ amp.}$$
$$I_{CD} (I_A - 70) \text{ A}$$
$$I_{DE} = I_A - 70 - 80 = [I_A - 150] \text{ A}$$
$$I_{EB} = I_A - 150 - 50 = [I_A - 200] \text{ A}$$

Voltage drop in various sections ;

$$V_{AC} = R_{AC} I_{AC} = 0.034 \, I_A$$
$$V_{CD} = R_{CD} I_{CD} = 0.051 \, (I_A - 70) = 0.051 \, I_C - 3.57$$
$$V_{DE} = R_{DE} I_{DE} = 0.017 \, (I_A - 150) = 0.017 \, I_A - 2.55$$
$$V_{EB} = R_{EB} I_{EB} = 0.034 \, (I_A - 200) = 0.034 \, I_A - 6.8$$

Voltage at point B, $V_B = V_A - V_{AC} - V_{CD} - V_{DE} - V_{EB}$

or
$$V_A - V_B = 0.0341\text{A} + 0.051 \, I_A - 3.57$$
$$+ 0.017 \, I_A - 2.55 + 0.034 \, I_A - 6.8$$

or
$$250 - 250 = 0.136 \, I_A - 12.92$$

or
$$I_A = \frac{12.92}{0.136} = 95 \text{ A}$$

Actual flow of current in various sections ;

$$I_{AC} = I_A = 95 \text{ A} \quad \textit{(from A to C)}$$
$$I_{CD} = I_A - 70 = 95 - 70 = 25 \text{ A} \quad \textit{(from C to D)}$$
$$I_{DE} = I_A - 150 = 95 - 150 = -55 \text{ A}$$
$$= 55 \text{ A} \quad \textit{(from E to D)}$$
$$I_{EB} = I_A - 200 = 95 - 200 = -105 \text{ A}$$
$$= 105 \text{ A} \quad \textit{(from B to E)}$$

The actual flow of current is shown in Fig. 4.58.

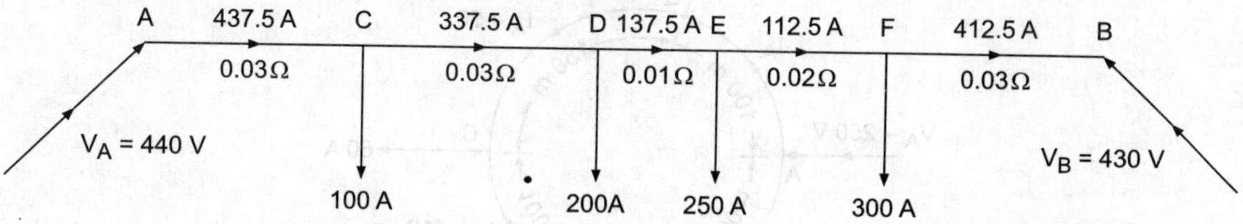

Fig. 4.58

Load point D is the point of minimum potential since it receives current from both sides.

Voltage at point D, $V_D = V_A - V_{AC} - V_{CD}$

$$= 250 - 95 \times 0.034 - 25 \times 0.051$$
$$= 245.495 \text{ V} \quad \textbf{(Ans.)}$$

Solution 3: Fig. 4.59 shows the single line diagram of the distributor with currents.

Resistance per 1000 m of distributor = 2 × 0.01 = 0.02 Ω

$$\text{Resistance of section } A_C,\ R_{AC} = \frac{0.02 \times 500}{1000} = 0.01\ \Omega$$

$$\text{Resistance of section } C_D,\ R_{CD} = \frac{0.02 \times 500}{1000} = 0.01\ \Omega$$

$$\text{Resistance of section } D_E,\ R_{DE} = \frac{0.02 \times 600}{1000} = 0.012\ \Omega$$

$$\text{Resistance of section } E_B,\ R_{EB} = \frac{0.02 \times 400}{1000} = 0.008\ \Omega$$

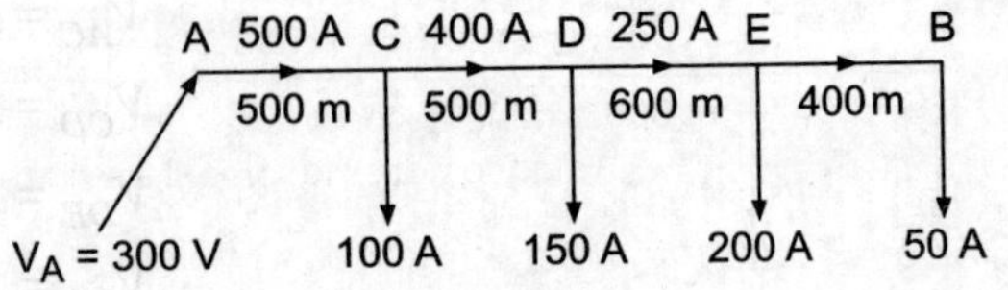

Fig. 4.59

Referring to Fig. 4.59, the currents in the various sections of the distributor are :

$$I_{EB} = 50\text{ A}$$

$$I_{DE} = 50 + 200 = 250\text{ A}$$

$$I_{CD} = 250 + 150 = 400\text{ A}$$

$$I_{AC} = 400 + 100 = 500\text{ A}$$

p.d. at load point C, V_C = Voltage at A – voltage drop in A_C

$= V_A - I_{AC} R_{AC} = 300 - 500 \times 0.01 = 295$ V **Ans.**

p.d. at load point D, $V_D = V_C - I_{CD} R_{CD}$

$= 295 - 400 \times 0.01 = 291$V **Ans.**

p.d. at load point E, $V_E = V_D - I_{DE} R_{DE}$

$= 291 - 250 \times 0.012 = 288$ V **Ans.**

p.d. at load point B, $V_B = V_E - I_{EB} R_{EB}$

$= 288 - 50 \times 0.008 = 287.6$V **Ans.**

Solution 4: The ring distributor is shown in Fig. 4.60.

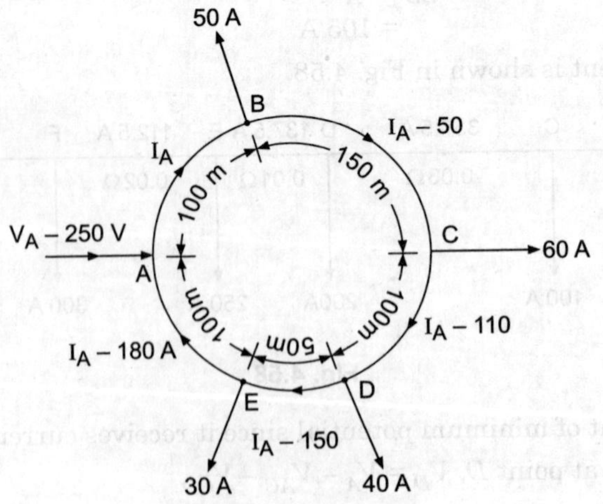

Fig. 4.60 Ring distributor

Resistance of various sections;

$$R_{AB} = \frac{pl}{a} = \frac{1.7 \times 10^{-6} \times 100 \times 100 \times 2}{1} = 0.304 \text{ ohm}$$

$$R_{BC} = 0.051 \text{ ohm}$$

$$R_{CD} = 0.034 \text{ ohm}$$

$$R_{DE} = 0.017 \text{ ohm}$$

$$R_{EA} = 0.034 \text{ ohm}$$

Let the current flowing through various sections be

$$I_{AB} = I_A \text{ amp.}$$

$$I_{BC} = (I_A - 50) \text{ A}$$

$$I_{CD} = I_A - 50 - 60 = (I_A - 110) \text{ A}$$

$$I_{DE} = I_A - 110 - 40 = (I_A - 150) \text{ A}$$

$$I_{EA} = I_A - 150 - 30 = (I_A - 180) \text{ A}$$

Voltage drop in various sections;

$$V_{AB} = I_{AB} R_{AB} = I_A \times 0.034 = 0.034 I_A$$

$$V_{BC} = 0.051 (I_A - 50) = 0.051 I_A - 2.25$$

$$V_{CD} = 0.034 (I_A - 110) = 0.034 I_A - 3.74$$

$$V_{DE} = 0.017 (I_A - 150) = 0.017 I_A - 2.55$$

$$V_{EA} = 0.034 (I_A - 180) = 0.034 I_A - 6.12$$

Total voltage drop in the distributor

$$= V_{AB} + V_{BC} + V_{CD} + V_{DE} = V_{EA}$$

$$= 0.34 I_A + 0.051 I_A - 2.55 + 0.034 I_A - 3.74 + 0.017 I_A$$

$$= -2.55 + 0.034 I_A - 6.10$$

$$= 0.17 I_A - 14.96$$

In a ring main distributor, total voltage drop in the distributor I zero.

$$0.17 I_A - 14.96 = 0$$

or

$$I_A = \frac{14.96}{0.17} = 88A$$

Actual flow of current in various sections;

$$I_{AB} I_A \; 88 \text{ A (from } A \text{ to } B)$$

$$I_{BC} = I_A - 50$$

$$= 88 - 50 = 38 \text{ (from } B \text{ to } C)$$

$$I_{CD} = I_A - 110$$

$$= 88 - 110 = -22 \text{ (from } C \text{ to } D)$$

$$I_{DE} = I_A - 150$$

$$= 88 - 150 = -62 \text{ (from } D \text{ to } E)$$

$$I_{EA} = I_A - 180$$

$$= 88 - 180 = -92 \text{ (from } E)$$

The actual flow of current in the distribution is shown. Since load point '*C*' receives current from both sides, therefore, load point *C* is the point of minimum potential.

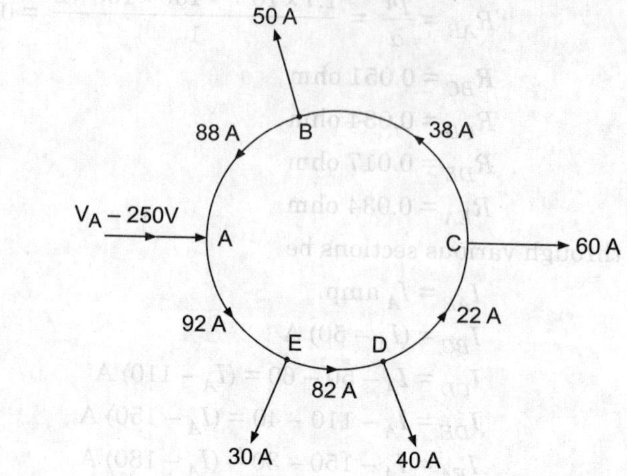

Fig. 4.61 Actual flow of current in distributor

∴ Voltage at load point *C*,

$$V_C = V_A - V_{AB} - V_{BC}$$

$$= 250 - 88 \times 0.034 - 38 \times 0.051$$

$$V_C = 245.07 \text{ volts} \quad \textbf{(Ans)}$$

Solution 5: Fig. 4.62 shows the single line diagram of the distributor

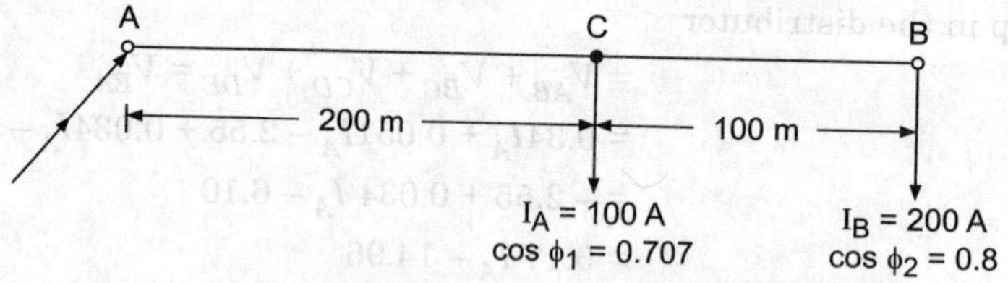

Fig. 4.62 Single phase ac distributor

Impedance of the distributor/km = (0.2 + *J*0.1)Ω

Impedance of section A_C, $\vec{Z}_{AC}$ = (02 + *J*0.1) × 200/1000 = (0.04 + *J*0.02)Ω

Impedance of section C_B, Z_{CB} = (0.2 + *J*0.1) × 100/1000 = (0.02 + *J*0.01)Ω

Load current at point *B*, $\vec{I}_2 = I_2 (\cos \phi_2 - J \sin \phi_2) = (200(0.8 - J\,0.6)$

$= (160 - J120)$ A

Load current at point *C*, $\vec{I}_1 = I_1 (\cos \phi_1 - J \sin \phi_1)$

$= 100\,(0.707 - J0.707) = (70.7 - J70.7)A$

Current in section C_B, $\vec{I}_{CB} = \vec{I}_2 (160 - J120)\,A$

Current in section A_C, $\vec{I}_{AC} = \vec{I}_1 + \vec{I}_2$

$= (70.7 - J70.7) + (160 - J120)$

$= (230.7 - J\,190.7)\,A$

Voltage drop in section *CB*, $\vec{V}_{CB} = I_{CB} Z_{CB} = (160 - J120\ (0.02 + J0.01)$

$= (4.4 - J0.8)$ volts

Voltage drop in section *AC*,

$$\vec{V}_{AC} = \vec{I}_{AC}\ \vec{Z}_{AC} = (230.70 - J190.7)\ (0.04 + J0.02)$$

$$= (13.04 - J3.01) \text{ volts}$$

$$\text{Voltage drop in the distributor} = \vec{V}_{AC} + \vec{V}_{CB} = (13.04 - J3.01) + (4.4 - J0.8)$$

$$\text{Magnitude of drop} = \sqrt{(17.4)^2 + (3.81)^2} = 17.85 \text{ V} \quad \textbf{Ans.}$$

EXERCISE

1. Distinguish between a feeder, distributor and service main in a distribution scheme.
2. Mention the relative advantages and disadvantages of the use of overhead lines and underground cables for distribution of electrical energy.
3. Draw the section of a 11 kV power cable. Label the various parts and explain in brief the functions of each part.
4. Describe briefly the procedure of lying an 11 kV underground power cable.
5. What are the advantages of a ring distribution system over radial distribution?
6. Name the different methods of lying underground cables and explain any one of them briefly.
7. Explain what is meant by primary distribution system and secondary distribution system.

❑❑❑

Substations

5

INSIDE THIS CHAPTER

- Introduction
- Functions of a Substation
- Types of Substations
- Layout of 33/11 kV Distribution Substation and Various Accessories Equipment
- Grid Substation
- Key Diagram of 220 kV Grid Substation
- Selection and Location of Site for Substation
- Equipment for Substations and Switchgear Installations

5.1 INTRODUCTION

A substation may be defined as an assembly of apparatus which is installed to control transmission and distribution of electric power.

Substations took place when it became possible to generate high voltage for transmission to load centres which were far away from the generating stations. The substations form the most important part of power system. The electric power is generated at the power stations, handled at several substations and then delivered to the consumers of electricity.

Some substations are simply switching stations where different connections between various transmission lines are made, others are converting substation which either convert ac into dc or vice versa. Substations are also provide some safety devices which may be installed to disconnect equipment in case of fault. Street lighting equipment as well as switching controls for street lights can be installed in a substation.

5.2 FUNCTIONS OF A SUBSTATION

A substation may be required to perform one or more of the following functions:

1. To switch on and off the power lines, the operation is known as *switching operation.*
2. To raise or lower the voltage, the operation is known as voltage *transformation operation.*
3. To convert ac into dc or vice versa, the operation is known as *power converting operation.*
4. To convert frequency from higher to lower or vice-versa, the operation is known as *frequency operating operation.*
5. To improve the power factor by installing synchronous condensers at the end of the line, the operation is known as *power factor correction operation.*

Out of these operations, probably the voltage transformation is the most important feature of a substation.

5.3 TYPES OF SUBSTATIONS

There are many ways of classification of substations as under :

1. According to system of supply.
   (a) D.C. substation (b) A.C. substation
2. According to the design
   (a) Indoor type (b) Outdoor type
   Outdoor type substation in further classified as
   (i) Pole mounted substation
   (ii) Foundation mounted substation.
3. According to the equipment in the substation.
   (a) Motor converter (b) Rotary converter
   (c) Mercury arc rectifier (d) Metal rectifier
   (e) Transformer
4. According to the system of operation.
   (a) Manual (b) Automatic

All the substations working on a.c. having transformer. These may be outdoor, indoor or pole-mounted type. The operation may be automatic or manual.

5.3.1 Types of Substations According to Design

According to design there are two types of substations:

(i) Indoor substations
(ii) Outdoor substations

(i) **Indoor Substations:** In these substations the electrical equipment is installed within the building of substation. Indoor substations are usually for a voltage upto 11 kV but can be erected for 33 kV and 66 kV volts when the surrounding atmosphere is contaminated with impurities, such as metal corroding gases and fumes, conductive dust etc. The major factor in the design of indoor substation is the minimization of the fire risk; sectionalizing by fire resisting wall is usually necessary and fire-extinguishing apparatus must be installed. Carbon dioxide is a very effective fire-extinguishing medium and causes no damage to sound equipment, the gas is stored in cylinder and released automatically by fusible plugs. Figure 5.1 gives the layout of a typical indoor type of substation having transformer with weather protection.

The main function of all sub-stations is to convert or transform energy for a variety of purposes. A sub-station is an assembly of apparatus the function of which is to perform any one or two or all the following operations :

1. Switching operations i.e., to switch on and off the power lines.
2. Voltage transformation operation i.e., to raise or lower the voltage.

3. Power converting operation i.e., to convert AC to DC or vice versa.

4. Frequency converting operation i.e., to change the frequency.

5. Power factor correction operation i.e., to improve the power factor by installing synchronous condensers at the end of the line.

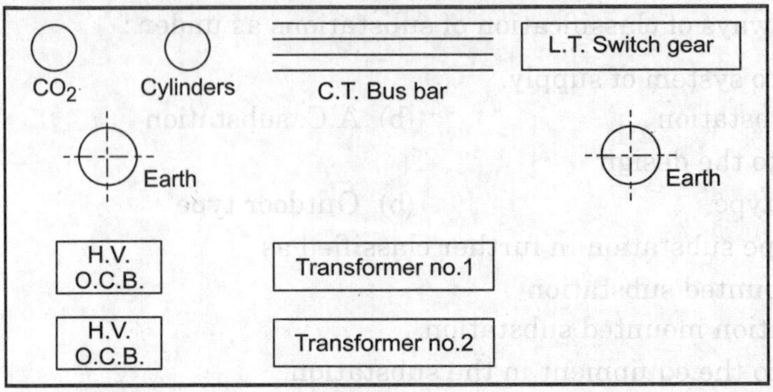

Fig. 5.1 Layout of indoor type substation

Main substations are seldom indoor type. Generally local substations beyond 230 kVA capacity controlling a large number of LT feeders are of indoor type. Fig. 1.10 gives the layout of a typical indoor type of substation having transformer with weather protection. The usual practice is to put the transformer out of doors and the switch gear inside a properly designed building.

The substation shown in Fig. 5.1 consists of two transformers say each of 500 kVA. The approximate size of the building for this type of substation is 8 metres × 5 metres. The usual primary voltage is 11 kV and the secondary is 440 volts. The switch gear on primary side will consist of oil circuit beakers only. The high voltage supply is given to the primary of the transformer through circuit breaker and isolator. The secondary is connected to the low voltage busbars. From the busbars various feeders emerge out. The panel for each feeder consists of an isolator switch and a circuit breaker. In addition to the isolator and circuit breaker, the panel is provided with the measuring instruments consisting of 3 ammeters for measurement of current through each phase, one voltmeter with selector switch, one wattmeter, one power factor meter and one energy meter. As regards protection of feeders usually reverse power relay is used. For the protection of oil filled transformers with conservator tanks. Buchholz's relay is most common. Buchholz's relay is provided with alarm circuit as well as trip circuit.

The auxiliaries of the indoor type of substations are :

(a) Storage batteries.

(b) Fire-fighting equipment.

(a) Large batteries of lead-acid type are very common both in generating stations as well as substations. Batteries are expensive and occupy considerable space but they are useful in the sub-station for the following applications.

(i) Operation of the protective gear and switch-operating solenoids.

(ii) Emergency lighting in case of failure of supply.

(b) Previously water and sand were the only fire-fighting media, but now a number of fire-extinguishers have been developed. Fire fighting equipment is useful after the fire has broken out and is absolutely necessary for an indoor substation, particularly near the oil circuit breakers and transformers. Best automatic medium for extinguishing fire is carbon dioxide or methyl-bromide. The greatest advantage of such gases is that they do not damage the insulation just like water. Also the dielectric strength of carbon dioxide is greater than air. It is stored in steel bottles in liquid from at about 60 kg per sq. cm. The system automatically operates when the temperature reaches about 150° F. At this temperature the fusible link melts and causes the liquid carbon dioxide to discharge.

The various compartments of an indoor substation are as under:

1. Control compartment.

2. Indicating and metering instruments protective device department.

3. Main busbar compartment.

4. Circuit breaker and operating mechanism compartment.

(ii) **Outdoor Substations:** In this type, the apparatus of the substations is installed in open and hence the name outdoor substation. Such substations can be designed to handle low, medium and extra high voltages.

The outdoor substations are cheaper than indoor type. The rating of transformers used in such sub-stations vary from about 5 MVA to 50 MVA. Generally oil-filled natural cooled transformer are used upto this rating. For proper voltage regulation on load tap changing transformers are used.

Outdoor substation may be further classified as:

(i) Foundation mounted substations

(ii) Pole mounted substations

5.3.2 Foundation Mounted Substations

Such substations are those which transmit electrical energy at 33 kV and above, including 400 kV. Transmission substation have a different design than distribution or pole mounted substations, which supply electrical energy at relatively low voltages. The transmission substations are designed to receive and transmit large blocks of electrical energy amounting to several hundred thousand kVA. Such substations are generally installed outside the city. The equipment required for such substations such as high kVA transformers, Bus bars for supporting conductor for taking the connections, supporting structures for CTS and CVTS, circuit breakers, Isolators and Isolators with switches. Foundation mounted substation is shown in Fig. 5.2.

Key Diagram of Foundation Mounted Sub-station

These substations are installed in the open area in outside the city. They transmit electrical energy at 33 kV and above. These substations are having large number of equipments. Fig.5.3 shows a line diagram of such a substation.

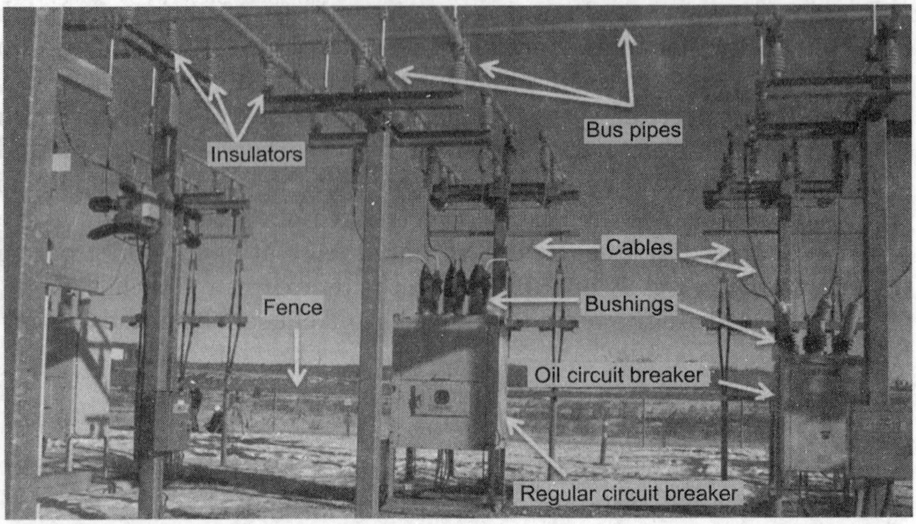

Fig. 5.2 Foundation mounted outdoor substation

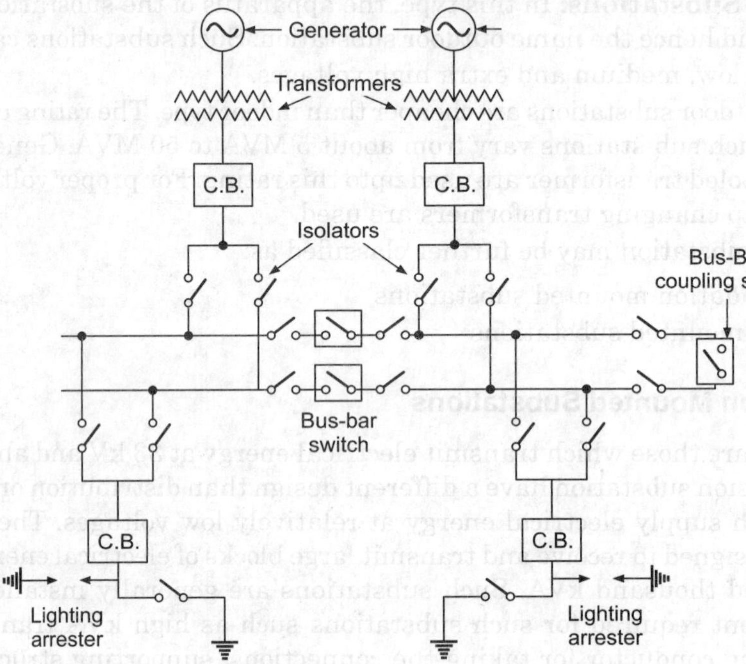

Fig. 5.3 Key diagram of foundation mounted substation

The equipment installed in the foundation mounted substation includes transformers, circuit breakers and control panel etc. Primary and secondary transmission of electric power is handled by these substations.

An outdoor substation saves building costs but requires a larger site and more maintenance. A major factor in the design is the provision of adequate clearance so that work of maintenance can be carried out without making more of the substation dead than is absolutely necessary. At and above 132 kV, outdoor construction is almost universal.

Usually outdoor type substations are used for primary and secondary transmission purposes. These substations are cheaper than indoor type substations. The rating of transformer used in such substations vary from 5 MVA to 50 MVA. The cooling generally **used is of natural** cooling type upto 10 MVA.

5.3.3 Pole Mounted or Distribution Substations

These type of substations require a H-type of structure. At a suitable height it is attached to the H-type of structure (pole), a platform of channel iron is erected for placing the transformer. The primary side of the transformer is connected through a Gang-operating switch (GOS) and HRC fuses of appropriate capacity. There is no need of circuit breaker (CB) on primary side, Lightning arresters are installed over the high voltage line to protect the transformer from the surges. Such substations generally receive power at 11 kV and delivers it at 400/230 V for distribution purposes.

Fig. 5.4 Pole mounted outdoor substation

These substations are cheap and simple and are erected in important localities of the city. These substations are erected in important locations of the yards. Such type of substations is suitable for low rating, say upto about 100 kVA. It does not require much attention for their operation. It is cheaper in first cost and the maintenance cost is also small. For the rural electrification work, distribution to small resident colonies and for medium size consumers. Pole mounted type of substation is more common. The maintenance cost of substation is low.

It should be born in mind that while erecting the pole mounted substation whatever installation is done, it should be carried out as per IEE regulations. Earthing should be provided to the substation at two or more places. One earth is provided for neutral and another earth is necessary for connecting all metal parts of the substation to the ground.

HT fuse unit is installed for protection of HT side and to control LT side, iron clad low tension switch of suitable capacity with fuses is installed.

Key Diagram of Pole-mounted Substation

These types of substations transformer are mounted on the pole. All other equipment are also mounted on a suitable height on the H-type pole on HT distribution lines. The primary side of a transformer is connected through a gang operating switch and fuses of suitable capacity.

Secondary side of transformer is controlled by a switch. Lightening arresters are installed on the H.T side for the protection of transformer from the surges. These substations receive power at 11 kV and step down to 400/230V for distribution purpose.

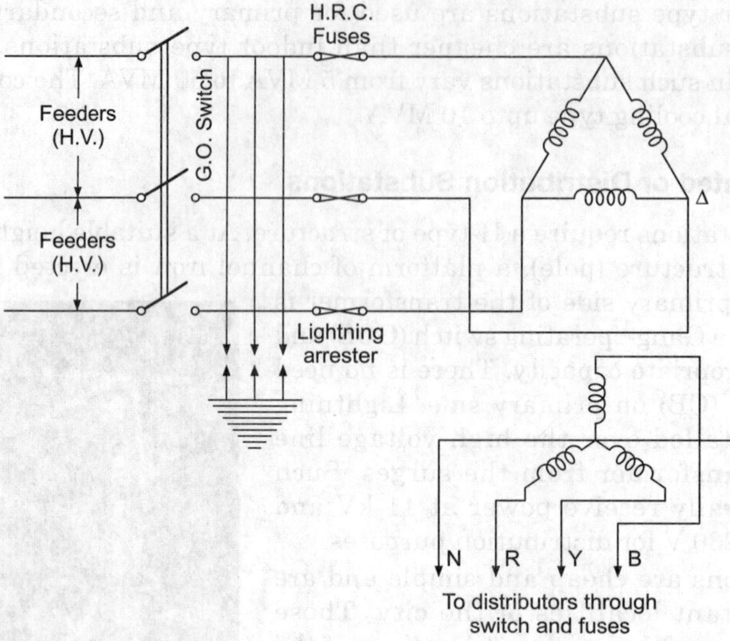

Fig. 5.5 Line diagram of pole-mounted or distribution substation

5.3.4 Components of 11/0.4 kV Pole Mounted Substation

Such substations are erected for distribution of power in localities.

A pictorial representation of pole mounted substation of outdoor type is shown in Fig. 5.6. The various components of such a substation are enlisted below:

1. **Steel Tubular Poles:** The pole which acts as a terminal or carries switch gears or transformers is usually of H-type.
2. **Transformer Plateform:** It is made of iron channel on which the transformer is placed. The channel size is 2.8 m × 7.5 cm × 1 cm. Normally for one pole-mounted substation six numbers of such channel irons are required.
3. **Transformer:** 11/0.4 kV step-down transformers 3-phase are used. The kVA capacity of such transformers to be installed will depend on the load requirement of the locality.
4. **Insulator (Pin Type):** 11 kV pin type insulators made of porcelain are used. These are mounted at the top of the pole structure and house the jumpers of 11 kV line.
5. **Jumpers:** These are made of ACSR conductors and are used for connecting 11 kV line conductors on either side of the pole structure not shown in Fig. 5.6.
6. **Fuses:** On the primary side of a transformer, each phase of 11 kV line is provided with a fuse for protection.
7. **Strain Insulators:** These are disc type insulators used for taking up the strain of the line and are connected to the line conductors on one side and to the channel iron fixed to the pole on the other side.
8. **Gang Operating (Go Switch):** Gang operating switch is used for switching on and off of H.T. transmission line and is installed on the primary side of the transformer.

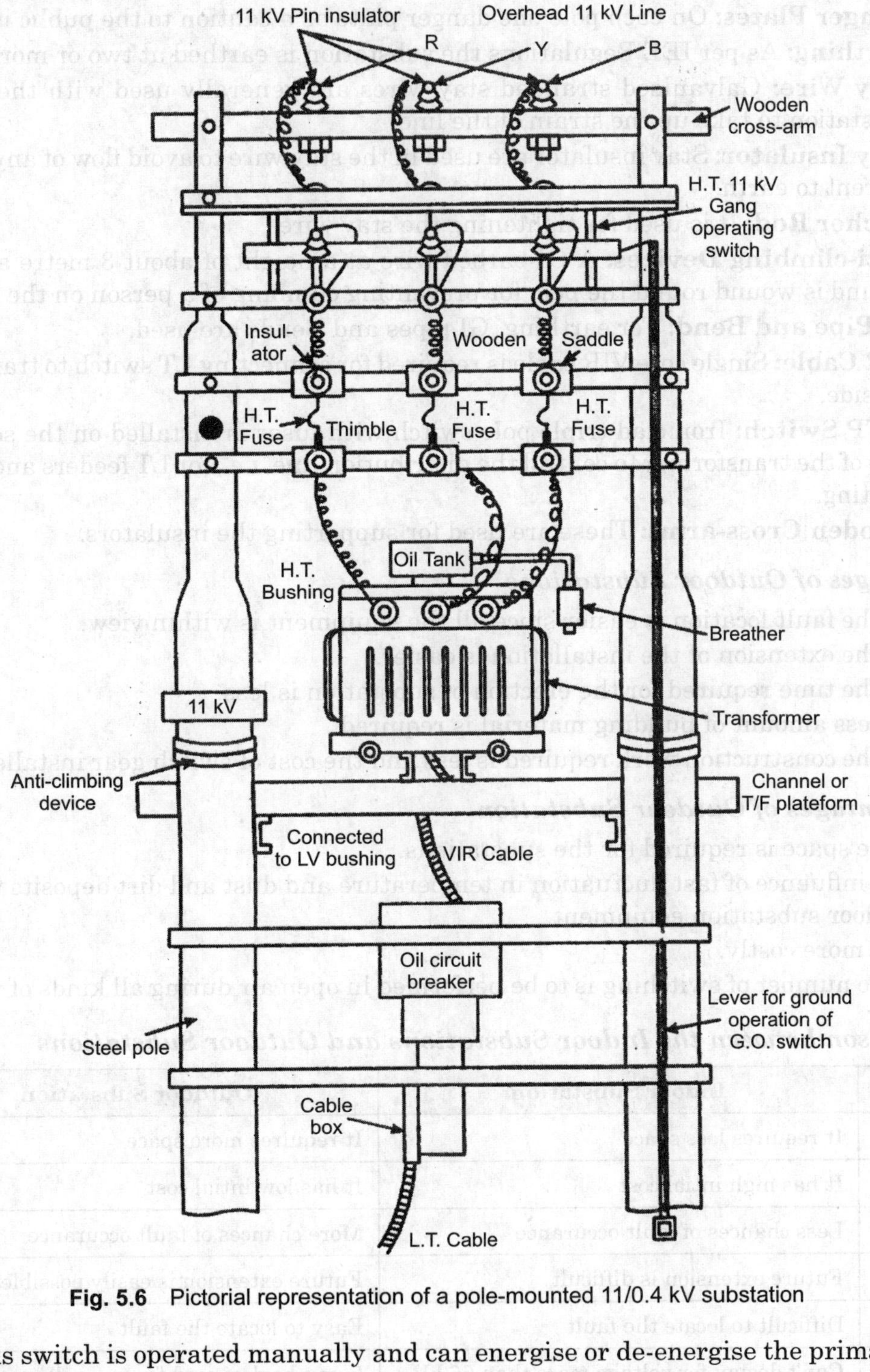

Fig. 5.6 Pictorial representation of a pole-mounted 11/0.4 kV substation

This switch is operated manually and can energise or de-energise the primary of the transformer.

9. **Parallel Grooved Clamps:** PG clamps are used for connecting the jumpers to the conductors.

10. **Danger Plates:** On each pole one danger plate as a caution to the public is fixed.
11. **Earthing:** As per IEE Regulations the substation is earthed at two or more places.
12. **Stay Wire:** Galvanised stranded stay wires are generally used with the poles of substation to take up the strain of the line.
13. **Stay Insulator:** Stay insulator are used in the stay wire to avoid flow of any leakage current to earth.
14. **Anchor Rod:** It is used for tightening the stay wire.
15. **Anti-climbing Devices:** A GI barbed wire at a height of about 3 metre above the ground is wound round the pole for preventing climbing of a person on the pole.
16. **GI Pipe and Bend:** For earthing, GI pipes and Bends are used.
17. **VIR Cable:** Single core VIR cable is required for connecting LT switch to transformer LT side.
18. **ICTP Switch:** Iron clad triple pole switch with fuses is installed on the secondary side of the transformer to control the distribution line, *i.e.*, for LT feeders and for load lighting.
19. **Wooden Cross-arms:** These are used for supporting the insulators.

Advantages of Outdoor Substations

(i) The fault location is easier since all the equipment is within view.
(ii) The extension of the installation is easier.
(iii) The time required for the erection of substation is less.
(iv) Less amount of building material is required.
(v) The construction work required is less and the cost of switch gear installed is low.

Disadvantages of Outdoor Substation

1. More space is required for the substations.
2. The influence of fast fluctuation in temperature and dust and dirt deposits upon the outdoor substation equipment.
3. It is more costly.
4. More number of switching is to be performed in open air during all kinds of weather.

Comparison between the Indoor Substations and Outdoor Substations

S.No	Indoor Substation	Outdoor Substation
1.	It requires less space	It requires more space
2.	It has high intial cost	It has low intial cost
3.	Less chances of fault occurance	More chances of fault occurance
4.	Future extension is difficult	Future extension is easily possible
5.	Difficult to locate the fault	Easy to locate the fault
6.	Can't design for voltage more than 66 kV	It can be designed for any voltage
7.	It requires long time for completion	It requires less time for completion
8.	Maintenance cost is high	Maintenance cost is low

Advantages and Disadvantages of Outdoor Substations Over Indoor Substations

The outdoor substations have the following main advantages over indoor substations.

(i) All the equipment is within view and therefore fault location is easier.
(ii) The extension of the installation is easier, if required.
(iii) The time required in erection of such substations is lesser.
(iv) The smaller amount of building materials (steel-concrete) is required.
(v) The construction work required is comparatively smaller and cost of the switchgear installation is low.
(vi) There is practically no danger of a fault which appears at one point being carried over to another point in the installation because the apparatus of the adjoining connections can be spaced liberally, without any appreciable increase in costs.
(vii) Repairing work is easy.

The disadvantages of outdoor installations in comparison of indoor installations are:

(i) The various switching operations with the isolators, as well as supervision and maintenance of the apparatus is to be performed in the open air during all kinds of weather.
(ii) More space is required for the substation.
(iii) Protection devices are required to be installed protection against lightning surges.
(iv) Length of control cable required is more.

5.4 LAYOUT OF 33/11 kV DISTRIBUTION SUBSTATION AND VARIOUS ACCESSORIES EQUIPMENT

OCB – Oil Circuit Breaker
LA – Lightning Arrester

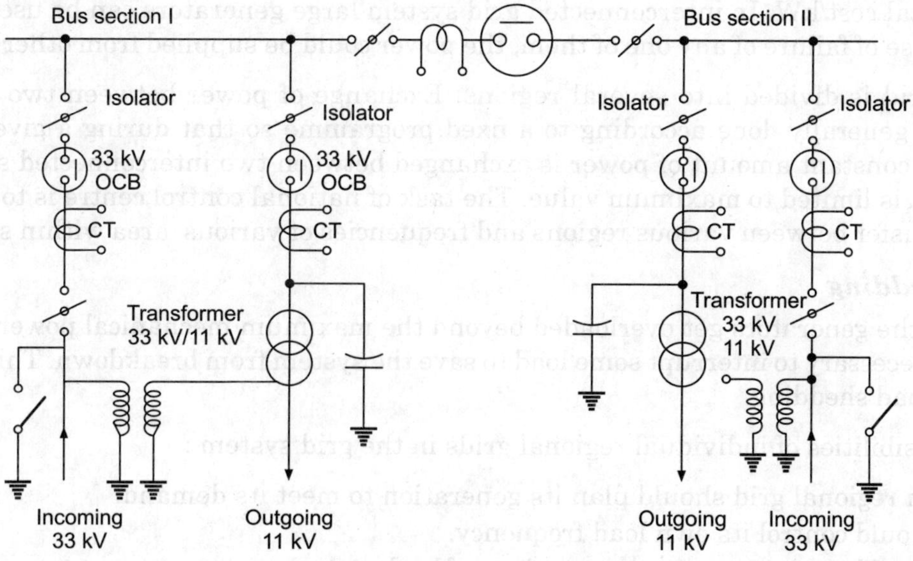

Fig. 5.7 Layout of 33/11 kV distribution sub-station

In such cases single bus bar system with sectionalization is used. Here single bus bar is divided into two sections and whole load is equally distributed on all sections. The two sections are connected with circuit breakers and isolators.

In this case there are two 33 kV incoming lines connected to sections I and II as shown through CB and Isolators. Each 11 kV outgoing line is connected to one section through CB and Isolators. Each 11 kV outgoing line is connected to one section through transformer (33 kV/11kV) and circuit breaker.

Advantages

1. If a fault occurs on any section of the bus, that section can be isolated without affecting the supply from other section.
2. Repair and maintenance of any section of bus bar can be carried out by de-energising that section only eliminating the possibility of complete shut down.

This arrangement is used for voltage upto 33 kV.

5.5 GRID SUBSTATION

Several generating stations are connected to each other to form an inter connected grid system. The operation of such a grid is controlled from a load control centre or load dispatch centre. There are several advantages of interconnecting the large generating stations such as :

1. By interconnecting the large generating station the amount of reserve plant capacity in the system is reduced and the load factor and efficiency of operation are improved.
2. The reliability of supply is increased.
3. As the load curves for different stations are different, therefore, diversity factor of the whole system is improved which increases the effective capacity of the whole system.
4. With interconnected stations generators of large size can be used which reduce the capital cost/kW. In interconnected grid system large generators can be used so that in case of failure of any one of them, the power could be supplied from other stations.

Each grid is divided into several regions. Exchange of power between two adjacent regions is generally done according to a fixed programme so that during a given period of time. A constant amount of power is exchanged between two interconnected system or the output is limited to maximum value. The task of national control centre is to keep the power transfer between various regions and frequencies of various area within set limits.

Load Shedding

When all the generators get overloaded beyond the maximum mechanical power input, it becomes necessary to interrupt some load to save the system from breakdown. This process is called load shedding.

Responsibilities of individual regional grids in the grid system :

1. Each regional grid should plan its generation to meet its demand.
2. It should control its own load frequency.
3. It should generate as per instructions of load control centre.
4. It should co-operate with other regional grids.

Regional Grids in India

1. Northern Region; 2. Western Region; 3. Southern Region; 4. Eastern Region; 5. North-Eastern Region

National load dispatch centre is at Delhi.

5.6 KEY DIAGRAM OF 220 kV GRID SUBSTATION

The Fig. 5.8 shows the key diagram of 220 kV grid substation. The grid substation gets its supply from another substation at 220 kV and in this substation it is stepped down at 132 kV. The energy is distributed to various load centres through 132 kV feeders.

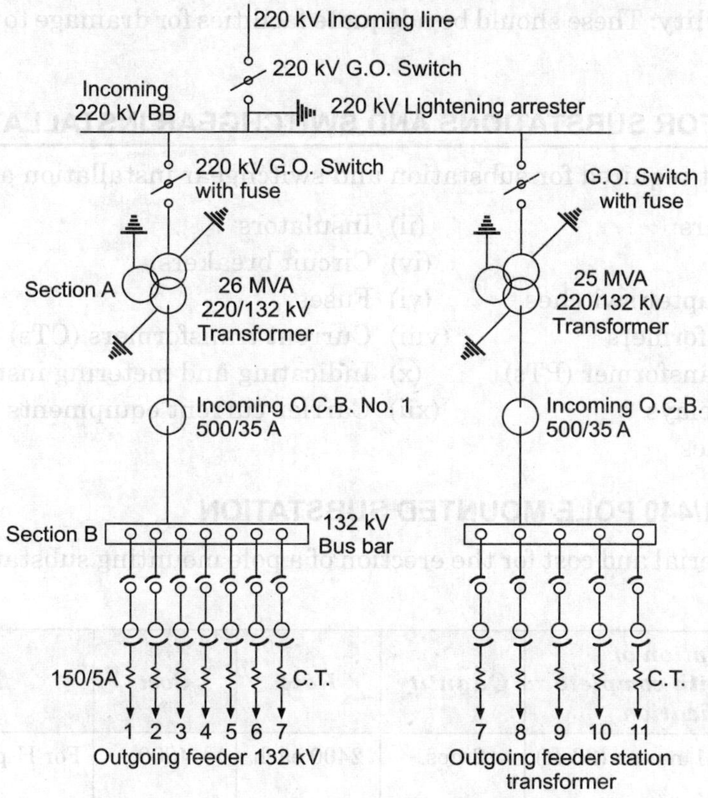

Fig. 5.8 Key diagram of grid substation 220/132 kV

In section of key diagram 220/132 kV, 25 MVA main transformer steps down the supply voltage from 220/132 kV. In-between various apparatus and circuit elements viz. bus bars, lightning arrester, isolator, oil circuit breaker, current transformer, potential transformer have been shown.

5.7 SELECTION AND LOCATION OF SITE FOR SUBSTATION

The following factors are considered while making site selection for a substation:

1. **Type of substation:** Step up station for long transmission should be located as close as to the generating stations in order to minimize the transmission losses.

2. **Availability of sufficient land:** The land selected for a substation should be such that approach of transmission lines and their take off can be possible and it should be sufficient in quantity.
3. **Communication facilities:** There should be suitable communication facilities for the selected land so that there is cheaper transportation.
4. **Atmospheric pollution:** The land selected should not be near the factories because they may produce gases, air, fumes, dust etc.
5. **Availability of essential amenties to the staff:** The side selected should be such where staff can be provided essential ementies like school, hospital, drinking water, market and housing etc.
6. **Drainage facility:** These should be adequate facilities for drainage to avoid pollution of air.

5.8 EQUIPMENT FOR SUBSTATIONS AND SWITCHGEAR INSTALLATIONS

The main equipment required for substation and switchgear installation are as under:

(i) Main bus bars
(ii) Insulators
(iii) Isolators
(iv) Circuit breakers
(v) Load-interrupter switches
(vi) Fuses
(vii) Power transformers
(viii) Current transformers (CTs)
(ix) Potential transformer (PTs)
(x) Indicating and metering instruments
(xi) Protective relays
(xii) Carrier-current equipments
(xiii) Control cables

ESTIMATION OF 11/440 POLE MOUNTED SUBSTATION

The quantity of material and cost for the erection of a pole mounting substation is estimate as below :

S. No.	*Description of material with complete specification*	*Quantity*	*Rate*	*Cost*	*Remarks*
1.	Steel poles, 11 meter (36 ft) long	2 nos.	2400 each	4800	For H-pole structure
2.	100 kVa, 11/0.4 kV 50 cycles transformer platform : For housing the transformer, channel iron 2.8 m × 7.5 cm × 1 cm (9' × 3" × 3/8") = 6 nos. + 3 nos. for switches, 2 nos. for climing + for GO switch, etc. say 12 nos. with clamps.	12 nos.	250 each	3000	For supporting transformer
3.	3 phase, 4 wire Δ/γ connected transformer	1 no.	40,000 each	40,000	

(Contd....)

S. No.	Description of material with complete specification	Quantity	Rate	Cost	Remarks
4.	Pin type insulator	6 nos.	400 each	2400	3 Nos. for incoming line and 3 Nos, for GO switch
5.	Jumpers (ACSR conductors)	3 nos.	80 each	240	Used for connecting 11 kV line conductors on either side of the GO switch
6.	11 kV fuse unit fitted with fuse elements	1 no.	2600 each	2600	
7.	Strain or disc insulators	6 nos.	500 each	300	These are fixed on wooden saddles.
8.	11 kV GO switch with fittings complete and mounted on channel iron.	1 no.	2000 each	2000	
9.	Wooden saddle.	6 nos.	10	60	These are mounted on cross arm to support the disc insulators
10.	Danger plates (11 kV) with clamps	2 nos.	30 each	60	
11.	Earthing sets.	2 nos.	1400	2800	Not shown in the diagram
12.	Stay rod set (complete) with anchor rod	2 nos.	400	800	Not shown in the diagram
13.	Stay insulators	2 nos.	10 each	20	do
14.	Anti-climing devices	2 nos.	40 each	80	Barbed wire approvingly 10 kg is used for anticlimbing device.
15.(a) (b)	G.I. pipe 63.5 mm dia. G.I. bends 63.5 mm dia.	5 meter 2 nos.	20 meter 1 = 50 each	100 10	For earthing do
16.(a) (b)	61/2.6 mm single core VIR cable. 19/1.63 mm single core VIR cable.	15 meters 6 meters	15 15/meter	225 90	For connecting LT switch to transformer LT side (phase) do (Neutral)
17.	LT main ICTPN switch of 200 amps. 500 volts with rewirable type porcelain fuse.	1 no.			For controlling LT lines
18.	Teak wood 5' × 4" × 4" Sundries	Lump sum	3000	3000	
			Total ₹ 64, 585 Say ₹ 65000		

SUMMARY

1. **Substation:** It is defined as assembly of apparatus which is installed to control transmission and distribution of electric power.
2. **Function of a substation**
   (i) To switch on and off the power lines
   (ii) To raise or lower the voltage
   (iii) To convert a.c. into d.c. or vice versa.
   (iv) To convert frequency from higher to lower or vice versa.
   (v) To improve the power factor by using synchronous condensers
3. **Types of substations**
   (i) Indoor substation, (ii) Outdoor substation
   (i) Indoor substation: It is installed within the substation building and having voltage upto 11 kV.
   (ii) Outdoor substation: It is installed in open hence the name and are designed to handle low, medium and extra voltages.
4. **Load shedding:** When all the generators are overloaded, then some load is interrupted to save the system from breakdown.
5. **Type of outdoor station**
   (i) Foundation mounted outdoor substation
   (ii) Pole-mounted outdoor substation
6. **Advantages of outdoor substation**
   (i) Easy location of fault
   (ii) Extension is simple
   (iii) Erection time is less
   (iv) Less building material required
   (v) Cost of switchgear is less.
7. **Disadvantages of outdoor substations**
   (i) The supervision and maintenance of all the apparatus to be performed in open air during all kinds of weather conditions.
   (ii) They require more space for installation.
   (iii) Equipment installed may get damaged during lightening.
   (iv) The climate conditions deteriorate the life of the equipment.
8. **Types of substations according to different categories.**

   1. According to design:
   (i) Indoor substation
   (ii) Outdoor substations

   2. According to type of supply
   (i) A.C. substations
   (ii) D.C. substations

Objective Type Questions

1. Multiple Choice Type Questions

1. The main function of the substation is
   (a) To control the distribution of electric power
   (b) To limit the current in the transmission lines
   (c) To transfer the voltage from higher to lower level.
   (d) Any one of the above.
2. Pole mounted distributed transformer is generally
   (a) Star-delta (b) Delta star
   (c) Star-star (d) Delta-delta
3. For indoor sub-station adequate area is required to ensure
   (a) Economy (b) Efficiency of transformer
   (c) Safety of operator (d) Maintenance
4. Pole mounted substation are installed where
   (a) Huge power is handled (b) Danger is there due to atmosphere
   (c) Small power in handled (d) All of the above.
5. When huge quantity of power at high voltages is handled, the substation needed is;
   (a) Foundation mounted substation
   (b) Foundation mounted outdoor substation
   (c) Pole mounted out door substation
   (d) None of the above

ANSWERS

1. (a) 2. (b) 3. (c) 4. (c) 5. (b)

2. True-False Type Questions

1. The outdoor substations are costilier than indoor substation in initial cost.
2. The maintenance cost of equipment is more in indoor substations than outdoor substations.
3. Substation control the distribution of electric power.
4. The pole mounted distribution transformer is generally star-delta.
5. G.O switch means gang operator switch.
6. There are two types of substation *i.e.*, indoor and outdoor.
7. Outdoor substation requires less space.
8. Fault location is easier in an outdoor substation than in indoor substation.
9. Power factor correction sub-stations are generally located at the sending end of a transmission line.
10. 132 kV/11 kV transformer is used in a distribution substation.
11. To distribute power in a locality, mostly pole mounted sub-stations are recommended.
12. The climate conditions may deteriorate the life span of the equipment placed in outdoor substations.

ANSWERS

1. False **2.** False **3.** True **4.** True **5.** True **6.** True **7.** False **8.** True
9. False **10.** False **11.** True **12.** True

3. Fill in the Blanks Type Questions

1. The substations may be indoor or __________ type.
2. The substation may be pole mounted or __________ mounted type.
3. The indoor substations are __________ than outdoor substations.
4. The maintaince of __________ door substation is more.
5. The pole mounted transformer is connected in __________
6. Expand G.O switch __________
7. The climate conditions usually decrease the life span of the equipment place in __________ substation.
8. The kVA rating of transformer in a pole mounted substations does not exceed __________
9. The areas where high voltage are handed __________ substations are recommended.
10. Mostly the substations are used to __________ the voltages.
11. Pole mounted substations are used for __________ distribution.
12. Outdoor substation requires __________ space.
13. 11/0.4 kV transformer is used in __________ substation.
14. Majority of distribution substations are of __________ type.

ANSWERS

1. outdoor **2.** foundation **3.** costlier **4.** out **5.** delta-star
6. gang operated **7.** outdoor **8.** 200 kVA **9.** outdoor
10. transfer **11.** secondary **12.** more **13.** pole mounted
14. pole mounted substation

SHORT ANSWER TYPE QUESTIONS

Q.1 What is substation?

Ans. An assembly of equipment which in installed to control transmission and distribution of electric power.

Q.2 List the function performed by substations.

Ans. (i) On/OFF the supply (ii) Changing the level of voltage
(iii) Improve the power factor (iv) Maintain the supply frequency
(v) Convert A.C. supply into D.C. supply

Q.3 Name the types of substations.

Ans. (i) Indoor substation
(ii) Outdoor substation

Q.4 What is an indoor substation?

Ans. In such substations, the apparatus are installed within the substation and are made for voltage upto 11 kV.

Q.5 What is an outdoor substations?

Ans. Here the apparatus installed in the open and used for handling low voltage.

Q.6 What is grid substation?

Ans. In a grid substation, a large number of generating stations are inter-connected to form a grid.

Q.7 What is GO switch.

Ans. It is gang operated switch. It is installed on primary side of transformer and are used for switching on and off a H.T. transmission lines.

Q.8 What are advantages of inter connection of substations?

Ans. (i) Reliability of supply in increased.

(ii) Load factor and efficiency in improved.

Q.9 State the two advantages of outdoor substation.

Ans. (i) Repair and maintenance is difficult.

(ii) These are subjected lightening surges.

Q.10 What is circuit breaker?

Ans. It is used to make and break the circuit under no load, full load and under fault conditions.

LONG ANSWER TYPE QUESTIONS

Q.1 Define pole mounted substation with suitable diagram.

Ans. 1. ***Transformer:*** Pole mounted substations are outdoor substation. In these substations 11 kV/400 V step down transformer is installed on H-type structure on suitable height. The primary is connected through GO switch and fuses.

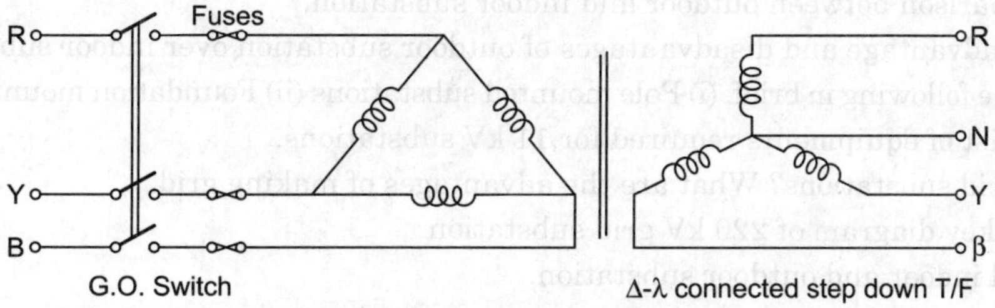

Fig. 5.9 Pole mounted substation

Transformer is delta/star connected at primary it received 11 kV and step down into 400 V at secondary side these substations are located near the load centre and provide three phase as well as single phase supply. The main parts are given below:

2. **Danger plate** is installed on pole mounted substation to give caution to public. It has red colour and danger is written on it.
3. **GO switch:** Such switch is connected on primary side of transformers by which supply can be switch ON/OFF. The operation of switch is manual.
4. **Anchor rod:** Anchor rod is used for tightening the stay wire.
5. **Stay wire:** Stay wire is dead wire to give support to the pole structure against strain of line.
6. **Earth wire:** Earth wire is used to provide earthing to pole and equipments.

Q.2 Explain the types of substation and compare indoor and outdoor substation.

Ans. (i) **Indoor substation:** In these substations, all the equipments are installed inside the building and hence the name. Such substations are usually for a voltage upto 11 kV.

(ii) **Outdoor substations:** In these substations, all the major equipments are installed in the open. Most of substations are such type as low intial cost, extension is possible.

Comparison between Outdoor and Indoor Substation

S. No	*Indoor Substation*	*Outdoor Substation*
1.	It requires less space	1. It requires more space
2.	It has high intial cost	2. It has low intial cost
3.	Less chance of fault occurance	3. More chance of fault occurance
4.	Difficult to locate the fault	4. Easy to locate the fault.
5.	Future extension in difficult	5. Future extension is easily possible.
6.	Maintenance cost is high	6. Maintenance cost is low.
7.	High capital cost	7. Low capital cost
8.	Operation is easy	8. Operation is difficult

EXERCISE

1. Define the term substation, state the reason for stabilising substation.
2. Name the types of substation used in power system.
3. Give comparison between outdoor and indoor substation.
4. State the advantage and disadvantages of outdoor substation over indoor substation.
5. Explain the following in brief. (i) Pole mounted substations (ii) Foundation mounted substations.
6. Give the list of equipments required for 11 kV substations.
7. What is grid substations? What are the advantages of making grid.
8. Draw the key diagram of 220 kV grid substation.
9. Compared indoor and outdoor substation.

□□□

Power Factor

6

INSIDE THIS CHAPTER

- Introduction
- Concept of Power Factor
- Disadvantages of Low Power Factor
- Causes of Low Power Factor
- Power Factor Improvement by Using Static Capacitor
- Economics of Power Factor Improvement

6.1 INTRODUCTION

The electric energy is almost generated, transmitted and distributed in the form of alternating current. Therefore, the question of power factor immediately comes into picture. Most of the loads, *i.e.*, 3-ϕ induction motors are inductive in nature and hence have low lagging power factor. The low power is highly objectionable as it causes an increase in current resulting in more losses.

In order to ensure more favorable conditions for a supply, it is most important to have power factor as close to unity as possible.

6.2 CONCEPT OF POWER FACTOR

Power Factor (P.F.)

(a) Power factor may be defined as cosine of angle between voltage and current.

(b) The ratio of resistance to impedance

i.e.,

$$\text{Power factor} = \frac{R}{Z} = \frac{\text{Resistance}}{\text{Impedance}}$$

(c) The ratio of real power to apparent power,

i.e.,

$$\frac{\text{Real power}}{\text{Apparent power}} = \frac{VI \cos \phi}{VI} = \cos \phi$$

The term cos ϕ is called power factor. Its value can never be more than one.

To obtain maximum power, the power factor in a circuit is made high as possible, *i.e.*, current is brought in phase with the applied voltage so that power factor nearly equal to unity. The leading and lagging power factor depends upto the phase of current vector with respect to voltage vector.

Consider an inductive circuit, which draw a current I from the supply mains lagging the supply voltage by an angle ϕ, known as phase angle the phasor diagram is shown in Fig. 6.1(*a*).

In case current lags the voltage, the power factor is lagging, if it leads the voltage, the power factor is leading. Thus current "*I*" lags the voltage "*V*" by an angle ϕ, as shown in Fig. 6.1(*a*) so the power factor of circuit is $\cos \phi$ lagging.

Let current *I* can be resolvent into two components, one along the phasor and other perpendicular to it. The component along the voltage phasor, $I \cos \phi$ is called the in-phase or active component of current, and one perpendicular to the voltage phasor, $I \sin \phi$ is called the out of phase or reactive component of current.

Let all these components are multiply by voltage *V*, the triangle so obtained is shown in Fig. 6.1(*b*) known as power triangle. All the three angles of the triangle still remain unchanged $VI \cos \phi$ in the phase component of voltage is called real power and is denoted by *P* $VI \sin \phi$ lagging voltage *V* by 90° is called reactive power and is represented and is represented by *VAR*.

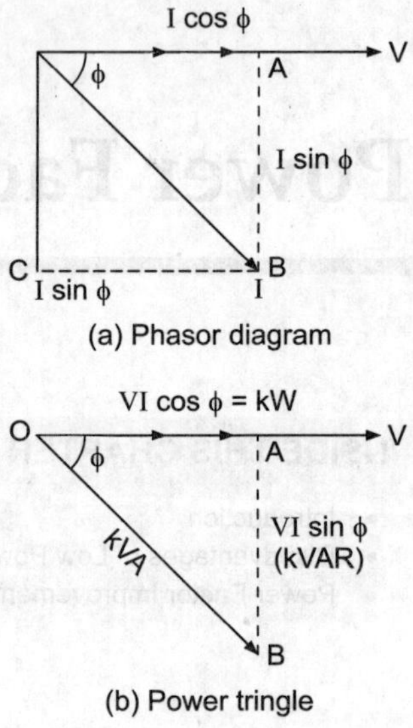

Fig. 6.1

VI is called apparent power and is represented by *VA*.

From power triangle *OAB* shown in Fig. 6.1(*b*)

$$OA = \text{kW component of power}$$

$$AB = \text{kVAR component of power}$$

$$\cos \phi = \frac{OA}{OB} = \frac{\text{kW}}{\text{kVA}}, \text{ the ratio of true power and apparent power.}$$

Thus if the power factor is to be made unity, ϕ should be made zero. This can be achieved if reactive power is made zero by supplying equal amount of leading reactive power so that resultant of leading and lagging components of reactive power of the load will be neutralised, hence power factor of the system is improved.

6.3 DISADVANTAGES OF LOW POWER FACTOR

Power consumed in an a.c. circuit depends upon power factor.

Power consumed is given by

$$P = \sqrt{3}\, V_L I_L \cos \phi$$

$$I_L = \frac{P}{\sqrt{3} V_L \cos \phi}$$

For fixed power and voltage, *P* and V_L load current is inversely proportional to the power factor. Lower the powr factor higher the current and results in following disadvantages.

(a) **Large kVA Rating of Equipment:** The electrical machinery, e.g., alternators, transformers are always rated in kVA.

$$\text{Power kW} = \text{kVA} \times \cos \phi$$

$$\text{kVA} = \frac{\text{kW}}{\cos\phi}$$

kVA rating of equipment is inversely proportional to the power factor.

For a given amount of power, kVA rating will be more for powr factor and vice versa.

(b) **Greater Conductor Size:** To transmit fixed amount of power at fixed voltage, the conductor will have to carry more current at low powr factor. Therefore, large size of conductor is required.

(c) **Large Copper Losses:** At low powr factor conductors have to carry larger current, therefore, $I^2 R$ losses are increased. This results in poor efficiency.

(d) Excessive heating of conductor materials.

Due to above disadvantages, low powr factor is an objectionable factor.

6.4 CAUSES OF LOW POWER FACTOR

1. A transformer draws a magnetizing current which remains constant at all loads. This magnetizing current makes the total current lag with respect to e.m.f. At normal loads, this magnetizing current is quite small as compared to load current and, therefore, does not effect the power factor much but at light loads (In case of distribution transformers supplying lighting load). The magnetizing current becomes good enough to cause the whole current to lag behind and thus make the power factor poor.
2. Induction motors, which work almost at the same principle as the transformers work at very poor power factor when running at lighter loads. But when running at full load they have power factor between 0.8 to 0.85 lagging.

   In fact the power factor at which induction motor works goes on decreasing with the decrease in load. It being approx. 0.85 at full load, 0.8 at 75% of full load, 0.7 at half load and so on, so much so that it is approximately 0.1 at no load.
3. Arc lamps operate at very poor power factor due to the inherent characteristics of the arc.
4. Industrial heating furnaces, such as arc and induction furnaces operate at very poor lagging power factor.
5. Increase in supply voltage during light hours such as during lunch time and during night time, results in more lagging current drawn by inductive reactances which further results in poor power factor.

6.4.1 Methods of Avoiding Low Power Factor

1. Synchronous motors may preferably be used as against inductions motor.
2. High speed induction motors may be preferred over low speed ones, as they have high power factors.
3. If possible no induction motor should be worked at less than full load. Group driving may be preferred as against individual driving, if induction motors are used. So that the group motor may be worked at near full load.

4. If 3-phase induction motors are to be used for longer periods at less than half load, stator windings normally in delta may switched over to star. This improves efficiency and also power factor.
5. If possible d.c. motors may be used, driven by synchronous motor generator set in preference to a.c. motors. This provides an added advantage of better speed control.

6.5 POWER FACTOR IMPROVEMENT BY USING STATIC CAPACITOR

One of the major applications of capacitor is to improve the power factor. For such purpose it is connected is parallel with the load responsible for low power factor. The capacitor connected in parallel is shown in Fig. 6.2(a).

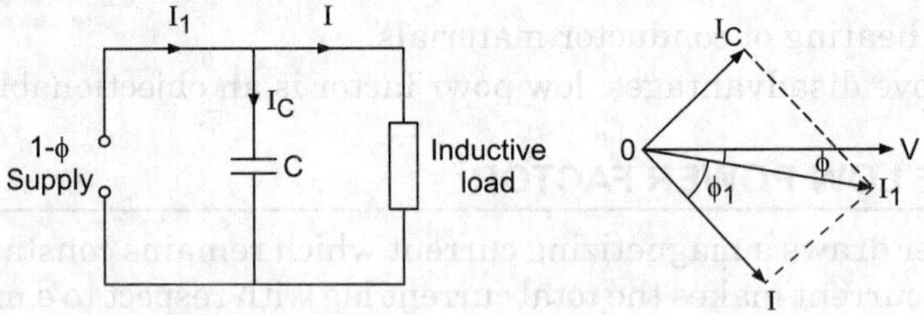

(a) Schematic diagram (b) Phasor diagram

Fig. 6.2 Power factor improvement by using static capacitor

It improves the power factor by neutralize the effect of inductive load the capacitor takes leading current I_C, where inductive load draws the lagging current and resultant current is shown by I. As shown in phasor diagram ϕ is less than ϕ_1 hence resultant power is improved.

Below in Fig. 6.3 shows the connection of capacitors used for 3-phase system. Generally capacitors are connected in delta in order to improve power factor of 3-phase load. However, capacitors can be connected in star connections but it demands larger size.

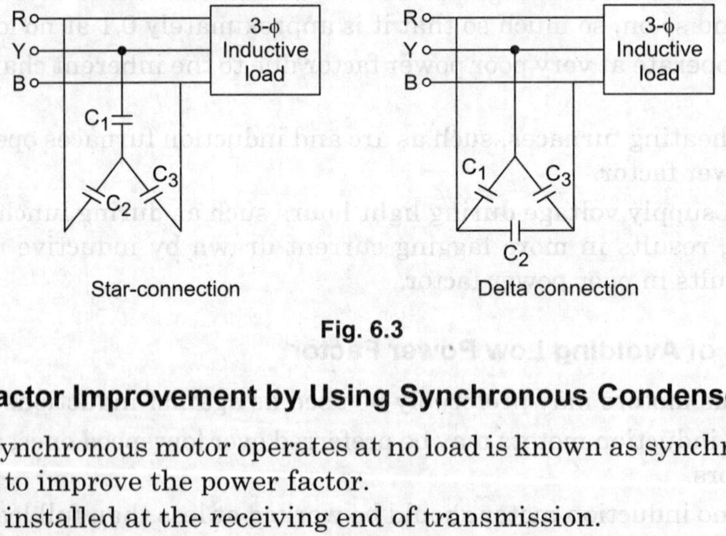

Star-connection Delta connection

Fig. 6.3

6.5.1 Power Factor Improvement by Using Synchronous Condenser

An over excited synchronous motor operates at no load is known as synchronous condenser that can be used to improve the power factor.

It is generally installed at the receiving end of transmission.

To illustrate how an synchronous motor seen in parallel with the load can improve the power factor. Consider the inductive load, without synchronous motor operates at power factor ϕ and draw lagging current I_L as shown in Fig. 6.4.

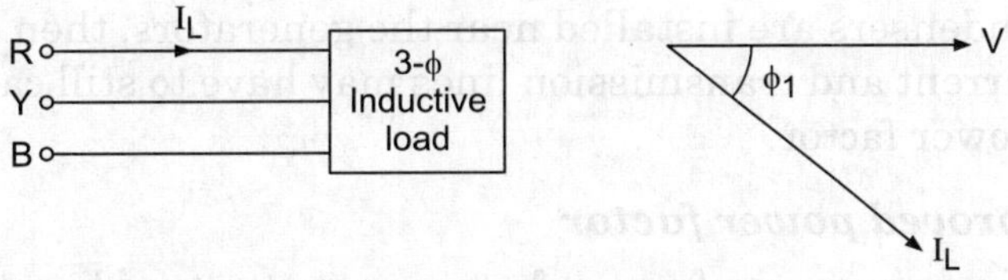

Fig. 6.4 Inductive load without synchronous motor

Now connect an over excited synchronous motor in parallel with load, that draws leading current I_S and total resultant current I and power factor is shown in Fig. 6.5.

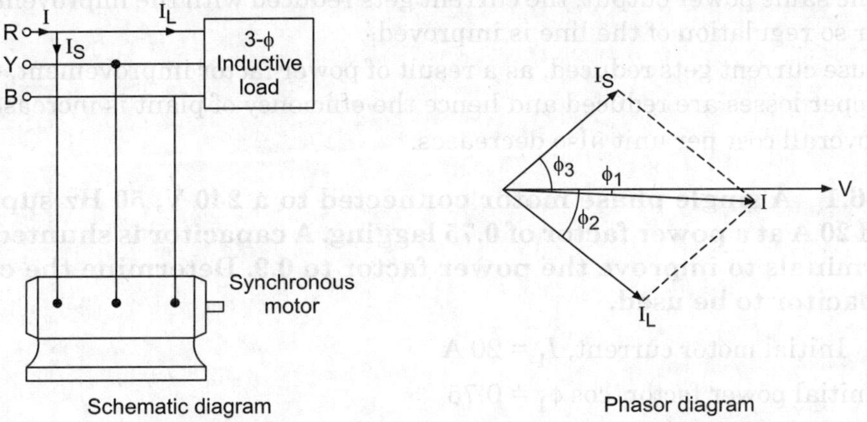

Fig. 6.5 Synchronous motor in parallel with load

Since ϕ is less than ϕ_1, hence power factor is improved. Power factor can be accurately be controlled by using this method. It is very costly method.

6.5.2 By the Use of Phase Advancers

The power factor of induction motor is poor because of the exciting current drawn by it from the mains which lags behind the voltage by 90°. This power factor can be improved by fitting with the set an a.c. excitor or phase advancer which supplies the exciting current to the rotor at slip frequency. Such an excitor can either be fitted on the same shaft as that of motor or it can be suitably driven from it. Use of phase advancers is generally not economical for a motor size below 200 HP.

6.5.3 Location of Power Factor Improvement Apparatus

The most appropriate location for the power factor improvement equipment is, where the apparatus responsible for low power factor is operating.

In case of transmission line, if the power factor is to be improved by installing synchronous condensers, then these should be installed at the receiving end of transmission line so that it is not only the generators and transformer which carry the reduced current as a result of improving the power factor but the transmission line is also relived of carrying excessive current.

If synchronous condensers are installed near the generators, then only generators shall carry the reduced current and transmission lines may have to still carry excessive current due to its own low power factor.

Advantages of improved power factor

1. Since with the improvement of power factor, current gets reduced, the same equipment now if carries the rated current at improved power factor its kW capacity shall get increased. Thus kW capacity of alternator, transformers and transmission lines is increased with the improvement of power factor.
2. For the same power output, the current gets reduced with the improvement of power factor so regulation of the line is improved.
3. Because current gets reduced, as a result of power factor improvement, of any plant, so copper losses are reduced and hence the efficiency of plant is increased.
4. The overall cost per unit also decreases.

EXAMPLE 6.1 A single phase motor connected to a 240 V, 50 Hz supply takes a current of 20 A at a power factor of 0.75 lagging. A capacitor is shunted across the motor terminals to improve the power factor to 0.9. Determine the capacitance of the capacitor to be used.

Solution: Initial motor current, $I_1 = 20$ A

Initial power factor, $\cos \phi_1 = 0.75$

Lagging reactive component of initial motor current

$$I_1 \sin \phi_1 = I_1\sqrt{1-\cos^2\phi} = 20\sqrt{1-0.75^2} = 13.229 \text{ A}$$

In phase component of initial motor current

$$= I_1 \cos \phi_1 = 20 \times 0.75 = 15 \text{ A}$$

Motor current after improvement of power factor

$$I_2 = \frac{\text{Active component of initial current}}{\text{Improved power factor}}$$

$$= \frac{15}{0.9} = 16.667 \text{ A}$$

Lagging reactive component of motor current after power factor improvement,

$$= I_2 \cos \phi_2 = I_2\sqrt{1-\cos \phi_2^2}$$

$$= 16.667\sqrt{1-0.9^2}$$

$$= 7.625 \text{ A}$$

Leading reactive component drawn by the capacitor,

$$I_C = I_1 \sin \phi_1 - I_2 \sin \phi_2$$

$$= 13.229 - 7.265$$

$$= 5.964 \text{ A}$$

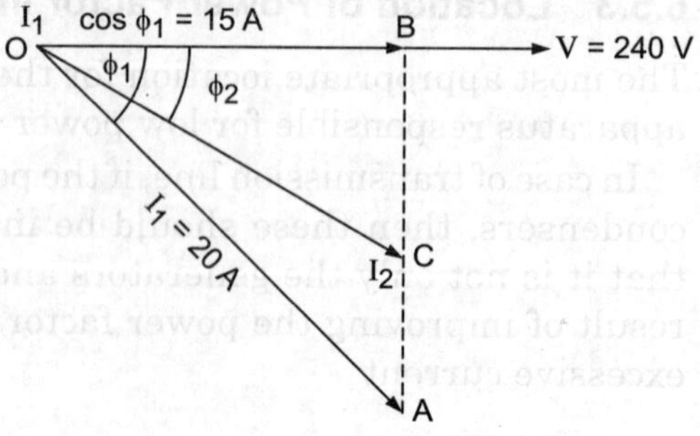

Fig. 6.6 Phasor diagram

Capacitance of the capacitor,

$$C = \frac{I_C}{2\pi f V}$$

$$I_C = 2\pi f C V = \frac{5.964}{2\pi \times 50 \times 240} = 791\ \mu F \quad \textbf{Ans.}$$

EXAMPLE 6.2 A 250 HP 3300 V, 50 c/s, 3 phase star connected induction motor has a full load efficiency of 86% and power factor of 0.707 lagging. It is desired to improve the power factor to 0.9 lagging by connecting 3 capacitors in the motor circuit. Calculate:

(i) The kVA rating of the capacitor bank.

(ii) The capacitance of each unit if the capacitors are connected: (a) in mesh, (b) in star.

Solution:

(*i*) Input of induction motor $= \frac{250 \times 735.5}{0.86} \times \frac{1}{1000} = 214$ kW

$$\cos \phi_1 = 0.707$$

$$\phi_1 = 45^\circ$$

$$\therefore \quad \tan \phi_1 = 1$$

$$\cos \phi_2 = 0.9$$

$$\phi_2 = 25^\circ\ 50'$$

$$\tan \phi_2 = 0.4841$$

Originally reactive power of the motor

$$= P_1 \tan \phi_1 = 214 \times 1 = 214 \text{ kVAR}$$

After improving the power factor,

Reactive power of the motor $= P_1 \tan \phi_2 = 214 \times 0.841 = 103.5$ kVAR

Therefore, reactive power supplied by bank of capacitors

$$= 214 - 103.5 = 110.5 \text{ kVAR}$$

Thus neglecting losses in the capacitors, the rating of the capacitor bank = 110.5 kVAR

(*ii*) (*a*) If the capacitors are mesh connected as shown in Fig. 6.7

then $\frac{\sqrt{3} V_L I_L \sin \phi}{1000} = 110.5$

$\sin \phi = 1$ as capacitors have current, leading voltage by 90°.

$$\sqrt{3} \times 3.3 \times I_L \times 1 = 110.5$$

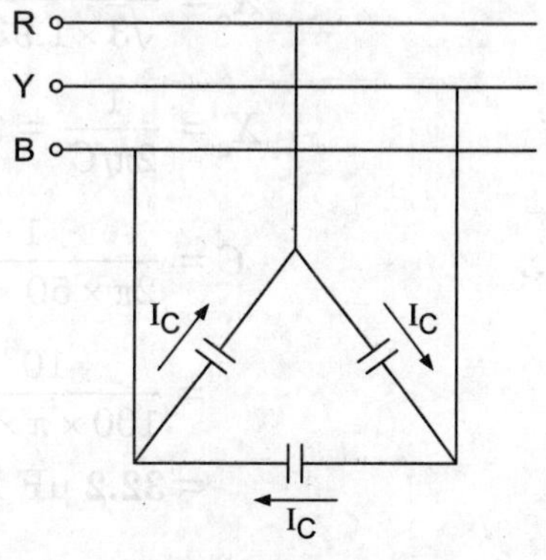

Fig. 6.7 Capacitor bank (delta connection)

$$I_L = \frac{110.5}{\sqrt{3} \times 3.3} = 19.3 \text{ A}$$

I_c = phase current

= current in the capacitor

$$= \frac{19.3}{\sqrt{3}} = 11.10 \text{ A}$$

$$\text{Reactance of each capacitor} = X_c = \frac{\text{Voltage across each capacitor}}{\text{Current in each capacitor}}$$

or $$X_c = \frac{3300}{11.10} = 297\ \Omega$$

∴ $$X_c = \frac{1}{2\pi f C} = 297$$

or $$C = \frac{1}{2\pi \times 50 \times 297} \text{ Farads}$$

$$= \frac{10^6}{100 \times \pi \times 297}\ \mu\text{F} = \mathbf{10.7\ \mu F} \quad \textbf{Ans.}$$

(*b*) If the capacitors are star connected as shown in Fig. 6.8 current in each capacitor

$$I_L = I_c = 19.3 \text{ A}$$

Voltage across each capacitor

= Phase voltage

$$= \frac{3300}{\sqrt{3}} \text{ V}$$

X_c = Reactance of each capacitor

$$= \frac{\text{Voltage across each capacitor}}{\text{Current in each capacitor}}$$

$$X_c = \frac{3300}{\sqrt{3} \times 1.93} = 98.8\ \Omega$$

$$X_c = \frac{1}{2\pi f C} = 98.8\ \Omega$$

∴ $$C = \frac{1}{2\pi \times 50 \times 98.8} \text{ Farad}$$

$$= \frac{10^6}{100 \times \pi \times 98.8} \text{ Micro farads}$$

$$= \mathbf{32.2\ \mu F\ Ans.}$$

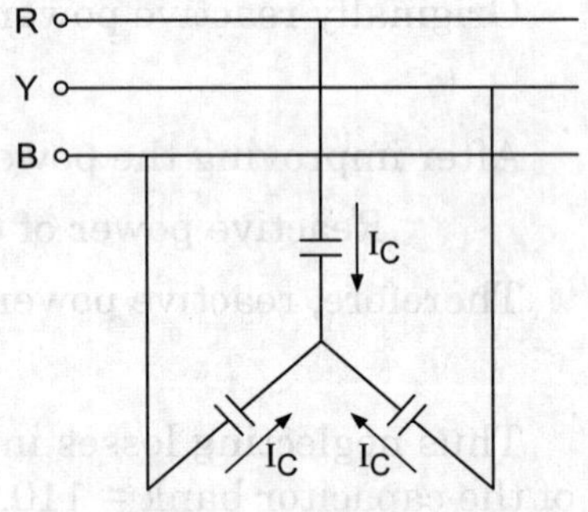

Fig. 6.8 Capacitor bank (star-connection)

6.6 ECONOMICS OF POWER FACTOR IMPROVEMENT

When the power factor is to be improved, power factor improvement plant is required to be installed which involves some expenditure. Improvement of power factor results in reduction of maximum demand which in turn reduced the maximum demand charges annually but extra expenditure is to be increased every year in the form of interest and depreciation on account of investment made over the power factor improvement equipment.

It the yearly interest and depreciation on power factor improvement plant is more than the annual saving on account of maximum demand charge, it is uneconomical to install power factor improvement plant but on the contrary the annual saving on account of maximum demand charge as a result of power factor improvement is more than the yearly interest and depreciation on power factor improvement plant, if is advisable to install the power factor improvement plant as it is economical.

The value of the improved power factor at which the net annual saving is maximum as called most economical power factor. Let P be the kW demand of the consumer represented by OC at power factor $\cos\phi_1$ shown in Fig. 6.9.

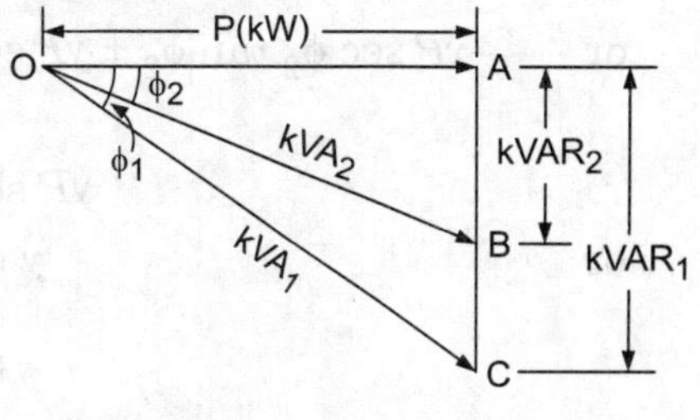

Fig. 6.9 Phasor diagram

$$\text{Reactive component of load} = CA = P\tan\phi_1$$

$$\text{kVA demand of the load} = OA = \frac{P}{\cos\phi_1}$$

If the power factor is improved to $\cos\phi_2$

New kVA of the load represented by

$$OB = \frac{P}{\cos\phi_2}$$

$$\text{New kVAR} = BC = P\tan\phi_2$$

As a result of power factor improvement from $\cos\phi_1$ to $\cos\phi_2$ reduction in kVA demand

$$= OA - OB = \frac{P}{\cos\phi_1} - \frac{P}{\cos\phi_2}$$

kVAR neutralized by phase advancing plant

$$= AB = AC - BC = P\tan\phi_1 - P\tan\phi_2$$
$$= P(\tan\phi_1 - \tan\phi_2)$$

If ₹ x is the annual cost per kVA of the maximum demand, and ₹ y is the annual cost of the phase advancing plant per kVAR, then

$$\text{Annual saving in max. demand} = x\left(\frac{P}{\cos\phi_1} - \frac{P}{\cos\phi_2}\right) = xP\left(\frac{1}{\cos\phi_1} - \frac{1}{\cos\phi_2}\right)$$

Annual expenditure on phase advancing plant

$$= yP(\tan\phi_1 - \tan\phi_2)$$

For most economical power factor, annual saving "S" should be maximum

$$\therefore \quad S = xP\left(\frac{1}{\cos\phi_1} - \frac{1}{\cos\phi_2}\right) - yP(\tan\phi_1 - \tan\phi_2)$$

$$= xP(\sec\phi_1 - \sec\phi_2) - yP(\tan\phi_1 - \tan\phi_2)$$

If "S" is to be maximum $\frac{ds}{d\phi_2}$ should be zero.

i.e., $$\frac{ds}{d\phi_2} = 0$$

i.e., $$\frac{ds}{d\phi_2}[xP(\sec\theta_1 - \sec\theta_2) - yP(\tan\phi_1 - \tan\phi_2) = 0$$

or $$-xP\sec\phi_2\tan\phi_2 + yP\sec^2\phi_2 = 0$$

(Assuming ϕ_1 as constant)

$$\therefore \quad yP\sec^2\phi_2 = xP\sec\phi_2\tan\phi_2$$

or $$y\sec\phi_2 = x\tan\phi_2 = x\sin\phi_2\sec\phi_2$$

$$\therefore \quad \sin\phi_2 = \frac{y}{x}$$

$$= \frac{\text{Annual cost of phase advancing plant per kVAR}}{\text{Annual cost per kVA of maximum demand}}$$

$$\therefore \quad \cos\phi_2 = \sqrt{1 - \sin\ \phi}$$

$$= \sqrt{1 - \left(\frac{y}{x}\right)^2}$$

Thus $\cos\phi_2$ represents the most economical power factor.

EXAMPLE 6.3 A factory takes a peak load of 2000 kW at a p.f. 0.707 lagging and is charged at ₹ 60 per year per kVA of the maximum demand. If the phase advancing plant costs ₹ 100 per kVAR, find the limit to which factory's power factor can be economically improved. Interest and depreciation totals 10% of capital cost of phase advancing plant.

Solution: Most economical power factor at which factory can work is given by

$$\text{cost}\ \phi_2 = \sqrt{1 - \left(\frac{y}{x}\right)^2}$$

where y = annual cost of phase advancing plant per kVAR

x = annual cost per kVA of max. demand

In the given problem

$$y = \frac{100 \times 10}{100} = ₹\,10 \text{ per kVAR per annum}$$

$$x = ₹\,60 \text{ per kVA/annum}$$

$$\therefore \quad \cos \phi_2 = \sqrt{1-(10/60)^2}$$

$$= \sqrt{1-1/36} = \sqrt{35/36}$$

$$= \mathbf{0.987\ Ans.}$$

EXAMPLE 6.4 A consumer takes a steady load of 500 kW at 0.707 power factor lagging and pays ₹ 80 per kVA of maximum demand per annum static capacitors cost ₹ 200 per kVA. Determine the rating of the capacitors required for minimum overall expenditure. Take interest and depreciation as 10% per annum.

Solution: For minimum overall expenditure, power factor should be most economical and condition for power factor $\cos \phi_2$ to be most economical is that

$$\cos \phi_2 = \sqrt{1-\left(\frac{y}{x}\right)^2}$$

where $x =$ ₹ 80 per kVA per annum

$$y = \frac{₹\,200 \times 10}{100} = ₹\ 20 \text{ per kVAR per annum}$$

(for capacitors kVA and kVAR are same)

$$\cos \phi_2 = \sqrt{1-(Y/X)^2}$$

$$= \sqrt{1-(20/80)^2} = \sqrt{\frac{15}{16}} = 0.97$$

$$\sin \phi_2 = \sqrt{1-(0.97)^2} = 0.25$$

$$\tan \phi_2 = \frac{\sin \phi_2}{\cos \phi_2} = \frac{0.25}{0.94} = 0.2575$$

Thus for minimum expenditure, power factor = 0.97

The given power factor is 0.707, *i.e.*,

$$\cos \phi_1 = 0.707, \tan \phi_1 = 1.0$$

Thus the power factor should be improved from 0.707 lagging to 0.97 lagging by static capacitor, therefore, rating of capacitors is given by BC as shown in phasor diagram of Fig. 6.10.

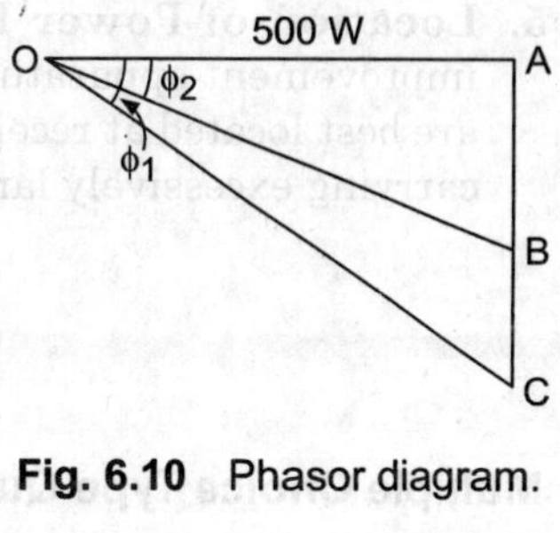

Fig. 6.10 Phasor diagram.

$$BC = AB - AC = 500\ (\tan \phi_1 - \tan \phi_2)$$

$$= 500\ (1 - 0.2575) = 500 \times 0.7425$$

$$= \mathbf{371.25\ kVAR \quad Ans.}$$

SUMMARY

1. **Power Factors (P.F.):** It is defined as cosine of angle between voltage and current. The ratio of resistance to impedance

$$\text{P.F.} = \frac{R}{Z} = \frac{\text{Resistance}}{\text{Impedance}}$$

2. **Disadvantages of Low Power Factor**
   1. Large kVA rating of equipment
   2. Greater conductor size
   3. Large copper loss
   4. Excessive heating of conductor materials
   5. Voltage regulation is poor
   6. Uneconomical power generation and transmission

3. **Causes of Lower Power Factor**
   (a) A transformer working on light loads draws magnetizing current at a low power factor.
   (b) Induction motors working at loads less than full load draw currents at low power factor, through the power factor of induction motor at full load is about 0.85.
   (c) Arc lamps work at low power factor due to their vary nature.

4. **Methods of Improving Power Factor**
   (i) By the use of static capacitor
   (ii) By the method of synchronous condenser
   (iii) By the use of phase advancers
   (i) **Static Capacitor:** Either star or delta connected. These are mostly used in shunt connection. Series connected capacitors create more operational problem and are bulky in size.
   (ii) **Synchronous Condenser:** Synchronous motors working with over excitation draw leading currents thus compensating for the lagging current component. Such motors works at no load and very high speeds (to obtain an economical design).
   (iii) **Phase Advancers:** A special machine which may be connected in the rotor circuit of induction motor to improve its power factor.

5. **Location of Power Factor Improvement Apparatus:** Best location for power factor improvement apparatus causing low power factor. If synchronous condensers are used they are best located at receiving end this would reletive generators and also transmission lines of carrying excessively large lagging currents causing great losses.

Objective Type Questions

1. Multiple Choice Type Questions

1. Power factor is defined as
   (a) The ratio of resistance and reactance of the circuit
   (b) Angle between voltage and current
   (c) The ratio of power and energy in a circuit
   (d) All of the above

2. The value of power factor may be
   (a) More the one (b) Less than one
   (c) More than two (d) None of the above
3. The power factor of an inductive circuit is called
   (a) Leading power factor (b) Lagging power factor
   (c) None of the above
4. For a particular power the current drawn by the circuit is minimum when value of power factor.
   (a) 0.8 lagging (b) 0.8 leading
   (c) unity (d) None of these
5. Low power factor decreases the efficiency of
   (a) Generator (b) Transmission line
   (c) Prime mover (d) All of the above
6. To improve the power factor of 3-phase circuit, the size of each capacitor when connected in delta with respect to when connected in star is :
   (a) $\frac{1}{6}$th (b) $\frac{1}{4}$th
   (c) $\frac{1}{2}$ (d) $\frac{1}{3}$rd
7. A under excited synchronous motor operates at :
   (a) Leading power factor (b) Unity power factor
   (c) Lagging power factor (d) All of the above
8. The power factor improvement equipment is always placed.
   (a) Near the apparatus responsible for low power factor
   (b) At generating station
   (c) Near the transformer (d) Near the bus bass

ANSWERS

1. (a) 2. (b) 3. (b) 4. (c) 5. (b) 6. (d) 7. (c) 8. (a)

2. True-False Type Questions

1. Power factor is the ratio of resistance to reactance.
2. Power factor of a circuit should be less than one.
3. Low power factor decreases the efficiency of generator.
4. For improving power factor static capacitor is connected in parallel with load.
5. Low power factor has good regulation.
6. An overexcited synchronous motor working on no load in called synchronous condenser.
7. An under excited motor has a leading power factor.
8. Capacitor takes leading current.
9. The induction motor operate at high power factor
10. The current drawn by a circuit is minimum when power factor is unity.

ANSWERS

1. True	2. True	3. False	4. True	5. False	6. True	7. False	8. True
9. False	10. True						

3. Fill in the Blanks Type Questions

1. The __________ of the angle between voltage and current is called power factor.
2. The power factor is also difined as true power divided by __________ power.
3. The induction motors operate at __________ power factor.
4. The capacitor takes __________ current.
5. An over excited synchronous motor working at __________ load is called synchronous condenser.
6. The value of power factor cannot be __________ than one.
7. An inductive circuit has a __________ power factor.
8. The causes of low power factor is due to __________ motors.

ANSWERS

1. cosine	2. apparent	3. low	4. leading
5. no	6. more	7. lagging	8. induction

SHORT ANSWER TYPE QUESTIONS

Q.1 Define power factor.

Ans. Power factor can be defined as the rates of resistance to impedance $\cos \phi = \frac{R}{Z}$.

It has no unit.

Q.2 Name the quipment used in transmission and distribution to lower the power factor.

Ans. (i) Transformer (ii) Induction motor

Q.3 Name the equipment used for power factor improvement

Ans. (i) static capacitor (ii) synchronous condenser.

Q.4 State the disadvantages of low power factor.

Ans. (i) Large copper losses (ii) Greater conductor size (iii) Large kVA rating of the equipment.

Q.5 What is the most appropriate location for the installation of power factor improvement apparatus.

Ans. The power factor improvement plant is installed where the apparatus responsible for low power factor.

Q.6 What are the advantages of improving low power factor?

Ans. (1) Small conductor size

(2) Smaller copper losses and improved efficiency

(3) Less voltage drop and better regulation

(4) For same kW output smaller kVA rating of various equipment of the power system.

LONG ANSWER TYPE QUESTIONS

Q.1 What is the necessity of improving power factor?

Ans. We know that power consumed in an a.c. circuit

$$P = VI \cos\phi \quad \text{(for 1-phase circuit)}$$

$$\therefore \quad I = \frac{P}{V\cos\phi}$$

and $$P = \sqrt{3}\, V_L I_L \cos\phi \quad \text{(for 3-phase circuit)}$$

$$\therefore \quad I_L = \frac{P}{\sqrt{3} V_L \cos\phi} \quad \text{(when other factors are constant)}$$

or $$I_\alpha \frac{P}{\cos\phi}$$

It is clear from the above equation that for fixed power and voltage, load current is inversely proportional to the power factor. Lower the power factor, higher is the load current and vice-versa. The higher load current at low power factor results in the following disadvantages :

(i) **Greater conductor size:** To transmit or distribute a fixed amount of power at fixed voltage, the conductors will have to carry more current at low power factor. This necessitates a large conductor size.

(ii) **Large copper losses:** Since at low power factor, the conductors have to carry more current, therefore, I^2R losses are increased. This also results in the poor efficiency of the power system.

(iii) **Poor voltage regulation:** Low lagging power factor results in the large voltage drops in alternators, transformers, transmission and distribution lines. This leads to poor voltage regulation. Therefore, power factor improvement equipment is required to keep the voltage drop within permissible limits.

(iv) **Large kVA ruting of equipment:** The electrical machinery e.g., alternators, transformers, switch gears etc., are always rated in kVA.

We know $$\text{kVA} = \frac{\text{kW}}{\cos\phi}$$

Thus, kVA rating of the equipment is inversely proportional to the power factor. For a given amount of power, kVA rating will be more for low power factor and vice-versa. Therefore, at low power factors, the equipment of higher kVA rating have to be installed which increases the capital cost.

Q.2 What are the causes of low power factor?

Ans. Causes of Low Power Factor

Low power factor is undesirable from economic point of view. The following are the causes of low power factor :

(i) A transformer is an inductive device and draws a magnetizing current which causes the total current to lag behind the voltage *i.e.*, it operates at lagging power factor. At normal loads, magnetizing current does not effect power factor much, but at light loads magnetizing current decreases the power factor effectively.

(ii) Most of the a.c. motors are of induction type (1-phase and 3-phase induction motors used for industrial purposes), which have low power factor. Though, power factor of an induction motor is reasaonably high (0.85 lagging) at full load, it decreases to a low value (0.3 to 0.5 lagging) at small loads.

(iii) Arc lamps and industrial heating furnaces (induction and are furnaces) operate at low lagging power factors.

PROBLEMS

Q.1 A single phase motor takes a current of 10 A at power factor of 0.707 lagging from 230V, 50 Hz supply. What value must a capacitor have to raise power factor to unity? **(Ans.** 97.85 μF)

Q.2 Find the rating of capacitor bank required to improve the power factor of an induction motor from 0.65 to 0.85 lagging. The motor takes 4 kW. **(Ans.** 2.197 kVAR)

Q.3 Find the rating of capacitor bank required to improve the p.f. of 20 HP induction motor from 0.7 to 0.85 lagging consider motor efficiency 85% and supply is 3-ϕ, 400V, 50 Hz. **(Ans.** 3.464 kVAR)

Solution of Problems

Solution 1.

Current draw by motor, $I_m = 10\ A$

Power factor of motor, $\cos\phi_1 = 0.707$ lagging

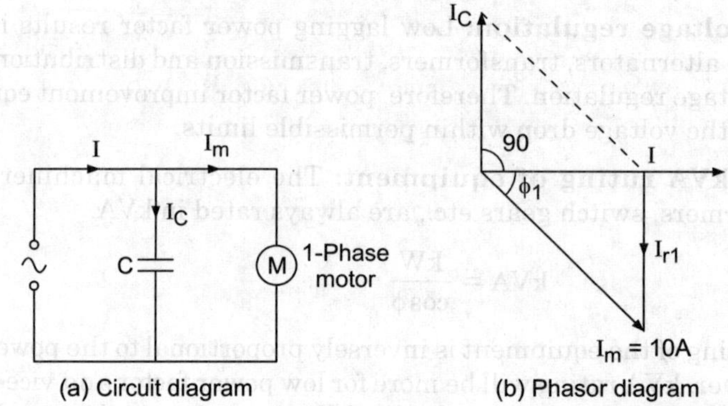

(a) Circuit diagram (b) Phasor diagram

Fig. 6.11

Let a capacitor of capacitance C farads be connected across the motor to improve power factor unity.

At power factor, $\cos\phi_1 = 0.707$

$\sin\phi_1 = \sin\cos^{-1} 0.707$

Reactive component of current, $I_{r_1} = I_m \sin\phi_1 = 10 \times 0.707 = 7.07$ A

When power factories improved to $\cos\phi_2 = 1$

Reactive component of current, $I_{r2} = 0$

Current drawn by the capacitor, $I_c = Ir_1 - Ir_2 = 7.07 - 0 = 7.07$A

Now $$I_C = \frac{V}{X_c} = \frac{V}{1/2\pi f_c} = 2\pi fCV$$

$\therefore$ $$\text{Capacitance, } C = \frac{I_c}{2\pi fV} = \frac{7.07}{2\pi \times 50 \times 230} = \textbf{97.85 Ans.}$$

Solution 2. Active power of the motor, $P = 4\text{kW}$

Power factor of the motor, $\cos\phi_1 = 0.65$ lagging

now $\cos\phi_1 = 0.65$,

$\tan\phi_1 = \tan\cos^{-1} 0.65 = 1.169$

Reactive power of the motor, $Pr_1 = P\tan\phi_1 = 4 \times 1.169 = 4.676$ kVAR

Let C be the capacitance to improve power factor from 0.65 to 0.85 lagging.

$\cos\phi_2 = 0.85$; $\tan\phi_2 = \tan\cos^{-1} 0.85 = 0.6197$

Reactive power at improved power factor,

$P_{r_2} = P\tan\phi_2 = 4 \times 0.6197 = 2.479$ kVAR

Reactive power supplied to capacitor rating of, capacitor

$Pr_c = Pr_1 - Pr_2 = 4.676 - 2.479 = 2.197$ kVAR **Ans.**

Solution 3. Motor input = 10 HP

$\cos\phi_1 = 0.7$ lag

$\cos\phi = 0.85$ lag

$$\text{Power input to the motor, } P = \frac{10 \times 735.5}{0.85} = 0.8653 \text{ kW}$$

Now, $\cos\phi_1 = 0.7$

$\tan\phi_1 = \tan\cos^{-1} 0.7 = 1.02$

Reactive power of the motor, $Pr_1 = P\tan\phi_2 = 8.653 \times 1.02 = 8.826$ kVAR

Let Pr_c be the rating of capacitor

Now, $\cos\phi_2 = 0.85$

$\tan\phi_2 = \tan\cos^{-1} 0.85 = 0.6197$

Reactive power at improved p.f $= Pr_2 = P\tan\phi_2 = 8.653 \times 0.6197 = 5.362$ kVAR

Rating of capacitor bank, $Pr_c = Pr_1 - Pr_2 = 8.826 - 5.362 = 3.464$ kVAR **Ans.**

EXERCISE

1. What do you understand by power factor? What are the causes of low power factor?
2. How power factor of a system can be improved by the use of static capacitors?
3. What are the disadvantages of low power factor?
4. Discuss the various methods for power factor improvement.
5. What are the advantages of power factor improvement?
6. What is power factor? How it improved in transmission line?
7. Write short notes on the following:
   (i) Power factor improvement by synchronous condenser
   (ii) Disadvantages of poor power factor.

□□□

Faults

7

INSIDE THIS CHAPTER

- Introduction
- Faults in Underground System
- Location of Cable Faults
- Testing of Faults in Underground Cables
- Maintenance Schedule of Overhead Lines
- Types of Faults in Overhead Systems
- Causes of Cable Faults
- Location of Faults in Overhead Transmission Lines
- Types of Faults
- Causes of Electrical Faults

7.1 INTRODUCTION

In an electric power system a fault current is the abnormal current. A fault in an electric power system can be defined as any abnormal condition of the system that invalues the electrical failure of the equipment such as transformers, generators, busbars etc. The fault occurs also involves in insulation failure and conducting path failures which results shorts circuit and open circuit of conductors.

Under normal operating conditions, the electric equipments in a power system network operating at normal voltage and current ratings. Once the fault takes place in a circuit voltage and current values deviates from their normal values.

The faults in power system causes over current under voltage, unbalance of the phases and high voltage surges. This results in the interruption of the normal operation of the network, failure of equipment, electrical fires etc. Usually the power system networks are protected with switch gear protection equipments such as circuit breaker and relays in order to limit the loss of service due to the electrical failure.

There are various types of faults which may occur, in the system during transmission and distribution of electric power. If the faults occurs efforts should be made to rectify it as early as possible for economy, safety and reliability of power system.

7.2 TYPES OF FAULTS IN OVERHEAD SYSTEMS

The most common faults that occur in the overhead lines is the short circuit fault. The main reason of this fault is insulation failure due to over voltage caused by lightning, and due to broken conductors.

The following are the various faults which can occurs in the 3-phase overhead transmission lines and can be explained with the help of Fig. 7.1.

1. **Single Phase to Ground:** This may occur when one of the conductors of transmission line breaks and falls on the ground. This is shown by arrow *AB* in Fig. 7.1.
2. **Phase to Phase:** If one of the conductors of the 3-phase lines breaks and fall on the other conductor, it forms a phase-to-phase fault. This is shown by arrow *OD* in Fig. 7.1.
3. **Two Phases to Ground:** If two conductors of 3-phase transmission line break and fall on the ground it constitutes 2-phases to ground fault.
4. **Phase to Phase and Third Phase to Ground:** This is combination of faults shown at number 1 and 2, *i.e.*, if one conductor breaks it fall on the second and if third breaks it falls on the ground.

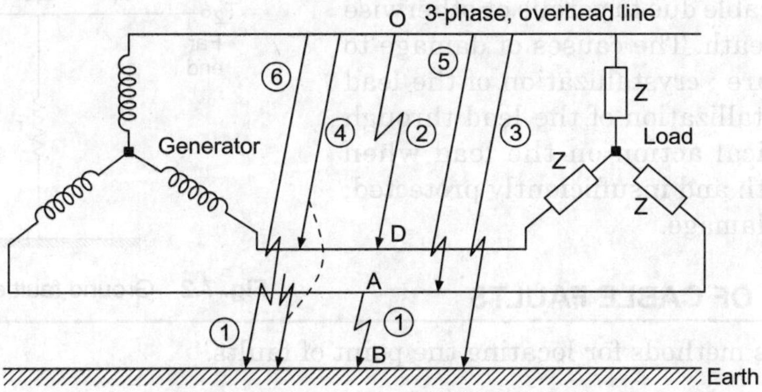

Fig. 7.1 Faults in overhead systems

5. **All the Three Phases Shorted:** This may occur if two conductors of transmission line fall on the third conductor.
6. **All the Three Phase to Ground:** In this type of fault, all the three conductors break and fall on the ground or fall on any other object which is further grounded.

7.3 FAULTS IN UNDERGROUND SYSTEM

The faults which are most likely to occur in the cables are :

1. **Ground or Earth Faults:** When the insulation of the cable get damaged, the current starts flowing from core to earth or to cable sheath. Such faults are known as *ground or earth faults.*
2. **Cross or Short-Circuit Faults:** When the insulation between two cables or between two cores of a multicore cable get damaged, the current starts flowing from one cable to another cable or from one core to another core of a multicore cable directly. Such faults are known as *short-circuit faults.*
3. **Open-Circuit Faults:** When the conductor of a cable is broken, there is no current in the cable. Such faults are known as *open-circuit faults.*

First the nature of fault is determined and then the point of fault is located. For determination of nature of faults, the insulation resistance of each core to ground and between cores is measured with the help of meggar. The low value of insulation resistance between any core and earth indicates the ground fault whereas the low value of insulation resistance between two cores (with far ends of the cable isolated from load) indicates short-circuit fault.

For determination of open-circuit fault, the far end of the cable, in case of single cable, is earthed (or the far ends of the cables are interconnected), an ammeter is inserted in series with the cable and low voltage supply is connected across the cable and earth or cables. Zero deflection in ammeter indicates open-circuit fault.

7.4 CAUSES OF CABLE FAULTS

Most faults are caused by dampness in the paper insulation of the cable due to porous or otherwise damaged lead sheath. The causes of damage to the lead sheath are : crystallization of the lead sheath are : crystallization of the lead through vibration; chemical action on the lead when buried in the earth and insufficiently protected; and mechanical damage.

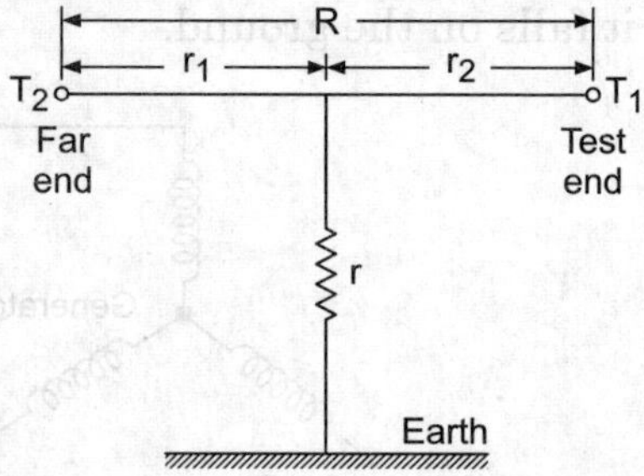

Fig. 7.2 Ground fault of a single cable.

7.5 LOCATION OF CABLE FAULTS

There are various methods for locating the point of faults.

7.5.1 Ground Fault of a Single Core Cable

Blavier's test is used to locate the ground fault of a single cable.

This test is performed with the aid of a low voltage supply and either an ammeter or voltmeter or a bridge network. In this test resistance between one end of the cable T_1 and earth is measured first with the far end T_2 isolated from earth and then with the far end T_2 earthed. Let the two readings R_1 and R_2 respectively.

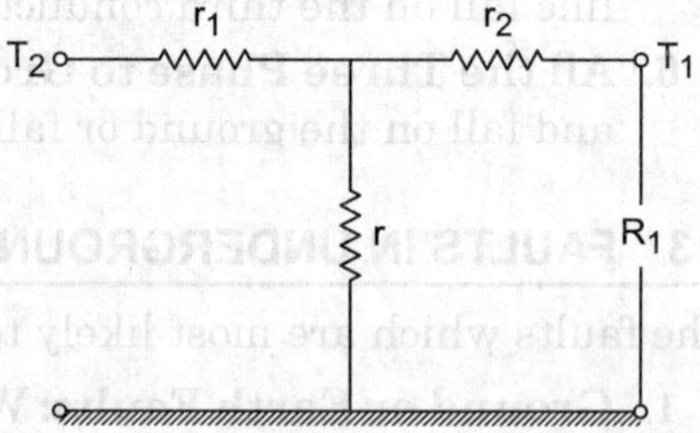

Fig. 7.3 Ground fault of a single cable

If r_1 and r_2 are the conductor resistances of the lengths of cable "far end" to fault and "test end" to the fault respectively and r is the resistance of fault to earth then

$$R_1 = r_1 + r \quad \text{...(i)}$$

and
$$R_2 = \frac{1}{\frac{1}{r} + \frac{1}{r_1}} + r_2 = \frac{rr_1}{r + r_1} + r_2 \quad \text{...(ii)}$$

The total resistance of conductor,

$$R = r_1 + r_2 \quad \text{...(iii)}$$

By solving the above three equations, we can get the value of r, r_1 and r_2.

If the total length of the cable is L metres, the length of cable between far end and fault is L_1 metres, length of cable between test end and fault is L_2 metres and cross-section of conductor is uniform then

$$\frac{L_1}{L_2} = \frac{r_1}{r_2}$$

and
$$\frac{L_1 + L_2}{L_2} = \frac{r_1 + r_2}{r_2}$$

or
$$L_2 = L \times \frac{r_2}{r_1 + r_2}$$

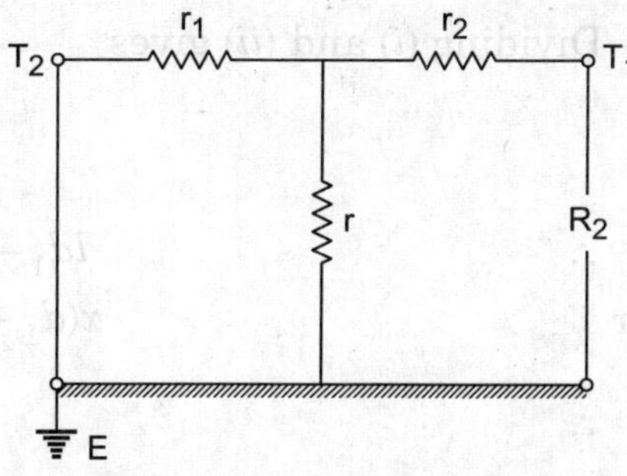

Fig. 7.4

Thus the distance of fault from test end can be determined.

7.5.2 Core to Core Fault

(i) Measure the resistance between cores from end A with the other ends open circuited. Let it be R_A

Z = Fault resistance

$$\therefore \quad R_A = 2rx + z = 2rx + z \qquad ...(i)$$

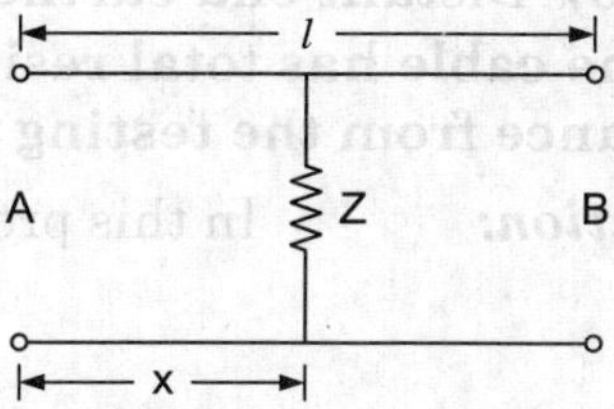

Fig. 7.5 Core to core fault

(ii) Measure the resistance between cores from end B with end A open circuited. Let it be R_B.

$$\therefore \quad R_B = Z(l - x)r + Z \qquad ...(ii)$$

Subtracting (*ii*) from (*i*) gives

$$R_A - R_B = 2rx + Z - 2(l - x)r - Z = 2rx - 2rl + 2rx = 4rx - 2rl$$

$$\therefore \quad 4rx = (R_A - R_B) + 2rl$$

$$\therefore \quad x = \frac{R_A - R_B}{4r} + \frac{1}{2}$$

7.5.3 Open Circuit Fault

B.G. = Ballistic Galvanometer

C = Capacitance per unit length

(i) The cable is charged upto a potential V by putting switch in position 1 at end A. Then the switch is put in position 2 and is discharged through BG. The kick of B.G. is given by $Q = CV$

$$d_1 = KC_x V \qquad ...(i)$$

where K = constant of galvanometer

(ii) Similar procedure is repeated for end B. Let the kick of B.G. in this case be d_2.

$$\therefore \quad d_2 = KC(l - x)V \qquad ...(ii)$$

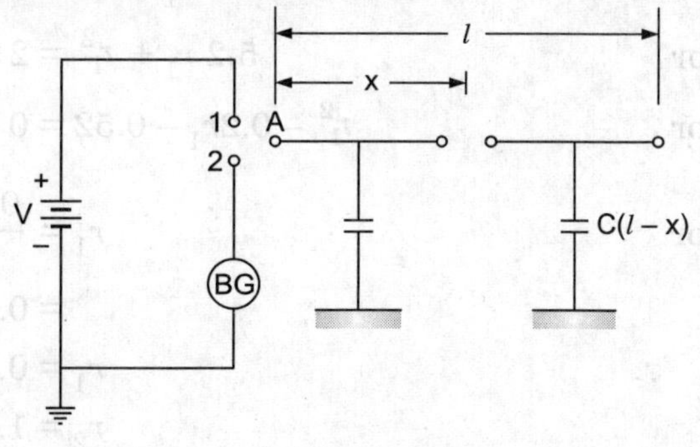

Fig. 7.6 Open circuit fault

Dividing (*i*) and (*ii*) gives

$$\frac{d_1}{d_2} = \frac{KC_xV}{KC(l-x)V} = \frac{x}{l-x}$$

$\therefore$ $$ld_1 - xd_1 = xd_2$$

or $$x(d_1 - d_2) = ld_1$$

$\therefore$ $$x = \frac{d_1}{d_1 + d_2} \cdot l$$

EXAMPLE 7.1 A feeder cable 500 metres long has a fault to earth. The fault is localized by the following resistance measurements between earth and one of the cable.

(*a*) Distant end insulated, 7.0 Ω

(*b*) Distant end earthed 1.7 Ω

The cable has total resistance of 1.8 Ω. Find the resistance of the fault and its distance from the testing end.

Solution: In this problem $R_1 = 7.0\ \Omega$

$$R_2 = 1.7\ \Omega$$
$$R = 1.8\ \Omega$$

If r_1 and r_2 are the conductor resistances of the length of cable far end to fault and test end to fault respectively and r is the resistance of fault to earth then

$$r_1 + r_2 = R = 1.8\ \Omega \qquad \text{...}(i)$$

$$r + r_2 = R_1 = 7.0\ \Omega \qquad \text{...}(ii)$$

$$\frac{rr_1}{r + r_1} + r_2 = R_2 = 1.7\ \Omega \qquad \text{...}(iii)$$

Substituting $r_2 = 1.8 - r_1$ from equation (*i*) and $r = 7.0 - r_2 = 7.0 - (1.8 - r_1) = 5.2 + r_1$ from equations (*i*) and (*ii*) in equation (*iii*), we have

$$\frac{(5.2 + r_1)r_1}{5.2 + r_1 + r_1} + 1.8 - r_1 = 1.7$$

or $$5.2\,r_1 + r_1^2 = (r_1 - 0.1)\,(2r_1 + 5.2)$$

or $$5.2\,r_1 + r_1^2 = 2r_1^2 + 5r_1 - 0.52$$

or $$r_1^2 - 0.2r_1 - 0.52 = 0$$

or $$r_1 = \frac{0.2 \pm \sqrt{(0.2)^2 - 4 \times (-0.52)}}{2} = \frac{0.2 \pm 1.455}{2}$$

$$= 0.8725\ \Omega \text{ as } -0.6275\ \Omega \text{ is impracticable figure}$$

$\therefore$ $$r_1 = 0.8275\ \Omega$$

$$r_2 = 1.8 - r_1 = 1.8 - 0.8275 = 0.9725\ \Omega$$

$$r = 5.2 - r_1 = 5.2 + 0.8275 = 6.0275\ \Omega$$

$\therefore$ Resistance of fault, $r = 6.0275\ \Omega$ **Ans.**

$$\text{Resistance per meter length} = \frac{1.8}{500} = 0.0036\ \Omega$$

$$\therefore \quad \text{Distance from testing end} = \frac{r_2}{\text{Resistance per meter length}}$$

$$= \frac{0.9725}{0.0036} = 270.14 \text{ metres} \quad \textbf{Ans.}$$

7.6 LOCATION OF FAULTS IN OVERHEAD TRANSMISSION LINES

Overhead line, are generally subjected to various troubles, lightning, snow and ice being perhaps the most prevalent. Lightning will induce a high voltage in a line, irrespective of the working voltage of the circuit. It causes less trouble on extremely high tension lines than on those work at lower pressures. This is because of the heavier insulation of the former.

For location of faults, overhead lines are patrolled regularly by skilled linemen, whose job is to notice even the smallest visible defect. This work is added by binoculars. In addition, the lineman keeps an eye for anything which might lead to trouble, such as growth of trees, building work going on in the neighbouring place of the line, the erection of radio and television aerials.

The comparatively few interruptions of current show the general reliability of equipment and do credit to those whose duty is to maintain supply.

7.7 TESTING OF FAULTS IN UNDERGROUND CABLES

The tests for locating faults in underground cables are given below:

1. Murray loop test
2. Varlay loop test
3. Fall of potential test

7.7.1 Murray Loop Test

This test is performed for the location of either an *earth fault or short circuit faults* in *underground cables* provided that a sound cable runs along with the faulty cable or cables. This test employs the principle of Wheatstone bridge.

The conection diagram to locate earth fault by Murray Loop Test method is shown in Fig. 7.7.

For earth fault in Fig. 7.7, G is a galvanometer, B is battery, K_B is battery key and K_G is galvanometer key.

The faulty cable is connected to a sound cable through low resistance link at the far end. Bridge is balanced by adjusting the resistance of ratio arms P and Q until the galvanometer indicates zero. In balanced condition of bridges.

$$\frac{P}{Q} = \frac{R}{X}$$

where X = Resistance of faulty cable from test end to fault point F

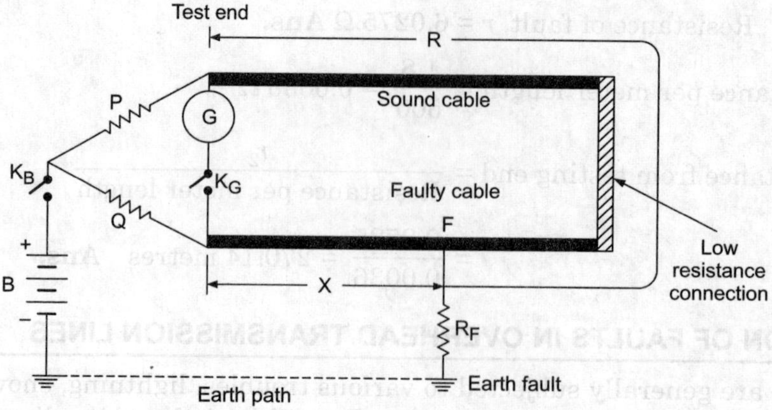

Fig. 7.7 Murray loop test (Earth fault)

or $$\frac{P}{Q}+1=\frac{R}{X}+1$$

or $$\frac{P+Q}{Q}=\frac{R+X}{X}=\frac{2r}{X}$$

(where r is resistance of one of the cables when free from fault).

or $$X=\frac{Q}{P+Q}\times 2r$$

Since resistance per metre length of cable $= \frac{r}{l}$, where l is the length of cable in metres.

$\therefore$ Distance of fault from testing end $= \dfrac{X}{(r/l)} = \dfrac{X\cdot l}{r} = \dfrac{Q}{P+Q}\times 2r.\dfrac{l}{r}$

$$= \frac{2Q}{P+Q}\cdot l \text{ metres}$$

The connections for short-circuit are practically the same as in earth fault test except that a portion of one of the short circuiting cables is used instead of earth as return path in the battery circuit. Balance is obtained as before.

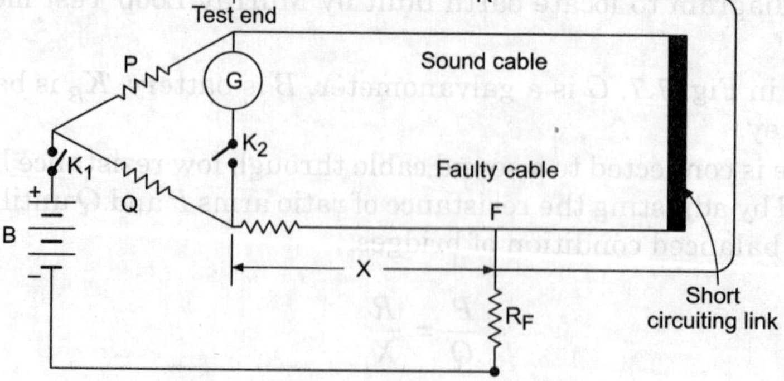

Fig. 7.8 Murray loop test (short circuit)

In balanced condition of bridges.

$$\frac{P}{Q} = \frac{R}{X}$$

$$\therefore \quad \frac{P+Q}{Q} = \frac{R+X}{X}$$

or
$$X = \frac{Q}{P+Q} = (2r)$$

where 'R' is the resistance of each cable, when free from fault.

Since resistance per meter length of the cable $= \frac{r}{l}$ where l is the length of each cable.

$\therefore$ Distance of fault point F' from the testing end

i.e.,
$$\frac{X}{r/l} = \frac{lX}{r} = \frac{Q}{P+Q} \times 2r\,\frac{Xl}{r} = \frac{2Q}{P+Q} \cdot l \text{ meters}$$

or
$$\frac{P}{Q} + 1 = \frac{R}{X} + 1$$

$$\therefore \quad X = \left[\frac{Q}{P+Q}\right](R+X)$$

where $(R + X)$ is the total resistance of the loop and is assumed to be known.

Since P, Q and the total resistance of the loop is known so X and hence the distance of fault from lower end of Q can be determined.

7.7.2 Varlay Loop Test for Short-circuit and Ground Faults

The circuit diagrams for this test, which is used for locating either ground or short-circuit faults, are shown in Fig. 7.9(*a*) and (*b*). These circuits are, again, essentially Wheatstone Bridge networks in which the ratio arms P and Q are fixed resistances. Balance is obtained by adjusting the variable resistance S, which is connected to the end of the faulty core of the cable. The throw-over switch is connected such that the battery gets connected to contact c.

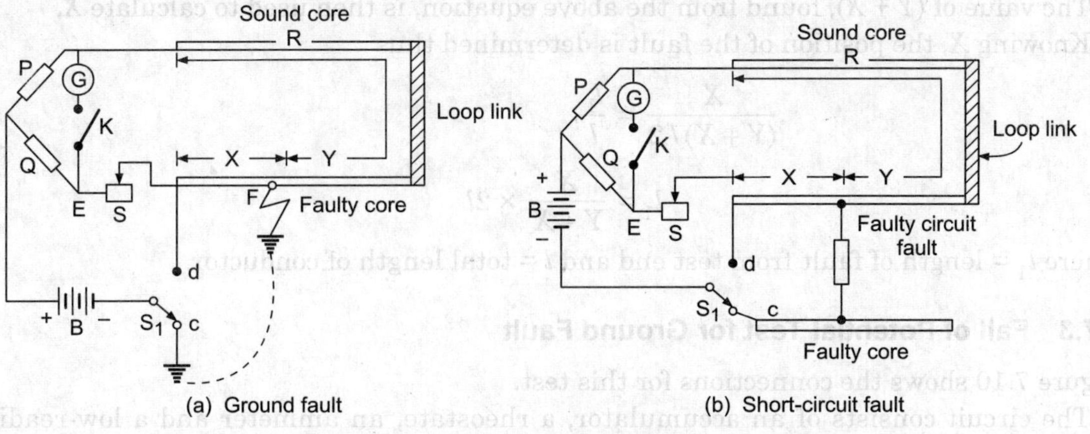

Fig. 7.9 Varley loop test (a) for ground fault, (b) for short-circuit fault.

At balance, in either the ground or short-circuit test, and with the throw-over switch connected to contact *c*, we have from Fig. 7.9(*a*) and (*b*).

$$\frac{P}{Q} = \frac{Y}{X+S}$$

or $$\frac{P}{Q} + 1 = \frac{Y}{X+S} + 1$$

or $$\frac{P+Q}{Q} = \frac{Y+X+S}{X+S}$$

or $$X + S = \frac{Q(Y+X+S)}{P+Q}$$

or $$X = \frac{Q(Y+X+S) - S(P+Q)}{P+Q}$$

or $$X = \frac{Q(Y+X) - S \times P}{P+Q} \qquad ...(i)$$

In equation (*i*) the values of S, P and Q are known. The value of X can be calculated from this equation provided the value of $(Y + X)$, *i.e.*, the total loop length is also known. In the Murray loop test, the value of $(Y + X)$ in equation (*i*) was taken from the known length of the cable. In the Varlay loop test, the value of $(Y + X)$ is found by electrical measurement. This is done by connecting the throw-over switch to the contact *d* and then again adjusting the value of S for balance.

At balance, with the throw-over switch connected to contact *d*, we have from Fig. 7.9(*a*) and (*b*)

or $$\frac{P}{Q} = \frac{Y+X}{S_1}$$

where S_1 is the new value of S for balance.

Thus $$(Y+X) = \frac{P}{Q} \times S_1$$

The value of $(Y + X)$, found from the above equation, is then used to calculate X. Knowing X, the position of the fault is determined thus

$$\frac{X}{(Y+X)/2} = \frac{l_1}{l}$$

or $$l_1 = \frac{X}{Y+X} \times 2l$$

where l_1 = length of fault from test end and l = total length of conductor.

7.7.3 Fall of Potential Test for Ground Fault

Figure 7.10 shows the connections for this test.

The circuit consists of an accumulator, a rheostate, an ammeter and a low-reading moving-coil voltmeter. A large steady current, depending upon the rating of the cable, is passed through the loop, formed by the sound and faulty cables jointed together at the distant end by a low resistance link *BC*.

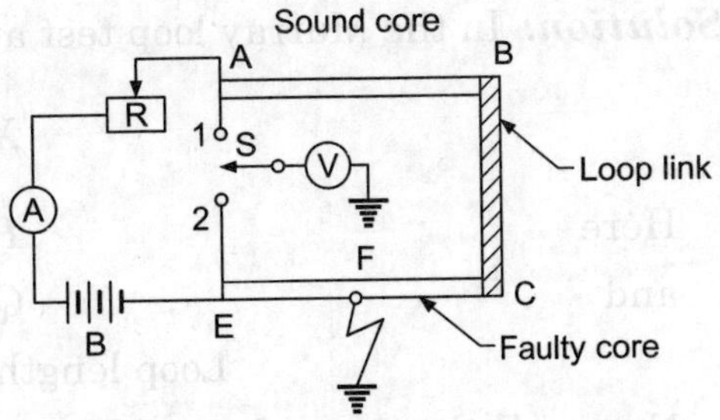

Fig. 7.10 Fall of potential test for ground fault

The current is regulated by means of the variable resistor *R*. When the throw-over switch is in position 1, the voltmeter reads the voltage drop in *ABCF*. Let this voltage drop be V_1. When *S* is thrown to position 2, the voltmeter will read the voltage drop in *EF*. Let this voltage drop be V_2.

Now $\quad V_1 = I \times \text{resistance of } ABCF$

and $\quad V_2 = I \times \text{resistance of } EF$

where *I* is the current flowing through the loop including the portions *ABCF* and *EF*.

or $$\frac{V_1}{V_2} = \frac{\text{Resistance of } ABCF}{\text{Resistance of } EF}$$

or $$\frac{V_1}{V_2} + 1 = \frac{\text{Resistance of } ABCF}{\text{Resistance of } EF} + 1$$

or $$\frac{V_1 + V_2}{V_2} = \frac{\text{Resistance of } ABCF + \text{resistance of } EF}{\text{Resistance of EF}}$$

or $$\frac{V_1 + V_2}{V_2} = \left(\frac{\text{Resistance of the whole loop formed by two conductors } AB \text{ and } CE}{\text{Resistance of } EF}\right)$$

If the cross-section of two conductors is the same, the resistance can be expressed in terms of length. Thus

$$\frac{V_2}{V_1 + V_2} = \frac{\text{Length of } EF}{\text{Length of the whole loop, i.e., } AB + CE}$$

or $$\text{Length of } EF = \frac{V_2}{V_1 + V_2} \times (\text{length of the loop } ABCE)$$

EF is the distance of fault position *F* from the test end. Thus the fault position is located.

Since the resistance of the fault forms part of the voltmeter circuit, it is essential that the resistance of the voltmeter should be large in comparison to the resistance of the fault. Hence the use of an electrostatic voltmeter is very desirable for this test.

The accuracy of this test is not as high as that of the Murray loop test.

Example 7.2 The use of the Murray loop test resulted in the location of an earth fault in a cable. Particulars of the test are as follows :

Length of cable = 400 m

At balance, the resistance connected to the fault core was set at 12 Ω and the resistance of the resistor connected to the sound core was 33 Ω. Determine the distance of the fault from the test end.

Solution: In the Murray loop test at balance, following condition is applicable.

$$X = \frac{P}{P+Q} \times \text{loop length}$$

Here $P = 12\ \Omega$

and $Q = 33\ \Omega$

Loop length = 400 m

Now, substituting values of P, Q and loop length in the equation applicable at balance, we get

$$X \text{ (distance of fault from test end)} = \frac{12}{(12+33)} \times 400 = \mathbf{106.6\ m\ Ans.}$$

Example 7.3 The Murray loop test is used to locate an earth fault on one core of a two-core cable. The other core is used to complete the loop. When the network is balanced, the resistance connected to the faulty core has a value of 3.2 Ω. The other resistance arm has a value of 11.8 Ω. It is estimated that the fault is 42.7 m from the test end. Find the length of cable.

Solution: In the Murray loop test for ground fault, at balance

$$X = \frac{P}{P+Q} \times \text{loop length}$$

$$\text{Loop length} = \frac{X(P+Q)}{P} = 42.7 \times \frac{(11.8+3.2)}{3.2} = \frac{15}{3.2} \times 42.6$$

$$= 200.15 \text{ m}$$

$$\text{Length of cable} = 100.075 \text{ m} \approx 100 \text{ m}$$

Example 7.4 A Varley loop test is used to locate an earth fault on a telephone line of route length 10 km. The resistance per km of single line is 280 Ω. The loop is completed with a line similar to that of the faulty one. At balance, the variable resistor connected to the faulty core is set at 86 Ω and the fixed resistors have equal values. Calculate the distance of the fault from the test end.

Solution: In case of ground fault $X = \dfrac{Q(Y+X) - S \times P}{P+Q}$

It is given that $P = Q$, $S = 86\ \Omega$ and $(Y + X) = 280 \times 2 = 560\ \Omega$. Now substituting values in the above equation, we get

$$X = \frac{Q(Y+X) - SQ}{2Q} = \frac{Y+X-S}{2}$$

or $2X = Y + X - S$

or $2X = 560 - 86 = 474\ \Omega$

$\therefore$ $X = 237\ \Omega$

The distance of fault from test end is thus $X = \dfrac{237}{280} = 0.846$ km.

7.8 TYPES OF FAULTS

Electrical fault is the deviation of voltages and currents from nominal values under normal operating conditions, power system equipment or lines carry normal voltages and currents which results in a safer operation of the system.

But when fault occurs, it cause excessively high currents to flow which causes damage to equipments and devices. Fault detection is necessary to select suitable switch gear equipments, circuit breakers etc.

There are mainly two types of faults in the electrical power system. Those are symmetrical and unsysmmetrical faults.

7.8.1 Symmetrical Faults

These are very severe faults and occur infrequently in the power systems. These are also called as balanced faults and are of two types namely, line to line to line to ground ($L - L - L - G$) and line to line to line ($L - L - L$) only 2 to 5 percent of system faults are symmetrical faults. If these faults occur, system remains balanced but results in severe damage to the electrical power system equipments. Above figure shows two types of three phase symmetrical faults. Three phase fault information is required for selecting set-phase relays, repturing capacity of the circuit breakers and rating of the protective switch gear.

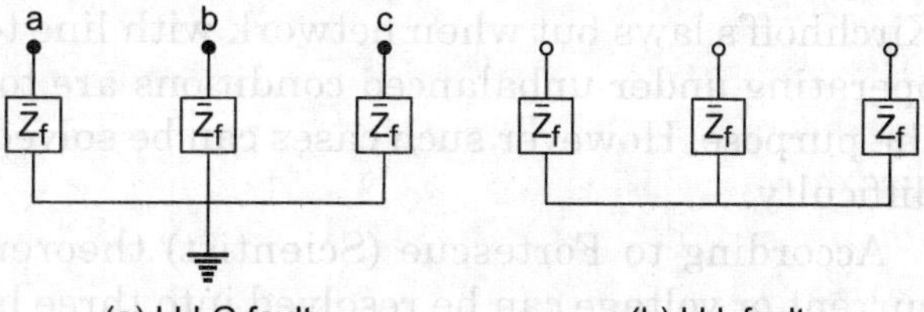

Fig. 7.11 Symmetrical faults

In brief fault is known as symmetrical fault, when equal fault current with equal displacement flows through all the three phases. The rating of the circuit breaker installed on line depending upon the symmetrical fault e.g., all three phase short circuited with ground.

7.8.2 Unsymmetrical Faults

These are very common and less severe than symmetrical faults. There are mainly three types namely, line to ground ($L - G$) line to line ($L - L$) and double line to ground ($LL - G$) faults. Line to ground fault ($L - G$) is most common fault and 65 – 70 percent of faults are of this type.

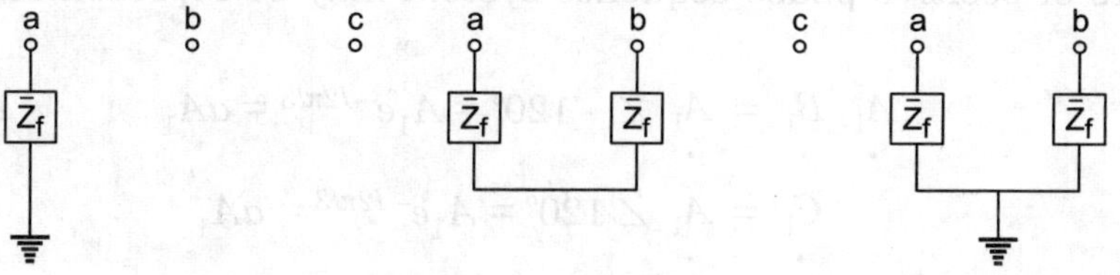

Fig. 7.12 Unsymmetrical faults

It causes the conductor to make contact with earth or ground. 15 to 20 percent of faults are double line to ground and causes the two conductors to make contact with ground.

Line to line faults occur when two conductors make contact with each other mainly while swinging of lines due to winds. These faults are 5 to 10%.

These faults are also called unbalanced fault since their occurance causes unbalance in the system.

Unbalance of the systems means that the impedance values are different in each phase causing unbalance current to flow in the phases.

To summarized when fault occurs on over head line and unequal current flows or having different phase displacement is known as unsymmetrical fault.

For example, single line to ground, line to line, double line to ground faults.

Symmetrical Components, Positive, Negative and Zero Sequence Networks

Simple unbalanced three phase a.c. circuit can be solved conveniently by application of Kirchhoff's laws but when network with line to line and line to earth faults and machines operating under unbalanced conditions are to be dealt with, these methods cannot serve the purpose. However such cases can be solved by the method of symmetrical without any difficulty.

According to Fortescue (Scientist) theorem, any unbalanced three phase system of current or voltage can be resolved into three balanced systems of vectors which are called symmetrical components. The symmetrical components differ in phase sequence, that is, the order in time in which the phase quantities go through a maximum. There are three sequence networks for a given power system namely.

1. Positive sequence networks
2. Negative sequence networks
3. Zero sequence network.

1. Positive Sequence Network

A balance system of three phase vectors having the same phase sequence as the original set of three unbalanced vectors, *i.e.*, $A \rightarrow B \rightarrow C$, is called the positive phase sequence components are marked by suffix 1. The three vectors of the positive phase sequence system are equal in magnitude, displaced from each other by 120° apart. The positive sequence network of a given power system, the main points are:

(*i*) All the resistance and magnetizing currents for each transformer are neglected for simplicity.

(*ii*) Shunt capacitances and resistances are generally neglected transmission lines.

The three vectors of positive phase sequence system may be represented in complex from as follows :

$$\underset{\bullet}{A_1}, \underset{\bullet}{B_1} = \underset{\bullet}{A_1} \angle -120^\circ = A_1 e^{-J2\pi/3} = aA_1$$

and

$$\underset{\bullet}{C_1} = \underset{\bullet}{A_1} \angle 120^\circ = A_1 e^{-J2\pi/3} = aA_1$$

The complex number $e^{-J2\pi/3}$ in above expression is called the operators of the three phase system and is denoted by letter 'a'. Multiplication of a vector by $e^{J2\pi/3}$ turn it through 120° counterclockwise. Multiplying a vector by a^2 turn it through 240° in counterclockwise direction and position of a vector remains unchanged if multiplied by a^3.

2. Negative Sequence Network

A balanced system of three phase vectors having phase sequence opposite to that of the original unbalanced vectors, *i.e.*,

$A \to C \to B$, is called negative phase sequence system. The negative phase sequence components are mark by suffix 2.

Figure 7.13 shows a vector diagram for all the three phase sequences of the symmetrical components.

Figure 7.13 symmetrical components of an unbalanced three phase system negative phase sequence, a like positive phase sequence are of equal magnitude and displaced by 120°. These are represented in complex form as follows :

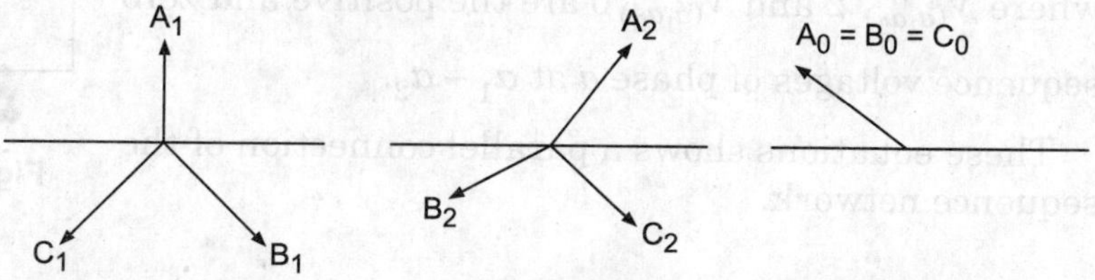

Fig. 7.13

$$A_2 \,;\; B_2 = A_2 \angle 120^\circ = A_2 e^{-J2\pi/3} = aA_2$$

and

$$C_2 = A_2 \angle -120^\circ = A_2 e^{-J2\pi/3} = a^2 A_2$$

For static devices such as transmission lines and transformers, the negative phase sequence impedances have the same value as the corresponding positive phase sequence impedances.

3. Zero Sequence Network

A system of three vectors equal in magnitude and with zero phase displacement from each other is called the zero or uniphase sequence system. The zero phase sequence components are marked by suffix 0. The three vectors of zero sequence system are expressed as

$$A_0 = B_0 = C_0$$

Open Conductor Fault

The open conductor fault is taken to a fault in series with the line. There are two types of open conductor or faults.

1. One conductor open
2. Two conductor open

1. One Conductor Open

Let us assure that conductor a is open as $a_1 - a_2$ point as shown in Fig. 7.14.

The currents and voltages are thus given by

$$I_a = 0$$

$$V_{b_1 b_2} = V_{c_1 c_2} = 0$$

i.e.,

$$I_{a_1} + I_{a_2} + I_{a_0} = 0$$

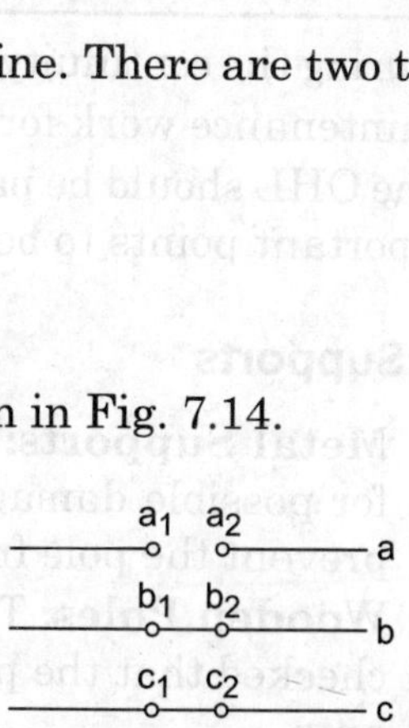

Fig. 7.14 One conductor open faults

i.e.,
$$V_{(a_1a_2)1} = V_{(a_1a_2)2}$$
$$= V_{(a_1a_2)0}$$
$$= \frac{1}{3} V_{a_1a_2}$$

where $V_{(a_1a_2)}$ 2 and $V_{(a_1a_2)}$ 0 are the positive and zero sequence voltages of phase a at $a_1 - a_2$.

These equations shows a parallel connection of the sequence network.

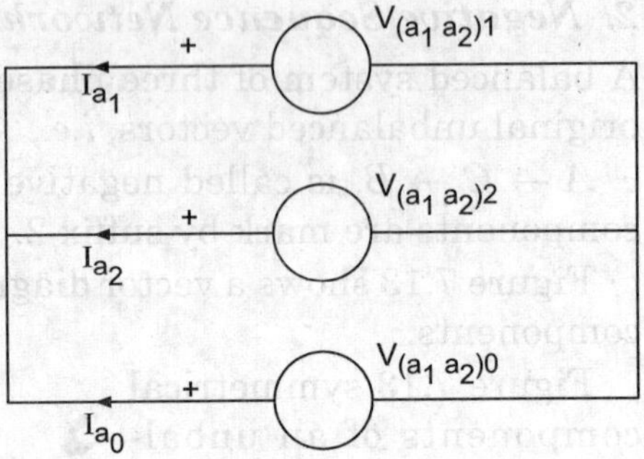

Fig. 7.15 Sequence network of one conductor open fault

2. *Two Conductor Open Fault*

Figure 7.16 shows the two conductor open fault.

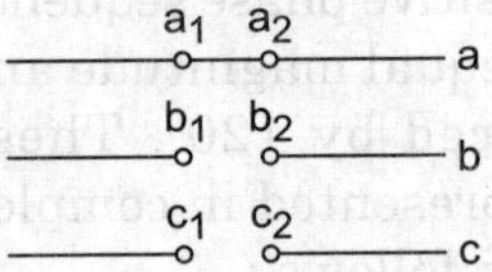

Fig. 7.16 Two conductors open fault.

The current and voltage of this circuit is given by

$$V_{a_1a_2} = 0$$
$$I_B = I_C = 0$$

In terms of symmetrical components,

$$V_{(a_1a_2)}1 + V_{(a_1a_2)}2 + V_{(a_1a_2)}0 = 0$$

and
$$I_{a_1} = I_{a_2}$$
$$= I_{a_0} = \frac{1}{3} I_a$$

These equations show a series connection of sequence networks as shown in Fig. 7.17.

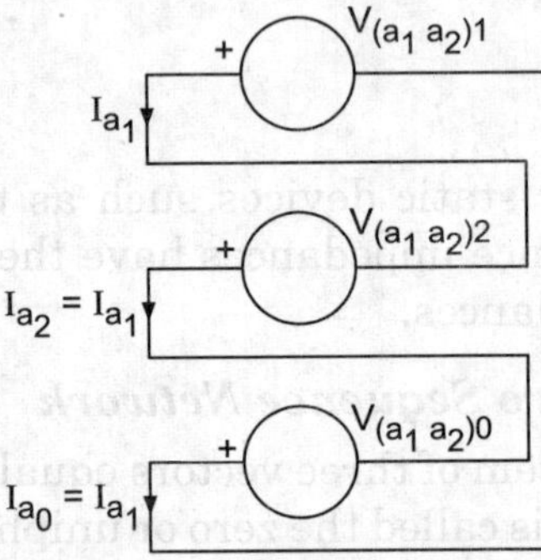

Fig. 7.17 Sequence connection of two conductors open fault

7.9 MAINTENANCE SCHEDULE OF OVERHEAD LINES

For ensuring the continuity of power supply through OHL regular maintenance is necessary.

A maintenance work for the OHL consists of the following.

All the OHL should be patrolled regularly each month at ground level while the line live. The important points to be noted are:

7.9.1 Supports

(a) **Metal Supports:** The condition of the concrete foundation should be examined for possible damage. If any soil erosion takes place at foundation, set it right to prevent the pole from tilting and falling.

(b) **Wooden Poles:** The poles should be checked for correct plumb. It should also be checked that the pole below the ground should be healthy and not eaten by white ants.

(c) **RCC Poles:** It should be checked for cracks.

7.9.2 Cross-arms

It should be checked whether the X-arm (metallic) are rusted. A wooden *X*-arm may be tilted or decay owing to rot.

7.9.3 Insulators and Fittings

It should be checked for following defects :

1. Broken porcelain
2. Tilted Insulator.
3. Accumulation of dust, etc., on the insulators.
4. Rusting of fitting
5. Burnt and fused spots on the glaze of insulator.

Damaged Insulators should be replaced, tilted insulators should be set right and dirty insulators cleaned after disconnecting the line from the supply.

7.9.4 Conductors and Earth Wires

Clearance of phase wires and earth wire to ground, clearance between phase wires and that between the various phase wires and the earth wire as per Electricity rules. In case the clearances are not correct the sag should be adjusted after disconnecting the line from the supply. Any foreign objects found on conductors and earth wire should be removed.

7.9.5 Conductor Fittings and Joints

The line should be checked for the following defects :

(i) The loosening of the binding of insulators and at joints.
(ii) The slipping of the conductor from the insulator seat.
(iii) Broken strands should be repaired.
(iv) Burnt jumpers and loose fitting of parallel groove clamps should be tightened.

The remedial measures for the above are:

Slipped conductors should be placed on the insulator seat and bound again but after disconnecting of line from supply. Broken strands should be repaired by providing aluminium conductor repair sleeves. Burnt jumpers should be replaced and the loose fitting of clamps should be tightened.

7.9.6 Guys and their Accessories

Guys should be checked for the following defects :

(i) Loose guys
(ii) Broken or chipped guy insulators
(iii) The earthing arrangement of guys broken or missing
(iv) The corrosion of guy rods
(v) The condition of the guy anchoring.

Any anchoring should be filled with earth. Loose guys should be tightened and the earthing arrangement restored and broken guy insulators should be replaced.

7.9.7 Gang-operated Switch and Fuse Unit on 11 kV Line

The following defects may be observed :

(i) A defective switch
(ii) A missing or broken earth wire
(iii) Cracked or chipped insulators
(iv) Burning or overheating of contacts
(v) Damaged arcing contacts.

Adjustments should be made for contact alignment and adequate contact pressure. Damaged contacts should be repaired and replaced. Earth connection if broken should be restored. Bearings should be lubricated for correct and smooth operation of the moving parts.

7.9.8 Lightning Arresters

The line lead of the lightning arrester should be firmly connected with the phase wires. The earth connection should be tight and the earth resistance of earth wire should be less than 10 Ω.

7.9.9 Tree Clearance

Trees or branches coming close to the lines should be felled or trimmed. A minimum clearance of 1.8 m should be maintained on each side of the line.

7.9.10 Special Inspection

Interruptions and breakdowns on overhead lines are generally more frequent during the rainy season owing to the rains and thunderstorms. Therefore, it is worthwhile to conduct a special inspection of lines just before the monsoon period. Any defects should be removed and a general improvement be carried out.

An inspection of this nature should also be carried out after heavy rains and thunderstorms to detect any damage or breakage which may lead to major breakdown or accidents.

Periodic say bimonthly night inspections for overheating of conductor joints, loose jumpers and sparking on GO switches should be carried out.

7.9.11 Emergency Inspection

Whenever an overhead line trips on a sustained fault, an immediate inspection should be made to find out the nature of the fault. The tripping may be on account of a loose sag, snapping of conductors, tree branches touching the line conductors, falling on cross-arms etc. The necessary repairs should be carried out to avoid the re-occurrence such faults.

7.10 CAUSES OF ELECTRICAL FAULTS

1. **Weather Conditions:** It includes lighting strikes, heavy rains, heavy winds and snow and ice accumulation on transmission lines, etc. These environmental conditions interrupt the power supply and also damage the electrical installations.

2. **Equipment failure:** Various electrical equipments like generators, motors, transformers, reactors, switching devices etc., causes short circuit faults due to malfunction, agency, insulation failure of cables and winding. These failures result in high current to flow through the devices which further damages it.
3. **Human Errors:** Electrical faults also caused due to human errors such as selecting improper rating of equipment and switching the circuit while it is under servicing etc.
4. **Smoke or fire:** Ionization of air, due to smoke particles. Surrounding the overhead lines results in spark between the lines. This flashover causes insulators to lose their insulating capacity due to high voltages.

Effects of Electrical Faults

The following are effect of electrical faults.

1. Over current flow
2. Danger to operating personnel
3. Loss of equipment
4. Electrical fires

Faults Limiting Devices

Some of the fault limiting devices are given below:

1. Fuse
2. Circuit breaker
3. Relay
4. Limiting power protection devices

SUMMARY

1. **Short Circuit Fault:** This short-circuit occur due to faults in power system. This fault usually occur due to insulation failure of the system. Insulation failure can be caused due to system over voltage.
2. **Types of Fault**
   - (i) Single phase to ground
   - (ii) Phase to phase
   - (iii) Double line to ground fault
   - (iv) 3-phase to ground fault
   - (v) Open conductor fault.
3. **Types of Faults in Underground Cables**
   1. Breakdown of cable insulation
   2. Short-circuit fault
   3. Open circuit fault
   1. **Breakdown of the Cable Insulation:** When insulation of cable damaged current flows from core to earth causes earth faults.
   2. **Short-Circuit Fault:** This fault is due to damaged of two cores of multi-core cable, the current flowing from one cable to another cable.
   3. **Open Circuit Fault:** When the conductor of cable broken, no current flow in cable, such faults are open circuit faults.
   4. **Testing of underground cables:** The tests of location faults in underground cable are given below:
      - (a) Murray loop test
      - (b) Varley loop test
      - (c) Fall of potential test

4. **Symmetrical Components of 3-phase System:** In unbalanced system of three vectors I_a, I_b, I_c or V_a, V_b, V_c can be resolved into three balanced systems of vectors, the vectors of the balanced system are called symmetrical components of the original system. The following are the three symmetrical components of 3-phase system.

   1. **Positive sequence components:** $I_{a_1}, I_{b_1}, I_{c_1}$ or $V_{a_1}, V_{b_1}, V_{c_1}$ comprising three balanced system of vectors displaced mutually by 120° and having the same phase sequence as that of the original system.

Objective Type Questions

1. Multiple Choice Type Questions

1. Short-circuit currents are due to
   (a) Single-phase to earth fault (b) Phase-to-phase fault
   (c) All the three phase-to-earth fault (d) any of the above
2. The magnitude of fault current depends upon
   (a) Total impedance up to fault
   (b) Voltage at the fault point
   (c) Load current being supplied before occurrence of fault
   (d) both (a) and (b)
3. The most common type of fault is
   (a) Single phase-to ground (b) Phase-to-phase
   (c) Two-phase-to ground (d) Three phase to ground
4. The most serious major uncleared short-circuit fault could be
   (a) Blowing of fuse (b) Fire
   (c) Heavy voltage drop (d) none of these
5. Which of the following results in a symmetrical fault?
   (a) Single phase-to earth (b) Phase to phase
   (c) All the three phases to earth (d) Two phase to earth
6. In underground system the earth fault in located by
   (a) Blavier's test (b) Murray loop test
   (c) Varlay loop test (d) all (a), (b) and (c)
7. The basic principle applied in murray loop test is :
   (a) Thevenins theorem (b) Kelvin's law
   (c) Wheatstone bridge (d) All of the above
8. Which fault is very rare in overhead system.
   (a) open circuit fault (b) Short circuit fault
   (c) Single phase to earth fault (d) Phase to phase fault

ANSWERS

1. (d) **2.** (d) **3.** (a) **4.** (b) **5.** (c) **6.** (d) **7.** (c) **8.** (a)

2. Fill in the Blanks Type Questions

1. Short-circuit faults are __________ occur
2. Murray loop test are based on the principle of __________
3. In order to locate __________ Fault in single core cable, Blavier's test is used
4. Varley test is used to locate an __________ fault in a cable.
5. The fault location is easy in __________ system.
6. The __________ circuit fault is very rare in overhead system.
7. In order to locate __________ fault in an underground cable Murray test is used.
8. When all the three phases are short circuited the fault is called __________
9. When one of the conductor breaks and fall on the other line conductor, the fault is a __________
10. Blavier's test is used to locate the __________ fault of a single core cable.

ANSWERS

1. mostly	2. Wheatstone bridge	3. ground
4. earth	5. overhead	6. open
7. short circuit	8. symmetrical fault	9. phase to phase
10. ground fault		

3. True-False Type Questions

1. The most common fault occurs in overhead lines is short circuit fault.
2. It is easier to locate fault in underground system.
3. Insulation resistance is measured with the help of an earth tester.
4. When all the three phases are short circuited the fault is called symmetrical fault.
5. Balvier test is used to earth fault in multicore cables.
6. The frequency of faults occurring in overhead system is more than underground system.
7. Open circuit fault is very rare in overhead system.
8. In underground system, the earth fault may be located by Varley loop test.
9. When all the three phases are short circuited then fault is unsymmetrical.
10. The frequency of occurance of three-phase fault is lower than that of line-to-line fault.

ANSWERS

1. True	2. False	3. False	4. True	5. False	6. True	7. False	8. True
9. False	10. True						

SHORT ANSWER TYPE QUESTIONS

Q.1 What are the faults that are likely to occur in cables?

Ans. The faults which are likely to occur in cables are open circuit, short circuit and ground faults.

Q.2 What is meant by ground fault, in cables?

Ans. When the current starts flowing from core to earth because of damage to the cable insulation, the fault is known as ground or earth fault.

Q.3 What is meant by short circuit?

Ans. When two line wire (phase to phase, phase to neutral come in direct contact short circuit occurs.

Q.4 Name the tests used for location and testing of underground cables.

Ans. (i) Murray loop test
(ii) Varley loop test
(iii) Fall of potential test

Q.5 What is meant by open-circuit fault in cables?

Ans. When the conductor of a cable is broken the fault is open circuit fault.

Q.6 What principle do Murray loop and Varlay loop tests employ?

Ans. Murray loop and varley loop tests employ the principle of Wheatstone bridge.

Q.7 List the common types of faults in overhead lines.

Ans. (i) Single phase to ground
(ii) Phase to phase
(iii) Two phase to ground
(iv) All the three phases shorted
(v) All the three phase to ground

Q.8 How will you locate the faults in cables?

Ans. For location of cable faults varley loop test is employed.

Q.9 What is the essential difference between Murray and Varlay loops tests?

Ans. The difference between Murray and Varley loop tests is that in Varley loop test provision is made for the measurement of total loop resistance instead of obtaining it from the relation $R = \rho l/a$.

Q.10 In what way Varlay loop test is advantageous over Murray loop test?

Ans. In Murray loop test sound cable resistance must be known where as in Varlay loop test it is not so.

LONG ANSWER TYPE QUESTIONS

Q.1 Explain the various types of faults in overhead system and underground system.

Ans. The various faults occurs in overhead system are following:

***(i)* Single phase to earth:** When a single conductor of any phase breaks and falls on earth wire it is known as single phase to earth fault.

***(ii)* Phase to phase fault:** When a conductor falls on the other phase conductor, it is known as phase to phase fault.

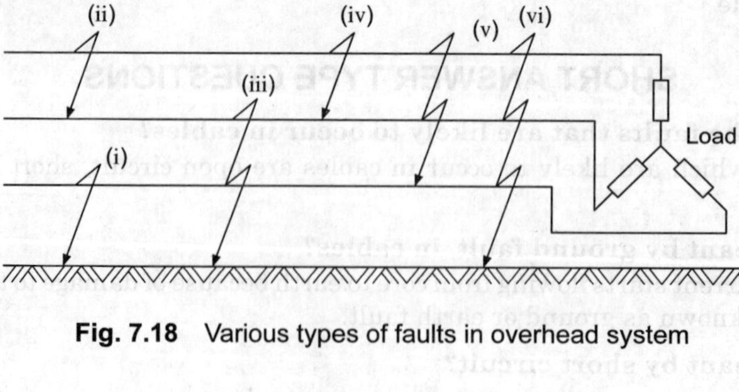

Fig. 7.18 Various types of faults in overhead system

(iii) **Two phase to earth fault:** When two phase conductors fall on earth or ground wire, it is known as two phase to earth fault.

(iv) **Phase to phase and third phase to earth fault:** When one conductor falls on the other phase conductor and third phase falls on earth wire, it is known as phase to phase and third phase to earth fault.

(v) **All the three phases short circuited:** This may occur when two of the line conductors break and fall on the third conductor.

(vi) **All three phases to earth:** This may occur when insulators of all the three line conductors fail simultaneously.

Types of fault in underground system: The various types of faults occur in underground cable are following.

(i) **Ground fault:** Such faults occurs, when due to failure of insulation current starts to flow from core to cable sheath instead of flowing to load.

(ii) **Short circuit fault:** Such fault occurs, when insulation failure occurs between two cores of multi core cable. Thus current starts to flow between two cores instead of flowing to the load.

(iii) **Open circuit fault:** Such fault occurs, when cable conductor breaks and there is no current flow in the cable.

Q.2 Describe Varlay loop test for location of short circuit and ground fault in underground cable.

Ans. The circuit diagram for this test, which is used for locating ground is shows in Fig. 7.19. This circuit is, again, essentially Wheatstone bridge networks in which the ratio arms *P* and *Q* are fixed resistance. Balance is obtained by adjusting the variable resistance *S*, which is connected such that the battery gets connected to contact *C*.

At balance with the throw-over switch connected to contact *C*, we have

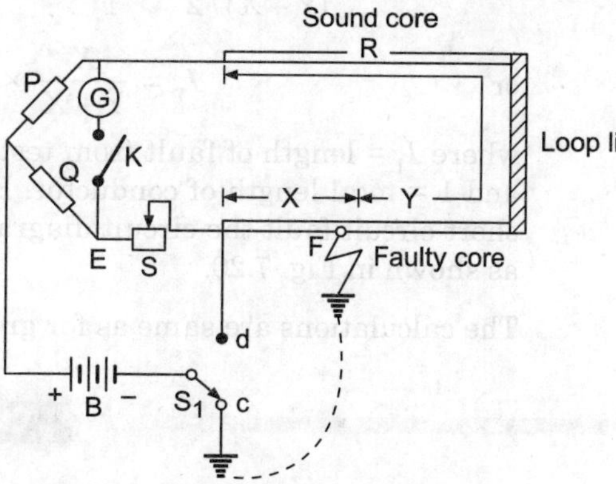

Fig. 7.19 Varlay loop test for ground fault

$$\frac{P}{Q} = \frac{R}{X+S}$$

or $$\frac{P}{Q} + 1 = \frac{Y}{X+S} + 1$$

or $$\frac{P+Q}{Q} = \frac{(Y+X+S)}{X+S}$$

or $$X+S = \frac{Q(Y+X+S)}{P+Q}$$

or $$X = \frac{Q(Y+X+S) - S(P+Q)}{P+Q}$$

or $$X = \frac{Q(Y+X) - S \times P}{P+Q} \quad \ldots(i)$$

In eqn. (*i*) the values of S.P. and Q are known. The value of X can be calculated from this equation provided the value of $(Y + X)$, *i.e.*, the total loop length is also known. The value of $(Y + X)$ is found by connecting the throw over switch to the contact d and then again adjusting the value of S for balance.

At balance, with the throw over switch connected to contact d, we have

$$\frac{P}{Q} = \frac{Y + X}{S_1}$$

where S_1 is the new value of S for balance.

Thus $$(Y + X) = \frac{P}{Q} \times S_1$$

The value of $(Y + X)$, found the above equation, is then used to calculate X. Knowing X, the position of the fault is determined thus

or $$\frac{X}{(Y + X)/2} = \frac{l_1}{1}$$

or $$l_1 = \frac{X}{Y + X} \times 21$$

where l_1 = length of fault from test end and 1 = total length of conductor. For a short circuit fault the circuit diagram is as shown in Fig. 7.20.

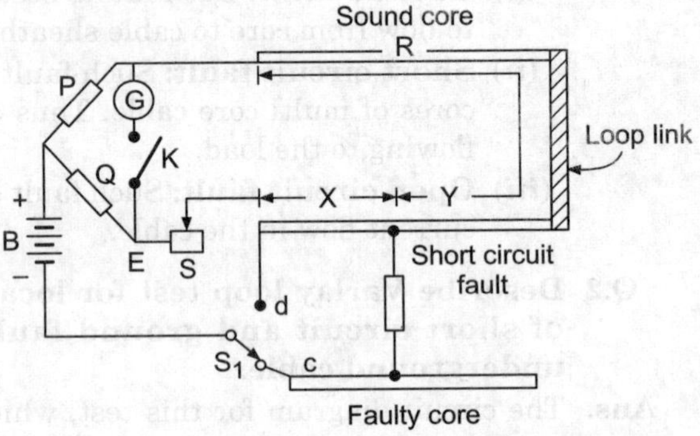

Fig. 7.20 Varley loop test for short circuit fault

The calculations are same as for ground fault.

PROBLEMS

Q.1. In a test by Murray loop for ground fault on 1,000 metres of cable having a resistance of 1.6 Ω per km, the faulty cable is looped with a sound cable of the same length and cross section. If the ratio of the other two arms of testing network at balance are in the ratio of 3:1, calculate the distance of the fault from the testing end of the cable. (**Ans.** 500 metres)

Q.2. In a test for an earth fault on a 500 metre cable having a resistance of 1 Ω per 1,000 metres the faulty cable is looped with a sound cable of the same length but having a resistance of 2.25 Ω per 1,000 metres. The resistance of the other two arms of the testing network, at balance are in the ratio of 2.75:1. Calculate the distance of the fault from the testing end of the cable. (**Ans.** 433.3 metres)

Q.3. In a Murray loop test for earth fault location on a 500 m long cable having a resistance of 1.2 Ω per km, the faulty cable is looped with a sound cable of the same length and area of *X*-section. If the ratio of the other two arms of the testing network are in the ratio 2.5 : 1, find the distance of the fault point from the test end of the cable. (**Ans.** 285.7 metres)

Q.4. A Varlay loop test is used to locate an earth fault on a telephone line of route length 4 km. The resistance per km of single line is 20 ohms. The loop is completed with a line similar to that of the faulty one. At balance, the variable resistor connected to the faulty core is set at 80 Ω and fixed resistors are in the ratio of 1 : 1. Calculate the distance of the fault from the test end. (**Ans.** 2 km)

Solution of Problems

Solution 1. The ratio of two arms,

$$\frac{P}{Q} = 3$$

or

$$\frac{P+Q}{Q} = 3 + 1 = 4$$

$$\text{Total resistance of loop, } (R + X) = \frac{1.6}{1,000} \times 2 \times 1,000 = 3.2\ \Omega$$

$$X = \frac{Q}{P+Q}(R + X) = \frac{1}{4} \times 3.2 = 0.8\ \Omega$$

$$\text{Distance of fault from testing end} = \frac{X}{r/l} = \frac{0.8}{1.6/1,000} = 500 \text{ metres } \textbf{Ans.}$$

Solution 2. The ratio of two arms,

$$\frac{P}{Q} = 2.75$$

or

$$\frac{P+Q}{Q} = 2.75 + 1 = 3.75$$

$$\text{Total resistance of loop, } (R + X) = \frac{1}{1,000} \times 500 + \frac{2.25}{1,000} \times 500 = 1.625\ \Omega$$

$$X = \frac{Q}{P+Q}(R + X) = \frac{1.625}{3.75} = 0.4333\ \Omega$$

$$\text{Distance of fault from testing end} = \frac{X}{r/l} = \frac{4.4333}{1/1,000} = 433.3 \text{ metres } \textbf{Ans.}$$

Solution 3. The value of ratio arm, $P = 2.5$

Value of ratio arm, $Q = 1$

$$\frac{P+Q}{Q} = \frac{2.5+1}{1} = \frac{3.5}{1}$$

Total resistance of the cable = $(R + X)$

Also total resistance of cable = Resistance per metre length X of the loop of the cable

$$= \frac{1.2}{1000} \times 500 \times 2 = 1.2\ \Omega$$

$\therefore$ Resistance of cable upto fault point, $X = \dfrac{Q}{P+Q}\ X\,[R + X]$

$$X = \frac{1}{2.5+1}(1.2) = \frac{1}{3.5} \times 1.2 = 0.342\ \Omega$$

$$\text{Distance of fault point} = \frac{X}{\text{Resistance per metre length of cable}}$$

$$= \frac{0.342}{1.2} \times 1000 = 285.7 \text{ metres } \textbf{Ans.}$$

Solution 4. Length of the telephone line = 4 km

Resistance of the line per km = 20 Ω

∴ Total resistance of single line = 20 × 4 = 80 Ω

When the stud is set at 1.

Then,
$$X = \frac{Q(R+X) - PS_1}{P+Q}$$

The value of variable resistor, S_1 = 80 Ω

Since the arm ratio : $Q = 1$

∴
$$\frac{P}{Q} = 1$$

or
$$P = 1$$

Total resistance of loop ($R + X$) = 80 × 2 = 160 Ω

$$\text{By putting the values, } X = \frac{1 \times (160) - 1 \times 80}{1+1} = \frac{80}{2} = 40\ \Omega$$

$$\text{Distance of fault from test end} = \frac{40}{20} = 2 \text{ km} \quad \textbf{Ans.}$$

EXERCISE

1. Explain the various types of faults in overhead system.
2. Explain the types of faults in underground cable.
3. Explain the Murray loop method to find the faults in underground cables.
4. What is Varlay loop test? Explain the procedure of locating a fault on a cable by this test.
5. What is Meant by ground fault in cable?
6. Explain in brief for determining the cable faults :
   (i) Open circuit fault
   (ii) Short circuit fault
   (iii) Ground fault
7. Write a note on symmetrical and unsymmetrical faults.

❑❑❑

8

Various Types of Tariffs

INSIDE THIS CHAPTER

- Introduction
- Types of Tariffs
- Characteristics of Tariff
- Difference between Flat Rate Tariff and Block Rate Tariff

8.1 INTRODUCTION

Electrical energy produced by the power system is delivered to a large numbers of customers. The tariff becomes the attention for the electric supply company. The company has to ensured that the tariff such that it is not only recovers total cost of producing electrical energy but also earns profit on the capital investment.

The rate at which electrical energy is supplied to a consumer is known as tariff. The supplier invests lot of amount of money on building, equipment and salaries of staff etc., in order to supply electrical energy to various consumers. In view of this the supplier expects some return and thus he does by charging the consumer for the energy consumed by him. For charging the consumer, some basis is to be fixed and this basis is called Tariff. This basis of charging differs from consumer to consumer. Tariff depends upon:

1. Fixed and running charges
2. Purpose for which electricity consumed : such as heating or lighting.
3. Simplicity

Characteristics of Tariff

1. The tariff must be simple enough to be understood by all the consumers.
2. Consumers should be in a position to pay the tariff.
3. The annual cost of production of electricity, i.e., total of fixed and running charges. If this cost is high, tariff fixed should also be high and vice versa.
4. Type of service rendered, i.e., whether the power is to be supplied to domestic consumers or to industrial consumers. Industrial consumers are in a position to pay more but they consume more energy and if tariff fixed is high, cost of production in the factory shall go up and hence industrial consumers are charged at lesser rate. Domestic consumers on the other hand consume less of energy and so even if they are charged at higher rate, it may not pinch them and hence domestic consumers are charged at higher rates.

8.2 TYPES OF TARIFFS

There are several types of tariffs. However, the following are the commonly used types of tariffs.

8.2.1 Simple Tariffs

When there is a fixed rate per unit of energy consumed, it is called a simple tariff. In this tariff, the price per unit is constant and does not very with increase or decrease in number of units. The units are recorded by energy meter.

Advantages

1. It is simplest type
2. It is easy to understand
3. Consumer pay as per consumption

Disadvantages

1. No distinction is made between bulk consumer of electricity and smaller one.
2. Cost of electricity calculated per kWh comes out to be on the higher side than the one calculated by other methods.

8.2.2 Flat Rate Tariff

This type of tariff differs from the simple one in a sense that different types of consumers such as domestic consumers and industrial consumers are charged at different rates. The rate for domestic load such as light load and fan load etc., is slightly higher than the power load. The rate for each type of consumers is arrived at by taking into account its load factor and diversity factor. This type of tariff has an advantage that it can be understood by all types of consumers since calculations involved are quite simple.

If the consumer has both types of loads say:

1. Light and fan load
2. Power load

then two separate meters are required to be installed at the premises of the consumer and the consumer shall have to pay monthly rent for both the meters and this may be considered as a disadvantage of this type of tariff. In order to understand this tariff, let it be supposed that the two metres i.e., domestic load meter and power load meter show consumption of 40 units and 100 units of energy respectively. If the rate of light and fan load (domestic load) is 20 paise per unit and that for power load is 10 paise per unit then the consumer shall have to pay a monthly bill of ₹ $\frac{40 \times 20}{100} + \frac{100 \times 10}{100}$ ₹ 18 plus the meters rental charges of ₹ 1.50 if monthly rental charges of each meter is 75 paise.

Advantages

1. This is also simple and easy to calculate.
2. Larger consumer encourage to consume more power.

Disadvantages

1. The power company got no return, if in any month consumer consume no energy.
2. Different types of energy meters are required to install.

8.2.3 Block Rate Tariff

In this type of tariff, as the number of units generated increases the tariff falls with the result that the consumer who consumes more of energy has to pay less. This is obvious also as the increased generation results in spreading of fixed charges over greater number of units thus reducing the total over all cost. Thus if a consumer consumes 120 units of energy in one month and if the rate for first 20 units is 30 paise per unit and the rate for next 40 units is 20 paise per unit and the rate for all other additional units is 10 paise per unit, then his monthly bill shall be

$$₹\ \frac{20 \times 30 + 40 \times 20 + 60 \times 10}{100} = ₹\ 20.00.$$

Advantages

1. Consumers are motivated to use more energy.
2. Since consumer uses more energy hence reduces per unit cost.

Disadvantages

1. The power company does not get any return if consumer uses no power in any month.

8.2.4 Two Part Tariff

In this type of tariff system as the name suggests, charges are made in two parts.

(*i*) Fixed charge
(*ii*) Running charge.

Fixed charges depends upon the maximum demand of the consumer when as running charge depends upon the energy consumed. Maximum demand for calculating the fixed charges is ascertained either by calculating the total connected load at the premises of the consumer or by any other method. Thus each consumer has to pay a fixed sum proportional to the maximum demand which is proportional to the energy consumed by him. It is expressed as

$$E = ₹\,(A \times \text{kW} + B + \text{kWh})$$

where A is the charged per kW of maximum demand expressed in rupees and B is the charge per kWh of energy consumed. Thus amount A per kW recovers the fixed charges and amount B per kWh recovers the running charges from the consumer.

The only disadvantage of this particular tariff is that even if a premises is closed for a month, full fixed charges are to be paid by the consumer although running charges shall be zero with the result that the consumer shall have to pay a disproportionately high over all price per unit of energy consumption.

Advantages

1. The power company gets some return even if consumer uses no power.
2. It is easy to understand.

Disadvantages

1. It is difficult to measure maximum demand.
2. The consumer have to pay even if he uses no power.

8.2.5 Power Factor Tariff

The efficiency of power plant and equipment is dependent upon power factor; so to increase the utility of plant and equipment to maximum, the plant must be operated at most economical power factor. The following types of power factor tariffs are recommended by State Electricity Board for those consumers who use energy at low power factor.

8.2.6 Maximum Demand Tariff

This type of tariff is similar to two part tariff with the only difference that the maximum demand instead of being calculated by rateable value is measured by putting actual "maximum demand indicator" in the circuit. Thus the disadvantage noticed in the two part tariff no longer exists in this tariff as the maximum demand indicator shall no longer show any reading if premises remains locked through the month. Thus fixed charges shall get reduced to zero and running charges are already zero as the consumer has no longer consumed any electrical energy throughout the month. This tariff is advantageous from the point of view of the consumer. This tariff is written as :

$$₹\ (A \times \text{kVA} + B \times \text{kWh})$$

8.2.7 kWh and KVArh Tariff

In such type of tariff both kWh and kVArh of consumer are metered separately by two separate meters and are charged accordingly. The kVArh will reduce with the increased power factor so that the consumer is tempted to use energy at better power factor.

8.2.8 Average Power Factor Tariff

In this tariff 0.8 lagging power factor is considered as reference. A surcharge is levied if the power factor falls below 0.8 and however discount can be allowed by which the average power factor rises above 0.8.

Difference between flat rate tariff and block rate tariff

Sr. No.	*Flat rate tariff*	*Block rate tariff*
1.	Generally applied to domestic consumers	Generally applied to domestic and small commercial consumers
2.	It is simple method	Complex as compared to flat rate
3.	Different types of consumers are charged at different uniform rate	First block of energy is charged at given rate and succeeding blocks are changed progressively reduced rates
4.	Consumers are not encouraged to consume more power	Consumers are encouraged to consume more power
5.	Different energy meters are required for light and power load.	Only one energy meter is required to measure power

EXAMPLE 8.1 A factory has a maximum load of 300 kW at 0.72 power factor with an annual consumption of 40000 units, the tariff is ₹ 4.50 per kVA of maximum demand plus 2 paise per unit. Find out the average price per unit. What will be the annual saving if the power factor be improved to unity.

Solution:

$$\text{Maximum demand in kVA} = \frac{300}{0.72} = 416.67$$

$$\text{Annual consumption} = 40000 \text{ units}$$

$$\text{Total annual charges} = ₹\ \frac{9}{2} \times 416.67 + ₹\ \frac{2}{100} \times 40000$$

$$= ₹\ 1875 + ₹\ 800 = ₹\ 2675$$

$$\therefore \quad \text{Average price per unit} = \frac{\text{Total annual cost}}{\text{Units consumed per annum}}$$

$$= ₹\ \frac{2675}{40000} = ₹\ 0.0668 = 6.68 \text{ paise}$$

If the power factor is improved to unity,

$$\text{Maximum demand in kVA} = \frac{300}{1} = 300 \text{ kVA}$$

Annual consumption in kWh remaining the same, maximum demand in kVA has reduced from 417 to 300 on the improvement of power factor.

$$\therefore \quad \text{Annual saving} = ₹\ \frac{9}{2} \times (416.67 - 300)$$

$$= ₹\ \frac{9}{2} \times 116.67 = ₹\ \mathbf{525\ Ans.}$$

EXAMPLE 8.2 Calculate the amount of annual bill in the case of a consumer, whose load is 120 kW. Average power factor 0.8 lagging, load factor 80%, the tariff used is ₹ 6 per kVA of maximum demand (MD) per month and 3 paise per unit.

Solution: (*a*) given,

$$\text{Load} = 120 \text{ kW}$$

$$\text{Average p.f.} = 0.8 \text{ lagging}$$

$$\text{Load factor} = 80\%$$

Tariff = ₹ 6/kVA of maximum demand/month + P3/kWh

$$\text{We have, maximum demand} = \frac{\text{Load, kW}}{\text{p.f.}} \text{ kVA}$$

$$= \frac{120}{0.8} = 150 \text{ kVA}$$

$$\text{Annual energy consumption} = \text{p.f.} \times \text{M.D.} \times 8760 = 0.8 \times 120 \times 8760$$

$$= 8,40,960 \text{ units}$$

$$\therefore \quad \text{Annual charges} = ₹\left(6 \times 150 \times 12 + 840960 \times \frac{3}{100}\right)$$

$$= ₹\ (10800 + 25228.80) = ₹\ \mathbf{36,028.80\ P\ Ans.}$$

EXAMPLE 8.3 The cost of generation at a station is ₹ 500/kW plus 5 paise/unit. Calculate the overall cost/unit if the load factor is

(i) 100%

(ii) 50%

(iii) 20%

Solution: Given, cost of generation = ₹ 500/kW + 5 P/unit

Let maximum demand = 1 kW

(*i*) Load factor = 1.0

Energy consumed = 8760 kWh/year

$$\therefore \quad \text{Annual charge} = ₹\left(500 \times 1 + \frac{5}{100} \times 8760\right) = ₹\,(500 + 438.0)$$

$$\therefore \quad \text{Overall cost/unit} = ₹\,938 = \frac{₹\,938}{8760} = \mathbf{10.7\ P\ Ans.}$$

(*ii*) Load factor = 0.5

Energy consumed = p.f. × MD × 8760 = 4380 kWh/year

$$\therefore \quad \text{Annual charge} = ₹\left(500 \times 1 + \frac{5}{100} \times 4380\right)$$

$$= ₹\,(500 + 219.0) = ₹\,719$$

$$\therefore \quad \text{Overall cost/unit} = \frac{₹\,719}{4380} = \mathbf{16.4\ P\ Ans.}$$

(*iii*) Load factor = 0.2

Energy consumed = 0.2 × 8760 = 1752 kWh

$$\therefore \quad \text{Annual charge} = ₹\left(500 \times 1 + \frac{5}{100} \times 1752\right)$$

$$= ₹\,(500 + 87.6) = ₹\,587.4$$

$$\therefore \quad \text{Overall cost/unit} = \frac{₹\,5876}{1752} = \mathbf{33.5\ P\ Ans.}$$

Figure 8.1 shows the effect of load factor on overall cost per unit generated.

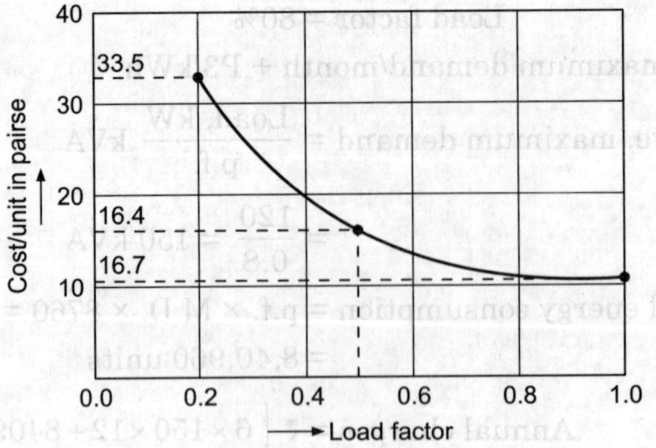

Fig. 8.1 Effect of load factor on cost/unit.

EXAMPLE 8.4 What will be the annual bill of a consumer whose load factor is 70% and has a maximum load of 500 kW at 0.8 power factor lagging? The following data is available regarding the two part tariff of the supply system to which he is connected.

(i) The fixed charges are ₹ 80 per kVA of the maximum demand of the consumer.

(ii) Running charges are 5 P/kWh consumed.

Solution: Given,

$$\text{load factor} = 70\% = 0.7$$

$$\text{Maximum load} = 500 \text{ kW}$$

$$\text{p.f.} = 0.8 \text{ lagging}$$

$$\text{Fixed charges} = ₹\ 80/\text{kVA of MD}$$

$$\text{Running charges} = ₹\ 5 \text{ P/kWh}$$

We have,

$$\text{energy consumed} = 0.7 \times 500 \times 8760 = 307 \times 10^6 \text{ kWh/annum}$$

$$\therefore \quad \text{Annual bill} = ₹\left(\frac{500}{0.8} \times 80 + \frac{5}{100} \times 3.07 \times 10^6\right)$$

$$= ₹\ (5 + 15.35) \times 10^6 = ₹\ \mathbf{20.35 \times 10^4 \text{ Ans.}}$$

EXAMPLE 8.5 Calculate the number of units to be consumed which will justify the two part tariff over flat rate tariff from the following data :

Maximum demand 5 kW, Two part tariff ₹ 100 per annum per kW of maximum demand plus ₹ 0.1 per unit consumed. Flat rate tariff ₹ 0.15 units.

Solution: Given,

$$\text{Maximum demand} = 5 \text{ kW}$$

$$\text{Two part tariff} = ₹\ 100 \text{ kW/annum} + ₹\ 0.1/\text{unit}$$

$$\text{Flat rate tariff} = ₹\ 0.15 \text{ per unit.}$$

Let number of units consumed by N

then annual charges/as per two part tariff = ₹ $(5 \times 100 + 0.1 \times N)$ = ₹ $0.15 \times N$

Both should be same.

$$\therefore \quad 5 \times 100 + 0.1 \times N = 0.15\, N$$

$$\text{or} \quad 0.05\, N = 500$$

$$N = \frac{500}{0.05} = \mathbf{1000 \text{ units Ans.}}$$

∴ The annual charges by both the tariffs will be same if 1000 units are consumed in a year.

EXAMPLE 8.6 A generating station has a connected load of 40 MW and a maximum load 20 MW, the units generated being 60 × 10⁶ per annum. Calculate the load factor and demand factor. If the tariff is ₹ 50 per kW + ₹ 0.03 per kWh consumed, calculate the annual bill.

Solution: Given,

$$\text{connected load} = 40 \text{ MW}$$

$$\text{Maximum load} = 20 \text{ MW}$$

$$\text{Units generated/annum} = 60 \times 10^6$$

$$\text{Tariff} = ₹\ 50\ \text{kW} + ₹\ 0.3/\text{kWh}$$

We have,

$$\text{Demand factor} = \frac{\text{Maximum load}}{\text{Connected load}} = \frac{20}{40} = \mathbf{0.5\ Ans.}$$

$$\text{Load factor} = \frac{\text{Units generated/annum}}{\text{Max.demand} \times 8760}$$

$$= \frac{60 \times 10^6}{20 \times 10^3 \times 8760} = \frac{3}{8.76} = \mathbf{0.343\ Ans.}$$

$$\text{Annual bill} = ₹\ (50 \times 20 \times 10^3 + 0.03 \times 60 \times 10^6)$$

$$= ₹\ (1 + 1.8) \times 10^6 = ₹\ \mathbf{2.8 \times 10^6\ Ans.}$$

SUMMARY

1. **Tariff:** The rate of payment by which the cost of electricity is charged from the consumer is known as *tariff*.
2. **Types of tariff**
   (i) Simple type of tariff
   (ii) Flat rate tariff
   (iii) Block rate tariff
   (iv) Two part tariff
   (v) kVA maximum demand tariff
3. **Principal factors involved in fixing of a tariff**
   (i) The tariff must be simple
   (ii) Easy for calculating the bill
   (iii) Tariff should depend upon the rendered
   (iv) The tariff should be easily understood by the consumer
4. **Block rate tariff:** In block rate tariff the bulk consumers are charged at lower rates as the net increases, the cost of energy decreases.
5. **Load factor:** It is defined as the ratio of average load to maximum load.
6. **Factors considered while fixing tariff.**
   (i) The tariff should be simple
   (ii) Consumers should be in a position to pay the tariff.
   (iii) Type of service *i.e.*, domestic or industrial.
7. **Three part tariff:** When the total charges from the consumer are to be made in three parts *i.e.*, fixed charge.
8. **Flat rate tariff:** In flat rate tariff different types of consumers such as domestic and industrial consumers are charged at different rates. Rate of domestic load is higher than rate of industrial power load.
9. **Two part tariff:** In a two part tariff the charges are splet into two parts
   (i) Fixed charges
   (ii) Running charges

It is expressed as $E = A \times \text{kW} + B \times \text{kWh}$

where 'A' is the charge per kW of maximum demand and B = charge per kWH of energy consumed

10. Merits of two part tariff

(i) It is easily understood by consumers.

(ii) The supplier recovers the fixed charges which depend upon the maximum demand.

11. Maximum demand tariff: The tariff in which electrical energy is charged on the basis of maximum demand of the consumers and the units consumed by him is called maximum demand tariff.

12. Power factor tariff: The tariff in which power factor of the consumer's load is taken into consideration is known as power factor tariff.

Objective Type Questions

1. Multiple Choice Type Questions

1. What is the objective of the tariff?
   (a) A satisfactory return of cost of operation supplies and maintenance of equipment.
   (b) Recovery of cost of capital investment in generating equipment transformer.
   (c) All the above two.

2. What is the meaning of tariff?
   (a) The rate at which electrical energy is supplied to a consumer.
   (b) Quantity of electrical energy consumed.
   (c) To calculate the load on the basis of kW.

3. Which type of tariff is used in case of maximum demand?
   (a) Power factor tariff
   (b) Maximum demand tariff
   (c) Block rate tariff

4. Tariff is defined as :
   (a) Monthly bill of the consumer (b) The yearly bill of the industry
   (c) The rate at which electrical energy is sold to a consumer
   (d) All of the above

5. The tariff in which electrical energy is charged on the basis of maximum demand of the consumer and the units consumed by him is called.
   (a) Two part tariff (b) Block rate tariff
   (c) Three part tariff (d) Power factor tariff

6. The power factor tariff is charged on the basis of
   (a) Maximum demand in kW and units consumed
   (b) Maximum demand in kVA and units consumed
   (c) Maximum demand in kVA
   (d) Maximum demand in kW only

7. The tariff (₹ 50/kVA of maximum demand plus 5 paise per unit) as a
   (a) Flat rate tariff (b) Maximum demand tariff
   (c) Block rate tariff (d) Power factor tariff

8. The demand factor of a power system is defined as
   (a) The ratio of average to maximum load.
   (b) The ratio of maximum load to connected load
   (c) The ratio of maximum load to average load
   (d) None of the above
9. Domestic consumers are usually charged
   (a) Flat demand tariff (b) Flat rate tariff
   (c) Block rate tariff (d) Off peak tariff
10. Two part tariff is charged on the basis of
   (a) Connected load (b) Units consumed
   (c) Maximum demand (d) Both (a) and (b)

ANSWERS

1. (c) **2.** (b) **3.** (b) **4.** (c) **5.** (a) **6.** (c) **7.** (d) **8.** (b) **9.** (c)
10. (d)

2. True-False Type Questions

1. The tariff in which the rate per unit of energy is fixed is called block rate tariff.
2. The ideal tariff for any type of consumer is three part tariff.
3. Tariff is also low of power factor is low.
4. Tariff is rate of selling commodity.
5. A consumer who consumes more electrical energy should pay more fixed charges per unit.
6. The tariff in which different types of consumers are charged at different uniform per unit rate is called flat rate tariff.
7. For agriculture, simplest tariff is applicable.
8. Power factor tariff is charged the basis of maximum demand in kVA.
9. The maximum kVA demand of the consumer is directly proportional to power factor.
10. In two part tariff energy charges do not depend on power factor.

ANSWERS

1. False **2.** False **3.** False **4.** True **5.** False **6.** True **7.** True **8.** True
9. False **10.** True

3. Fill in the Blanks Type Questions

1. The flat rate for lighting load is generally _________ than power load.
2. The block rate tariff is mostly applicable to _________ consumers.
3. The ideal tariff for any type of consumer is _________
4. The maximum kVA demand of the consumer is _________ proportional to the power factor.
5. In block rate tariff the rate of energy in first two block is _________
6. Schedule of rates framed for supply of energy to various consumers is called _________
7. Two-part tariff is mostly applicable for medium _________ consumers.
8. The consumption of electrical energy is recorded by _________
9. If power factor is low, the tariff is _________

10. The tariff in which different consumers are charged at different rates in ________ tariff.
11. The tariff in which the rate per unit of energy is called ________
12. The consumers should be ________ to use electricity.
13. The ideal tariff for any type of consumer is ________ part tariff.
14. Ratio of average load to maximum load is called ________
15. Maximum demand tariff is applied on ________

ANSWERS

1. higher	**2.** domestic	**3.** three part	**4.** inversely
5. high	**6.** tariff	**7.** industrial	**8.** energy meter
9. high	**10.** flat rate	**11.** simple tariff	**12.** encouraged
13. two	**14.** load factor	**15.** bulk supplies.	

SHORT ANSWER TYPE QUESTIONS

Q.1 What is meant by tariff?

Ans. Tariff means the schedule of rates framed for supply the electrical energy to different classes of consumers.

Q.2 Name the different types of tariff.

Ans. (*i*) Simple tariff (*ii*) Fast rate tariff
(*iii*) Block rate tariff (*iv*) Two part tariff
(*v*) Maximum demand tariff (*vi*) Power factor tariff
(*vii*) Three part tariff

Q.3 What are the objectives of tariff?

Ans. (*i*) Recovery of cost of generation.
(*ii*) Recovery of cost of transmission and distribution.
(*iii*) Recovery of cost of meters bill and miscellaneous service provided.
(*iv*) To get retrun on invest.
(*v*) Consumer gets energy at low rate and motivate to use more energy.

Q.4 Why is tariff less for power than lighting load?

Ans. Power load spreads the fixed charges over a greater number of units, thus reduces the overall cost of generation of electrical energy. Lighting load has low load factor and therefore cost of generation of electrical energy is higher. Due to this reason power tariff is less costly than lighting load.

Q.5 What type of tariff is employed for domestic consumers?

Ans. Block rate tariff.

Q.6 What is two part tariff?

Ans. In the two part tariff, total charge is divided into two parts. In this, consumer have to pay fix charges depending upon maximum demand plus energy consumed.

Q.7 For which category of consumers two part tariff is used?

Ans. Two part tariff is mostly applicable to medium industrial consumers.

Q.8 What type of tariff is usually applied to bulk consumers?

Ans. Three part tariff.

Q.9 What is flat rate tariff?

Ans. In flat rate tariff different types of consumers such as domestic consumers and industrial consumers are charged at different rates.

Q.10 What are the advantages of flat rate tariff?

Ans. (*i*) This is also simple and easy to calculate.

(*ii*) Larger consumer encourage to consume more power.

LONG ANSWER TYPE QUESTIONS

Q.1 Explain various types of tariffs. What are their advantages and disadvantages?

Ans. There are several types of tariff out of which the most commonly are described below.

1. **Simple Tariff:** The tariff in which the rate per unit of energy is fixed, is called simple tariff. This is a simplest possible tariff. The rate per unit of energy consumed by the consumer is fixed irrespective to the quantity of energy consumed by the consumer. The energy consumed by the consumer is measured by installing an energy meter at the consumer's premises.

Advantages

(*i*) It is simplest type

(*ii*) It is easy to understand

(*iii*) Consumer pay as per consumption.

Disadvantages

(*i*) There is no difference between smaller and larger consumers.

(*ii*) The rate per unit is very high.

(*iii*) The power company get no return, if in any month consumer consumes no power.

2. **Flat Rate Tariff** : The tariff in which different types of consumers are charged at different uniform per unit rates is called flat rate tariff. This type of tariff is similar to simple tariff. Only difference is that consumers are grouped into different classes and each class of consumers is charged at a different uniform per unit rate. For example, flat rate for fan and light loads is slightly higher than that for power loads.

Advantages

(*i*) This is also simple and easy to calculate.

(*ii*) Larger consumer encourage to consume more power.

Disadvantages

(*i*) The power company get no return if any month consumer consume no power.

(*ii*) Different types of energy metre are required to install.

3. **Block Rate Tariff:** The tariff in which first block of energy is charged at a given rate and the succeeding blocks of enrgy are charged at progressively reduced rates is called block rate tariff.

   In this type of tariff, the energy units are divided into number of blocks and the rate per unit of energy is fixed for each block. The rate per unit of energy for the first block is the highest and reduces progressively with the succeeding blocks. For example, the first 40 units may be charged at the rate of 50 paise per unit. The next 60 units may be charged at the rate 35 paise per unit and the remaining additional units may be charged at the rate of 25 paise per unit.

Advantages

(*i*) Consumers are motivated to use more energy.
(*ii*) Since consumer uses more energy hence reduces per unit cost.

Disadvantages

(*i*) The power company does not get any return is consumer uses no power in any month.

4. **Two-part Tariff:** The tariff in which electrical energy is charged on the basis of maximum demand of the consumer and the units consumed by him is called two-part tariff.
   In this tariff, the total charges to be made from the consumer are split into two components namely, fixed charges and running charges. The fixed charges are independent of energy consumed by the consumer and depend upon the maximum demand, whereas the running charges depend upon the energy consumed by the consumer.
   The maximum demand of the consumer is assessed on the basis of the kW capacity of all the consuming devices owned by a particular consumer or on the connected load.

Thus, the consumer is charged at a certain amount per kW of maximum demand plus a certain amount per kWh of energy consumed i.e., total charges = ₹ ($a \times$ kW + b kWh)

where, ₹ a = charge per kW of maximum demand
₹ b = charge per kWh of energy consumed

Advantages

(*i*) The power company get some return even if consumer uses no power.
(*ii*) It is easy to understand.

Disadvantages

(*i*) It is difficult to measure maximum demand.
(*ii*) The consumer have to pay even he uses no power.

5. **Maximum Demand Tariff** : The tariff in which electrical energy is charged on the basis of maximum demand (actually measured) of the consumer and the units consumed by him is called maximum demand tariff. In fact, this tariff is similar to two-part tariff with the only difference that the maximum demand is actually measured by installing a maximum demand indicator meter in the premises of the consumer instead of assessing it on the basis of rateable value. Thus the draw-back of two part tariff is removed.
   The tariff is mostly applied to bulk supplies and large industrial consumers.
6. **Power Factor Tariff** : The tariff in which power factor of the consumer's load is taken into consideration while fixing, it is called power factor tariff.
   Power factor plays an important role in an a.c. system. A low power factor increases the rating of the power plant equipment and decreases the efficiency of the system because of higher losses. Therefore, in order to increases the utility of the plant and equipment to the maximum, the plant must be operated at the most economical power factor. Therefore, consumers are advised to operate their loads at higher power factor. Sometimes, they are penalized by applying the following power factor tariffs:

   (i) kVA Maximum Demand Tariff: It is a modified from of two-part tariff. In this case, the fixed charges are made on the basis of maximum demand in kVA instead of kW. Since maximum demand in kVA = $\frac{\text{kW}}{\text{P.F.}}$, therefore, a consumer having low power factor has to pay more fixed charges. Thus the consumers are encouraged to operate their loads at higher power factor.

(ii) kWH and kVArh Tariff : In this tariff, the consumers are charged for kWH and kVArh separately. Since kVArh = kWh × tan ϕ (where tan $\phi = \tan^{-1} \phi$) and the value of kVArh increases with the decrease in p.f. therefore a consumer having low power factor shall have to pay more charges.

Q.2 Define the following terms :

1. Maximum demand
2. Diversity factor
3. Peak load hours

Ans. 1. **Maximum Demand:** The greatest of all demands (load) which occur during a given period is called maximum demand.

2. **Diversity Factor:** The ratio of sum of individual maximum demands of all the consumers connected to the generating station to the maximum demand on the power station is called diversity factor.

$$\text{Diversity factor} = \frac{\text{Sum of individual maximum demand}}{\text{Maximum demand on the power station}}$$

3. **Peak load hours:** The hours (time) during which the load on the generating station is maximum are called Peak load hours. Usually Peak load hours occur between 6 AM to 10 PM.

The time between 10 PM to 6 AM may be called as off peak load hours as the load is minimum during this time.

Q.3 Which type of tariff is recommended for tube-well connections? Write short note on it.

Ans. For tubewell connection, generally simple tariff is recommended as it is the simplest form and easily understood by rural consumers.

Simple Tariff: The tariff in which the rate per unit of energy is fixed, is called *simple tariff*. This is a simplest possible tariff. The rate per unit of energy consumed by the consumer is fixed irrespective of the quantity of energy consumed by the consumer. The energy consumed by the consumer is measured by installing an energy meter at the consumer's premises.

Advantages:

(*i*) It is an simplest form and easily understood by the consumer.

(*ii*) Consumers is to pay as per his consumption.

Disadvantages:

(*i*) Consumer is to pay the same rate per unit of energy consumed irrespective of the number of units consumed by him. Hence, consumers are not encouraged to consume more energy.

(*ii*) The cost per unit delivered is high.

PROBLEMS

Q.1 A consumer has an annual consumption of 70,080 kWh. The charge is ₹ 100/kW of maximum demand plus 5 paise/kWh.

(i) Find the annual bill and the overall cost per kWh if the load factor is 40%.

(ii) What is the overall cost per kWh if the consumption was reduced by 25% with the same load factor? **(Ans. (*i*) 7.85 *P* (*ii*) 7.85 *P*)**

Q.2 An industrial undertaking has connected load of 200 kW. The maximum demand is 150 kW. On average each machine works for 70% of time. Find yearly expenditure on electricity if the tariff is ₹ 3,000 + ₹ 700 per kW of maximum demand per year + ₹ 0.60 per kWh.

(Ans. ₹ 843840)

Q.3 The annual consumption of domestic customer is 1500 × 10^3 units and the annual load factor is 40%. What will be the saving in the average unit cost is the load factor improves to 100%. The two part tariff is ₹ 500 per kW of maximum demand per year + 40 paise per kWh.

(Ans. paise 8.56/kWh)

Q.4 An industrial consumer has single phase 230V supply. His monthly energy consumption is 2,020 kWh. A maximum demand indicator installed at his premises indicates 40 A which is charged at unity power factor for 2 hours daily at ₹ 3.50 per kWh. The remaining units are charged at ₹ 1.80 per kWh. Find the monthly bill for 30 days and average tariff per kWh.

(Ans. ₹ 2.265 per kWh)

Q.5 An industrial consumer having a maximum demand of 100 kW, maintains a load factor of 60%. The tariff rates are ₹ 900 per kVA of maximum demand per annum plus ₹ 1.80 per kWh of energy consumed. If the average power factor is 0.8 lagging, calculate the total energy consumed per annum and the annual electricity bill. Also workout the overall cost per kWh consumed.

(Ans. ₹ 2.02)

Q.6 A consumer takes a steady load of 250 kW at a power factor of 0.8 lagging for 10 hours per day and 300 days per annum. Estimate the annual payment under each of the following tariffs.

(i) ₹ 1.20 per kWh + ₹ 1,200 per kVA per annum.

(ii) ₹ 1.20 per kWh + ₹ 1,200 per kW per annum + 25 paise per kVArh.

(Ans. *(i)* ₹ 12,75,000, *(ii)* ₹ 13,40,625)

Q.7 Calculate the number of units to be consumed so that the annual bill on the basis of two part tariff is same from the following data :

Maximum demand = 10 kW

Two part tariff ₹ 1,200 per annum per kW of maximum demand plus ₹ 1.80 per unit consumed.

Flat rate tariff ₹ 2.40 per unit.

(Ans. 20,000 units)

Q.8 What is the effect of load factor on tariff. The cost of generation at a station is ₹ 500/kW + 5 paise/unit. Calculate the overall cost per unit if the load factor is

(i) 100%, (ii) 50%, (iii) 20% **(Ans.** (i) 10.7 P, (ii) 16.41 P, (iii) 33.48 P)

Solution of Problems

Solution: 1. (i) Annual energy consumption = 70,080 kWh

Annual load factor, LF = 40% or 0.4

$$\text{Average load} = \frac{\text{Annual energy consumption}}{8{,}760}$$

$$= \frac{70{,}080}{8{,}760} = 8 \text{ kW}$$

$$\text{Maximum demand, MD} = \frac{\text{Average load}}{\text{LF}} = \frac{8}{0.4} = 20 \text{ kW}$$

Annual energy consumption bill = Demand charges/annum + energy charges/annum

= ₹ 100 × 20 + ₹ 0.05 × 70,080

= ₹ 2,000 + ₹ 3,504 = ₹ 5,504 **Ans.**

$$\text{Overall cost per kWh} = \frac{\text{Annual energy consumption bill}}{\text{Annual energy consumption}}$$

$$= ₹\ \frac{5,504}{70,080} = \text{Re } 0.0785 \text{ or } 7.85 \text{ paise } \textbf{Ans.}$$

$$\text{(ii) Annual energy consumption} = (1 - 0.25) \times 70,080$$

$$= 52,560 \text{ kWh}$$

$$\text{Average load} = \frac{52,560}{8,760} = 6 \text{ kW}$$

$$\text{Maximum demand, MD} = \frac{\text{Average load}}{\text{Load factor}} = \frac{6}{0.4} = 15 \text{ kW}$$

$$\text{Annual energy consumption bill} = ₹\ 100 \times 15 + ₹\ 0.05 \times 52,560$$

$$= ₹\ 1,500 + ₹\ 2,628 = ₹\ 4,128$$

$$\text{Overall cost per kWh} = ₹\ \frac{4,128}{52,560}$$

$$= ₹\ 0.0785 \text{ or } 7.85 \text{ paise } \textbf{Ans.}$$

Solution 2. $$\text{Yearly energy consumption} = 200 \times 0.7 \times 365 \times 24$$

$$= 1,226,400 \text{ kWh}$$

$$\text{Fixed charges/annum} = ₹\ 3,000$$

$$\text{Demand charges/annum} = ₹\ 700 \times 150 = ₹\ 105,000$$

$$\text{Energy, charges/annum} = ₹\ 0.60 \times 1,226,400 = ₹\ 735,840$$

$$\text{Yearly expenditure on electricity} = ₹\ 3,000 + ₹\ 105,000 + ₹\ 735,840$$

$$= ₹\ 843,840 \quad \textbf{Ans.}$$

Solution 3. $$\text{Annual energy consumption} = 1,500 \times 10^3 \text{ kWh}$$

$$\text{Average load} = \frac{\text{Annual energy consumption}}{365}$$

$$= \frac{1,500 \times 10^3}{365 \times 24} = 171.233 \text{ kW}$$

$$\text{Load factor} = 40\% = 0.4$$

$$\text{Maximum demand} = \frac{\text{Average load}}{\text{Load factor}} = \frac{171.233}{0.4} = 428 \text{ kW}$$

In case the consumer improves the load factor to 100 per cent, his maximum demand will be reduced to $\frac{171.233}{1}$ *i.e.*, 171.233 kW

$$\text{Annual energy bill with 40\% load factor} = ₹\ 500 \times 428 + ₹\ 0.40 \times 1,500 \times 10^3 = ₹\ 814,000$$

$$\text{Unit cost} = ₹\ \frac{814,000}{1,500 \times 10^3}$$

$$= \text{Re } 0.5427 \text{ or paise } 54.27$$

$$\text{Annual energy bill with 100\% load factor} = ₹\ 500 \times 171.233 + ₹\ 0.40 \times 1,500 \times 10^3$$

$$= ₹\ 685,616.50$$

$$\text{Unit cost} = ₹\ \frac{685{,}616.50}{1{,}500 \times 10^3} = ₹\ 0.4571 \text{ or paise } 45.71$$

Saving in the average unit cost = Paise 54.27 – paise 45.71

= Paise 8.56/kWh **Ans.**

Solution 4. Monthly energy consumption corresponding to maximum demand

$$= \frac{\text{Voltage} \times \text{maximum demand of current} \times \text{pf} \times \text{working hour} \times 30}{1{,}000}$$

$$= \frac{230 \times 40 \times 1 \times 2 \times 30}{1{,}000} = 552 \text{ kWh}$$

Cost of energy corresponding to maximum demand

= ₹ 3.50 × 552 = ₹ 1,932

Energy cost for remaining energy consumption

= ₹ 1.80 × (2,020 – 552) = ₹ 2,642.40

Total monthly bill = ₹ 1,932 + ₹ 2,642.40 = ₹ 4,514.40 **Ans.**

$$\text{Average tariff} = \frac{\text{Monthly energy cost}}{\text{Monthly energy consumption}}$$

$$= ₹\ \frac{4{,}514.40}{2{,}020} = ₹\ 2.265 \text{ per kWh } \textbf{Ans.}$$

Solution 5. Maximum demand = 100 kW

Average power factor = 0.8

$$\text{Maximum demand in kVA} = \frac{\text{Maximum demand in kW}}{\text{Average power factor}} = \frac{100}{0.8} = 125$$

Load factor = 60% or 0.6

Total energy consumed per annum = Maximum demand in kW × load factor × 8,760

= 100 × 0.6 × 8,760 = 525,600 kWh **Ans.**

Annual demand charges = ₹ 900 × 125 = ₹ 112,500

Annual energy charges = ₹ 1.80 × 525,600 = ₹ 946,080

Annual electricity charges = ₹ (112,500 + 946,080) = ₹ 1,058,580 **Ans.**

$$\text{Overall cost per kWh supplied} = ₹\ \frac{1{,}058{,}580}{525{,}600} = ₹\ 2.02 \textbf{ Ans.}$$

Solution 6. Maximum demand = 250 kW

Annual energy consumption = Steady load in kW × working hours per day × working days per annum

= 250 × 10 × 300 = 750,000 kWh

$$\text{Maximum demand in kVA} = \frac{KW}{PF} = \frac{250}{0.8} = 312.5$$

kVARh consumed per annum = kWh × tan ($\cos^{-1}$ pf)

= 750,000 × tan ($\cos^{-1}$ 0.8)

= 750,000 × 0.75 = 562,500

(*i*) Annual payment under tariff = ₹ 1.20 × 750,000 + ₹ 1,200 × 312.5
= ₹ 1,275,000.00 **Ans.**

(*ii*) Annual payment under tariff = ₹ 1.20 × 750,000 + ₹ 1,200 × 250
+ ₹ 0.25 × 562,500
= ₹ (900,000 + 300,000 + 140,625)
= ₹ 1,340,625.00 **Ans.**

Solution 7. Maximum demand = 10 kW

Let the consumption be x units to that the annual bill on the basis of two part tariff and flat rate tariff is the same.

Annual bill under two part tariff = ₹ 1,200 × 10 + ₹ 1.80 × x
= ₹ $(1.8x + 12{,}000)$

Annual bill under flat rate tariff = ₹ 2.40 × x = ₹ $2.4x$

Annual bill will be same if $(1.8x + 12{,}000) = 2.4x$

or $$x = \frac{12{,}000}{(2.4-1.8)} = 20{,}000 \text{ units} \quad \textbf{Ans.}$$

Solution 8. Let the maximum demand on the generating station = x kW.

Annual fixed charges = ₹ $500x$

(*i*) Load factor = 100%

Average load = Load factor x max. demand

$$= \frac{100}{100} \times x = x\text{kW}$$

Electrical energy generated/year = 8760 × kWH

$$\text{Annual running charges} = ₹\ \frac{8760x \times 5}{100} = ₹\ 438\ x$$

Total generating cost/year = ₹ $(500x + 438\ x)$ = ₹ $938x$

$$\text{Generating cost/unit} = ₹\ \frac{938x}{8760x} = 10.7 \text{ P } \textbf{(Ans.)}$$

(*ii*) Load factor = 50%

$$\text{Average load} = \frac{50}{100} x = 0.5x \text{ kW}$$

Energy generated/year = $0.5x$ × 8760 = $4380x$ kWH

$$\text{Annual running charges} = ₹\ \frac{4380x \times 5}{100} = ₹\ 219x$$

Total generating cost/year = ₹ $(500x + 219x)$

Total generating cost/year = ₹ $719x$

$$\text{Generating cost/unit} = ₹\ \frac{719x}{4380x} = 16.41 \text{ P } \textbf{(Ans.)}$$

(*ii*) Load factor = 20%

$$\text{Average load} = \frac{20}{100} x = 0.2x \text{ kW}$$

$$\text{Energy generated/year} = 0.2x \times 8760 = 1752x \text{ kWH}$$

$$\text{Annual running charges} = ₹\ \frac{1752x \times 5}{100} = ₹\ 87.6x$$

$$\text{Total generating cost/year} = ₹\ (500x + 87.6x) = ₹\ 587.6x$$

$$\text{Generating cost/unit} = ₹\ \frac{587.6x}{1752x} = 33.48 \text{ P } \textbf{(Ans.)}$$

EXERCISE

1. What is tariff? Explain different types of tariff.

2. What are the factor involved in fixing a tariff?

3. What is a two part tariff?

4. Distinguish between flat rate and block rate tariff.

5. Write short notes on the following:

(i) Two part tariff

(ii) Three part tariff

(iii) Block rate tariff

6. Why tariff for power load is less than lighting load?

7. Enumerate the various tariff system used and discuss their merits and demerits.

8. How does three part tariff differs from two-part tariff?

9. What are the various types of tariff? Explain them briefly.

❑❑❑

Miscellaneous Questions and Answers

1. Define resources.

Ans. A resources may be defined as any useful information, service or material.

2. Name the different types of natural sources.

Ans. (*i*) Renewable resources.

(*ii*) Non-renewable resources.

3. What are the different forms of energy.

Ans. (*a*) Electrical energy

(*b*) Mechanical energy including potential energy, kinetic energy etc.

4. What are the classification of energy resources?

Ans. The various sources of energy can be classified as under:

(*a*) Commercial primary energy resources–coal, lignite, oil and natural gas, hydroelectric and nuclear fuels can be grouped as primary energy resources.

(*b*) Renewable sources of energy the main attention has to be directed to the following source of renewables namely, (*i*) solar photovoltaic (*ii*) wind (*iii*) hydrogen fuel cell

(*c*) New sources of energy.

The most prominent new sources of energy are tidal energy ocean waves, geothermal energy etc.

5. What are the advantages and disadvantages of renewable sources?

Ans. Advantages

(a) They are inexhaustible

(b) Use for local processing and applications

(c) There is no pollution problem.

Disadvantages

(a) Efficiency is low

(b) Large investment is required

(c) More chances of environment pollution.

6. Define Solar energy.

Ans. Solar energy is the most promising of the unconventional energy sources. The energy from the sun in the form of radiations in called solar energy.

7. Name the two types of solar collector.

Ans. (*a*) Flat place collector
(*b*) Concentrating collector

8. What is solar cooker?

Ans. Solar cooker is used to prepare the food.

9. Describe Solar Photovoltaic.

Ans. Photovoltaic are device which directly convert incident solar radiation to electric current.

10. What are various types of solar thermal power plants?

Ans. 1. Parabolic trough solar power plant
2. Central receiver solar power plant.

11. What are the applications of solar ponds?

Ans. The main applications of solar ponds are :

1. Power generation
2. Process heat
3. Crop drying

The main limitation are availability of water and sunny climate.

12. What is wind energy?

Ans. The wind energy is the kinetic energy of the air flow.

13. What are the main components of wind power plant?

Ans. 1. Wind mill of suitable size and shape
2. Coupling
3. Wind direction follow up device
4. Hydraulic transmission
5. Electric generator
6. Tower

14. Write classification of wind power plants.

Ans. 1. By axis of rotation
2. By size of machine.

15. What are main applications of wind mills

Ans. 1. Pumping
2. Grinding grains
3. Saw milling
4. Electric generation.

16. Name power station you know in India of different types.

Ans. (*i*) **Hydro Power Stations:** Bhakra, Pong, Dehar, Koyna, Sreesailam and sivasamudram

(*ii*) **Thermal power stations:** Bhatinda, Rajghat power station, Neyveli, Panipat power station, Super thermal power stations, Ropar.

(*iii*) **Diesel Power Plants:** These are small size installed at necessary load centre.

(*iv*) **Nuclear Power Station:** Tarapore, Kota, Kalpakam (Chennai)

17. What are advantages of hydro power plants?

Ans. 1. Simple in construction.
2. Can be put in service instantly
3. No stand by losses
4. Low running cost.

18. What points are taken into consideration for selection of site of nuclear power plants?

Ans. 1. Adequate water supply
2. Nearness to load centres
3. Away from populated areas
4. Approach to the site by rail and road.

19. Define the term 'Transmission.'

Ans. The system by which bulk power is delivered from power station to load centres (sub stations) is called transmission.

20. Define the term Distribution.

Ans. The part of the power system by which electric power is distributed among consumers for their use is known as Distribution.

21. Why high voltage transmission is preferred?

Ans. High voltage transmission has the following advantages:

(i) With increase in the transmission voltage the volume of conductor material decreases. This decreases the cost of the line.

(ii) If voltage is high, the current is reduced which reduces the line losses. Thus the efficiency of transmission is improved.

(iii) High voltage also improves the regulation of the line.

22. State and explain Kelvin's law for transmission lines. How the most economical size of conductor is calculated?

Ans. Kelvin's Law: The most economical area of cross-section of conductor is that for which annual cost of transmission line is minimum. This is known as Kelvin's law. This is used to calculated cross-section of the conductor.

Explanation: The total annual cost of a line can be divided into :

(i) *Annual charges on capital outlay:* They include the charges of annual interest and depreciation on capital cost of the conductors.

$$\text{Annual charges} = (P_1 + P_2\, a) \qquad \ldots(i)$$

where P_1 and P_2 are constants and a is the cross-section of the conductor.

(ii) *Annual cost of energy wasted:* This is the cost of energy lost in the conductor due its resistance *i.e.*, $I^2 R$. losses.

$$\text{This is equal to } \frac{P_3}{a} \qquad \ldots(ii)$$

where P_3 is a constant

Adding exp. (*i*) and (*ii*), we get,

$$\text{Total annual cost, } C = P_1 + P_2\, a + \frac{P_3}{a} \qquad \ldots(iii)$$

The total annual cost will be minimum if the differentiation of exp. (*iii*) with respect to variable '*a*' is zero

i.e.,
$$\frac{dC}{da} = 0$$

or
$$\frac{d}{da}\left(P_1 + P_2 a + \frac{P_3}{a}\right) = 0$$

or
$$P_2 - \frac{P_3}{a^2} = 0$$

or
$$P_2 = \frac{P_3}{a^2}$$

or
$$P_2 a = \frac{P_3}{a}$$

i.e., Variable part of annual charges = Annual cost of energy wasted or $a = \sqrt{\frac{P_3}{P^2}}$

Hence, the conductor size under this condition will be most economical. Thus, Kelvin's law can also be stated as :

The most economical area of *x*-section of conductor is that for which the variable part of annual charges are equal to the cost of energy wasted.

23. What are the conductor materials employed for OH transmission? Discuss their electrical and mechanical properties.

Ans. The conductors carry electric power from the sending station to the receiving station. Usually the following materials are used for conductors:

(i) **Copper:** Hard Drawn Bare Copper (HDBC) is usually used. It has high conductivity and tensile strength. Copper is ductile and reasonably good against atmospheric troubles. Copper is an ideal conductor for transmission but due to heavy cost and non-availability, it is rarely used.

(ii) **Aluminium:** Its conductivity and tensile strength is poor than cooper. Due to less conductivity cross-section of aluminium is lighter in weight therefore supports (poles) need not to be too heavy as in case of copper. Due to light in weight and cheaper in cost, Aluminium is fast replacing copper nowa-days.

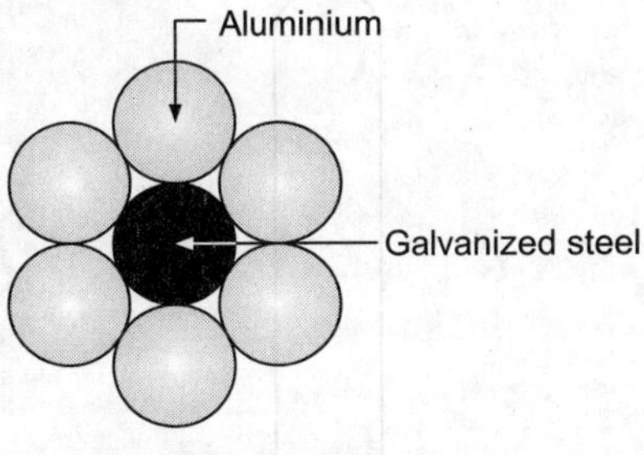

Fig. 1

(iii) **ACSR:** That is aluminium conductor with steel reinforcement has many advantages. It has less sag and therefore more suitable for larger spans. It has more tensile strength. The galvanished steel core in the centre makes it more stronger and at the same time cheaper than aluminium.

24. Mention various transmission line supports and discuss the types of lines for which they are suitable?

Ans. The purpose of supports is to carry the line. Various supports used in transmission are as under:

(i) **Steel Poles:** They may be steel tubular poles, rail or in the shapes of rolled steel joist, they passess greater mechanical strength and permit use of long spans (60 – 80 meters). They have long life (50 yrs). They are generally 9 to 11 metres high. Their use is upto 11 kV line.

(ii) **RCC Poles:** The Reinforced cement conerete poles have greator mechanical strength, larger life and permit large span (upto 200 m) than steel poles. They need little maintenance (Painting etc.) and also need not to be earthed, it is preferred to manufacture them at site to avoid heavy cost of transportion. They can be used upto 11 kV. (Fig. 2)

(iii) **Steel Towers:** Narrow base towers are used for lines upto 33 kV. The brood base towers are used beyond 66 kV. They have greater mechanical strength and permit very long spans (more than 300 m). Hence they are carry single circuit as well as Double circuit. (Fig. 3)

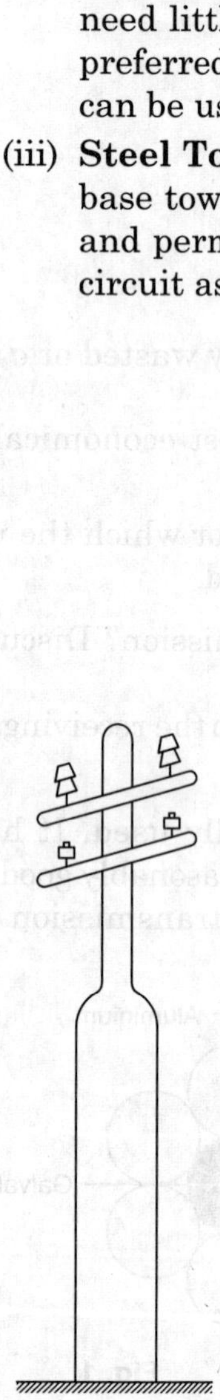

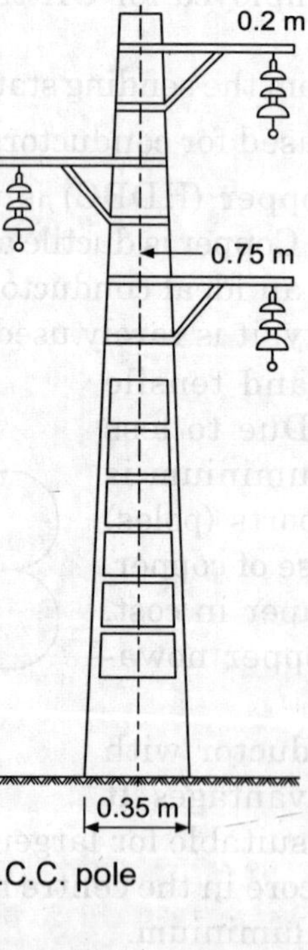

Fig. 2 R.C.C. pole

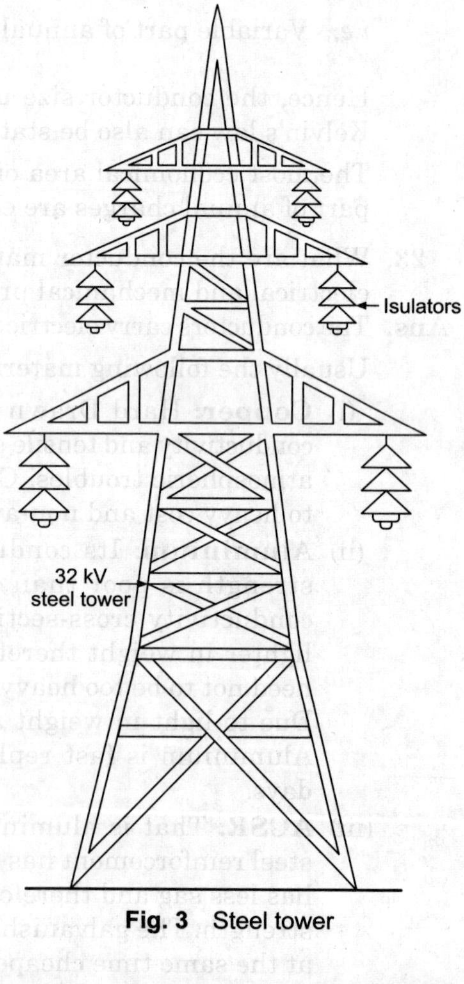

Fig. 3 Steel tower

25. **Name the various type of insulators used on transmission line. Draw their neat sketch and mention the field of application of each?**

Ans. The purpose of insulators is to isolate the conductor from the pole. The most commonly used insulators in OH line are as follows:

(i) **Pin Type Insulator:** Pin type insulator is screwed on to a galvanise steel bolt which in turn is installed on the cross arm of the pole. These insulators are easily used upto 11 kV line but some time upto 33 kV.

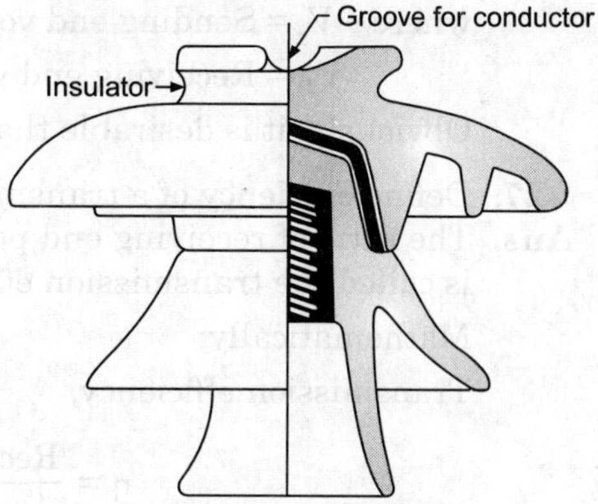

Fig. 4 Pin type insulator

(ii) **Suspension Type:** Above 33 kV, suspension type insulators an used. They consist of number of porcetain discs in series by metal links, Each disc is designed for 11 kV, hence by increasing number of discs very large voltage can be carried over. They are hanged vertically down.

(iii) **Strain Insulators:** At dead ends, sharp turns and corners, where line is subjected to greator strains, Insulators are used. Many number of discs (suspension) is series make a string which is put on pole horizontal to earth.

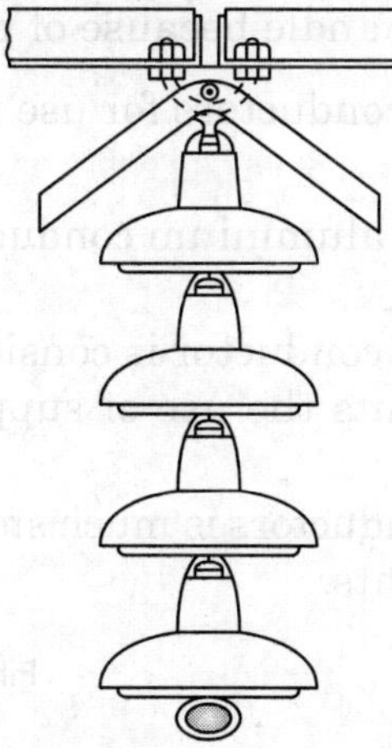

Fig. 5 Suspension type insulator

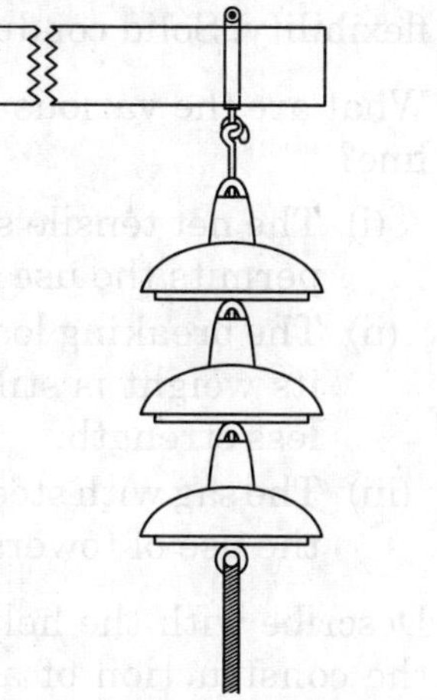

Fig. 6 Strain insulator

26. **Define voltage regulation of a transmission line.**

Ans. The rise in voltage at the receiving end, when full load is thrown off and the sending end voltage remaining the same, is called voltage regulation. It is expressed as a percentage of receiving end voltage.

When whole of the load is thrown of i.e., when the line is supplying no load, the receiving end voltage becomes equal to the sending end voltage.

Mathematically;

$$\text{Percentage regulation, \% Reg.} = \frac{V_s - V_R}{V_R} \times 100$$

where V_s = Sending end voltage (phase value in case of 3-phase lines)

V_R = Receiving end voltage (phase value in case of 3-phase lines)

Obviously, it is desirable that the regulation of a transmission line should be low.

27. Define efficiency of a transmission line.

Ans. The ratio of receiving end power to the sending end power of a transmission line is called the transmission efficiency of the line.

Mathematically;

Transmission efficiency,

$$\eta = \frac{\text{Receiving end power}}{\text{Sending end power}} \times 100 = \frac{V_R I \cos\phi_R}{V_S I \cos\phi_s} \times 100$$

where V_R = receiving end voltage (phase value)

I = current flowing through each conductor

$\cos\phi_R$ = receiving end p.f.

V_S = sending end voltage (phase value)

$\cos\phi_S$ = sending end p.f.

28. Why are the conductors for transmission line stranded?

Ans. The conductor used for OH transmission are stranded in order to increase the flexibility. Solid conductors are difficult to handle because of poor flexibility.

29. What are the various advantages of ACSR conductors for use in OH transmission line?

Ans.

(i) The net tensile strength of steel cored aluminium conductors is more, which permits the use of longer spans.

(ii) The breaking load of such a composite conductor is considerably greater and its weight is still smaller which permits the use of supporting structure of less strength.

(iii) The sag with steel cored aluminium conductors is much smaller which permits the use of towers having smaller heights.

30. Describe with the help of a neat sketch the construction of a multicore 11 kV under-ground cable?

Ans. A Multicore (3 core) 11 kV underground cable has been shown in Fig. 7. The cable has following parts?

1. **Core or conductors:** A three-core cable has three conductors as shown. These conductors are made of copper or aluminium and are usually stranded to make the cables flexible. The copper conductors are always

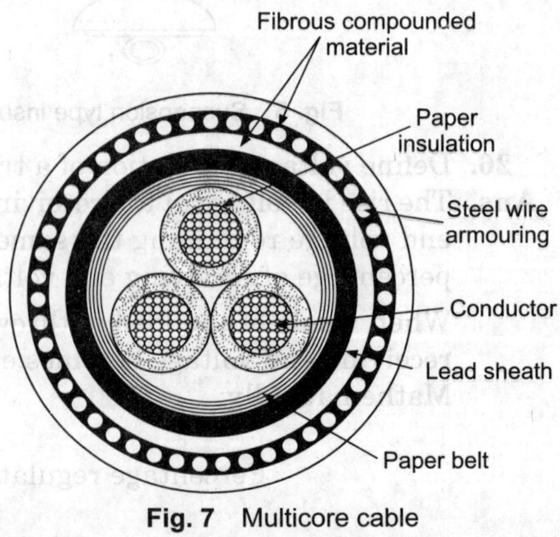

Fig. 7 Multicore cable

tinned otherwise they may react with the chemical compounds used in the insulation placed around them.

2. **Insulation:** Each core or conductor is provided with a suitable thickness of insulating material. The thickness of layer of the insulation depends upon the voltage to be withstand by the cable. Generally used material for insulation of 11 kV cable is impregnated paper tape.
3. **Sheath:** In order to protect the cable from moisture, gases or other damaging liquids (acids, alkalies) in the soil and atmosphere, a metallic sheath of lead or aluminium is provided over the insulation.
4. **Bedding:** In order to protect the metallic sheath against corrosion and from mechanical injury due to armouring, a layer of bedding is provided over the sheath. The bedding consists of a fibrous material like jute or hessian type.
5. **Armouring:** Over the bedding, armouring is provided to protect the cable from mechanical injury while laying it and during the course of handling. Armouring usually consists of one or two layers of galvanized steel wire or steel tap.
6. **Serving:** To protect the armouring from atmospheric conditions, a layer of fibrous material similar to bending is provided over the armouring. This is known as serving.

31. Name the various methods of laying underground cables and explain any one method in detail.

Ans. Laying of Underground Cables: The following are the three methods of laying underground cables :

1. Direct laying.
2. Draw-in system
3. Solid system

Direct Laying: This method of laying ground cables is simple and cheap and is much favoured in modern practice. In the method of laying, a trench about 1.5 meters deep and 45 cm wide is dug. The cable is laid in the trench over a sand bedding which is then covered with soil. The cable may be protected by planks, bricks, tiles or concrete slabs. In most of the cases, digging and trenching arwe done manually, but in places free from obstruction, machine methods can be used.

The Fig. 8 shows a cable in a trench with concrete cover for protection. When more than one cable is to be laid in the same trench, a horizontal or vertical inter-axial spacing of at least 30 cm is admisable in order to reduce the effect of mutual heating, and also to ensure that a fault occurring on one cable does not damage the adjacent cable.

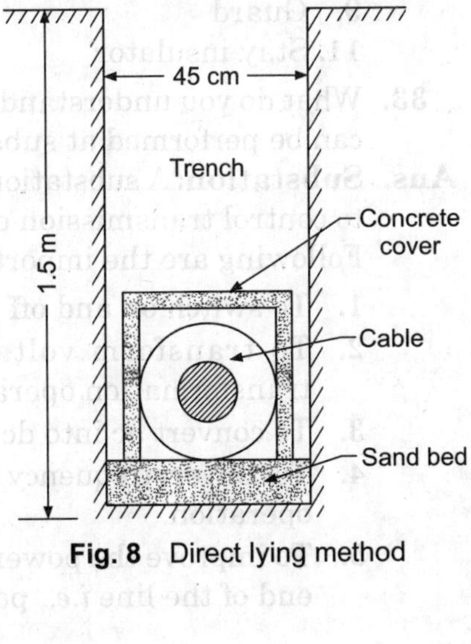

Fig. 8 Direct lying method

32. Draw a neat sketch of a LT pole and lable the important components.

Ans. The Fig, 9 shows a pole of a LT 400/230 V line. The various components are :

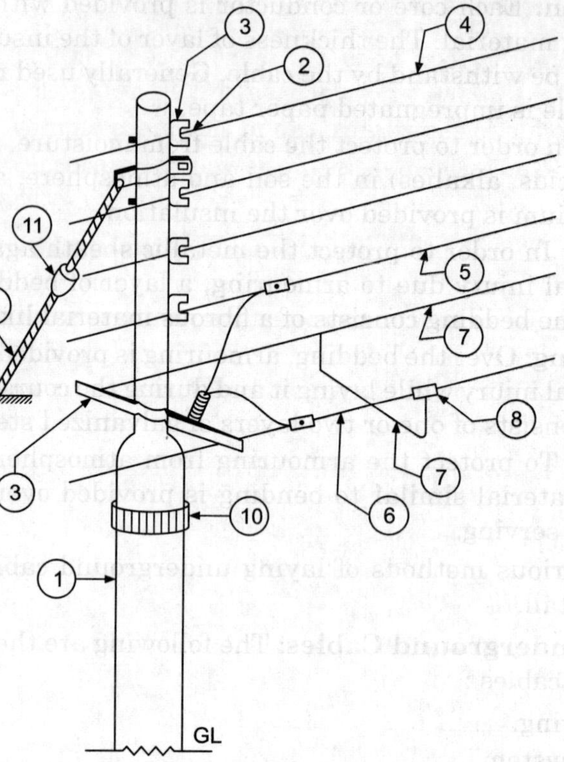

Fig. 9 L.T. pole

1. Pole
2. Insulators
3. Clamp
4. Phase wire
5. Street wire
6. Earth wire
7. Neutral
8. Reel insulator
9. Guard
10. Pole clamp
11. Stay insulator

33. What do you understand by a substation? What are the important functions which can be performed at substation?

Ans. Substation: A substation is essentially an assembly of apparatus which is installed to control transmission or distribution of electric power.

Following are the important functions which are performed at the substations:

1. To switch on and off the power lines *i.e.*, switching operations.
2. To transform voltage from higher to lower or vice-versa *i.e.*, voltage transformation operation.
3. To convert ac into dc or vice-versa *i.e.*, power converting operation.
4. To convert frequency from higher to lower or vice-versa *i.e.*, frequency correcting operation.
5. To improve the power factor by installing synchronous condensers at receiving end of the line *i.e.*, power factor correction operation.

34. State the advantages and disadvantages of outdoor substations over indoor substations?

Ans. Marits and Demerits of Outdoor Substations: The outdoor substations have the following advantages and disadvantages over indoor substations.

Advantages

(i) Fault location is easier, since all the equipment is within view.
(ii) The extension of the installation is easier when required.
(iii) Less time is required for their erection.
(iv) The cost of civil engineering work (building etc.) is less.
(v) There is practically no danger of a fault which appears at one point being carried over the another point in the installation because the apparatus of the adjoining connection can be spaced liberally, without any appreciable increase in costs.

Disadvantages

(i) The supervision and maintenance of all apparatus to be performed in open air during all kinds of weather conditions.
(ii) They required more space for installation.
(iii) The climate conditions deteriorate the life of equipment.

35. What do you understand by power factor? Explain in the necessity of improving power factor?

Ans. Power Factor: It can be defined in three ways:

(i) The cosine of the angle between voltage and current in an ac circuit is called power factor.
(ii) The ratio of true power to the apparent power is known as power factor.
From power triangle

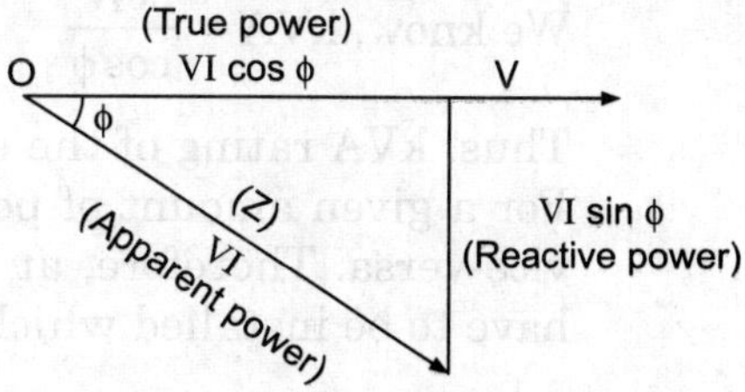

Fig. 10

$$\cos\phi = \frac{VI\cos\phi}{VI} = \frac{\text{True power}}{\text{Apparent power}}$$

(iii) The ratio of resistance and impedance of an ac circuit is known as power factor. From impedance triangle :

$$\cos\phi = \frac{R}{Z}$$

36. What is the necessity of improving PF (or Disadvantages of poor PF)?

Ans. We know that power consumed in an a.c. circuit

$$P = VI\cos\phi \quad \text{(for 1-phase circuits)}$$

$$\therefore \quad I = \frac{P}{V\cos\phi}$$

and

$$P = \sqrt{3}\, V_L I_L \cos\phi \quad \text{(for 3-phase circuits)}$$

$$\therefore \quad I_L = \frac{P}{\sqrt{3}V_L \cos\phi} \quad \text{(when other factors are constant)}$$

It is clear from the above equation that for fixed power and voltage, load current is inversely proportional to the power factor. Lower the power factor, higher is the load current and vice-versa. The higher load current at low power factor result in the following disadvantages :

(i) **Greater Conductor Size:** To transmit or distribute a fixed amount of power at fixed voltage, the conductors will have to carry more current at low power factor. This necessitates a large conductor size.

(ii) **Large Copper Losses:** Since at low power factor, the conductors have to carry more current, therefore, I^2R losses are increased. This also results in the poor efficiency of the poor system.

(iii) **Poor Voltage Regulation:** Low lagging power factor results in the large voltage drops in alternators, transformers, transmission and distribution lines. This leads to poor voltage regulation. Therefore, power factor improvement equipment is required to keep the voltage drop within permissible limits.

(iv) **Large kVA Rating of Equipment:** The electrical machinery *e.g.*, alternators, transformers, switch gears etc., are always rated in kVA.

We know, $\text{kVA} = \frac{\text{kW}}{\cos\phi}$

Thus, kVA rating of the equipment is inversely proportional to the power factor. For a given amount of power, kVA rating will be more for low power factor and vice-versa. Therefore, at low power factors, the equipment of higher kVA rating have to be installed which increases the capital cost.

37. What are the causes of low P.F.?

Ans. Causes of Low Power Factor

(i) A transformer is an inductive devices and draws a magnetizing current which causes the total current to lag behind the voltage, i.e., it operates at lagging power factor much, but at light loads magnetizing current decreases the power factor effectively.

(ii) Most of the a.c. motors are of induction type (1-phase and 3-phase induction motors used for industrial purposes), which have low power factor. Though, power factor of an induction motor is reasonably high (0.85 lagging) at full load, it decreases to a low value (0.3 to 0.5) lagging) at small loads.

(iii) Arc lamps and industrial heating furnaces (induction).

38. A single-phase motor takes a current of 10 A at a power factor of 0.707 lagging from a 230 V, 50 Hz supply. What value must a shunting capacitor have to raise the power factor to unity.

Ans. Current drawn by motor, $I_m = 10\ A$

Power factor of motor, $\cos\phi_1 = 0.707$

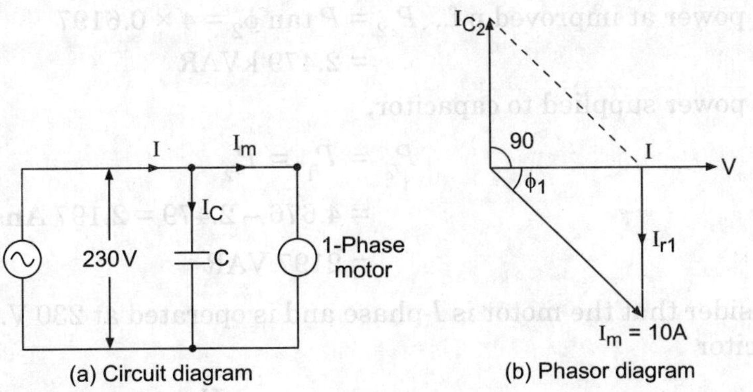

Fig. 11

Let a capacitor of capacitance C farads be connected across the motor as shown to improve the p.f. to unity. The phasor diagram is also shown.

At power factor, $\cos \phi_1$ 0.707; $\sin \phi_1 = \sin \cos^{-1} 0.707$

$= 0.707$

Reactive component of current, $I_{r_1} = I_m \sin \phi_1$

$= 10 \times 0.707 = 7.07$ A

When the p.f. is improved to $\cos \phi_1 = 1$

Reactive component of current, $I_{r_2} = 0$

Current drawn by the capacitor, $I_C = I_{r_1} - I_{r_2} - 7.07 - 0 = 7.07$A

Now, $$I_C = \frac{V}{X_C} = \frac{V}{1/2\pi fC} = 2\pi fCV$$

$$\text{Capacitance, } C = \frac{I_C}{2\pi fV} = \frac{7.07}{2\pi \times 50 \times 230}$$

$= 97.85$ μF **Ans.**

39. Find the rating of capacitor required to improve the power factor of an induction motor from 0.65 to 0.85 lagging. The motor takes 4 kW.

Ans. Active power of motor, $P = 4$ kW

Power factor of the motor, $\cos \phi_1 = 0.65$ lagging.

Now, $\cos \phi_1 = 0.65$; $\tan \phi_1 = \tan \cos^{-1} 0.65 = 1.169$

Reactive power of motor, $P_{r1} = P \tan \phi_1$

$= 4 \times 1.169 = 4.676$ kVAR

Let a capacitor of capacitance C farads be connected across the motor to improved the p.f. to $\cos \phi_2 = 0.85$ lagging.

Now, $\cos \phi_2 = 0.85$; $\tan \phi_2$

$= \tan \cos^{-1} 0.85 = 0.6197$

Reactive power at improved p.f., $P_{r2} = P \tan \phi_2 = 4 \times 0.6197$

$= 2.479$ kVAR

Reactive power supplied to capacitor,

$$P_{r_c} = P_{r_1} = P_{r_2}$$

$$= 4.676 - 2.479 = 2.197 \text{ Ans.}$$

$$= 2197 \text{ VAR} \qquad ...(i)$$

If we consider that the motor is *I*-phase and is operated at 230 V. Power drawn by the capacitor

$$= VI_C = V\frac{V}{X_C} = 2\pi fCV^2 \qquad ...(ii)$$

or

$$C = \frac{P_{r_c}}{2\pi fV^2}$$

(**Note:** Capacitors are also rated in KVAR.)

40. What do you understand by the term Tariff? Describe the various methods employed for fixing a tariff.

Ans. Tarriff. The rate at which electrical energy is sold to a consumer is called tariff the various methods employed (or factor) in fixing a tariff are under:

(*i*) The tariff should ensure the recovery of the total cost of generation transmission and distribution etc.

(*ii*) The tariff should be simple, cheap and capable of easy explanation to consumers.

(*iii*) The tariff should be attractive so that consumers are encourage to make more use of electrical energy.

(*iv*) The tariff should be such that it would earn a reasonable profit.

(*v*) The tariff must be fair and the consumers should be charged according to the cost of the energy.

41. Which type of Tariff is recommended for tube well connections? Wire short note on it.

Ans. For tube well connection, generally simple Tariff is recommended as it is the simplest for easily understood by rural consumers.

Simple Tariff: The tariff in which the rate per unit of energy is fixed, is called *simple tariff.*

This is a simplest possible tariff. The rate per unit of energy consumed by the consumer is fixed irrespective of the quantity of energy consumed by the consumer. The energy consumed by the consumer is measured by installing an energy meter at the consumer's premises.

Advantages

(*i*) It is an simplest form and easily understood by the consumers.

(*ii*) Consumers is to pay as per his consumption.

Disadvantages

(i) Consumer is to pay the same rate per unit of energy consumed irrespective of the number of units consumed by him. Hence, consumers are not encouraged to consume more energy.

(ii) The cost per unit delivered is high.

42. A load of 500 kW at 0.8 power factor lagging is taken by an industrial concern. The tariff is ₹ 100 per kVA of maximum demand per year plus 25 paise per kWH. The cost of installation of capacitor is ₹ 150 per kVAR and the interest and depreciation is 11%. Find the most economical power factor and rating of capacitor bank to improve the power factor to this value.

Ans.

Load of the industry = 500 kW

Power factor, $\cos \theta_1 = 0.8$ logging

Annual max, demand charges, x = ₹ 100/kWA

Cost of capacitors = ₹ 150/kVAR

Interest and depreciation = 11%

Annual expenditure on p.f. improvement equipment.

$$y = ₹\ \frac{11}{100} \times 150 = ₹\ 16.50$$

$$\text{Most economical p.f., } \cos \theta_2 = \sqrt{1 - \left(\frac{y}{x}\right)^2} = \sqrt{1 - \left(\frac{16.50}{100}\right)^2}$$

$$= 0.9863 \text{ lag. } \textbf{Ans.}$$

❑❑❑

STATE BOARD EXAMINATION PAPERS

Transmission and Distribution (Electric Power-I)

Time Allowed : 3 Hrs. *Maximum Marks : 100*

SECTION A

Attempt any ten question from this section 10 × 2

1. (*i*) What are the various sources of energy in nature?
(*ii*) What is meant by power factor?
(*iii*) What is meant by two-part tariff?
(*iv*) What are the mains of diesel electric station?
(*v*) What are the types of turbines used in hydel station?
(*vi*) What are the advantages of inter-connection of power station?
(*vii*) What are the advantages of high voltage transmission?
(*viii*) What are the unsymmetrical faults in power system?
(*ix*) What is skin effect?
(*x*) Name the components of an overhead transmission line.

SECTION B

Note: Attempt any five parts. 5 × 6

2. What is the difference between a thermal power station and nuclear power station?

3. (*a*) Describe any one method of improving the power factor.
(*b*) A single phase 400 V, 50 Hz motor takes a load current of 50 A at 0.8 p.f. lagging. The p.f. is to be improved to unity by connecting a condenser in parallel. Find the capacity of condenser.

4. Discuss the difference sources of energy available in nature.

5. Describe some of the important types of tariff commonly used.

6. Compare the volume of conductor material required in d.c. single phase and 3-phase a.c. system.

SECTION C

Note: Attempt all question from this section. 5 × 10

7. Draw the layout on Nuclear Power station labelling clearly each part.

8. Discuss the various types of supports.

9. (a) What is corona effect?
(*b*) Explain the various methods of improving string efficiency.

10. Compare the merits and demerits of underground system versus overhead system.

OR

11. Explain positive sequence current, negative sequence current and zero sequence current.

12. Explain with a diagram the Murray Loop test method for finding ground fault.

STATE BOARD EXAMINATION PAPERS

Transmission and Distribution (Electric Power-I)

Time Allowed : 3 Hrs. *Maximum Marks : 100*

SECTION A

Note: Attempt any ten questions. 10 × 2 = 20

1. (*i*) What is a feeder?

(*ii*) What is transposition of conductors?

(*iii*) What is draw-in-system in underground cables?

(*iv*) What is maximum demand tariff?

(*v*) What is the effet of spacing between the conductors on the inductance of line?

(*vi*) The highest transmission line voltage in India is

(a) 220 kV

(b) 440 kV

(c) 11 kV

(*vii*) The colour of the neutral of 3-core flexible cable is

(a) red

(b) black

(c) blue

(*viii*) Location of lighting arrester is near

(a) the generator

(b) the bus bar

(c) the transformer

(*ix*) Fault diverters are basically

(a) Relays

(b) Circuit breaker

(c) Fuses

(d) Fast switches

(*x*) For remote operation, the circuit breaker must be equipped with

(a) Time delay trip

(b) Shunt trip

(c) Inverse time trip

(d) None of these

(*xi*) Insulation resistance of HV circuit breakers is more than

(a) 100 Ω

(b) 500 Ω

(c) 1 Mega Ω

(d) 100 Mega Ω

(*xii*) Skin effect exists in

(a) A.C. transmission only

(b) D.C. transmission only

(c) Both (a) and (b)
(d) None of these

SECTION B

2. What are the disadvantages of low power factor?
3. What is the importance of sag?
4. What are the advantages of three phase system over single phase system?
5. What are the advantages of inter-connecting the three phases?
6. What is maximum demand tariff?
7. What are the faults on over-head transmission lines?

SECTION C

Note: Attempt all questions. **5 × 10 = 50**

8. What are the advantages of H.V. for transmission?
9. What is power factor? How is it improved in transmission line?
10. What are the constructional features of transmission line?
11. List the various components of 11/0.4 kV pole mounted substation and describe briefly about them.
12. Explain block rate, flat rate and two part tariff. Which is the most commonly used and why?

OR

Explain corona, factors affecting it and method of reducing corona loss.

Index

P

R

S

T

U

V

W

X

❑❑❑

Win Prizes!

ATTENTION READERS

We request you for your frank assessment regarding some of the aspects of the book given as under:

TRANSMISSION AND DISTRIBUTION (ELECTRICAL POWER-I)

By

Er. Tarlok Singh

Please fill up the given space in neat capital letters.

(i) What topics of your syllabus that are important from you examination point of view are not covered in the book ?

....

....

....

....

(ii) What are the chapters wherein the treatment of the subject matter is not systematic or organised or updated ?

....

....

....

....

(iii) Have you come across misprints/mistakes/factual inaccuracies in the book? Please specify the chapters and the page numbers.

....

....

....

....

(iv) What other books on the same subject have you found/heard better that the present book? Please specify in terms of price and quality.

....

....

....

....

(v) Further suggestions and comments for the improvement of the book:

....

....

....

....

(PS: If need be please attach a separate sheet to write your views.)

Other Details :

(i) Who recommended you the book ? (Please tick in the box near the option relevant to you.)

☐ Teachers ☐ Friends ☐ Bookseller

(ii) Name of the recommending teacher, his designation and address.

....
....
....
....

(iii) Name and address of the bookseller you purchased the book form:

....
....
....
....

(iv) Name and address of your institution (Please mention the University or Board, as the case may be)

....
....
....
....

(v) Your name and complete postal address:

....
....
....
....

(vi) Course you are enrolled in:

....
....
....
....

The best assessment will be awarded each month. The award will be in the form of our publications as decided by the Editorial Board.

Please mail the filled up coupon at your earliest to:

S.K. Kataria & Sons®

4885/109, Prakash Mahal, Dr. Subhash Bhargav Lane,
Opposite Delhi Medical Association, Daryaganj, New Delhi-110002
Phones: +91-11-23243489, 43551243; Mobile: +91-9871775858
e-mail: katariabook@gmail.com; katariabooks@yahoo.com
Website: www.skkatariaandsons.com